INTRODUCTORY FILM CRITICISM

A HISTORICAL PERSPECTIVE

Frank M. Scheide
University of Arkansas

KENDALL/HUNT PUBLISHING COMPANY
4050 Westmark Drive   Dubuque, Iowa 52002

Cover photo is of Émile Reynaud's "Théâtre Optique," c. 1892. One of the earliest known projection devices for screening animated cartoons of between five and fifteen minutes in length. From Hopkins's *Magic*.

This book is dedic   Marco

Dr Vest

TABLE OF CONTENTS

Chapter Three
Motion Picture Pioneers and the Evolution of Film Form and Film Style

Chapter Four
Charlie Chaplin, Auteur and Mise-en-Scene Criticism, and *The Gold Rush*

Chapter Five
The Experimental Film

Chapter Six
German Cinema in the 1920s and the Importance of Camerawork as an Element of Film Style

Chapter Seven
Film Form and Continuity Editing

Chapter Eight
Sergei Eisenstein and Montage

Chapter Nine
"Talking Pictures" and Film Genres

Chapter Ten
Censorship

Chapter Eleven
Documentary

Chapter Twelve
Case Study: *Citizen Kane*

Acknowledgments

To properly show appreciation to everyone who helped me with this book is impossible. I will attempt to cite some of the people whose time, talent, and support contributed so much to its completion. Let me begin by thanking Charles Reed Mitchell and Ken Stout, for proofreading various chapters of this book. My appreciation, too, to Kathy Mandrell Van Laningham, who offered her insights and support when we talked about co-writing a textbook like this several years ago. Thanks also to Thomas S. Frentz, for his input and helpful suggestions.

As with all other aspects of this undertaking, the people who helped me with the research are many. Stephen Bottomore, Charles and Penny Chilton, Anne and Peter Fraser, Tony Merrick, David Robinson, and Winifred Thompson assisted me with various forms of useful information when I was visiting England, in 1993. The British Film Institute was very helpful in making available a number of the illustrations we have included. My thanks, too, to the Museum of Modern Art in New York; the Philadelphia Museum of Art; and the Oslo Nasjonalgaleriet, for granting me permission to reproduce artwork from their collections. I particularly appreciate Jo Wiegand's efforts in obtaining these permissions. Two other sources, who generously agreed to let me use their printed material, were my friends Daniel Boyd and Steve Gilliland.

The majority of photographs appearing in this book would not be included if it were not for the efforts of several collaborators. Carl Hitt reproduced most of the frame enlargements and took many of the original photographs. Chad Eby is another artist/technician whose expertise helped us capture a number of the more illusive images that did not seem to want to be taken. Many thanks to Michael Peven and Christine Hilker for making their darkrooms available to us. Nor do I wish to forget the patient and photogenic people who agreed to appear in these photographs--Shannon Piggee, Kristy Moore, Carl Hitt, and, particularly, Cindy Arnaud. My thanks to you all.

In closing I would like to thank my family--my sister and brother-in-law, Kathy and Steve Metzenbauer, and parents, Milo and Genevieve Scheide, for their never failing encouragement and support. Finally, thanks to my wife, Susan, who helped me get this manuscript finished under the most tiresome and tedious circumstances. Her patience, and good humor, never fail to amaze me.

CHAPTER ONE

THE FILM EXPERIENCE

COURSE OBJECTIVES: *Identify a rationale for film criticism and some basic types of film study, define the primary questions a "film consumer" needs to ask when watching a movie, and introduce the reader to the approach of this text.*

I. *The Rationale for Film Study*

The "motion picture" is just barely a century old. Consequently, film scholars have not had as long a time to define their discipline as have educators in most other fields of learning. Despite the brevity of film study's existence, its inclusion in educational curricula is justifiable for at least five reasons.

1) **Film is an important part of our lives.** No matter how one feels about the quality of movies and television, no one can deny that film is an important part of our culture. Every time we turn on a TV we confront visual messages attempting to entertain, inform, or persuade us. "Hollywood" is a billion dollar industry that has been manufacturing entertainment films for decades. News broadcasts use moving images to convey what is happening in our world daily. Commercials use film to persuade us to buy products. Because of these applications, film is a major medium we use to interact with our culture. To better understand the process of this interaction we should know how film works, as a medium of communication, and be aware of how film has been used and misused.

2) **Film has been used to document the history of the twentieth century**. Since the 1890s, the motion picture has recorded history in a manner unlike any medium before it. This visual record contains information relative to the appearance, lifestyles, and attitudes of the world's cultures. (See fig. 1.1.) Important events shaping international history have been preserved on film. All this information enables us understand the past and better comprehend why societies and attitudes exist the way they do today. The better we understand how film works as a medium of communication, the better we can interpret the historical data it has preserved.

3) **Film is constantly being used to manipulate us--to get us to think in particular ways**. Even if we have no interest in becoming filmmakers or historians we are all film consumers. Part of this consumption involves dealing with propaganda. Television commercials continuously

attempt to convince us of the desirability of products available for purchase. Politicians and special interest groups use film to persuade us to follow certain patterns of thought. At times we may consciously or subconsciously accept ideas communicated on film or television that we might, with more careful consideration, ignore or reject.

The fact that filmmakers have used their medium to encourage audiences to accept ideas, which may or may not be in a person's or society's best interests, has made film a powerful tool for persuasion. The concerned film consumer should be aware of how the medium attempts to manipulate us into accepting a film's message. We also should be aware of the ramifications which acceptance or rejection of film messages may have on our lives and the well-being of society.

4) **The motion picture is an important medium for communicating <u>information</u>**. When the word "movies" is mentioned many people think of entertainment on television or at the theater. Yet film is also used to inform an audience. While newspapers and radio are important news sources, most people rely on television for at least some of their knowledge concerning what is happening in the world. As film consumers the more we understand how movies work, the better we can digest and assess the quality and content of the information they communicate.

5) **The more we know about film, the more we can <u>appreciate</u> what film is communicating**. Anyone can watch a movie and legitimately claim to understand and enjoy the content. The complexity

1.1   A Lumiére cameraman filming little girls in the 1890s. An image from a culture different from our own.   From Hopkins's *Magic*.

1.2   Interior of a 1890s camera which doubled as a projector--the Demeny chronophotographe.   (See fig. 1.4.) From Hopkins's *Magic*.

of a person's viewing experience, however, can vary greatly from individual to individual. The better one can observe and appreciate what is happening in a movie, the richer and more enjoyable that viewing experience will be. People who have studied how to become better film consumers should get more enjoyment from a picture than they would experience if they had not taken a film course. This aspect of film study is concerned with increasing one's *aesthetic* appreciation of the motion picture as an art form. The word "aesthetic" refers to the philosophy or study of beauty. An aesthetic appreciation of film pertains to the beauty or spiritual uplifting experienced when watching some movies. Those pictures that continue to move their audience, years after they were made, are called "classics." [1]

These five arguments suggest that a basic understanding of film and film study is desirable for anyone who wishes to enjoy, and be informed about, the world around us as communicated through the motion picture medium. To become a better film consumer a person must have a general understanding of how film functions as a medium of communication and the audience's relationship to that process. The first step in becoming a competent film consumer is knowing how movies work.

II. How Do We Perceive Film?

Essentially "**film**" is a strip of transparent acetate with individual still images printed upon it called "**frames**." (See fig 7.1). Moving pictures do not actually "move" but are flashed past our eyes as still images at the rate of 24 frames per second. These pictures are first formed by exposing light sensitive motion picture film stock in a movie camera. The film is "**shot**"

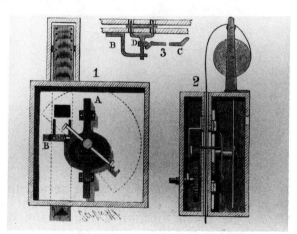

1.3 The gate of an 1890s Lumiére camera. As the shutter ("A") turns and covers the opening in the gate, a claw advances the film a perforation which equals one frame. The frame is exposed to light until the shutter covers the gate and the claw advances the film another frame. From Hopkins's *Magic*.

when the camera transports it through a "**gate**" located behind a **lens**, where each frame is exposed to light . (See fig. 1.2 and fig. 1.3).

When a frame enters the gate a **shutter** in the camera opens up allowing light to come through the lens. This light imprints an image on the frame, resembling the subject before the camera. A visual record of the previous movement before the camera is now documented on a series of exposed frames. Each frame contains a still image recording an individual phase of the action. The film is then processed and ready to be projected.

Motion picture projection is accomplished in a manner similar to the way we described film being transported in the camera. (See fig. 1.4 and fig. 2.5). The film travels through the projector and each frame is in the gate for a fraction of a second. A shutter opens up and the individual frame is subjected to a light source located behind the lens. The lens magnifies the image as it is projected on a screen. The shutter then closes, concealing the movement of the traveling film. It does not open again until the succeeding frame is positioned in the gate where it is illuminated by the light source. As the audience watches these individual frames, revealed by the opening shutter, an illusion of movement is created that seems to duplicate the action

1.4 This ingenious 1890s setup allowed the camera, shown in fig. 1.2, to open in the back and function as a projector. A light source behind the camera/projector focused its beam through a water tank that absorbed some of the heat that might damage the film. After passing through the water tank the light beam was centered on the gate of the "chronophotographe," illuminating an image that was enlarged and projected by the lens at the front. From Hopkins's *Magic*.

seen at the time it was photographed.

The moving picture is in motion only insofar that the film travels through the gate as it is spooled off one reel and wound up on the projector's take up reel. We do not see the pictures move, we just "think" we do. What we really see are individual still images interspersed with a shutter that temporarily cuts off the light projected on the screen. Part of the time we are seeing still images and part of the time we are looking at the closed shutter. We see the picture but are unaware of the shutter. Because of some physiological process in our brains we ignore, or are unable to see, the shutter but perceive the still photographs as a "moving image."

The mechanical methods reproducing this action are relatively simple, but the physiological process by which we perceive "movies" as "moving" is complex and not completely understood. Given the way motion picture film is projected, there are questions as to why this effect should work. It seems we should either comprehend these pictures as individual images, interspersed with the shutter, or see nothing more than a blur. One explanation for why the effect works is that the human brain can retain the memory of an image for a fraction of a second while the shutter is closed. Before the picture fades in our mind it is replaced by the visual information in the next frame. During this process our minds can isolate a pattern from these flashing images that we comprehend as motion. This physiological process has been described by some theorists as the "**phi-phenomenon**."

Filmmakers have always been fascinated with the mystery of how we perceive still images as moving. Many experimental films and special effects have been developed, exploring how we respond to these flashing images and light. Some intriguing results have occurred from these experiments. Filmmaker Tony Conrad isolated some interesting phenomena, relating to visual perception, in his 1965 motion picture *The Flicker*. When projecting alternating black and white frames arranged in certain patterns, Conrad found audiences perceive strobe effects, the appearance of color, and oscillating movements. He also found that this movie induces "photogenic epilepsy" in one out of every 15,000 viewers. Because of the way they physiologically perceive pulsating light in *The Flicker*, some individuals experience a type of epileptic seizure while viewing the film.

The type of physiological responses viewers experience when watching Tony Conrad's *The Flicker*, raises several intriguing questions about how our eyes and brains process film images. Most people who view *The Flicker* do not have epileptic seizures. Yet the fact that this and other psychological and physiological responses occur forces us to wonder just what happens to us when we watch any film. On a very basic level are the intermittent flashes, between light and shutter, lulling us into a kind of

5

trance? Is this condition similar to the "daydreaming" one can experience while staring at a fire? If we are in a dreamlike state how, if at all, does it effect our perception of the information being projected? Are we attracted to, or "hypnotized" by, the flashing light like moths drawn to a flame?

Conversely, can it be argued that our response to these flashing lights actually is one of greater sensory stimulation and heightened consciousness? Can we comprehend *more* from this medium by virtue of the physiological process? Or is our consciousness no more affected by the way this medium works than it would be if we were getting the information from the printed page? Until behavioral psychologists better understand *how* and *why* we perceive still images as moving, the nature of our relationship to this "cerebral film processing" is subject to question.

All filmmakers are aware that an audience physiologically interacts with the projected image of a movie. Most are more interested in how people react to the information conveyed in the images. The viewer's *emotional* and *intellectual* reaction to a movie's content are as important to the way we relate to a film as the subconscious physiological processing of the images that make "movies" work. The filmmaker may not fully understand how a person perceives still images moving. He or she is very involved with structuring the emotional and intellectual stimuli to which the viewer responds.

As we will see in our examination of the early history of film in Chapter Three, the invention of the motion picture in the late nineteenth century resulted from experiments relating to image perception. After the ability to create the effect of a "motion picture" was perfected, filmmakers considered what could be done with this illusion. It was then that they explored ways film could stimulate the emotional and intellectual involvement of the viewer.

By the early twentieth-century narrative **"photoplays"** were designed to engage the audience emotionally. Viewers were asked to empathize and respond to the characters in these movies--laugh at their antics, feel concerned about their misfortunes, and applaud their victories. The filmmakers developed carefully calculated moods to get the audiences emotionally involved in these story films. The medium of the theater, which has been striving for this response for centuries, served as a model for the filmmakers. "Hollywood" was eventually created because of audience interest in this "emotionally absorbing" form of cinema.

By now filmmakers also recognized that the motion picture could *intellectually* stimulate an audience. Film's ability to record the illusion of reality prompted filmmakers to use the medium to document the world around them. Important events, lifestyles, problems, and their proposed solutions were portrayed on film designed to inform and educate audiences. The **"documentary"** or **"nonfiction"** film grew out of the motion picture medium's ability to "document" or "record" that which it photographed. Rather than have audiences respond only to emotionally charged fictional imagery, the documentary asked its viewer to think about subject matter existing in a "*real*" world. The question of how objective film can be in recording *"the real world"* will be considered in this text.

Reviewing the above we can conclude that audiences respond to movies in essentially three ways: physiologically, emotionally, and intellectually. The first condition is something that is not really understood. The second two considerations involve carefully calculated responses which filmmakers attempt to elicit from their audience. If, as film consumers, we wish to better comprehend what a particular motion picture is communicating, we need to understand *how* and *why* the filmmaker has used the medium in the fashion chosen. We must be able to figure out just what emotional and intellectual responses the film is attempting to get from us, when we are watching it, and the filmmaker's rationale for trying to get us to respond this way.

III.   *The Nature of Film Criticism*

Viewers perceive film through their physiological, emotional, and intellectual responses to a given motion picture. Criticism is the process by which we assess these perceptions. The value of any communication lies in the experience one accrues from it. If a particular viewing experience is enjoyable, thought provoking, or spiritually rewarding the film that produced it can be assumed to be of sufficient value to warrant criticism. The term "criticism" might be taken as synonymous with the word "appreciation." A person criticizes a movie in an attempt to identify the appreciable experience one can get from viewing that picture. The purpose of the critic is to define the nature and degree of appreciation available in a work.

A critic is supposed to identify the *quality* of the film viewing experience. This is not accomplished in every review. Successful film criticism and the qualifications of a critic are dependent upon the values used to judge the aesthetics of a film. Too often we may rightfully question a reviewer's criteria, believe that an assessment of a movie is incorrect or unfair, and feel that we could do a better job analyzing that film ourselves.

Exposure to unsatisfactory criticism prompts one to ask how someone can justify calling him or herself a "film critic." Anyone can have an opinion. When is one individual's opinion of a movie "better" than that of someone else? Isn't the artist, who made the movie, the most qualified person to talk about the intent of the film and its value? How can a critic, totally uninvolved in the making of a picture, claim to have any knowledge of that work? What service do these people provide? Are they "parasites" of the arts, using the labors of others to gain recognition for themselves? Is the "critic" who accepts or dismisses a movie with "cute" or "sarcastic" phrasing accomplishing anything other than trying to impress us with his or her attempts at being clever? Are not some "critics" really little more than salespeople paid to promote a product? "Bad criticism" makes some "reviewers" guilty of these charges. "Good criticism" goes beyond such accusations.

Good critics inform potential viewers about what movie audiences will enjoy. They also point out ways we can better appreciate these films as we watch them. A good critic will make the film experience richer for the viewer than it would have been if that person had seen the movie without benefit of the review. Good criticism should enable the viewer to better comprehend and enjoy a film during the immediate viewing experience and beyond. Literary theorist Northrop Frye described the purpose of criticism in his book *Anatomy of Criticism*. Frye was largely addressing literary criticism, in his collection of essays, but what he said can be applied to film criticism as well.

Criticism should exist in its own right, Northrop Frye maintains, since it is necessary to formulate "cultural direction." [2] Taken in this context, film criticism should be concerned with more than just identifying what we like or dislike. Anyone can form that opinion. It also should isolate what is culturally significant in motion pictures. All of us may enjoy a popular film of the moment for its own sake on some level. We may be unable to say much about its significance beyond the immediate experience. To be a critic a person must be knowledgeable about the nature and history of that art. Based on this knowledge, the good critic should be capable of assessing recent trends in this art's expression and identify the cultural direction in which it is going.

According to Northrop Frye, without the critic's sense of cultural direction one either has "art for art's sake" or "pop" art. The "art for art's sake" category is concerned with a body of work with no apparent cultural context or direction. "Pop" art refers to "popular" work whose worth is determined by whatever is commercially successful. Frye believes neither the approach of pop art or art for art's sake has produced schools of art in the past. He also believes there is no reason to feel they will do so in the future. A critic, then, is needed to identify and help direct the artistic and cultural tendencies of that time. [3] The good film critic is a barometer who encourages and applauds the filmmaker for using the film medium to its fullest potential. The critic does this by considering alternatives to the artist's approach, and reminding us of what film is capable of expressing when it is not doing it. The box-office will tell us what is popular. Criticism should point out what is artistically and culturally significant.

The filmmaker's knowledge and experience with film, and intentions when making a particular movie, would seem to make that person most qualified to function as critic. Artists can provide enlightening critical information but criticism should not be limited to those producing a given art. In *Anatomy of Criticism* Northrop Frye argues that the capacity for criticism should not exist solely with the producing artist. According to Frye, " . . . criticism is a structure of thought and knowledge existing in its own right with some measure of independence from the art it deals with." [4] While the artist is concerned with achieving certain goals in his or her individual expression, the critic should concentrate on identifying its value in a broader cultural context. The creating artist should not serve as final arbiter of a work because that individual cannot always be objective.

The primary function of the filmmaker is to make films--a very time consuming process. The film critic's purpose is to understand a film, in and of itself, and within broader cultural contexts. The critic must view many films, the good as well as the bad, and decide where they all fit in the cultural scheme of things. This takes a great deal of time. The filmmaker does not always have the time, nor the desire, to function in the role of the critic. Even artists who have the time and interest in being critics are sometimes limited in the way they can criticize their art and the work of others.

Being intimately involved with the production of a film may make it difficult for filmmakers to be unbiased about their work. This bias is comparable to the way certain parents are unable to be objective about the qualities and deficiencies of their children. Even if filmmakers have reservations about their movies they might not care to express them. Talking about the weaknesses of one's own picture could dissuade potential viewers from seeing it, thereby effecting that film's earning potential. By being an honest critic a filmmaker could lose money and jeopardize opportunities to make films in the future. The filmmaker/critic could also be accused of trying to damage the competition after giving a negative review of someone else's film. Thus, while filmmakers are qualified to be film critics in one sense, conflicts of interest can prevent them from being effective in performing this function.

Creating artists should not serve as final arbiters of their art because they cannot always be unbiased about their work. Legitimate critics outside the filmmaking process, unprejudiced by financial gain or personal involvement with the work, are needed to evaluate films objectively. The first priority of film criticism is to be sensitive to what an individual film says and how well it says it.

Reviews based solely on personal opinion, or made only to espouse other causes, generally are not satisfactory as film criticism. Too often they fail to recognize what a movie is trying to say or how well the information is communicated. One may not like what a picture is expressing. This message does not necessarily make that film a bad movie. Not everything one needs to know in life is pleasant. We might not enjoy hearing a physician's diagnosis but still need to listen and use the information to make important adjustments in our lives. A critic should be able to review a film in the same unbiased way a doctor diagnoses a patient. The critic must objectively review how well a film articulates its information and then ascertain the validity of the message. The legitimate critic is an interpreter who assesses the identity and quality of film communication, not someone who uses this position to promote personal bias.

To obtain legitimacy the critic must know how film works as a medium. He or she should also be aware of how individual films compare with others that have been made before it. The only way to prove this legitimacy is for the critic to become acquainted with his or her art. This is done by making an inductive survey of the specific works in the field. Knowledge of these works is then used to shape one's critical principles. Northrop Frye describes this process as a means for formulating a *scientific schema* for criticism. It is the responsibility of those working within a critical discipline to identify this schema and justify its use.

The identity of any science involves the collection and organization of data relating to the phenomena pertaining to it. A "science" becomes legitimate only after the phenomena is interpreted as data and an order or structure is imposed upon it. This task, in part, involves the concerns of film history--the study of film from its origins to the present.

Because millions of films have been made, during the last hundred years, we are talking about a substantial amount of data. Each movie may contain information useful to the historian for identifying social attitudes relating to the time the picture was made. These films also reflect a myriad of ways filmmakers have used the medium to communicate. Some conceptual framework is needed to organize all this data. No one has the time to look at this huge number of movies. Even if someone did view everything the activity could end up being meaningless. Some criteria must be established, to assess the nature and importance of each picture in relation to the others, if the examining process is to have value.

IV. *Ways of Categorizing Movies*

A critic must have a knowledge of film history but cannot view every piece of data in the discipline. One general way the critic can start organizing this data is by grouping the films in categories that reflect their content and cultural orientation. All motion pictures can be placed in three general categories--**narrative**, **documentary**, and "**experimental**." Of the three general film categories the narrative will be the most discussed in this text. Narrative films are fictional movies that tell a story. Documentaries are nonfiction films associated with documenting "reality." We will consider the history and content of the documentary in Chapter Eleven. The experimental category is somewhat more difficult to describe.

"Experimental," "abstract," and "avante-garde" are all terms used to describe essentially the same category of film. In essence, experimental cinema generally does not depend upon a story or actuality for its communication the way films in the other two major groupings do. Rather, these motion pictures often explore the properties of the film medium itself and the unique cinematic effects it can create. The experimental film may manipulate time and space. It can make cartoons animated. Experimental films create environments and visual contexts that do not really exist. They also investigate how the viewer responds to various visual stimuli and effects. Tony Conrad's movie *The Flicker*, previously described, is an example of an experimental film. The "music video" could be placed in this general classification as well. Chapter Five will examine the category of experimental film by considering its relationship to important modern art movements and artists during the late nineteenth and early twentieth centuries.

The narrative, documentary, and experimental designations provide some general groupings for identifying movies but there are other ways of categorizing motion pictures. One convenient means for classifying pictures is to recognize their country of origin. Because of cultural diversities an American movie can often be quite different from a British film even though the countries of origin share a common language. The 1939 Hollywood picture *Gone with the Wind*, for example, has distinct cultural differences that are not shared by the 1937 British film *Fire Over England,* which also stars English actress Vivien Leigh.

Another way the critic and historian can group movies is according to narrative forms known as "**genres.**" Examples of familiar movie genres include the western, horror, gangster, and musical film. Common "generic elements" allow the critic to take the 1903 American picture *The Great Train Robbery* and compare it with a western like *Butch Cassidy and the Sundance Kid* (1969), made over half a century later. Classifying a film by genre can be a very effective way of helping viewers get a general sense of what a picture is about, even before he or she looks at the movie. We will consider genre criticism further in Chapter Nine.

Still another way to classify movies is by grouping them according to director. In this instance one identifies the film with the filmmaker. This critical approach is known as "**auteur criticism**"--auteur" being the French word for "author." Following the second world war some French critics found, after watching many films, that the movies they liked best often were made by the same filmmakers. They established a list of auteur film directors, which included John Ford (1895-1973) and Alfred Hitchcock

(1899-1980), and advanced the argument that every movie made by these filmmakers was critically significant. Though some of the auteur movies were not as good as others, these French critics argued, everything the auteur filmmakers made should be examined to better isolate the important characteristics of their total work. A "minor" auteur film, for example, might contain attitudes and stylistic tendencies of its director useful for better understanding that filmmaker's major pictures. Critics have also grouped films by screenwriters, photographers, actors, and other filmmaking disciplines.

By categorizing films according to national cinema, genre, and director, among other methods of classification, the critic can develop general perspectives for understanding the vast amount of data contained in countless thousands of motion pictures. Such approaches enable us to put these pictures into groups. These broad divisions do not suggest what makes a movie good or bad. Not all movies are equal in terms of historical, cultural, or aesthetic relevance. Indeed, the auteur critics made a case for looking at "bad" films by certain directors. They justified this activity by saying it helped them look for that which was "good." Many viewers, however, prefer to spend their time looking at good movies rather than bad ones. Clearly some system is needed for separating the two.

How does one separate "good" films from "bad?" How does a critic judge the quality of even a small group of motion pictures made by a single auteur? By what standards can one dismiss a "bad" movie? The broad categorizations we have listed establish some general film groupings but do not answer these questions. Once these categories are recognized some standard is needed for assessing the quality of the movies we see. One way to establish a standard of film quality, in a group of films, is to compare these pictures with the "**classics**."

V.   *The Importance of Film Classics in Film Criticism*

Critics limit the data they explore, and assess the quality of a film, based on their understanding of the "classics." No matter what the critical grouping a critic uses, the body of work explored will contain a handful of films recognized as classic. Who has not heard of a classic foreign film? A classic horror movie? A classic "Hitchcock?" Sometimes the word "classic" is used too freely in identifying a memorable film. Though enjoyable, a "classic" Roy Rogers western, Bowery Boys comedy, or "beach blanket" romp does not have the qualities of certain other films that have been identified as great pictures. What differentiates these "classics" from the truly classic film is that the latter contains something extra which makes it stand out from the average movie. This "extra something" allows an "old" classic to remain fresh and interesting through time.

A movie becomes designated as a classic largely because the experience it imparts stirs the viewer in a unique and intriguing fashion. When a work of art is successful the observer experiences a feeling that the film director and theorist Sergei Eisenstein (1898-1948) called "ecstasy." [5] The artistic expression of that work is so strong that the film literally comes alive. For the sensitive critic the memory and feelings produced by a true classic remain undimmed by the passage of time or repeated viewings. The same experience will be true for other people exposed to this classic at a later period. The content and communication of a classic both reflects and transcends the time in which it was made.

Classics often serve as models for filmmakers wishing to duplicate their success. It is not surprising to find the influence of a successful film in many later movies. Yet, while the classic may inspire a formula that is repeated in succeeding pictures, these sequels and imitations are seldom as good as the original. Why Eisenstein's "ecstasy" will exist in one movie and be totally lacking in another, even when both films are made by the same artist, is one of the mysteries of creative expression. There seems to be no foolproof way to manufacture classics. The classics can offer artistic guidelines, but filmmakers cannot always replicate their quality.

The failure to reproduce the ecstasy of the great motion pictures may frustrate the filmmaker. It is this failure, that separates the classic from the average movie, which provides the critic with a conceptual framework for examining film. As indicated, whenever a critic reviews a movie he or she should judge that picture based on a criterion for cinematic excellence. This criterion involves a knowledge of classic films and the unique forms of cinematic experience they have been able to generate. The individual worth of each movie the critic examines, then, should be determined according to how it measures up to other films, both average and classic. In this manner the critic can ascertain how "good" or "bad" a particular movie is by comparing its quality with that of the best--classic--films of its type. Such ranking also helps to define the cultural direction film is taking as an art form.

While recognizing the importance of the critic, in determining what films are good and/or bad, the film consumer must be wary about allowing any person or group of people dictate what should or should not be seen. The critical ranking of movies by anyone should not solely determine what everyone should like, dislike, want to see, or learn about. This responsibility belongs to each individual.

This book relies heavily on the examination of certain classic films to illustrate its points. The text will identify why these movies are considered important and encourage you to reassess their worth. The classics chosen for this task certainly are not the only ones that could be used as examples. Other critics would suggest different choices. Few would question that these films are not worthy of serious study. Many of these movies are ones that you might not ordinarily look at or may not even like. All of them should help you explore important concepts that will assist you in becoming a better film consumer--to better judge the quality of the film experience for yourself.

VI.   *How Does One Become a Better Film Consumer?*

Experiencing is the foundation of film criticism.   Film classics provide the best film experience that critics have isolated. This does not mean that a film has to be a classic to be enjoyed. We should not have to depend upon someone knowledgeable of the classics to tell us what to experience when we watch a movie. Nor should we have to assume that the critic's assessment is infallible. A critic may have seen hundreds of classics and still be insensitive to the quality of some movies when reviewing them. The most important thing about experiencing film is the experience itself. The critic is only a potential guide in the pursuit of that experience. We are responsible for the experience we get from watching a movie. To fully experience a film we must be sensitive to what the filmmaker is saying and be aware of how that motion picture is expressing this communication. This critical sensitivity is something we must develop for ourselves.

The experience a person has when viewing a movie is one's own. Each of us is responsible for the quality of that experience. The first rule in becoming a better film consumer is to trust one's own reactions to a film experience. If we like or dislike a movie, find it confusing, frivolous, thought-provoking or distasteful, we should explore these impressions and make a thoughtful assessment based upon our own reactions. Someone else may have seen more classics and had more practice in film criticism. Others may be more knowledgeable about film history. Their appreciation may add to our experience. Ultimately the experience that we get from a film is more important than what they can tell us about it.

In a democracy it is the responsibility of everyone to think for oneself and to monitor what our society is doing. No one should have to tell us what to think, what movies to watch, or how we should respond to them. We should make responsible decisions for ourselves. If criticism determines the direction of a culture, it is the job of each conscientious person in society to decide where we want our culture to go. Not everyone can have the background of the professional critic, but we can learn how to become better, more sensitive, film consumers. Such erudition comes from knowing what questions to ask when watching a movie. By having a basic understanding of how film works as a medium of communication we can learn how to better assess the experience we get from viewing a movie. It is the goal of this text to help the reader become more receptive to these concerns.

14

Clearly there are technical aspects of film criticism we must learn if we are to become better film consumers. Yet even without this knowledge there are four basic questions anyone can ask, when watching a movie, which will increase his or her appreciation of the film experience. Before exploring the intricacies of film study we should identify these fundamental questions. Every critic, consciously or unconsciously, asks these four questions when reviewing a motion picture.

VII.   *The Four Basic Questions of Film Criticism*

Before you can begin to examine something you must have some general idea about what is being discussed. The first question you should ask is **what is the film about?** In every movie there is a basic idea or effect that the filmmaker is trying to communicate. Your first concern is to isolate and identify the nature of the subject matter in the movie and what the filmmaker is trying to say about it. Is the film a narrative, a documentary, or an experimental motion picture? Is it American, foreign, a genre picture, or made by an auteur? Considering a movie by type helps to isolate the filmmaker's objectives.

Once you have defined what the film is generally about the next question to be asked is **why is the filmmaker interested in stating the ideas being expressed?** Just what are the reasons for the filmmaker going to the effort of making a film of this sort? In this instance you try to ascertain the *purpose* behind the motion picture that you are reviewing. Your problem here is to determine **why** a film like this would be made.

The first two questions identify the subject matter. The second two questions are more specific in evaluating just what the reviewer believes the film is communicating and how. After identifying your subject, and what you believe the film is saying, you should try to figure out the methods the motion picture uses to communicate its particular ideas. In other words, **how is the film conveying its information?** To answer this question you must analyze how the filmmaker has used the properties of film expression to accomplish the particular effect that we experience when viewing his or her film. Such an examination calls for an investigation of a film's **"form"** (or structure) and its **"style"** (appearance.)[6] The following chapters will be specifically concerned with identifying these important critical approaches. This third question, then, is concerned with how the film medium is used to express its information.

Our fourth and final question involves an assessment of the communication process. **What effect has the film had on its audience?** What has been accomplished? Was the film successful in the way it communicated its information? Does the audience respond well to the message? Why or why not? This final question summarizes one's

15

critical findings.

Though deceptively simple in appearance, these questions can raise some complex issues. Even on the most elementary level they can force us to think more fully about the film experience when watching any movie. The more we know about what to look for, of course, the more thorough our answers to these questions are going to be. In total these four questions review a communication process in which a message is being conveyed and received. To understand this process the filmmaker must know how to communicate messages, using this medium of film, and the audience must understand how to receive them. The critic, in interpreting the messages, must be sensitive to all aspects of the communication process. Such sensitivity entails some knowledge of how film form and style can be manipulated to convey information.

We will identify ways to analyze the form and style of a motion picture, and the responsibility of the viewer and filmmaker regarding this communication process, in the chapters ahead. Before embarking upon our investigation we will spend some time examining, in Chapter Two, the general process that determines how a film gets made and exhibited.

ENDNOTES

1. I wish to thank Ms. Kathy Mandrell VanLaningham for her contributions to this chapter during discussions we had on this topic.

2. Northrop Frye, *Anatomy of Criticism: Four Essays*, (Princeton: Princeton University Press, 1957), pp.4, 115, 344-49.

3. Ibid., p.4.

4. Ibid., p.5.

5. Sergei Eisenstein, *Film Form* and *The Film Sense*, (New York: Meridian Books, 1968), pp.166-7.

6. I first became interested in developing an approach to introductory film criticism while working as a graduate student under Professor David Bordwell, at the University of Wisconsin, Madison. Over the years Dr. Bordwell has influenced the development of many students' critical skills, including my own, and has made innumerable contributions to the advancement of film study on an international scale.

CHAPTER TWO

THE FILM PRODUCTION PROCESS

CHAPTER OBJECTIVES: *Examine the film production process from the initial idea for a film to the time it is ready for exhibition.*

I. Film Communication and the Preproduction Process

As noted in the previous chapter, one way to better understand how film works is by viewing it as part of a communication process. Any form of communication requires a **transmitter**, a **receiver**, and a **medium of communication**. When the medium of communication is film, the transmitter is a filmmaker and the receiver is an audience. For this process to function properly the filmmaker must know how to communicate messages, using film, and the audience must understand how to interpret this information. The better aware the transmitter and receiver are of how the communication process works, the better the communication. A critic is someone who is especially interested in the *quality* of communication of a particular medium. Before we consider how the critic relates to this process, some time should be spent discussing how the filmmaker uses the motion picture medium for purposes of communication.

Every medium of communication has certain formal properties that can be used by the communicator to convey messages. The communicator's choice of medium will partially determine the specific form his or her communication will take. Because of its peculiar nature the medium of sculpture, for example, communicates information differently than music, theater, dance, writing, radio, or film. Though sculpture conveys information differently from the other media, some of its formal properties may be similar. For example, theater, dance, and film, like sculpture, communicate information by using posed figures. The closer one looks at how the figures are posed in each medium, however, the more differences one can find in the nature of the communication. Sculpture is three-dimensional where film has a two-dimensional form. Theater and dance use breathing figures of flesh and blood while sculpture depends upon entities composed of some inert material such as wood, plaster, or stone. Those wishing to communicate with a given medium, or interpret what that medium is expressing, need to understand the properties peculiar to it. The filmmaker, for whatever reason, chooses to use the medium of film and its properties to communicate his or her message to an audience. Before this film message can be transmitted the filmmaker has to produce the film.

17

Every picture must pass through a five phase process before it can be seen. These stages, which will be discussed in this chapter, are **preproduction**, **production**, **postproduction**, **distribution**, and **exhibition.** Any movie, no matter what the form or when it was made, could not have been produced if someone had not had an idea which he or she wanted to turn into a film. The "preproduction" phase begins with the initial idea and includes all the planning before the film is actually shot.

Usually it is the "**producer**" who takes an idea, for a film, and guides if from its inception to completed picture. Where other filmmakers may be involved in only one of the phases, the producer is associated with the film through the entire filmmaking process. One of the most important responsibilities of the producer is to see that the process is financed throughout all these various stages.

Usually a producer does not have the financial resources to pay for the film to be made. He or she must get backing from someone else. Since even a modest commercial film can be very expensive, backers are hesitant about providing the financing unless they have a good sense of what the movie is about. One of the producer's first tasks is to explain to a potential backer, as quickly and briefly as possible, the basic nature of the film. The picture may contain complex character development and intricate plot twists that need lengthy explanation. However, the producer usually does not have the luxury of being able to fully describe the future film's content to a busy and impatient financier. The producer, then, has the difficult problem of succinctly defining a complicated film narrative without oversimplifying it. This task is attempted with what is called a "**one-liner.**"

A "one-liner" tries to summarize the nature of an entire film in one sentence. There is a story that the writer and television producer Gene Roddenberry was faced with the problem of finding the proper one-liner to sell a science fiction program, later known as *Star Trek,* to network producers in the1960s. His solution was to compare his series with a well known television western of the period. The resulting one-liner, that Roddenberry used to initially describe *Star Trek,* identified the series as "*Wagon Train* to the stars." While most viewers would no longer think of *Star Trek* in this context, Roddenberry tersely defined his idea in such a way that his backers immediately understood the concept behind his series. If the story is true, this early association also is grounds for considering *Star Trek* as a kind of "space western" or, at least, a form of narrative very much influenced by this earlier genre.

Clearly Gene Roddenberry's idea for his series was much more complicated than his one-liner would suggest. It did establish a sense of its essence in his abbreviated description. Producers may not be as successful as Roddenberry in coming up with a suitable and pithy sales pitch, but they should always be capable of identifying the basic nature of their product. Once backers have been sold on the product, the producer has the resources to further explore the feasibility of the project.

The "**treatment**" is the next aspect of the preproduction process following the idea and the one-liner. A "treatment" is a rough outline of the narrative of the movie. Usually this summary of the story is quite broad--no more than a paragraph or a couple of pages in length. The treatment is really the first step in developing the "**script**" that will be used for shooting the film. Sometimes the same treatment will be submitted to more than one "**scriptwriter.**" This is often done so the producer can get a more extensive perspective of how his or her idea might be realized on screen. Usually a script will go through several drafts before it finally is deemed acceptable. The script, or "**screenplay,**" which will be used by the director during shooting is called the "**shooting script.**" (See fig. 2.1.) The shooting script contains all the shots and dialogue, and describes much of the action and camera setups, that will be included in the film. A filmmaker should be able to envision the entire picture from the information provided in the shooting script:

FADE IN

INT. DENTAL OFFICE - CLOSE ON HANDS - DAY

MUSAC plays over.
Holding a dental probe, hands move toward the mouth of

WIDER

Mrs. Clark: 50's/unpleasant/very overweight. As the instrument
touches her tooth, she jerks away.

> MRS. CLARK
> (whining)
> I can still feel it! I need more
> gas!

TWO SHOT

Reveals DR. WALTER BENNETT: early 30's/low end of average
height/slight of build/plain but pleasant. He wears a smock
that's a bit too large. He readjusts the gas tube on her space.

> WALTER
> (patiently)
> It's at the highest recommended level
> Mrs. Clark. You really shouldn't feel
> anything.

Mrs. Clark snaps. . .

MRS. CLARK
I told you, I have a very low threshold
to pain.

2.1 **Page from the script for**
Strangest Dreams **by
Daniel Boyd. Courtesy
Daniel Boyd.**

Once the producer and the backers are satisfied with the shooting script they must then decide who will be making the movie. During this part of the preproduction phase the cast and crew are chosen. The key person brought into the process at this time is the "**director**." The director is the individual who makes the artistic decisions relating to the film. It is the director's duty to determine who will be on the crew working behind the camera and, usually, the actors appearing in front of it. Typically the producer does not make these determinations but leaves them to the director. It is the producer's responsibility to provide the funding and other resources necessary for the director to make the picture. After the cast and crew have been chosen, the logistics of the shooting are worked out. This includes obtaining equipment needed for the shoot and identifying sites for the filming. Once this is accomplished, and funding for the project is assured, the production can begin.

II. The Production Process

The preproduction phase, as we have seen, is concerned with taking an idea and determining how it can be realistically adapted into a motion picture. Once the logistics for this are established on paper, the producer prepares to get the production underway. After it is ascertained that nothing more can be done to get ready for the upcoming production, the producer and director begin to shoot the film. How smoothly production proceeds often depends upon how well the participants made their plans during preproduction. If they are not adequately prepared, problems may arise that can be time consuming and expensive.

Production involves a cast and crew that were hired for the movie during the preproduction phase. The director, as we noted, is responsible for organizing and conducting the production process. It is the director who makes the artistic decisions that will determine how the film will ultimately look. The person who serves as liaison between cast and crew, and insures that the director's wishes are carried out, is the "**A.D.**" or "**assistant director**." Another crew member integral to the production process is the "**cinematographer**." The cinematographer works with the camera operators and "**lighting designer**" to insure that the scenes are shot to look the way the director envisions them. Often this activity involves a substantial amount of electricity that must be provided on the set, whether the shooting takes place in a studio or at a remote location. The electrician responsible for making it available is called a **gaffer**.

Before the filmmaker can shoot something he or she must have something to shoot. A **set designer** is responsible for staging the environment that will be shot. This involves the problem of seeing to the physical placement of properties on the set. The **key grip** coordinates the crew whose task it is to move the props and furniture so they will be where the director and set designer want them. Sometimes it will be necessary for someone to get something that has been overlooked. The person who is assigned to run and fetch such items is called a "**gofer**" or "**best boy.**" Other crew members important to a production include "**costumers,**" "**makeup,**" and "**special-effects**" technicians, among others.

2.2   Production still taken during the shooting of the German picture *Der Letze Mann (The Last Laugh)* (1925). Director F.W. Murnau, wearing a hat and watching from behind the camera, observes actor Emil Jannings's performance. Jannings plays a hotel doorman who loses his job because of advanced age--the doorman's dejected condition is clearly conveyed through the actor's body language. A technician behind the camera positions a light on Jannings. In the background, out of focus, is a set of city building fronts. Set designers constructed these exterior fronts for filming inside a building at the studio. German filmmakers of this period preferred to shoot everything inside because they had more control over the lighting and environment. Picture courtesy of the British Film Institute.

The producer coordinates the logistics of the shooting during the period that the movie is being shot. It is his or her responsibility to provide studio space, when it is needed, and sees to meeting the needs of cast and crew on location. Food, electricity, facilities, and permissions all must be dealt with before a company can go on location to shoot. The producer also makes sure that this often complicated undertaking continues to receive funding throughout all of its phases. Another concern is seeing that the cast and crew know what is expected of them, and where they are supposed to be, during the filming. One way this information is communicated is through a "**three-o'clock**." A "three-o'clock" is a timetable posted in the afternoon, often at various locations in the hotel where members of the production are staying. It identifies what is going to be done the following day and where.

III. Postproduction, Distribution, and Exhibition

After the crew has finished shooting, the producer must concentrate on the postproduction phase of the filmmaking process. Postproduction is primarily concerned with editing the film and putting the movie together in its finished form. With the possible exception of the director, the crew members involved in the preproduction and production phases usually are dismissed and do not work on postproduction. Again, the producer is concerned with the logistics and funding necessary to see the original idea realized in a completed picture. The producer hires the editor and staff and makes sure that an editing facility is available for them.

Very often the audience is not aware of how important editing is to the outcome of a completed picture. Sometimes the editing can take a picture, considered disappointing, and make it into a movie that is really appreciated. According to the Hollywood columnist James Bacon, the movie *High Noon* (1952) was not only salvaged but made into a classic through the efforts of the talented editor, Elmo Williams (1913-). *High Noon* was a western whose entire action takes place during the course of a single Sunday morning. It involves a sheriff who nervously awaits the arrival of an outlaw who is "coming to get him." Bacon claims that the original version of *High Noon* was too long and contained too many unmotivated close-ups of the attractive leading woman, Grace Kelly. To add to the problems the star, Gary Cooper (1901-1961), was suffering from an ulcer and looking miserable because of it in most of his shots. Williams shortened the film and cut out much of the material with Grace Kelly. He added footage of clocks that showed the actual time that transpired between the shots containing these timepieces. Williams also dubbed in the theme song, *Do Not Forsake Me, Oh My Darling*. He repeated the song over and over to the point that some describe its presence as irritating. Material which previously

22

had been ineffectual now helped give the film dramatic tension. The close-ups of Cooper looking miserable due to his ulcer, Bacon claims, now appeared to reflect the anxiety the sheriff was experiencing as he waited for the inevitable shoot out. One must always question the validity of anecdotal information coming out of Hollywood. Still, this story suggests how important the choice of footage and the way it is edited can be in influencing the outcome and appearance of a movie. [1]

During postproduction the editors piece the film together, mix the music and sound effects, and add the graphics. The film is now completed and ready to be seen. The producer at this time must figure out the best way to distribute the movies to viewers for maximum profit. At one time a producer's options for distribution would have been limited. During the period between the 1930s and 1950s most American producers would have been employees at the eight major Hollywood studios--MGM, Paramount, Twentieth Century Fox, Warner Brothers, Universal, Columbia, RKO, and United Artists. American filmmakers had to work with one of these studios if they wanted their movies exhibited in the United States and in foreign countries. Television, as we shall see, created new alternatives for distribution and exhibition.

The distribution phase is not only concerned with providing a means of getting films to the exhibitor. It also is involved with making audiences aware of the upcoming picture. The financial success or failure of a film may depend upon publicity and marketing. The "**preview**" or "**trailer**," that precedes the movie we have gone to see in the theater, is one time-honored way filmmakers inform their public about upcoming pictures. Movie posters, placed around the theater, newspaper advertisements (see fig. 2.3), and interviews with movie stars in fan magazines are other forms of publicity which filmmakers developed, early in the history of the industry, to publicize their product. Creating commercial **tie-ins** with books, music, toys, or candy associated with a picture is another way that filmmakers try to increase audience awareness, concerning their movie, and make money from this interest. (See fig. 2.4.)

Exhibition has changed dramatically over the last quarter-century. At first filmmakers depended solely upon domestic and foreign theatrical rentals to make a profit from their movies. Pictures would initially be released in large theaters in metropolitan areas at high rentals and then eventually made available to other venues, in the suburbs and small towns, at cheaper prices. Audiences, in these latter locations, would see the movies weeks and even months after they were shown in the larger cities. Foreign release would be substantially later as well. After a film completed this circuit its value to the producer might be seen as minimal. Many early films of this century were destroyed because they were believed to have no

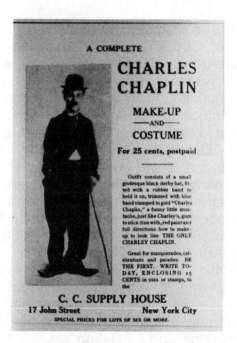

2.3 A 1915 trade journal advertisement announcing upcoming Chaplin films.

2.4 A commercial tie-in for Charlie Chaplin makeup published in 1915 fan magazines.

commercial value. Television eventually changed this attitude.

When television was first marketed, in the United States, it had an immediate two-fold impact on the movies. It competed for theater audiences and showed Hollywood's old movies. A film like *The Wizard of Oz* (1939), which did relatively well when first released, took on cult status from repeated screenings on television. As television technologies developed new markets and ways of looking at films evolved as well. Today a producer may figure that a film will generate revenue from domestic and foreign theatrical exhibition, cable channel franchises, "free television" transmissions, and videocassette purchase and rentals. All of these potential outlets determine how much a producer can spend in the expensive process of making a movie.

While these outlets have increased the ways a filmmaker can profit from a movie, and make it easier for audiences to see what they want to see, the changes in format do influence the aesthetics of the viewing experience. Films made before the advent of television were not intended to be shown in segments separated by commercials. Also, as noted in Chapter One, watching a movie on a small television does not provide the same effect as seeing it on a big movie screen. An epic picture like *Lawrence of Arabia*

(1962) can literally overwhelm a viewer when exhibited as a 70mm print projected on a big screen. When seen on television the viewer is bigger than the picture.

A recent controversial trend involves the "colorization" of what originally were black and white motion pictures. This is done to try and make them more marketable to certain audiences. Many critics believe this colorization process ruins aesthetic effects, accomplished by the filmmakers' manipulation of shadows and texture, that exist in the original black and white images. Converting a black and white theatrical movie to a poorly colored picture on the small screen, they argue, compromises the director's artistic intentions too much. The famous director Orson Welles (1915-1985), whom we will discuss in Chapter Twelve, directed two brilliant black and white films--*Citizen Kane* and *The Magnificent Ambersons*-- for RKO in 1941. A couple weeks before he died, Welles feared that media mogul Ted Turner would obtain the film and television rights to the RKO collection. Referring to *Citizen Kane* he asked a friend, "Please do this for me. Don't let Ted Turner deface my movie with his crayons." [2]

IV. Conclusion

In any communication process one must have a "transmitter" to convey information and a "receiver" that can comprehend it. The production process represents the various phases necessary to form, structure, and transmit a film message. Given the complex nature of the motion picture medium, film production involves several people and specialized processes so that this transmission can be completed. The remainder of this text will explore how film and filmmaker are important to this communication process. Because we are especially concerned with the film consumer --how *we* respond to the transmitted message--we will pay particular attention to the reception phase of the process. A key element to understanding this phase involves our awareness of **film form** and **film style**--the structure and appearance of a motion picture.

Anyone who has spent any time watching film or television has unconsciously developed some understanding of film form and film style. One hundred years ago early filmmakers, who did not have the benefit of our viewing experience, were faced with the problem of trying to use the motion picture as a medium of communication. The following chapter will explore how the meaning of film form and style evolved during motion picture history's earliest years. We will observe how the pioneer filmmakers learned to communicate with the medium, examine how they became more sensitive to this particular communication process, and consider how their early efforts at filmic expression can help us understand the basic skills needed to become better film consumers.

ENDNOTES

1. James Bacon, *Hollywood is a Four Letter Town,* (New York: Avon Books, 1976), pp.148-150.

2. Harlan Lebo, *Citizen Kane: The Fiftieth Anniversary Album,* (New York: Doubleday, 1990), p.194.

2.5   1890s film exhibition with an early Edison motion picture projector. From   Hopkins's *Magic.*

CHAPTER THREE

MOTION PICTURE PIONEERS AND THE EVOLUTION OF FILM FORM AND FILM STYLE

CHAPTER OBJECTIVES: *Examine the early history of the American and French film industries and show how these developments influenced film form and style.*

I. Thomas Alva Edison, the Invention of the Motion Picture, and Trends in Early American Film Exhibition, 1877-1900

Thomas Alva Edison (1847-1931) is often cited in the history books as principal inventor of the motion picture. A wizard at marketing and self-promotion, Edison tried to take credit for inventing the moving picture at the turn-of-the-century. Edison and his staff, especially W.K.L. Dickson (1860-1935), developed important aspects of the earliest motion picture technology but certainly not all of it. A number of inventors in Europe, usually working independently of one another, were responsible for many of the experimental cameras and projectors that evolved into the type of movie equipment used today.

Edison's interpretation of how he could market the motion picture was based upon his experience with the phonograph. Patented in 1877, the phonograph was one of Edison's most profitable and popular inventions. Instead of initially selling phonographs for home consumption, Edison placed the device in amusement parlors where individual patrons went from machine to machine, listening to the different recordings. Around 1889 Edison got the idea that it might be possible to synchronize moving pictures with phonographs. The strategy of restricting the motion picture to a penny-arcade format is indicative that this businessman saw no future for the movies other than as a mechanical curiosity. Edison, uncharacteristically, failed to recognize the financial potential of this technology. Instead of envisioning a multi-billion dollar industry arising from his invention, Edison dismissed it as a novelty. Thomas Edison's dream of talking pictures, ironically, was too visionary. The "talkies" would not be commercially viable until 1926.

Before images could be linked to the phonograph, Edison needed a workable camera. William Kennedy Laurie Dickson, one of Edison's

27

laboratory assistants, was given the task of developing such a machine. Dickson's exploration of the problem was influenced by the work of English-American photographer Eadweard Muybridge (1830-1904) in California, and physiologist Étienne-Jules Marey (1830-1904), in France.

Muybridge and Marey had been interested in studying how specific subjects looked when in motion. Muybridge created a prototype movie in 1872 at a Sacramento racetrack. He set up a row of still cameras on the track with strings attached one to a shutter. A series of photographs of a horse in various phases of motion were taken as the passing animal broke the individual strings. These images anticipated the future movie frames. In 1882 Etienne-Jules Marey, who was familiar with Muybridge's achievements, invented a photographic gun that took twelve pictures a second on a revolving glass plate. (See fig. 3.1 and 3.2). With this device Marey could photograph a bird in flight. Marey and Muybridge were interested in motion study and not the development of moving pictures as such. The outcome of their experiments, however, provided Dickson with the information that enabled him to develop a workable movie camera. It was for this camera that Edison sought a patent in 1891.

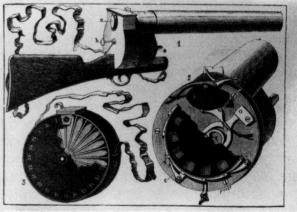

3.1 and 3.2   Étienne-Jules Marey's photographic gun.   From Hopkins's *Magic.*

Just how interested Edison was in developing and marketing his movie technology, at this time, is questionable. It was not until 1893 that he actually received a patent for his camera, or **"Kinetograph,"** and a device to exhibit his movies, called a **"Kinetoscope."** The Kinetoscope was a peep-hole projector that allowed one person to view a movie at a time. Historians have claimed that Edison did not want to project a large moving image because non-paying viewers might get to watch the movies for free. On April 14, 1894 the first Kinetoscope parlor opened in New York City, at 1155 Broadway.

The early movies, shown at the Kinetoscope parlors, were purchased from Edison. They were largely short segments of vaudeville acts or boxing films. The screening time for the individual subjects was under one minute. Dickson shot the movies using the Kinetograph--which was so large and bulky it took two people to move it--in a tar-paper studio called the "Black Maria." Located in West Orange, New Jersey, the Black Maria was constructed on a circular track with a roof that could be partially opened. This enabled the building to be rotated so the sun served as the principal source of lighting.

According to historian Gordon Hendricks, 973 Edison Kinetoscopes were manufactured by 1899, but purchase of the machines had already begun to decline by 1895. [1] The loss of audience was largely due to the fact that this format exhibited movies as a novelty. The Kinetoscope films were too short for viewers to become involved in the subject matter. Once people became accustomed to the curiosity of watching pictures that moved, they had no great desire to see films that offered little more than movement for movement's sake. Edison's policy of selling his movies, rather than renting them, also limited their commercial potential. Exhibitors were more likely to show movies they had on hand than buy new ones. Viewers soon tired of seeing the same pictures at these establishments. Because of this waning interest, Edison eventually concluded that projecting his motion pictures might be profitable after all.

As an experiment, Koster and Bial's Music Hall in New York projected movies on a large screen between vaudeville acts, on April 23, 1896. Although little more than a two or three minute novelty in vaudeville theaters, enthusiasm for the large projected moving image was positive. (See fig. 2.5). Soon Edison competitors, like American Mutoscope and Biograph--later known simply as American Biograph--were also projecting movies (see fig. 3.3). Edison, recognizing that he had failed to properly protect and exploit the commercial potential of this technology, tried to regain control of the market. He took the rival film companies to court for patents infringement. This costly and complicated litigation would, as we shall see, influence the evolution of the fledgling American film industry.

Meanwhile audience and market demand was evolving, irrespective of Edison's attempts to structure it in the courtroom.

The exhibition of movies at this time was strongly influenced by a forerunner of the slide projector--the "magic lantern." A Jesuit priest named Father Athanasius Kircher described the magic lantern, as early as 1645, in his book *Magnus Lucis et Umbrae*. Using pictures painted on glass, and illuminated with oil lamps or candles, the church utilized the magic lantern as a dramatic way to illustrate lectures. Showmen employed the device for more secular purposes in the 18th century. By the 19th century magic lantern presentations were rather sophisticated. The slides were often delicately hand-colored and quite attractive to look at. Shown with live commentary and accompanied by music, the magic lantern presentation frequently involved dramatic narratives in which each slide served as an integral scene in the story.

Familiarity with the magic lantern allowed inventors and showmen to explore the projection and exhibition of the moving image. This earlier entertainment was a model for the movies in several ways. As early as 1896 the frames of some films, like the magic lantern slides, were individually hand-colored. Eventually separate shots served a narrative function, comparable to that of the individual magic lantern slides, as "tableaus" or scenes in a story. In some countries the motion pictures were shown with live commentary similar to a magic lantern presentation. Seen by themselves these very early films might appear slow and somewhat incomprehensible today. This may be due to the fact that information, once provided by a live commentator, is no longer present. [2]

As the motion picture exhibition evolved, from peep-show to large screen, the traditional movie audience developed. Between 1896 and 1903 the movies ceased to be treated as a scientific curiosity and novelty for the American middle-class in the cities. A more promising commercial outlet was emerging among the urban poor. Middle and working-class viewers, living outside the metropolitan areas, were also developing as a movie audience. Entrepreneurs took projectors on the road for exhibition in small town America as early as 1895. This market soon expanded and by 1900 numerous traveling showmen were projecting motion pictures at fairs and public gatherings across the country.

After 1900, as the practice of showing films between live acts lost its novelty in the vaudeville theaters, penny-arcade owners bought their discarded motion picture equipment. Instead of restricting movies to a peep-show format, the arcades increasingly provided space where the films could be projected. That there was a decline in the popularity of projected movies, in large urban vaudeville theaters of 1900, reflects a continuing problem with the motion picture at this time--too many movies with unimaginative content.

3.3 An open air stage built on the roof of the American Mutoscope Company in New York in the 1890s. Note that the set is supposed to be the interior of a room even though the film is being shot outdoors. From Hopkins's *Magic*.

Too often entrepreneurs treated the projected film image of 1896 as a novelty rather than as something that could be developed for its interesting content. The movies being projected were actually the same ones that had been shown in the Kinetoscope parlors. The projected format created renewed interest among audiences. As we noted in Chapter Two, viewing a picture on a large screen provides a much different experience than seeing the same movie in a situation where the person watching is bigger than the image. Viewing tiny people on a small screen does not have the same psychological impact as observing them several sizes larger than real life. Audiences were literally overwhelmed by these giant images at first but lost interest as their peculiarity became familiar. Again the problem was not with the medium, or its potential, but with the way it was being marketed as a curiosity.

Sophisticated middle-class audiences in the metropolitan areas had the opportunity and resources to demand quality entertainment. They found it in vaudeville and the theater. The urban poor, and people outside the cities, had fewer options to amuse themselves. Because these individuals had access to fewer novelties, motion picture showmen could attract and keep them as an audience.

By 1900 Edison was made aware of the demand coming from this market, and began turning out large quantities of movies in an effort to supply it. Edison also had a director working for him, Edwin Stanton Porter (1870-1944), who was interested in creating a film product that audiences wanted. The quality of the product was not as high a priority for Edison, however, as his concern for the quantity of films he sold and his efforts at controlling the market through coercion and litigation. Eventually Edison's refusal to take film content seriously forced him out of the movie business altogether. Between 1900 and 1907, however, Edison and Porter produced some very innovative films. Before discussing Edwin S. Porter's importance, to the evolution of narrative film, we should recognize some pioneer French filmmakers who were influencing the way the motion picture was developing as a medium of communication at this time.

II. The "Home Movies" of Louis and Auguste Lumière and the Narrative Filmmaking of Georges Méliès

Even as Thomas Edison was trying to figure out the best way to commercially exploit motion picture production and exhibition in the United States, entrepreneurs were manufacturing and exhibiting movies in Europe. The French inventor and filmmaker Louis Lumière (1864-1948) was particularly instrumental in devising some of the first practical achievements in motion picture photography and projection. A manufacturer of photographic plates, along with his father and brother, Lumière perfected a workable movie camera and projector by 1895. His popular films showed workers leaving the Lumière factory (see fig. 3.4), a train coming into a station, a baby being fed, and simple jokes staged for the camera.

Not intended as historical documents, the Lumière moving pictures now provide a fascinating record of a different world. No one today travels on the types of trains, or wears the kind of clothing, shown in the Lumière movies. Although familiar to Louis Lumière this was not, of course, the world known to everyone living in the late nineteenth century either. Few individuals owned factories like Louis Lumière and his family. Many of the first Lumière films are, in fact, early home movies made by people who were clearly well-to-do. Wealth aside, the way this inventor used his new photographic toy reveals a fascinating link between ourselves and the interests of a filmmaker of one hundred years ago. Acting just like the owner of a new camcorder today, Lumière shot pictures of his business and family, and persuaded friends to "clown" before the camera.

The immediate response to Louis Lumière's home movies in the 1890s was enthusiastic and widespread. Public interest was so positive that Louis and his older brother Auguste (1862-1954) made their films available for international distribution a few months after their 1895 Paris premiere. As early film audiences became more familiar with the medium

32

3.4   Frame enlargement from the 1895 Lumiére film *La Sortie des ouvriers de l'usine (Workers Leaving a Factory).*

they demanded more from its content. It does not take long for home movies of someone else's baby being fed to become tedious for most viewers. If the Lumières had shot nothing more than home movies they soon would have lost their audience. Before people got tired of their films, the Lumières concentrated on shooting something else. Their choice of new subject matter again parallels the situation of the family with the camcorder of today.

When the novelty of the new camcorder wears off, people are less likely to shoot video of their daily routines. After a relatively short time the new camcorder is usually put away and only brought out for special occasions like family vacations. Eventually the Lumiére films went beyond their "home movie phase" and sought more specialized material to shoot. Anticipating audience demand for more exciting and unique subject matter, Lumière cinematographers began shooting documentary scenes all over the world. Their subjects included such special events as the 1897 inauguration parade of President William McKinley in the United States.

The content of turn-of-the-century movies, by other inventors and filmmakers, was similar to that found in the Lumière pictures. The early cameramen filmed short, usually nonfiction, footage of a few seconds duration. These scenes were spliced together, without concern for the order or consistency of subject matter, and exhibited to a curious public. Because of their efforts we can still see movies of Queen Victoria of England, Kaiser Wilhelm II of Germany, Czar Nicholas II of Russia, battle footage of the Spanish American War, devastation from the 1906 San Francisco earthquake, and the execution by electricity of a circus elephant who had killed a person. Such subjects were filmed because of their fame or novelty. Movies gave audiences their only opportunity to see these people and situations. The resulting short movies are quite similar to the type of film and video stories today's television journalists choose to produce.

Contemporary television pieces, called **"actualities,"** are visual documents relating to a newsworthy event or human interest story. The actuality is shown as a short segment on the news, with background commentary provided by the reporter or anchor. The audience's motivation, for watching the Lumière pictures, parallels the interests of today's newscast viewer. People in the 1890s wanted to be informed about news events and see exotic subjects and places.

Louis and Auguste Lumière decided, by 1897, to restrict themselves to the manufacture and sale of photographic equipment and film stock. They had helped create a market for the movies, with the exhibition of their films, and proven the satisfactory technical quality of their products in the process. The Lumières now left the production, distribution, and exhibition of motion pictures to others. No longer filmmakers, their pioneer efforts at filmmaking had anticipated what others would continue to do. By 1910 the Lumière form of nonfiction actuality had evolved into a format known as the **"newsreel."** Through the 1950s, and even into the 1960s, movie audiences expected to see a ten minute newsreel of news and novelty stories before viewing the feature film in a theater. Today we see similar nonfiction formats on television news programs. Lumière movies also anticipated the narrative motion picture.

As noted, the earliest Lumière movies were not just home movies of everyday routines or exotic footage of special events from faraway places. The Lumières also staged jokes for the camera using non-professional actors. In their famous sketch *L'Arroseur arrosée* (*The Hoser Hosed*), a boy steps on a gardener's hose as the latter waters some plants. (See fig. 3.5). When the gardener looks at the nozzle the boy lifts his foot so the gardener gets a face full of water. The gardener drops the hose, catches the boy, "spanks" him lightly in mock rage, and then picks up the hose to resume his watering. Clearly staged for the camera this little half minute sequence, with its rudimentary plot, is not a nonfiction film but a narrative. Staging situations for the camera would actually be the trend of the future. Until 1907 the majority of the movies produced in the world were nonfiction. After 1907 most films were narratives. A major pioneer in narrative filmmaking was another Frenchman, Georges Méliès (1861-1938).

During the latter part of the 1890s Georges Méliès ran a theater in Paris, the Theatre Robert-Houdin, where he put on magic performances for the public. Recognizing the film medium's potential, Méliès wanted to buy a Lumière camera after seeing the 1895 premiere of their films. His offer was refused. Undaunted, Méliès purchased an English movie projector which he had converted into a camera. By April of 1896 Georges Méliès was successfully exhibiting his own movies at his theater. What separated Méliès from many early filmmakers was his background in show business. Thomas Edison and Louis and Auguste Lumière were business people and inventors with little or no background in showmanship. Méliès was a magician and showman who knew what his audiences wanted and made movies that addressed their interests.

Audience demand for his films became so great that Méliès eventually built a film studio. This specially constructed facility allowed him to recreate the lighting and theatrical illusions, on film, that audiences saw in his stage shows. Méliès's background as a magician also prompted him to experiment with ways in which fantasy effects could be created using the properties peculiar to the motion picture medium. Because of his success with these experiments some historians have labeled Georges Méliès the "Father of Trick Photography." Edwin S. Porter would be one of the most important directors to be immediately influenced by Méliès's accomplishments.

III. Edwin S. Porter's Career at Edison, 1896-1909

Edwin Stanton Porter was hired as a technician and filmmaker by the Edison company in 1896. When enthusiasm for the movies was threatening to decline around 1900, Porter believed story films would attract audiences. He was especially interested in exploring how narrative continuity could be incorporated, in his pictures, and began experimenting with continuity film editing as early as 1901. Instead of shooting one subject one shot, Porter developed his narratives in much the same way that comic strips and magic lantern shows used a series of successive images to convey their information.   Most of his movies were restricted to fewer than a half dozen shots. In 1902 Edwin S. Porter made his most ambitious film to date--a charming version of *Jack and the Beanstalk,* which told its story in a series of nine shots. This film used trick photography, and a rather elaborate set design for the period, to create the proper fairy tale atmosphere in a style owing a great deal to the influence of Méliès.

New storytelling methods and technical breakthroughs were changing the way the way movies were being shot by 1902. In the early 1890s Dickson was limited to filming vaudeville acts and whatever else could be staged in the Black Maria. The camera could not be moved so the action had to come to the Kinetograph. The Lumière camera was much lighter than the bulky Edison apparatus. Its portability enabled filmmakers to shoot on location, rather than restrict them to the studio. Méliès had access to a light camera but preferred studio shooting. He found the studio gave him greater control over his set design, lighting and, most importantly, his elaborate special effects and trick photography. Instead of going outside to shoot his exteriors, Méliès recreated them in his studio.

Porter's *Jack and the Beanstalk,* which had been influenced by the work of Méliès, was also made in the studio. By 1902 the Edison equipment had become much lighter, allowing Porter to take his camera on location the way the Lumières had done. Despite the early emphasis on studio shooting, the trend for American filmmaking between 1900 and 1915 was to shoot outdoors. Given their preference for natural lighting, directors even had indoor sets built outside. (See fig. 3.3). Consequently viewers will sometimes see, even in a 1914 feature film like *The Birth of a Nation,* curtains and candles of interior settings being blown by the wind.

Porter's most famous film was *The Great Train Robbery,* which he directed in 1903. Ever on the lookout for subjects that would please an audience, Porter and his crew decided that a western might make an interesting movie. At this time the wild west was not a distant memory for many Americans. Famous western outlaws and gunfighters like Emmett Dalton, Frank James, and Wyatt Earp were still alive. Butch Cassidy and the Sundance Kid were continuing to "work" as robbers, although feeling compelled to move to South America if they were to continue their "profession." Butch and Sundance's old "hunting grounds" were becoming too civilized to support this older lifestyle. Buffalo Bill Cody's (1846-1917) wild west show was going from town to town at this time, giving outdoor performances in tents in a manner similar to the type of exhibition being done by the Ringling Brothers circus. Dime novels and stage productions of fictional western accounts were also very popular in 1903. Such familiarity with the western enabled Edwin S. Porter to structure his film, using this genre's well known conventions, in a manner that would make its narrative understandable to contemporary audiences.

The Great Train Robbery was shot on location in a rural area, outside Orange, New Jersey, that resembled western terrain. The eight minute movie's success proved that the motion picture could work well as a medium for telling this type of story. Porter knew what an audience wanted from a western and fashioned his plot to address these expectations. Dramatic situations and types of action, associated with the genre, made the picture quite exciting for 1903 viewers. *The Great Train Robbery* was a critical and commercial successful.

Instead of immediately advancing narrative filmmaking techniques, *The Great Train Robbery* ended up being a bit ahead of its time. Until about 1907, filmmakers recognized that the movie worked well but could not figure out exactly why. Many tried to make pictures like *The Great Train*

36

Robbery-- even to the extent of retelling its story and copying its setups--but few directors were able to duplicate this film's dramatic achievement. Ironically, Porter himself was never able to make a film that repeated the stylistic success of *The Great Train Robbery* . We will discuss this picture in greater length in Chapter Seven.

IV. The MPPC, the Decline of the Edison Film Company, and the Rise of Hollywood

As noted, Thomas Edison was more concerned about controlling the market, and selling a large quantity of films to meet this growing demand, than he was interested in making quality motion pictures. By 1907 over a million people were paying five cents a day to see the movies. Earlier Edison pictures had been individually crafted. Edison now encouraged his employees to use the ideas of mass production, pioneered by industrialists like Henry Ford, to create "assembly line movies." This emphasis resulted in Porter being pressured into producing several films quickly, rather than taking the time needed to make a few motion pictures well. According to film   historian Charles Musser, in his documentary *Before the Nickelodeon,* it took Porter six weeks to make the eight minute movie *Jack in the Beanstal*k in 1902. By 1909 the studio was expected to turn out fifteen films every three days. [3]

Edison's priority of quantity over quality suggests that he did not believe a movie could be of interest to a serious viewer. Porter, unhappy with this arrangement, left Edison in 1909 to form a film company called Rex. Thomas Alva Edison, in the meantime, came up with a new plan to dominate the American film industry.

By September of 1908, there were between eight and ten thousand nickelodeons showing movies in the United States. Most were projecting their films. When Edison found he could not beat his major competitors in court, he agreed to join them by forming an organization designed to control the market. On December 8, 1908, Edison and Biograph joined Pathe Freres, Vitagraph, Essanay, Kalem, Lubin, Star Film, Selig Polyscope, and Kleine Optical, to establish the Motion Pictures Patents Company or MPPC. As a combination this group shared sixteen important American patents relating to moving picture technology. They also received an exclusive contract from Eastman-Kodak supplying them with raw film stock. The MPPC attempted to control all aspects of the film business through special licensing agreements. Only parties authorized by the MPPC could manufacture or use their equipment, obtain Eastman-Kodak film stock, and buy or exhibit their movies. In 1910 the "trust" created the General Film Company which licensed the distribution of motion pictures to exhibitors.

Quite powerful during its first years of existence, the effectiveness of the Motion Pictures Patents Company was severely impaired by 1914. The MPPC's attempt to gain control of the distribution and production of the motion picture market resulted in the organization being accused of operating as an illegal trust. By October 1, 1915, the Motion Pictures Patents Company was declared to be an illegal combination, in violation of the Sherman Anti-Trust Act, by the District Court of the United States for the Eastern District of Pennsylvania. Even if it had not been challenged by the government, for attempting an illegal restraint of trade, the MPPC was not effectively competing with the companies that it had been unsuccessfully attempting to exclude from the market.

Before this 1915 ruling the legal existence of film companies, other than those within the MPPC, was a matter of continuous litigation in the courts. Any company attempting to manufacture or distribute motion pictures, using equipment containing patents owned by the MPPC, was in danger of prosecution by that organization. The MPPC's legal right to control the American film industry continued to be successfully challenged in the courts, particularly after 1912. As the MPPC's dominance weakened, an increasing number of independents got into the motion picture market. Hundreds of independent motion picture producers entered the business by 1914, with little fear of judicial censor. The popular product of the independents, and the 1915 anti-trust court decision challenging the MPPC's position in the American film market, severely limited this corporation's profit-making effectiveness. By 1918 the Motion Picture Patents Company went out of existence altogether.

The Motion Picture Patents Company had tried to base its control of the film market on the ownership of patents used in the equipment necessary to manufacture and exhibit motion pictures. Their position in the market allowed them to dictate the type of film they wanted to produce. The independents had to rely on audience reaction to guide the form and content of the films that they introduced to the public. To gain an audience for their product, the independents experimented with methods of servicing American film audiences that differed from those of the MPPC. Consequently, the independents gained ascendancy in the industry as the Motion Picture Patents Company went into decline.

Historians have isolated three differences between the product of the Motion Pictures Patents Company and the films associated with the independent companies. One early innovation of the independents was the introduction of feature length films. The MPPC preferred to produce and distribute short subjects that seldom ran beyond twenty-five minutes in length. Several independent companies, by 1912, were manufacturing and exhibiting feature length films that ran forty minutes or longer. The new length gave the filmmaker an opportunity to develop more complexity in a film's narrative. This special length also enabled the public to differentiate these pictures from the often thematically inferior MPPC short subjects.

A second important development, that the independents were marketing, was the idea of the "film star." The actors in the MPPC films often were not given billing because the companies feared they would demand larger salaries if they became popular with the public. By 1910 the independents were using stars as a means of attracting audiences to their films. These popular actors could, as the MPPC had indeed feared, command larger salaries.

A final market consideration, that separated the independent product from the films of the MPPC, was a concern for quality. The MPPC was more interested in the quantity of films it could rapidly produce than it was with the quality of their content. The independents recognized that audiences were becoming more discriminating in their film tastes and, unlike the MPPC, tried to give viewers the type of movies they seemed to want.

The independents totally usurped the film market by 1918. The MPPC members had now either gotten out of filmmaking altogether, like Edison, or broken away from this company to make films in the manner of the independents. With the growing ineffectiveness and eventual death of the MPPC, each of the independent film companies sought ways to gain commercial advantage in the market. Since no one was in a position to dictate what the consumer would see, between 1914 and 1918, the industry now relied on audience reaction to suggest what type of product should be made.   Consequently, the filmmaker or star who achieved box-office recognition could obtain financial reward and artistic freedom based on the demand for his or her product. It can be argued that quality of product was not always the highest priority for Edison and other members of the MPPC. Still, some attention should be given to the way these companies, in America and France, pioneered the evolution of film aesthetics prior to 1918.

V. The Lumière's Use of the Motion Picture as a Medium of Communication

As we noted in Chapter Two, every medium of communication has certain formal properties that can be used to convey messages. The communicator's choice of medium will influence the particular form his or her communication will take. Those wishing to communicate with a given medium, or interpret what it is expressing, need to have an understanding of its particular properties. An examination of some early Lumière films reveals that these filmmakers were using elements peculiar to film, for purposes of communication, from the very first.

The Lumières recognized that their moving pictures enabled them to document--or make visual records--of the world in front of their camera. This information was similar to what could be expressed in the two-dimensional visual depiction found in paintings and photographs. Given the nature of the motion picture medium, there were some unique differences. Paintings were restricted to one size. The Lumière pictures could be projected so the image ranged from the dimensions printed on the film to larger than life. Photographs could also be printed on slides, and projected so their size would vary, but still images do not move. The motion picture medium not only reproduced a visual facsimile of its subject, that could be varied in size, it could duplicate movement. Instead of freezing a moment in time the Lumières could capture several seconds. Today we can still use the Lumière movies to study and interpret the subjects they recorded.

Despite the similarity in appearance these early films have to their subjects, we must remember that they can be misleading in terms of what we think they have documented. It clearly would be incorrect for us to assume, from these films, that the France of the late 1890s existed in black and white rather than color, or that its people moved in a somewhat jerky fashion in a silent and two-dimensional world. It would also be very wrong to judge the intelligence and sophistication of the individuals in these movies by what, to us, are fairly crude standards of moving picture technology and filmmaking. The Lumières duplicated aspects of the reality around them but not the reality itself. Any medium is limited to what it can interpret. Even if they had access to sound, color, and three-dimensional photography, the Lumières could only depict aspects of the subjects they chose to document. Today's filmmakers and video producers have better technology. What information can be recorded is still limited, however. No matter how truthful one attempts to be, the medium a communicator uses will distort "reality" during the process of recording its subject. It is the responsibility of the receiver, viewing this visual communication, to assess the fidelity of the information and the distortion that prevents the facsimile from fully capturing the truth.

The Lumière brothers' recognition of some of the basic communicative properties of their new medium influenced their pioneer efforts at making both nonfiction and narrative films. The act of telling a story, and the special properties of the narrative itself, puts demands on the fiction filmmaker much different from those experienced by the director of nonfiction films. By shifting their concern from film's ability to chronicle reality, to exploring how the medium can be used to tell a story, the turn-of-the-century filmmakers changed the form and content of their filmic communication. For their nonfiction pictures the Lumières were influenced by the film medium's capacity for making two-dimensional black and white moving images of actual real life subjects and occurrences such as the feeding of a baby, a train coming into a station, and workers leaving a factory. Interest in this subject matter was based upon how well the movies duplicated the appearance of activities actually happening before the camera rather than how well something was staged for it. This concern structured the content of their early nonfiction films. The form, appearance, and intent, of the Lumière documentaries, consequently, are substantially different from what we find in their narratives like *The Hoser Hosed*--one of the first situation comedies ever made. This dramatization of a practical joke, involving a gardener getting squirted with his hose, would characterize the type of humor found in many comedies made between 1895 and 1900.

As stated previously, it is unfair to gauge the sophistication of the 1890s by the content of the Lumière movies. Given the literary achievements of the day it is also false to say that the narrative of *The Hoser Hosed*, though one of the first story sequences on film, represents the highest quality of 1890s fiction. When the Lumières made this movie Shakespeare's plays, for example, were already three-hundred-years-old. The Lumière movies were seen in the 1890s, as they are today, as a novelty. The content of these pictures would not have been considered at all sophisticated when compared to work being done in such contemporary media as the theater and the novel. Novelty aside, if given a choice, most 1890s audiences would have preferred to experience their fiction in a medium other than the motion picture. But narrative film, like the nonfiction film, had potential. The pioneer filmmakers got better at telling stories using film as they became more familiar with the properties of their medium.

VI. Film Form and Film Style in Early French and American Films

Like most tangible entities, any movie can be described in terms of its "form," or structure. The form an object takes is partially determined by the principal properties it shares with others of its type. The form a person can take, for example, is largely determined by one's species, race, sex, and age. Each human being exists as a unique individual but still shares characteristics in common with other people of comparable genetic makeup, species, race, sex, age, and nationality.

The greater the number of formal elements we use to describe an entity, the clearer our understanding of it. For example, identifying a person as a five-foot-two, ninety pound, eighty-five-year-old female Eskimo (or Inuit, as these people prefer to call themselves), tells us more about that person than referring to her simply as a human being. The more formal elements we are given, the more precise the form that woman will take in our minds. Each element identifies an aspect of that individual. With each additional category of information, taken in combination with the others, our understanding of a person's form increases.

In the same respect every film shares certain characteristics with every other movie but is also unique onto itself. Analyzing a film according to its form involves the recognition of the various formal elements relating to that movie's identity. *The Hoser Hosed*, for example, is a silent 1895 black and white French film comedy, about thirty seconds in length, involving a gardener and a little boy. Each formal element listed here identifies a context that we can cite to better envision the content of *The Hoser Hosed*, even if we haven't seen it.

The form and content of the Lumière documentaries are an outgrowth of the film medium's ability to duplicate aspects of visual information presented before the camera. A film narrative's form usually involves a plot. A film's plot can be likened to a skeleton, or frame, around which the content of that movie is structured. The plot, or skeleton of a narrative, can be better understood if it is broken down into its constituent parts: the three primary segments being the beginning, middle, and end of the movie. The plot of *The Hoser Hosed* could be described as having a beginning, in which a boy steps on a gardener's hose as a practical joke; a middle, involving the gardener getting squirted and spanking the perpetrator; and an end, where the gardener resumes his hosing as the boy leaves the scene. By breaking the narrative form of this movie down into plot segments, and showing their relationship to one another, we can develop a pretty fair understanding of what *The Hoser Hosed* is about. This is true even though our description does not consider many other important elements of the picture like composition and camera placement.

A film's form pertains to the structure of that movie. Film "style" relates to the appearance of a picture. The content of an image's composition, its color or gradations of black and white, the behavior and costume of the characters within the scene, and the way sound is incorporated, are some stylistic elements that can be used to convey information while giving that movie its particular appearance. The style of *The Hoser Hosed* is determined by such things as the setting of the garden in which the action takes place; the inclusion of a garden hose and the relationship of two people to it; the clothing of the characters, their age, motivations, and behavior.

Our examination of the Lumière films suggests that these filmmakers understood some properties of the motion picture and that the structure and appearance of their movies were influenced by the way they used the medium for communication. The form, style, and content of the Lumière films were rudimentary, however. These pioneers let others explore how the new medium could be used for purposes of more sophisticated communication. Eventually four basic stylistic properties of film were identified that could be manipulated for purposes of conveying information to the viewer. The elements of film style are image composition or **"mise-en-scene,"**

3.5 Frame enlargement from the 1895 Lumiére film *L'Arroseur arrosée (The Hoser Hosed).*

camerawork, **editing**, and **sound**.

Film mise-en-scene includes such elements as setting, lighting, costumes, props, the behavior of the actors and their position in the composition. Although the earliest narrative films, like *The Hoser Hosed*, relied almost exclusively on mise-en-scene for the picture's communication, most filmmakers had few ideas about the many ways this element could be used. In later films the directors learned how to manipulate set design, lighting, costume, and screen acting to enhance their cinematic expression. Until that time filmmakers were restricted to a pretty basic use of mise-en-scene. The potential of the three other major properties of filmic expression--camerawork, editing, and sound--remained almost totally unexplored until after the turn-of-the-century. Because of problems with the technology, sound films would not be extensively made until the 1920s. An examination of early movies by the Lumières and some of their contemporaries reveals how little camerawork and editing were used before 1907.

Film mise-en-scene bears similarities to its counterpart in the theater. The early filmmakers utilized theatrical conventions to help guide them in developing filmic equivalents. Film action, at first, was blocked for the camera in much the same way that theater was staged for its audience. This tendency resulted in the camera being placed in a stationary position, similar to where a member of the audience might be seated in the theater, where it observed whatever was placed in front of it. When used in this fashion the camera was more of a recording device than it was an element that interacted with the subject. A good example of the limitations resulting from such a stationary camera perspective can be seen in the chariot race sequence of the 1907 American movie, *Ben Hur*, directed by Sidney Olcott (1873-1949) for the Kalem company. Considered something of a spectacle when it came out in 1907, because of its emphasis on costume and use of locale, *Ben Hur* does not stand up well when judged by what we regard to be a well-made motion picture today. [4]

The chariot race, involving the story's principal characters of Ben Hur and Messala, was a major narrative sequence in the original 1880 Lew Wallace novel. This race was also a climactic part of the 1899 play and three film versions of *Ben Hur* made in 1907, 1926, and 1959. The description of the chariot race in the book continues to interest readers today. Turn-of-the-century reviews of the play describe a technically intricate staging of the race that thrilled contemporary audiences. The chariot race in the 1926 and 1959 movie versions of *Ben Hur*, made by Metro-Goldwyn-Mayer, still make for exciting viewing. The camera's depiction of the chariot race in the 1907 film, however, is more interesting for what it does not show than for any excitement the race might generate. A review of the chariot race in the 1907 version of *Ben Hur* can make us more aware of the types of camerawork and editing we have come to expect, from such sequences, but fail to see in this adaptation.

Interestingly, given the way the 1907 chariot race of *Ben Hur* is filmed and edited, we could get almost as much information from a still photograph of this camera setup as we can by watching the movie. Like most motion pictures of the day the camera, which does not move, is placed in one position--in this case in the center of the racetrack facing spectators at the beginning and finishing line. The chariots in the race do move, however. Were we actually standing in the middle of the track, where the camera was located, we could have turned our bodies to follow the action. From their vantage point the people facing the camera could observe the entire race as it was happening with a minimal amount of movement. For most of the chariot race sequence all we can see, as viewers of this film, is the audience reacting to the race and an occasional passing chariot.

In later pictures, for a scene of this sort, a director would use the camera to film the action from a variety of placements and perspectives. This movie allows us to observe the information from just one viewpoint. Given the way the camerawork presents--or more accurately fails to present--the action, we miss at least 80% of the race. We do not know who is winning or losing. We do not know which chariot belongs to Messala, the villain, or to Ben Hur, the hero. For an exciting situation the chariot race in the 1907 film of *Ben Hur* is not very thrilling today. The form and style of the movie do not allow the narrative to realize its dramatic potential. This is due, in part, to the director's failure to use more than one **shot** in this scene to advance the story.

A "shot" is what is filmed during a continuous run of the camera, beginning at the point where the camera starts shooting and ending when the camera stops filming. In most early films made before 1900, like the Lumière pictures, the subject matter usually was filmed one shot per scene. Once a single shot Lumière film, like *The Hoser Hosed,* finished going through the projector, it would be followed by another shot/scene of a substantially different movie, like *Le Répas de bébé (Feeding Baby).* A Lumière program, consequently, consisted of a series of single shot short subjects spliced together, with no real rationale for the order, or continuity between shots, regarding subject matter. Later film scenes would be comprised of a carefully chosen series of several integrated shots. These shots were edited to help the audience understand how the information in the film progresses from part to part.

"Editing" is the element of style most instrumental in determining a picture's overall form. The form of a film is concerned with how the different parts of that picture are put together to create a cohesive whole. A film's form establishes that picture's subject matter by introducing a concept, or problem, which is then summarized or resolved. This progression--from identity to problem to resolution--is usually reflected in the three basic segments which the form of most films generally are divided. These three basic segments are the <u>beginning</u>, where the identity of the movie and a principal problem is established; the <u>middle</u>, where the content of the film is most frequently developed; and the <u>end</u>, where the problem is resolved or a summary is provided. As can be determined from the movies we have examined, the "shot" is a particularly important basic unit relating to motion picture editing and film form. A structural problem with many early "photoplays," judging by the standards of today, is that the editing was too rudimentary. A good example of a movie where the editing potential remains generally unexplored is the 1907 film version of *Ben Hur.*

The 1907 *Ben Hur* does have a narrative form developed around individual scenes loosely taken from the plot of the novel. As seen in our review of the chariot race, this film incorporates an editing strategy using one shot per scene instead of breaking these sequences into individual shots. When reviewing the subject matter of the novel, from which this movie is based, this editing style fails to create a form that adequately reflects the excitement or complexity of the narrative. Mise-en-scene and camerawork

45

could also be utilized more. Until narrative filmmakers knew how to use film form and style to tell a story, the content of their work would be inferior to more developed contemporary fictional media of their time, like writing and theater. One of the first pioneer directors to explore, effectively, the potential of telling a story with film was the French magician turned fantasy filmmaker, Georges Méliès.

VII. Georges Méliès and the Form and Style of His 1902 Film Narrative, *A Trip to the Moon*

One can get a good sense of the nature of the Méliès style of filmmaking by closely examining his most famous picture, *Le Voyage dans las lune (A Trip to the Moon)*. Adapted from a Jules Verne novel, Georges Méliès's 1902 *A Trip to the Moon* is one of the first successful screen narratives. Ironically, though made five years before *Ben Hur*, Méliès's *A Trip to the Moon* is a much better movie. When compared to most films made at this time, *A Trip to the Moon* is a very remarkable picture. A major reason for its success was that Méliès effectively explored the potential expressiveness of filmic mise-en-scene. More than just a situation that happens in the space of thirty seconds or so, *A Trip to the Moon* is a carefully developed story with a beginning, a middle, and an end. We see the basics of film editing used to develop this narrative progression. This movie does more than just string shots together. All the shots are linked to give the form of *A Trip to the Moon* a cohesive and calculated identity.

A general analysis of *A Trip to the Moon*, using the four principal questions for film evaluation listed in Chapter One, reveals how much this movie is dependent upon mise-en-scene for its filmic communication. The first question the critic should ask, when watching a movie, is concerned with identifying **what the film is about.** We can start answering this question by briefly reviewing the plot of *A Trip to the Moon*.

A Trip to the Moon begins with an astronomical meeting where a person describes, on a blackboard, his theory for taking a rocket to the moon. (See fig. 5.1). Despite the debate that his idea generates, a rocket is constructed and eventually launched. As the spacecraft leaves the earth, and approaches its destination, we discover the moon's face is that of a living entity who gets very upset when the rocket hits it in the eye. (See fig. 3.6-3.8). After landing on the moon the explorers leave their craft and fall asleep. "Heavenly bodies," in the form of beautiful women, appear and disappear above their heads. They awake and investigate the exotic landscape on foot, eventually meeting a moon person who explodes after being kicked by the head explorer.

The visitors are soon captured and taken to the court of the leader of the moon people. They escape when the head explorer breaks from his captors, grabs the moon leader, and causes him to explode by throwing him to the ground. In the resulting confusion the explorers run away to their spacecraft, located near the edge of a cliff. The head explorer grabs the end of the rope, tied to the craft, and drags the vessel to the cliff's edge as the other party members get inside. When the head explorer pulls at the rope, combined with a moon person jumping on the bottom of the craft, the ship is forced to fall over the edge. This fall enables the rocket ship to leave the moon's gravity and return to earth. The moon person clutches the bottom of the ship, and the head explorer holds on to the rope, throughout the journey. The ship lands in the sea, goes to the bottom, and returns to the surface. In the last scene we see the craft, the explorers, and the captured moon person, being towed to port by a boat.

The second question, in our series of four, is concerned with **why the filmmaker is interested in stating the ideas being expressed**. Given Méliès's background as a showman, and his knowledge of the public's interest in magic and fantasy, he undoubtedly found this subject appealing. This filmmaker's sensitivity to the type of magic show entertainment audiences enjoyed enabled him to recreate a similar atmosphere in his motion pictures. The reaction of the moon when it gets hit in the eye, the presence of the female heavenly bodies, and the exploding moon people help to establish that this is a fantasy excursion to a magic place involving realities much different from those found on earth. We can address the style of *A Trip to the Moon* when we ask our third question-- **how is the filmmaker trying to accomplish his or her purpose?**

Clearly the plot and the editing of *A Trip to the Moon* are much more complicated than any of the Lumière films we have considered. The lengthy duration of some shots, and the absence of subtitles, suggests that a commentator may have been providing narration during the exhibition of this movie. Even without verbal commentary we can follow the story with little difficulty. Each shot of this Méliès movie picks up where the last one left off, preparing us for information we will encounter in the succeeding shots. In some situations a particular action begins at the end of a shot and continues in the next one. The continuation of an action from one shot into the next is an editing technique known as a "**match-on-action**." A match-on-action is a particularly effective way for the filmmaker to maintain narrative continuity between shots.

Rhythm and timing are two other editing concerns that can be found in *A Trip to the Moon*. This is particularly true at the end of the picture during the chase scenes where the explorers run away from the moon people. The chase shots are not as long as the opening shots of the film. The shorter shots correspond to the increased speed of the explorers as they run from their pursuers.   Méliès, the director, is using the action of the chase to dictate the faster cutting of this part of *A Trip to the Moon*. The incorporation of this chase scene helps to give the end of the picture a much different rhythm than that found at the beginning of the film. Early filmmakers probably learned more about editing from the chase than any other narrative technique.   The chase became an important part of innumerable melodramas and slapstick comedies of the early 1900s.

There are also some interesting camera applications in *A Trip to the Moon*.   On one occasion the camera is used as more than just a recording device that documents what is happening on the Méliès stage. In the scene where the explorers land their rocket, the moon's face physically moves toward the camera subjectively simulating the progression of the decreasing distance between rocket and destination. (See fig. 3.6-3.8). The use of this camera effect makes the scene much more effective, dramatically, than if we merely saw the rocket hit the moon's "eye" from a fixed perspective.   The decreasing distance between camera and object photographed establishes a constantly changing perspective as we appear

3.6, 3.7, and 3.8   Three views from the shot of the rocket progressing towards the moon's eye in Georges   Méliès's *Le Voyage dans las lune (A Trip to the Moon)*. Frame   enlargements.

48

to get closer to the moon's face. Unlike earlier scenes in *A Trip to the Moon*, this particular camera manipulation creates a dramatic *filmic* effect that could not have been duplicated for members of an audience watching a live stage performance in the Méliès theater.

Georges Méliès's familiarity with the construction of stage illusions, involving such things as trick boxes and trap doors, prompted him to experiment with the mechanics of motion picture photography. By shooting a scene, stopping the camera, having a performer leave the stage, and resuming shooting, Méliès created the impression that the individual suddenly disappeared. This type of camera adjustment allowed Méliès to create fantasy effects that could not always have been reproduced on stage. This use of trick photography helped to establish the fact that the moon was a magic place much different from the environment and rules of nature found on earth.

Having assessed the form and style of *A Trip to the Moon*, we are in a better position to consider the last question in our series of four--**what effect does the film have on its audience?** This question can be answered in terms of how audiences responded to the movie in 1902 and how we react to the movie today. A quick review of the answers to the previous questions confirms that any viewer's understanding and appreciation of *A Trip to the Moon*, either contemporary or modern, is largely determined by this movie's mise-en-scene. Because stage magic had been Georges Méliès's primary medium of expression, theatrical mise-en-scene tends to be the dominant stylistic element of the film. The set design, lighting, and behavior of the characters are used to help us understand what is happening in the picture. These elements also do much to determine this movie's form. By redesigning stage magic to fit this film narrative, Méliès brought a sense of whimsy to *A Trip to the Moon* that still can be appreciated.

The editing and camerawork in *A Trip to the Moon* are more sophisticated than most films of the period and viewers must have been thrilled by its special effects. The potential of these stylistic properties would, of course, be explored in other ways by filmmakers after 1907. Today many critics describe this movie as a "primitive" despite its edge over the competition. Yet, despite its age and the crudity of some of its technique when judged by modern standards, *A Trip to the Moon* continues to charm audiences with its romantic fantasy and fun--the principal effect that Méliès wanted people to get from the movie. *A Trip to the Moon* still communicates a sense of humor and magic today.

VIII. The Importance of Pioneer Directors and Their Movies to Contemporary Film Study

An understanding of the background of the pioneer filmmakers, and the content of their movies, is important to students for several reasons. The production methods of the early directors, and the way they marketed and exhibited their motion pictures, established the foundation upon which future film industries were based. We can gain fascinating historical perspectives of turn-of-the-century cultures and concerns from the content of these early movies. Equally intriguing, and important from the perspective of this study, is how early attitudes towards film and its use parallels our relationship with the medium today. Examinations of "primitive" films can help us think about how and why *current* filmmakers use the medium for communication in the manner that they do.

The early Lumière movies, for example, show a world very different from our own. The attitudes and interests being expressed in these pictures are not completely unfamiliar. Many Lumière films are essentially home movies of people clowning before a camera. The Lumière pictures remind us that people are people no matter when and where they live. The content of home movies differs dramatically with the type of place one calls home, however. The social and cultural background of the Lumières is much different from our own, but it was this environment that influenced what was reality for them. The Lumières' background as bourgeois manufacturers in turn-of-the-century Paris profoundly affected the content of their movies. Fellow Parisian Georges Méliès came from a similar background but made films substantially different from the Lumières. This was due to Méliès's interests as a showman and magician. Because he wished to tell complex stories, Méliès developed a more advanced filmic expression than that found in the work of most of his contemporaries.

The background of the filmmaker, and his or her intentions when making movies, can influence the content of a given film. The capabilities and limitations of the medium also influence the form and style of a motion picture's expression. After 1907 filmmakers knew they wanted to tell stories with film but they had not yet learned the best way to do it. The act of telling an effective story, its length, and content, all put demands on the medium conveying the narrative. Even as they became more sensitive to how the unique properties of the motion picture--such as camerawork, editing, and sound--could be used, the pioneer filmmakers borrowed techniques from other media and applied them to film for purposes of personal expression. The slide presentations of the "magic lantern" programs, and the presence of the live commentator, strongly influenced the structure, content, appearance, and exhibition of the early motion picture. Filmmakers also paid particular attention to how mise-en-scene could be adapted for film narratives.

Chapter Four will concentrate on how film mise-en-scene was developed into a sophisticated stylistic element of the motion picture and discuss how we, as film viewers, can become more sensitive to its expression. Particular attention will be paid to the major film producer and internationally acclaimed master of mise-en-scene, comedian Charlie Chaplin, and his 1925 film *The Gold Rush*.

ENDNOTES

1.   Gordon Hendricks, "The History of the Kinetoscope," adapted by Tino Balio from *The Kinetoscope: America's First Commercially Successful Motion Picture Exhibition* (New York, 1966), for *The American Film Industry*, (Madison, Wisconsin: The University of Wisconsin Press, 1976), p.45.

2.   The author wishes to thank Mr. David Robinson and Mr. Norman Blackburn for pointing out the influence magic lantern presentations, and the live commentator, had on early film exhibition. They offered their observations at a seminar Mr. Robinson was giving on Georges Méliès, at the Museum of the Moving Image, London, England, on May 14, 1993.

3.   Charles Musser, director, *Before the Nickelodeon: The Early Cinema of Edwin S. Porter,* Film for Thought, 1982.

4.   I am grateful to Mr. Charles Reed Mitchell for first showing me the 1907 version of *Ben Hur* some twenty years ago. It was Mr. Mitchell who got me thinking about the differences between this film and the type of cinematic expression we expect from motion pictures today. The *Ben Hur* screening was one of the first of now countless instances where Mr. Mitchell's friendship, assistance, and expertise influenced my understanding of motion picture history and criticism.

CHAPTER FOUR

CHARLIE CHAPLIN, AUTEUR AND MISE-EN-SCENE CRITICISM, AND *THE GOLD RUSH*

CHAPTER OBJECTIVES: *Explore how the background and philosophy of a filmmaker can be used for an "auteur" study of that person's work; consider Charles Chaplin's importance to motion picture history; and show how mise-en-scene analysis can provide a better understanding of a film's aesthetics.*

I. The "Dickensian" Childhood of Charles Spencer Chaplin, 1889-1903

The background and interests of a filmmaker, as we have observed, must have an impact upon the content and quality of his or her work. Aspects of the lifestyle of Louis and Auguste Lumière are reflected in the subject matter of some of their home movies. Georges Méliès's interest and expertise in magic shows influenced the kind of motion pictures he made. Thomas Edison's lack of interest resulted in his company making films that were often unremarkable in their content. Charlie Chaplin's film style, as we shall see, was particularly influenced by his childhood.

4.1 Above: Charles Chaplin, in costume, lining up a shot during the production of his 1925 film, *The Gold Rush*. Courtesy the British Film Institute.

Charles Spencer Chaplin, the son of Charles (1863-1901) and Hannah (1865-1928) Chaplin, was born on April 16, 1889 in London, England. (See fig. 4.2). From working-class backgrounds, Chaplin's parents' economic situation improved dramatically, in the 1880s, when they sought employment in a form of variety entertainment known as "English music hall." Hannah was a singer and dancer while Charles was a comedian and singer. The family enjoyed a comfortable lower middle-class lifestyle during the early childhood of Charlie and his half-brother, Sydney (1885-1965.) When Charlie was four, however, their lives changed dramatically after Hannah and Charles separated. Problems with Hannah's voice prevented her from getting music hall engagements. Charles, an alcoholic, continued to have a career in variety but did not care to contribute to the financial support of his family.

The story of what happened to the Chaplins between 1892 and 1906 could have been written by the great English novelist, Charles Dickens (1812-1870). As Hannah Chaplin's music hall bookings became fewer their comfortable lodgings were replaced by cheaper and cheaper housing. The once stylish clothing Hannah and her boys had worn was sold, sewn into different garments, or showed the effects of repeated mending. Hannah Chaplin attempted to make a living from sewing. This labor took many hours, was hard on her eyes and health, and brought in little money. The three often had too little to eat. The fact they once enjoyed economic success probably heightened their embarrassment about living in modest

4.2   Charles Spencer Chaplin is believed to have been born on East Street in south London, in April of 1889.   As can be seen from this photograph taken in July of 1993, the street market that existed in Chaplin's time is still thriving.   Photo taken by the author.

dwellings and wearing less than fashionable clothing. The strain caught up with the family and, in June of 1895, Hannah became ill. She checked into a public hospital, Lambeth Infirmary, remaining there until the end of July. Sydney was placed in a school for poor children and Charlie was left in the care of relatives. The Chaplins would continue to experience substantial hardships.

Hannah Chaplin fought destitution by trying to make a living as best she could, pressing legal demands to get child support from her estranged husband, and committing herself and family to the public "workhouse." Of the major horrors suffered by London's poor, few were more dreaded than the workhouse. Set up as a form of welfare assistance to help those with no recourse to existing homeless on the streets, admission to the workhouse was viewed by many Londoners as a social disgrace comparable to serving a prison sentence. Some may have considered it worse. Most poor people would do almost anything to avoid going to the workhouse for help. (See fig. 4.3). [1]

While most individuals seeking assistance were willing to work, they could not help but object to the circumstances in which they were expected to do workhouse labor. In return for a minimal amount of money, food, and temporary lodging, those submitting to the institution agreed to be locked in the premises, both day and night. They also were subjected to long hours of hard work; housed in unpleasant and often foul-smelling facilities; and paid

4.3   Lambeth Hospital--the workhouse where Hannah Chaplin lived and labored as an inmate after applying for public assistance. When this photo was taken in 1993 the workhouse gates, Master's House, and some of the walls and buildings were still standing. Photograph taken by the author.

a wage well below what could be earned in the private sector if comparable jobs were available. Treated like prisoners, denizens of the Victorian workhouse were guilty of the "crime" of being poor. One difference between the pauper and the prisoner was that workhouse inmates could check themselves out at any time and suffer the sentence of poverty somewhere else. The workhouse where Hannah Chaplin filed for assistance appears to have been a support facility for Lambeth Infirmary. By agreeing to accept their aid, Hannah was expected to do such tasks as washing bed linens, cleaning, or working in the kitchen.

Hannah Hill Chaplin was to share another condition experienced by many of the impoverished in Victorian England. She had a mental breakdown in 1898. Over the years Hannah's mental illness would come and go. Eventually her sanity would become permanently afflicted. Between 1898 and 1912 Hannah spent much of her time in the depressing hospitals designed to accommodate poor people suffering from this malady. Where young Charlie Chaplin lived, between 1896 and 1898, depended upon his mother's health and financial situation. When he was not in an institution for poor children, Charlie was living with Hannah or with Charles Chaplin, Senior, and the latter's abusive mistress, Louise. Life with his mother meant sharing financial hardship, but Charlie preferred being with her to anyone else. Hannah was a devoted and loving mother who did the best she could for her sons under more than trying circumstances. Charlie learned, while living with Hannah, how to survive in the streets; found ways to hustle money to supplement the family's income; and dealt with the problems of inadequate food, clothing, and shelter. He also suffered the death of his father from alcoholism in 1901, and his mothers institutionalization during those instances when she lost her mind.

In May of 1903 Chaplin experienced one of the worst tragedies of his life. The fourteen-year-old had to take his mentally disoriented mother to the hospital and have her committed. Alone and with nothing to do, Charlie aimlessly roamed the streets of London, or sat crying in the small room where he and Hannah had been living. Several weeks before Hannah's confinement Charlie's brother, Sydney, had secured employment as a sailor and gone to sea. Upon returning home Sydney found Charlie in a ragged and pitiful state. After Charlie was fed and clothed the brothers visited their mother at the hospital. Her appearance and disturbed mental condition shocked and horrified them. Hannah would remain institutionalized with her illness until the January of the following year. The beginning of 1903 would be one of the worst times in Charlie Chaplin's life. It was also the year his poverty permanently ended.

II. English Legitimate Theater, the Music Hall, and Charlie Chaplin

Given his lack of education, combined with the physical hardship and traumas of his childhood, some might have prophesied a bleak future for Charlie Chaplin in 1903. Charlie was not so pessimistic. The son of variety performers, the younger Chaplin had also worked professionally as a "music hall artiste" between 1898 and 1900. Charles Chaplin, Senior, possibly believing his nine-year-old son's employment might lessen Hannah's demands for child support, helped get him a job with some juvenile dancers called the Eight Lancashire Lads. This experiences taught Charlie the rudiments and realities of show business.

He had not performed in variety for over two years, suffered from the effects of poverty, was nearly illiterate, and lacked experience working in the theater, but the fourteen-year-old thespian-to-be took it upon himself go to various London theatrical agencies to apply for employment on the legitimate stage. Shortly after Sydney rescued him from his penury Charlie Chaplin's luck changed, in true Dickensian rags-to-riches fashion, when he got a substantial part in a major theatrical production featuring the fictional detective, Sherlock Holmes. By July of 1903 a boy, who earlier would have been dismissed by "polite" society as a "street urchin," was getting good reviews in the trade journals. Two years later Master Charles Chaplin's performance in a Sherlock Holmes play was favorably reviewed in the October 4, 1905 issue of the prestigious *Times* of London. He continued to work in the theater until 1906.

There were two forms of stage entertainment in England during this period. The "legitimate theater" was part of a proud tradition that included the work of William Shakespeare. Distinguished, venerated, and not always commercially successful, it was this form of employment to which most actors aspired. There was another type of live stage entertainment that was not considered as socially respectable as the theater. This was the English music hall in which Charlie Chaplin and his parents had performed at the turn-of-the-century.

The English music hall started around 1828 when inns began to provide "song and supper rooms" for their customers. These rooms enabled the patron to eat, drink, and engage in the singing of bawdy songs. After a time the innkeeper attempted to provide some structure to the singing room activities by serving as the "chairman" who organized and oversaw the evening's events. Instead of depending solely upon amateurs for the entertainment, performers were hired. The space where the entertainers performed evolved from a raised platform to a stage. Tables and chairs were replaced by fixed seating and the space took on more the appearance of a theater than a room in a tavern. By the 1860s, what had begun as a spontaneous communal activity, became a unique form of variety entertainment.

The type of stage expression that emerged from the evolving English music hall was substantially different from that of the legitimate theater. Most theatrical productions are organized around a specific story which structures the overall play. During such performances the thespians, interacting among themselves, usually behave as if they are not being observed by the audience. With variety the general entertainment was broken down into a series of independent segments in which the performers often directly interacted with the audience in a manner similar to the way standup comedians work today. Audiences might see standup comedians, singers, dancers, acrobats, magicians, animal acts, and short sketches during one evening's entertainment, and the music hall program changed from week to week. It was *variety* entertainment in every sense of the word.

By the 1880s, when Charlie Chaplin's parents were variety entertainers, the English music hall was experiencing a period of great commercial popularity, though many in middle and upper-class society still believed it to be vulgar. The legitimate theater had the greater reputation, but the vibrant and energetic music hall attracted a larger audience. Many performers "working the halls" would have preferred acting in the theater but competition for these parts was great and the number of roles few--a fact that makes Charlie Chaplin's 1903 employment in the theater all the more remarkable.

Charlie's good reviews, and ability to keep working in the legitimate theater for three years, are indicative of his talent. Despite this success and his professional preference for the theater in 1906, Charlie Chaplin found that he, too, must embrace the other form of stage entertainment if he was to earn a living in show business. Born in the rowdy and bawdy atmosphere of the early song and supper rooms, variety was now being tailored for middle-class respectability. Besides comic singers, eccentric dancers, and acrobats, one also might see abridged sketches adapted from Shakespeare and Dickens. Both Charlie and his mother had once been dancers on the variety stage. When the younger Chaplin returned to vaudeville it was as an actor in comic skits. He eventually was hired by Fred Karno (1868-1941) (see fig. 4.5 and 4.6), the most successful producer of slapstick sketches in English variety. [2]

III. Fred Karno's Wordless Comedy and Charlie Chaplin's Comic Quaint

Fred Karno's activities in English variety, as was true for everyone else working in this form of entertainment, were strongly influenced by laws favoring the legitimate theater. In England certain theaters had exclusive licenses to put on plays with dialogue. Until 1912 show business establishments could be prosecuted if they staged performances legally restricted to the licensed theaters. Variety could feature singing, dancing, acrobats, and other types of entertainment as long as they were not interpreted as plays. Despite legitimate theater's monopoly on dramatic expression, short sketches were being produced in the music halls by the 1870s. Many of these sketches contained dialogue and were subject to prosecution. Karno got around these restrictions by performing his sketches in mime.

The execution and evolution of the Karno sketch was very different from that of the dramatic production found on the legitimate stage. Theatrical plays were structured around dialogue written in a script. Developing a Karno wordless sketch was similar to choreographing movements for an acrobatic routine or dance. The communication was based upon nonverbal expression rather than spoken words. Part of a stylized form of expression not pretending to duplicate reality, the eccentric characters of the Karno sketches wore comic dress and engaged in slapstick behavior. These red-nosed music hall comedians in baggy pants were called "quaints." (See fig. 4.4).

The quaint, as one observer noted in the 1920s, was a bizarre personality who " . . . may be tall or short, thin or fat, but he should appear to be not quite as other people. He has the right of hanging his hat on a painted peg and falling into the scenery . . . . All hats are alike to a Quaint provided they are too small or too big. White socks should be worn in full

4.4 A picture of a music hall "quaint" at the turn-of-the-century, Mr. George Beauchamp. Illustrations like this appeared on the covers of sheet music which these variety artists performed on stage. Beauchamp's costume and posture are typical of this sort of music hall comic. Charlie Chaplin's films and screen character were greatly influenced by his background as an English music hall performer. From the collection of the author.

dress together with a short cane or a broken umbrella." [3] For over thirty years Fred Karno's quaints and sketches were among the most popular on England's variety stage.

Karno's most successful sketch was *Mumming Birds*--or *A Night in an English Music Hall*, as it was known in the United States. Developed in 1905, *Mumming Birds* was a satire on English variety in which incredibly poor acts were booed and pelted with objects by "audience members" actually part of the act. This sketch was so popular, when Charlie Chaplin joined Fred Karno in 1908, that several Karno troupes were simultaneously performing *Mumming Birds* in England, Europe, and America. Sydney Chaplin was a *Mumming Birds* star. It was through Sydney's persuasion that Charlie was hired by the company, despite Karno's belief that the younger Chaplin was unsuited for this type of comedy.

4.5 and 4.6   Fred Karno (in black suit) visiting the Hal Roach Studio in Hollywood, about 1930. Hal Roach is wearing a sweater. The smiling man in the light suit is a former Karno employee, Stan Laurel. The photographs are from the collection of Mrs. Winifred Thompson, Mr. Karno's cousin. The author wishes to thank Mrs. Thompson, and Anne and Peter Fraser, for allowing us to reproduce these pictures.

Fred Karno's doubts about Charlie Chaplin's ability as a "wordless comedian" did not last long. The nineteen-year-old quickly proved himself and was Karno's headliner for two American engagements in 1910-1912 and 1912-1913. On both occasions Chaplin's understudy was a comedian named Arthur Stanley Jefferson (1890-1965). Jefferson later changed his professional name to "Stan Laurel" and became the thin half of the famous comedy team of Laurel and Hardy.

When Chaplin was appearing on stage in New York, during his first American tour, he was seen by Mack Sennett (1880-1960). Sennett had worked as a comic actor under the great director, D.W. Griffith (1875-1948) at Biograph. A year after seeing Chaplin, Sennett became manager of the new Keystone film company in California. Often featuring the famous "Keystone Cops," Sennett's comedies were soon recognized as the preeminent slapstick pictures in America, if not the world. On September 25, 1913, Charlie Chaplin signed his first film contract, agreeing to work at Keystone for one year. His salary of $150.00 per week was three times what he received from his contract with Fred Karno. Chaplin continued performing with the Karno troupe until November, joining Sennett in December of that same year.

The movies generally had not reached the artistic quality--nor the respectability--that the English music hall had achieved by 1913. There were now about 30,000 movie theaters in America, and independent producers made sixty-two pictures a week. At a time when 25 cents had the purchasing power of about $5.00 in 1990s money, the public paid $275,000,000 a year to watch the movies. Mary Pickford (1893-1979) (see fig. 4.9) was the most popular film star, earning a weekly salary of $500. [4] Charlie Chaplin did not think much of the "flickers," but appreciated the money and name recognition that an actor could get by working in film. Chaplin later claimed he planned to shoot film comedies for one year, make a great deal of money, and return to the stage for a very large wage. He did not know it but his stage career was to end in 1913.

Charlie Chaplin could not have found a better discipline for anticipating the demands of silent film comedy than the comic mime of Fred Karno's music hall sketches. In many respects Sennett's comedy resembled Karno's. The Sennett films featured pretty girls and eccentric looking males whose appearance was similar to the music hall quaint. During the course of a typical Keystone comedy the men got themselves in some type of trouble, resulting in a chase scene at the end of the picture. As with the Karno sketch, the actors had to execute the split-second timing and muscular control of an athlete performing an acrobatic routine. Everything was precisely choreographed and timed to create a specific rhythm and effect.

Mack Sennett fostered the myth that his movies were largely improvised, but this is not exactly true. The Keystone pictures were usually scripted and depended upon carefully thought out film effects for much of the comedy. As Méliès had done with pictures like *A Trip to the Moon,* Sennett used the film medium to create a world unlike that found in reality. By speeding up or slowing down the action when shooting his pictures, and increasing and decreasing the duration of the shots, Sennett imposed a calculated rhythm on his movies that carried the film characters--and the viewer--at a breathtaking pace. To be successful in Mack Sennett slapstick a comedian had to adapt to the frenetic rhythms and eccentricities of this world. All humor had to be communicated without sound. Actors could improvise within a shot, but needed to limit comic business to the short time between their characters' prearranged entries and exits before the camera. A Karno troupe would take six months to polish the tempo of a particular sketch. [5] Charlie Chaplin made thirty-five pictures for Sennett in one year.

Sennett's comedy was similar to Karno's, but Chaplin was not completely comfortable with it. The ex-music hall comedian missed having the time to refine the tempo, and opportunity to improvise better comic business, which the Karno troupes used to perfect their music hall sketches. Chaplin believed that Keystone's fast pace, and emphasis on chase, was done at the expense of developing the screen characters' personalities. He also preferred creating his comedy through improvisation during rehearsal rather than being restricted to someone else's script. These irritations aside, Charlie Chaplin's initial problem at Keystone was to come up with a workable screen character. His solution to that dilemma made film history.

4.7 Charlie Chaplin's "tramp" walking down a lonely country road with his back to the camera, at the end of the 1915 Essanay comedy, *The Tramp*. This picture of loneliness and isolation is one of the most famous images associated with Chaplin's screen character. Frame enlargement.

The character Chaplin used in his first picture for Sennett, a movie called *Making a Living,* was a seedy English con man with a monocle. While this British stereotype worked fine in Karno sketches, he did not fit in well with the American clowns at Keystone. Chaplin wanted a versatile screen personality who would blend into this world no matter what the circumstances. What he needed was a screen character, comparable to the eccentric music hall quaint, who was not quite like other people but similar enough to keep from looking out of place.

Before making his second film Chaplin went to the Keystone dressing room, experimented with makeup and fake mustaches, borrowed pieces of other people's costumes and, in one sitting, came up with the most famous screen characterization of all time. Everything about this character's appearance was a study in contrast. His derby hat was too small. His vest too tight. His pants too big and baggy. His shoes appeared to have been put on the wrong feet. His cane was rather pretentious for someone dressed in this fashion. Largely because of his ill-fitting clothing, critics began calling this figure "The Little Tramp." The character had been gainfully employed in most of the movies he appeared, but Chaplin began featuring him in "tramp" parts after 1917. Even then, it can be argued, this famous screen personality was as much a variation of the English music hall quaint as he was a comic tramp.

IV. Charlie Chaplin's Screen Career vs. the Evolution of the Hollywood Studio System, 1913-1966

The disintegration of the MPPC, and the rise of the independent company in the American film market between 1910 and 1919, changed the climate in which motion pictures were produced. During this time the freedom of the filmmaker's use of the medium was determined largely by the success of his or her pictures at the box office. Companies competed with one another for the services of Hollywood's most popular stars. Charlie Chaplin was directly affected by this competition. Between 1913 and 1923 Chaplin was a salaried employee, at different times, for four film companies-- Keystone, Essanay, Mutual, and First National. In 1913-1914 he worked at Keystone for the salary of $150 a week. When he went to Essanay in 1915, Chaplin demanded $1,250 a week plus a $10,000 bonus for joining the company (see fig. 4.8). His 1916 contract with Mutual earned him $10,000 a week, gave him a bonus of $150,000 for signing with the corporation, and made Chaplin one of the two highest salaried persons in the entire world. Another film star, Mary Pickford, competed with Chaplin for the claim of being the world's highest paid performer. Chaplin's 1918 contract with First National Exhibitors was for over a million dollars.

When they became tired of paying actors astronomical salaries the film companies, not surprisingly, looked for ways to save money. Besides outbidding one another for stars, these corporations experimented with other ways to dominate the film market, control expenses, and maximize profits. In 1919 Paramount Pictures bought a theater chain and became a "vertically integrated business" seeking to control all aspects of the production, distribution, and exhibition of its movies. Other companies followed Paramount's lead, became vertically integrated, and vied with their competition to see who could dominate the American film industry. This activity was, in fact, what Edison and the MPPC had tried to do earlier.

Efforts to conquer every aspect of the American film industry resulted, by 1925, in hundreds of independent companies being absorbed by a handful of major corporations. In the early 1930s the American film industry was dominated by five major studios--Metro-Goldwyn-Mayer, Paramount, Twentieth Century Fox, Warner Brothers, and Universal--and the three smaller concerns of United Artists, RKO, and Columbia. Not only did these eight studios effectively control the industry in America, their product was tremendously popular all over the world. Foreign film industries found it very hard to compete with American movies, even in their native countries, and often went out of business when they tried.

The hold the eight major Hollywood studios had over the American

4.8 The ABC of Essanay--1915 Essanay film stars Bronco Billy Anderson (on the right), Francis X. Bushman (on the left), and Charlie Chaplin. Anderson, who was from Pine Bluff, Arkansas, was one of the owners of Essanay and responsible for hiring Chaplin. The year Chaplin was at Essanay he made millions of dollars for the company and became one of the two most popular film stars in the world. Chaplin's principal competitor for most popular star was Mary Pickford. From the collection of the author.

motion picture market went unchallenged until 1948. That year the Supreme Court claimed that Paramount, and most of the other major studios, had been operating as an illegal trust unlawfully restraining trade. The studios could be involved in two of the three principal aspects of the business--production, distribution, and exhibition--but not all three simultaneously. Most of the companies decided to give up their theaters and continue the production and distribution of their films. The power of the old Hollywood broke up as new independent companies, and different types of filmmaking arrangements, were formed.

If most American filmmakers wanted to make movies, between 1925 and 1948, they had to work with the eight major Hollywood studios. Even if these independent producers could find someplace to shoot their pictures they still had to publicize their work and get them distributed to theaters for exhibition. These variables were controlled by the Hollywood system. After 1925 the film artist's salary, creative freedom, and choice of project was largely determined by the studio heads.

Charlie Chaplin was among those filmmakers whose careers flourished during the breakup of the MPPC and the rise of the Hollywood system. Between 1914-1919 Chaplin had more freedom than most filmmakers during the first half of this century, but his work still was subject to studio influence. Each time Chaplin signed a new contract with a film studio he not only asked for more money, he demanded greater control over his art. By 1918, however, Chaplin grew concerned that changes in the industry threatened his future creative and financial independence as a film artist. Filmmakers D.W. Griffith, Mary Pickford, and Douglas Fairbanks, Senior (1883-1939) shared his concerns. Rather than become subservient to the major corporations, they decided to become partners in film distribution themselves.

On January 15, 1919, Fairbanks, Pickford, Griffith, and Chaplin formed United Artists--a corporation that would publicize and distribute their films to theaters around the world. (See fig. 4.9). Eventually UA would own a chain of theaters as well. Since the studios where they produced their films were separate from the corporation, United Artists was not considered an illegal vertically integrated business, like Paramount, when the Supreme Court challenged Hollywood's business practices in 1948. The strategy of setting up United Artists to insure their independence anticipated how other filmmakers would make movies after the breakup of the Hollywood studio system. Chaplin remained a part owner of United Artists until 1955.

Although he helped form United Artists in 1919, contract obligations with First National prevented Chaplin from releasing movies through his own company until 1923. Upon completing his contractual obligation to First National, Chaplin had the financial, artistic, and corporate independence to make films any way he wanted.

Between 1923 and 1952 Chaplin released eight feature films through United Artists, four of which were talkies. Besides producing, writing, directing, and starring in his sound pictures, Chaplin also composed the film scores. With the passing years it took Chaplin longer and longer to produce a film. After 1952 he could not make movies in the United States at all.

Due to controversies involving his personal life, and his political views during the anti-communist period in America known as "McCarthyism," Chaplin was not allowed to return to the United States after making a short visit to England in 1952. Charles Chaplin and his family moved to Switzerland where he lived until his death on December 25, 1977. Chaplin spent the final twenty-five years of his life scoring and re-releasing some of his silent movies, writing his autobiography, and directing two more movies, *A King in New York* (1956) and *A Countess from Hong Kong* (1966.) *A Countess from Hong Kong*, which starred Marlon Brando and Sophia Loren, contained just two brief appearances by its famous director, and was Chaplin's only picture in color.

4.9   Forming their company in 1919--Charlie Chaplin signs the papers that will bind him with the other "United Artists." D.W. Griffith is on the left and Mary Pickford is on Chaplin's immediate right. The fourth partner, Douglas Fairbanks, Senior, is standing to Chaplin's left. Collection of the author.

The political controversy surrounding Chaplin abated in later years. Many Americans felt that Charlie Chaplin had been an innocent victim of the ideological witch hunts that swept their country in the '40s and '50s. Hollywood, desiring to honor one of the most famous film artists of all time, invited Charles Chaplin to visit the United States in 1972, to receive a special Oscar. Chaplin movies, unavailable to viewers for decades, were re-released to rave reviews. Three years later Queen Elizabeth II of England, knighted the eighty-six-year-old actor/director. Sir Charles Chaplin had come a long way from the Victorian workhouse he knew as a boy.

V. Charlie Chaplin as Film Auteur and Master of Mise-en-Scene

As we noted in Chapter One, "auteur" is the French word for "author." Critics in France developed "auteur criticism," following the second world war, to identify filmmakers whose unique cinematic style deserved individual attention. They made a list of auteur directors and advanced the argument that everything these filmmakers made was critically significant. Even when some of their movies were not as good as others, these theorists argued, such "minor" films should still be studied for attitudes and techniques relevant to appreciating the importance of that auteur's overall style.

A filmmaker's work must have a unique philosophy or film style if he or she merits the right to be called an auteur. Students of Chaplin claim his films qualify. Chaplin narratives reflect his experiences with poverty and "riches-to-rags/rags-to-riches" childhood in London. As a boy Charlie Chaplin, like the literary author Charles Dickens, knew the horrors of London poverty--inadequate food, shelter, clothing, and the hostility of that city's streets. Both artists used these themes in their work. Central to their art was a character, or characters, outside "accepted society"--persons not part of a predominant group. Chaplin revered Dickens as an artist and critics have pointed to similarities in their art. There are, however, important differences in their narrative styles.

The stories of Charles Dickens often feature a protagonist who, after intense suffering and social estrangement, escapes the horrors of poverty to live in material comfort as an accepted member of society. Once treated as an outsider, this person is financially rewarded and becomes part of the predominant social group--a rags-to-riches "happy ending." Dickens's stories vividly portrayed, and criticized, the conditions suffered by the poor while suggesting it was possible to escape this situation. Charlie Chaplin's life mirrored this scenario so closely it almost could have been written by Dickens. In Chaplin's movies, however, the character of his quaint--or tramp, if you will--is not always integrated into society. One of the most famous Chaplin images has this screen character wandering down a country road with his back to the camera--estranged, lonely, and with no particular destination. (See fig. 4.7).

A principal theme in all Charles Chaplin's movies is **Man vs. Society**. In his pictures Chaplin played a quaint who looked and acted differently than the other characters. He often was an outsider trying to beguile those, holding higher positions in society, who were otherwise predisposed to ignore one of his condition. The quaint of the Keystone films was self-centered, larcenous, lecherous, violent, and vulgar. This uninhibited, unsympathetic, anti-social, and often drunk exhibitionist was generally the person most responsible for creating the trouble in his world. His main purpose was to chastise, exploit, and cheat a society that chose to neglect or subdue him.

By his later pictures the goals and social attitudes of Chaplin's quaint broadened. The character now alternated between being both a victimizer and victim. Ever an outsider, this quaint continued to be a disruptive force in his world but was also someone society made to suffer--often through no fault of his own. Audiences could feel sorry for this character while still laughing at the situations in which he was embroiled. This quaint was less the instigator of the violence in his environment and much more vulnerable to the pain it created. By 1917 Chaplin was frequently adding pathos to his slapstick comedies. As his film career progressed, Chaplin's man vs. society themes increasingly showed the tragedy of social estrangement.

A unique aspect of Chaplin's comedy, like that of Dickens, is that the film comedian took tragic elements from his past and made them comic. Chaplin's father died of alcoholism yet his son played a comic drunk on stage and in film. Charlie Chaplin had been embarrassed as a boy because of his ill-fitting and ragged clothes. As an adult Chaplin developed a quaint whose disheveled wardrobe established him as a comic figure. The young Charlie Chaplin hustled for money on the street for his family's survival. In Chaplin's movies the quaint's hustling, and social and material deprivations, were played for humor.

There is a great deal of irony in Chaplin's comedy that challenges the priorities and values society uses to judge people. Rags-to-riches stories may be enjoyable, even comforting, to the "haves" of society when construed as proof that the poor can "pull themselves up by their own boot-straps." This belief supports the questionable attitude that those who have money need not feel responsible for the problems of others--an excuse for not bothering to help them. Having been in the position of both enjoying material comfort and knowing economic deprivation, Charlie Chaplin was not so comfortable with the idea that the poor are responsible for their hardship. He was very aware of the irony that people could shun him on the street, when he looked like a bum, but adore him in that role when on stage or screen. It is easy to like someone who is rich and famous. It is not as easy to like people who need help.

Chaplin was an auteur whose film narratives contain an identifiable philosophy. He also was a major cinematic stylist--a master of motion picture mise-en-scene. Film mise-en-scene, as defined in Chapter Three, relates to what we see in the picture. Elements of mise-en-scene include the appearance and behavior of the characters and their spatial position within the frame, setting and set design, lighting, props, and the color and texture of the image. Chaplin borrowed aspects of theater and English music hall mise-en-scene and adapted them to fit the demands of the motion picture medium. An excellent actor and mime, Charlie Chaplin knew how to stage nonverbal action from his work in comic sketches on the variety stage. His film character, an adaptation of the music hall quaint, has already been described. More than a recycled theatrical figure, however, Chaplin's quaint was cinematic as well as comic.

As the Greek philosopher Aristotle noted in his theory of aesthetics in 320 B.C., the appearance, personality, and behavior of a character in comedy is influenced by a "comic flaw" or "mark of the ridiculous." The "mark of the ridiculous" is a physical comic deformity, or a mistaken attitude, which the viewer does not associate with real pain despite the difficulties it creates for the humorous figure displaying it. Examples of physical "marks of the ridiculous" would be a clown's red nose or the costume and makeup of the music hall quaint. A famous example of a comic "mistaken attitude" would be Don Quixote's attack of a windmill, under the delusion it was a giant, in the classic novel *Don Quixote,* by Miguel de Cervantes. The behavior of a comic drunk is another example of the mark of the ridiculous. Though physical deformity, insanity, and alcoholism can be very tragic in real life, comics use variations of these conditions and situations in playful and non-hurtful contexts for purposes of comedy.

Charlie Chaplin did not restrict his comic sources to painful childhood memories. He could, for example, use aspects of filmmaking that bothered him and turn this irritation into brilliant comic effects. His comic quaint's most notable mark of the ridiculous was the way in which he walked--bowlegged with feet pointed outward. Funny in itself, this off-centered stride also parodied the motion picture medium.

A problem with many early movies was a "flicker" that made action look "jerky" rather than realistic. Such abnormal movement could be caused by improper registration of the raw footage as it went through the camera gate, poorly spliced film in the projector, or shooting or projecting the picture at an incorrect speed. Motion pictures projected under these conditions impose a ludicrous rhythm on the characters' movements, whether desired or not. Show an early Chaplin comedy in this manner, however, and the erratic action seems almost "normal" because it resembles the quaint's usual wobble. This comic character's mark of the ridiculous is especially cinematic, then, because it is a flaw shared by film technology of the time. By 1914 motion picture cameras and projectors were being refined so that the flicker was becoming less a problem--a development that heightened the crude and anachronistic appearance of earlier movies. Today Charlie Chaplin's famous "flickering shuffle" is a permanent reminder of the funny way many early silent movies looked.

Besides creating his famous cinematic saunter, Chaplin has been hailed as a film auteur for the way he used mise-en-scene to convey the quaint's relationship to his world. The plots of earlier movies we have discussed, like *Ben Hur* and *A Trip to the Moon*, center on a narrative situation rather than specific personalities. Chaplin's films focus on conflicts the quaint has with people and his surroundings. At Keystone the quaint was one of many self-centered antisocial individuals competing to see who could benefit most when tricking one another. In later films at other studios Chaplin's quaint was not always so "me-oriented." As pathos became increasingly associated with Chaplin films after 1917, the quaint became less a social irritant and more a vulnerable outsider victimized by a society that chose to ignore or exploit him.

Auteur and mise-en-scene criticism are supposed to help the critic analyze and appreciate film, individually or in groups. Knowing what we do about Chaplin's background, and given his reputation for being a master of cinematic mise-en-scene, we should be able to assess his films by looking for specific themes and images attributed to this auteur. The following examination will use auteur and mise-en-scene criticism to investigate *The Gold Rush* (1925), one of Chaplin's greatest artistic successes, to see how these approaches can be used as effective methods for doing film analysis.

VI. Case Study in Auteur and Mise-en-scene Analysis: *The Gold Rush*

Chaplin got the idea for *The Gold Rush* after seeing some pictures of prospectors taken during the Klondike gold rush of 1898, and from reading a book about the Donner tragedy of 1846. The Donner tragedy involved a group of immigrants who waited too long in the season to go through the Sierra Nevada Mountains on their journey to California. Trapped in the mountains without adequate supplies, members of the party survived by eating the bodies of those who had died. From this tragic incident involving cannibalism, Charlie Chaplin developed one of his most famous comedies. Before making this movie Chaplin took tragic situations from his childhood and turned them around to make comedy. His inspiration for *The Gold Rush* is another example of how this comedian made comedy out of tragedy. A plot synopsis can help us identify many of this picture's principal themes.

Synopsis

The Gold Rush begins with an extreme long shot of an extended line of prospectors heading up the Chilkoot Pass, from a tent city at the base of the mountains, on their way to the Yukon gold fields. The fragile appearance of the men and their flimsy shelter in such a harsh environment indicates that the desire for gold is a strong motivation. (See fig. 4.10 and fig. 6.16). This is no place for the ill-prepared. The almost documentary-like images of the Yukon are followed by comically stylized shots of Chaplin's quaint. He is by himself, inadequately clothed for the climate, and obviously

4.10   A publicity still from the opening shot of *The Gold Rush*. Chaplin's quaint does not actually appear in this master shot of the movie, but the director used the setup to devise this clever picture anyway. (See fig. 6.16).   Though he is appearing with a "cast of hundreds," Chaplin has blocked the picture so that our attention is directed towards the quaint and not something else. The quaint is shown as being isolated, even when with a group. Besides emphasizing the thesis of "man vs. society," the concepts of man vs. environment and new "city" vs. rugged country are also used as dialectic themes in this photograph. From the author's collection.

lost. The quaint is totally oblivious to the dangers around him, including a bear which turns off the path before our protagonist ever discovers it. The first time our hero recognizes he is in danger is when he stumbles across the grave of a "Jim Sourdough." The quaint suddenly becomes concerned when he reads that the victim "got lost in the snow." Shortly after that the quaint gets caught in a blizzard and is literally blown into the cabin of Black Larson, a fugitive pursued by the law.

Bigger and meaner than the quaint, Larson has no interest in sharing his shelter. Before he can throw out his unwanted guest a third party gets blown into the cabin--Big Jim, a prospector. When Black Larson tries to remove both callers he and Big Jim end up fighting over a gun. Larson is overpowered and Big Jim informs the criminal that both he and the quaint will stay. (See fig. 6.11). The problem of shelter has been resolved but there is still the need for food. They conclude that one of them must brave the storm to bring back provisions and decide who should go by drawing cards. Black Larson loses. He leaves with his dog, finds food, but never returns. Instead, Larson stumbles across the police who have been searching for him, kills them, and steals their provisions. Later, Larson finds Big Jim's claim which he intends to keep for himself. Meanwhile the situation of the two starving men in the cabin deteriorates to the point that Big Jim starts hallucinating and believes his little companion is a chicken. Before Jim's disturbed mental state results in his hurting the quaint, a bear wanders in the cabin which they kill and eat.

When the storm subsides Big Jim heads to his claim while the quaint gives up prospecting and returns to town. Broke and without a place to stay, the quaint finds temporary shelter in a dance hall. Everyone in this newly formed "boom town" is an immigrant. Yet even among this group the quaint is the person most out of place--an outsider among outsiders. Friendless and lonely, the quaint is attracted to a dance hall girl named Georgia. (See fig. 4.11). Georgia ignores the quaint until she dances with him to make Jack, her boyfriend, jealous. After getting into a fight with Jack, the quaint leaves the dance hall. Outside and still without shelter, he lies down in front of the door of a nearby cabin, pretending to be frozen stiff. The owner of the cabin, Hank Curtis, takes pity on the quaint and lets him look after his house while he is out prospecting. The quaint now has shelter, food, and met a woman he really likes.

One day, while he is minding the cabin, Georgia and some women from the dance hall stop by and see him. When they agree to come back on New Year's Eve, the quaint gets work shoveling snow to earn money for the party. They do not show up. Disappointed, the quaint dreams about a party that never happens. Awaking from his reverie, the quaint goes to the dance hall where everyone in town is partying except himself. He stands outside the dance hall window, lonely and forgotten. Unbeknownst to him Georgia, Jack, and the women later go to the cabin that evening when he is not there, discovering the elaborate meal and party favors he prepared for them. Jack is unaffected but Georgia is sorry that they have hurt the quaint's feelings.

Meanwhile Big Jim has returned to his claim and discovers Black Larson. The two fight and Big Jim is hit on the head. Larson leaves with a sled load of provisions and is killed shortly thereafter when he falls off a cliff. (See fig. 7.1). Big Jim, disoriented from getting hit on the head, wanders into town to file his claim but cannot remember where it is. Jim stumbles upon the quaint and persuades his former companion to take him back to the cabin, believing that once there he can find his lost claim. The two return to the cabin. This time, among their plentiful supplies, they have a side of beef and some whiskey, which makes the quaint drunk. During the night, while

4.11 In this publicity still from *The Gold Rush,* Chaplin introduces the last major theme of the film--the quaint's romantic feelings for Georgia. There seems little chance he will "get the girl." Ignored by everyone present, including Georgia, the character is socially and spatially isolated in this environment. Again the director has positioned the quaint so that he catches our attention in a crowd. One technique Chaplin uses, to accomplish this effect, is selective focus. Notice how people and objects behind the quaint are out of focus. This forces him to stick out from the background. Courtesy British Film Institute.

its occupants sleep, the cabin is caught in a blizzard and blown to the edge of a cliff where it remains, teetering dangerously. The quaint assumes the wobbling is a result of his hangover. Balancing on the brink of disaster, Jim and the quaint escape from the cabin and discover that they have been blown to Big Jim's claim.

Now rich, the two former prospectors take a ship back to America. The quaint has everything but Georgia. During the trip he is asked to put on his old mining clothes for photographs, gets separated from the reporters, and discovers Georgia is on board. Georgia, who is riding in steerage, hears that the ship's officers are looking for a stowaway. Seeing the quaint she assumes that he is the stowaway and tries to hide him. Caught trying to conceal her friend, Georgia agrees to pay for his passage before he is "put in irons" by the ship's officer. The reporters and the captain find the couple at this time and vouch that he is the partner of Big Jim, the multi-millionaire. Thrilled at the love interest that has developed, the reporters ask Georgia and the quaint to pose for the camera. While posing the two kiss, causing the photographer to complain that they have "spoiled the picture." The quaint dismisses this complaint with a wave of his hand, continuing to kiss Georgia as the movie ends.

Analysis

Any narrative film analysis should consider the motivations and conflicts of the characters in relation to the plot. One way to isolate these concerns is to figure out the significance of the title, and the first and last shots of the movie. A film's title usually gives us clues about the general content of the picture. The title of this picture suggests both a desire to strike it rich and the fact that we have a period picture. We usually associate "gold rush" with events in nineteenth century America, not 1925. The first shot of *The Gold Rush* establishes the hardship the prospectors must experience to realize their dream. The inhospitable environment, harsh weather, and man's fragile nature in the face of these obstacles are graphically depicted. The last shot shows that the quaint's goals have been fulfilled. He is rich, found love, and previous conflicts involving food, clothing, and shelter no longer are a concern.

Almost everything described in our synopsis of *The Gold Rush* is communicated to the audience visually. In analyzing the film, using auteur and mise-en-scene criticism, we find that *The Gold Rush* continues such Chaplin themes as man vs. society, lack of money, inadequate clothing, and the need for food and shelter. Using mise-en-scene criticism we can see how these themes are developed as visual motifs that give *The Gold Rush* its form and structure.

One of the first visual motifs explored in *The Gold Rush* centers on the harsh environment of the mountains. The difficulty of traversing this terrain is emphasized in the first shots. The movie then cuts from the hardship experienced by strong and warmly-dressed prospectors scaling the cliff-side to the quaint, blissfully ignorant of danger. The hazard of the cliffs will be repeated two more times in the film when Black Larson meets his end and when the cabin falls over the mountain. The need for shelter in this harsh environment is emphasized repeatedly as a theme in the picture as well. The quaint's discovery of the grave of Jim Sourdough who got lost in the snow; the blizzard that blows the quaint and Big Jim into Black Larson's cabin; Black Larson stumbling across the policemen's tent; the quaint ingratiating his way into Hank Curtis's life; and the wind blowing the cabin to the cliff's edge, are examples of how the need for shelter is used as a theme in the movie.

Once the quaint's need for shelter is satisfied, the film focuses on food as a motif. After getting blown into Black Larson's cabin the quaint hungrily chews on a bone that he finds. He later eats a candle and his shoe due to hunger. They are so hungry that the quaint mistakenly thinks, at one point, that Big Jim has eaten Black Larson's dog. (It also might be noted that Black Larson leaves the cabin with his dog but we do not see the animal later, suggesting that he may have eaten it.) The quaint is nearly killed and eaten himself when Big Jim starts hallucinating and believes his companion is a chicken. The bear, which presented a danger on the cliff and in the cabin, is another source of food and salvation. The way the quaint gets breakfast from Hank Curtis is also played for humor. When no longer a matter of death or survival, the social importance of food is emphasized during the quaint's preparation for his party. The last time food appears as a theme is when the quaint and Big Jim return to the cabin with more food than they probably would ever need--an indication of their vivid memories of once being hungry at that location.

An interesting aspect of *The Gold Rush* is its thematic progression from the physical and material needs of its principal character to social and romantic concerns. Aspects of organized society are introduced in the first shot of the film. The line of prospectors represents the systematic approach these people use to attack the wilderness while the quaint's actions, in contrast, are unorganized and sporadic. Law and order also exist in this frontier, as seen in the police's attempts to find Black Larson. Larson is an outlaw but even he has to conform to some rules of social behavior. When he attempts to throw the quaint and Big Jim out of his cabin he is defeated and an uneasy living arrangement is agreed upon by all three.

The theme of man vs. society is particularly emphasized after the quaint leaves the cabin and goes to live in town. Unlike in earlier pictures, where he created much of the tension around him, the quaint of *The Gold*

Rush is a sympathetic victim rather than a social irritant in his world. As noted in the synopsis, the quaint is an outsider among immigrants. Lonely and laughed at, his estrangement is made particularly poignant on New Year's Eve. Holidays are made special by society, family, and friends. The quaint's isolation is graphically shown when he watches the party through the dance hall window, separated from the group by more than a pane of glass. This possibly is the quaint's lowest moment in the picture. Chaplin's ability to combine pathos with comedy, in scenes such as this one, brought a distinct mood to his art not generally associated with slapstick. After the New Year's Eve scene the character's fortunes suddenly experience a dramatic reversal when it turns out that he has something others want. The first to embrace him is Big Jim, who needs the quaint's help to get back to cabin and claim.

The final sequence in the film is full of Chaplin irony. The quaint assumes the mannerisms of the idle rich but occasionally forgets himself. When someone throws away a cigar butt he picks it up for a smoke, as in days of old. He only throws it away after Big Jim admonishes and reminds him that he can smoke a new cigar any time he wants. We also see the quaint's past influencing his present actions when he takes off his elegant fur coat. He has another fur coat underneath it. Having known cold too well, the quaint flamboyantly savors the resources he has to stay warm. Some of the greatest irony in this sequence relates to social themes. Once rich the quaint is sought out by people who previously would have laughed at or ignored him. When he puts on his old clothes they want to throw him in irons.

The Gold Rush is ironic, in its social comments, but it is not cynical. The movie prefers to emphasize the idea of success over adversity rather than dwell on the possibilities for human failure. The film does this, paradoxically, by using themes taken from tragic incidents, such as those surrounding the Donner party and Chaplin's own childhood, and playing them for comedy. The film eventually gets away from these darker motifs by shifting its focus to the quaint's romantic involvement with Georgia. As noted, an interesting pattern in the film's narrative is the succession of character conflicts and motivations based on immediate priorities. Once a person's need for clothing, shelter, and food are satisfied, he or she has time to consider romance.

The Gold Rush is a unique romantic comedy in that the leading lady is not introduced until the picture is almost half over. The movie uses the character of Georgia to show the quaint's social estrangement, feelings of rejection, yearnings for romance, and ultimate success in love. Georgia ignores the quaint at first. She later uses him as an object of ridicule until she gets to know and respect him. By the end of the movie she shows her true affection for the quaint by agreeing to pay his passage on board ship. If we had seen Georgia befriending the quaint, after she discovered he was rich, we might be more pessimistic about the nature of her interest. As with all the other conflicts put in his path, the quaint wins the girl against all odds. These successes, it can be argued, would be unlikely or even impossible in reality. We can deal with this concern the same way that the quaint ignored the still photographer's disapproval at the end of *The Gold Rush*. When told he "spoiled the picture," by breaking his pose to kiss the girl, our hero simply waves this objection aside. In the-anything-can-happen atmosphere of comedy the observer is asked to temporarily set aside feelings of disbelief and enjoy the romance, even if it is implausible.

Ultimately it is the implausible which sets the tone of this movie. The harsh environment of the Klondike is first shown with documentary-like realism. The director might have used this setting--and the themes of inadequate clothing, lack of food, and need for shelter--to make a tragedy. Instead *The Gold Rush* is a highly stylized comedy structured around an eccentric figure whose behavior and dress is absurdly out of place--a quaint not quite of this world.

VII. Conclusion

At a time when most American filmmakers were part of the "studio system," Charles Spencer Chaplin worked as an independent. Chaplin is particularly famous for his popular screen character--a variation of a comic music hall personality known as a "quaint"--who appeared in comedies combining pathos with slapstick. Because his independence enabled him to make films with very personal narrative and visual styles, Charlie Chaplin's motion pictures particularly lend themselves to auteur and mise-en-scene analysis.

The repetition of themes, images, patterns of behavior, personality characteristics, and plot conflicts provide a film narrative with its overall structural form. When narrative and cinematic elements are repeated in a unique and articulate style in a filmmaker's total work, that director is said to be an auteur. Based on experiences from his childhood, Chaplin repeats themes involving food, clothing, shelter, romance, and "man vs. society," in the mise-en-scene of his pictures. As our examination of *The Gold Rush* confirms, an understanding of how Chaplin worked with mise-en-scene, as an auteur, can make the viewing of his films a more complete and enjoyable experience. Knowledge of how cinematic masters like Chaplin used mise-en-scene to tell a story also helps us better appreciate the way other directors employ this component of the medium to communicate. The more we know about how mise-en-scene works in a movie, the better we can take delight in that picture's expression.

The movie chosen for mise-en-scene analysis in this chapter was a narrative film. As we will see, mise-en-scene analysis also can be employed to examine films with a limited narrative or no story at all. Even as Charlie Chaplin sought to tell stories on film, other artists experimented with ways the unique properties of the medium--such as special effects, color, texture, shape, light, and time--could be used for non-narrative exposition. Chapter Five will examine some of these experimental forms of cinematic discourse, with particular emphasis being paid to a movement known as German expressionism.

ENDNOTES

1.   My appreciation and thanks to Mr. Tony Merrick of Kennington, London, for sharing his perspectives on the turn-of-the-century English workhouse and life in Lambeth. A lifelong resident of the area where Charlie Chaplin grew up, Mr. Merrick's grandfather was a music hall performer who knew Charles Chaplin, Senior. Mr. Merrick operates a flower shop across the street from the site of the pawnshop which Hannah Chaplin often had to frequent.

2.   The author wishes to thank Mrs. Winifred Thompson for sharing her memories, during the numerous times I have interviewed her, about her cousin, Fred Karno. I am also very grateful for the assistance that Mrs. Thompson's daughter and son-in-law, Anne and Peter Fraser, have given me when researching this important English variety producer. My thanks, too, to Gillian and Jerry Braban of Tagg's Island, Hampton Court, Middlesex, England, for helping me with my Karno research.

3.   Dion Clayton Calthrop, *Music Hall Nights*, (London: John Lane the Bodley Head, Limited), 1925, pp.99-100.

The noted music hall historians Charles and Penny Chilton have reservations about Calthrop's use of the word "quaint" for describing this type of music hall comedian. The Chiltons agree that the "red-nosed, baggy pants" comic performed in English variety, but feel the term "quaint" does not properly identify this characterization. They also question how extensively the word "quaint" was used to define this type of comedian.

I have found only one other source for this utilization of the word "quaint." In an old interview, broadcast on British television in the early 1990s, Stan Laurel discussed his early career as a music hall comic. He described himself as performing as a "quaint comedian" at that time. A poster with Laurel's picture, with the words "quaint comedian" underneath, was shown on the screen as he was speaking.

I believe Mr. and Mrs. Chiltons' points are well taken. Since I know of no one else who has come up with another term to describe the "quaint" and his/her brand of comedy, however, I am deferring to the Calthrop definition. More important than the choice of word, for defining the characterization, is the recognition that this type of comedian did, in fact, exist. There is no question that such comics were familiar and popular figures on the variety stage in England and the United States at the turn-of-the-century. This subject definitely deserves further study if people wish to better understand the work of comedians like Charlie Chaplin and Stan Laurel.

4. *Variety*, July 25 1913, p.4; "A Billion is Invested in Movie Enterprises," *Variety,* October 10 1913, p.15; and "Mary Pickford, Picture Star," *Variety*, May 16 1913, p.13.

5. Charles Chaplin, *My Autobiography*, (New York: Pocket Books, 1966), p.117.

CHAPTER FIVE

THE EXPERIMENTAL FILM

CHAPTER OBJECTIVES: *To define the experimental film, explore how movements in modern art influenced the first major works in experimental filmmaking, and consider how German expressionism influenced the history of the motion picture.*

I. The Urge to Experiment and Abstract

There are essentially three types of movies which a filmmaker can make: narrative, documentary, and experimental. Documentary filmmakers record something which already exists and then organize that information so the audience will think about the subject. A nonfiction or documentary motion picture goes to reality to determine its form whereas the narrative film, as we saw with *A Trip to the Moon* and *The Gold Rush,* is structured around a fictional story which has been staged for the camera. Documentary focuses on depicting reality. The narrative movie centers around a story. The experimental film explores a specific effect or concept often based on the unique properties of the motion picture medium itself. The experimental film generally is less concerned with telling a story, or duplicating something which exists in the real world, than it is with challenging the way we think; investigating how and what audiences perceive; or exploring how the medium can convey filmic effects involving, but not limited to, such elements as color, texture, shape, light, and time.

Experimental films, as a category, is difficult to define. We can get a sense of the incredible diversity of this type of motion picture by considering a few random examples of experimental films. For example, the form and intent of Tony Conrad's *The Flicker,* discussed in Chapter One, reflects this filmmaker's interest in how people physiologically perceive individual images imprinted on film and projected as "moving images." Where Conrad explored people's perceptions and physiological reactions to alternating black and white frames, the artist Andy Warhol (1928-1987) asked audiences to consider their relationship to the subjects of the film, in his movies *Sleep* (1963) and *Empire* (1964).

Sleep is a six hour movie of a person sleeping, shot from one camera position. *Empire* documents the existence of the Empire State Building, again shot from a single stationary perspective, during an eight hour period. Warhol's unorthodox style of filmmaking in these two pictures, which requires the audience to watch one thing over a long duration of time, forces a viewer to consider such things as his or her relationship to the subject; one's expectations when watching a film; and what constitutes valid perspective and interpretation.

Other experimental films concentrate on the types of images, textures, or "special effects" which can be created using this medium. Many MTV videos might be considered in this context. By editing various colors, shapes, and pictures to the rhythm of a popular song, the MTV video may be less concerned with using images to convey a clear narrative interpretation of the lyrics than it is with the visual impact, on the observer, of the filmic effects. The music video can create an alternative world in which its subjects can interact, in time and space, in ways not possible in "reality."

The diversity of forms which experimental films can take prevents these pictures from immediately allowing us to place them in a common category. One consideration a critic can use, to separate experimental cinema from other types of motion picture, is based upon *"mimesis"* and *verisimilitude*. According to the Greek philosopher Aristotle, people have an innate need to mimic that which is around them. This concern with "mimesis," or act of imitation, defined western art since before the time Aristotle wrote his theory of aesthetics, *Poetics*, in 330 B.C. "Verisimilitude" is defined as something *appearing* to be real or true. Considered from these perspectives, a film might be examined in terms of how "realistically" or "truly" it mimics its subject. The critic must be careful how these concepts and definitions are applied, however.

What makes mimesis and verisimilitude debatable criteria, as analytical perspectives, is that the *appearance* of being "real" or "true" is different from *actually* being real or true. In any analysis the critic should treat the object being evaluated as a *representation* of its subject. If this distinction is not carefully considered the verisimilitude oriented analysis, as can be seen in the following example, will be inherently flawed.

Using the condition of verisimilitude as a gauge, a continuum might be constructed in which the most "realistic" surface depiction of subjects are placed on one end while "stylized," or highly abstract renderings, are ranked on the other. Based on this verisimilitude criteria, the surface appearance of a detailed painting of a man by someone like Michaelangelo (1475-1564), might be described by some observers as more "realistic" than an "abstract" stick figure representing the same subject. Michaelangelo's attention to such anatomical concerns as the interpretation of muscles and flesh color would allow his rendition to have certain similarities to a "real man" which the abstract figure would lack. Yet to say the Michaelangelo painting is "more real" than the abstract stick figure raises questions regarding the nature of "reality." The stick figure will lack aspects of anatomical detail found in the Michaelangelo rendition, but may still express aspects of the man--a feeling, a pose, a state of mind--absent in the "realistic" painting. The stick figure does not reflect some of the surface reality of Michaelangelo's interpretation, but is it not also "real and true" in its own fashion?

Duplicating how we see surface reality is one effect an artist may try to achieve, but it is not the only one nor necessarily the "best." Truth and reality exist beyond the "realistic" mimetic depiction of a subject appearing in a "straightforward" photograph. "Reality" is a complex manifestation which exists, and can be depicted, in innumerable forms and interpretations. Recognizing this complexity, and being sensitive that a mimetic bias towards surface mimesis does not negatively blind us to the value of alternative depiction, a criterion based on verisimilitude can still be used to identify "realistic" documentaries and fictional movies on one end and the "unrealistic," "stylized" or highly "abstract" experimental films on the other. The more realistic a nonfiction film appears to be, for example, the more likely some people are to believe it is depicting the truth. If a fictional film is supposed to be a truthful depiction of a subject, we expect it to be very realistic. However, as we saw in our above example with the Michaelangelo painting and the stick man rendition, outward appearance should not be the sole criterion for determining reality and a "realistic" depiction may actually conceal truths that a more abstract rendering can reveal.

Placing films on a "verisimilitude continuum" is one means to get us to question just how "realistic" a given motion picture actually is, and what constitutes "truth" and "reality." Such questions are useful because, too often, viewers accept what they see as real rather than as a flawed or mediated representation. Using our film verisimilitude continuum also enables us to recognize that many films use a combination of stylized and mimetic traits in their expression instead of existing as pictures which completely gravitate towards one of the two ends of the spectrum. When a story is fanciful and stylized audiences still may want believable or appealing characters presented in a convincing environment, even if that world has never actually existed, so the viewer can suspend feelings of disbelief and go along with the dramatic premise of the story. This can be seen by examining some of our responses to *The Gold Rush*.

The Gold Rush features realistic settings and many ordinary looking characters, but Chaplin's quaint sticks out as someone who is not quite of this world. The quaint's appearance, movement, and behavior are different from those of other people. By combining realistic elements with very fanciful ones, the film creates a unified world with its own rules, tragedies, and successes.

The Gold Rush employs mimesis and verisimilitude but it also uses comic imagery which would not be found in any "real world." As Chaplin's comedy suggests, even as artists and storytellers have an innate need to imitate and duplicate what they see around them, they also have a desire to lampoon and distort reality--to investigate truths which may be lurking behind what may be deceptive surface appearances. Truth sometimes can be revealed through duplicating the real world in one's art. It also may be found by creating artistic alternatives to realistic depiction as seen in experimental films at the opposite end of the verisimilitude continuum.

5.1 Georges Méliès employs an interesting use of linear perspective in this publicity still from the opening shot of *A Trip to the Moon.* **Note how the crowd is positioned to form a kind of triangle. The top of this triangle, and some of the peaked hats, points to the open window and the moon. An even more pronounced use of linear perspective involves the way the chalk drawing curves towards the astronomical instrument hanging on a column. This instrument, a pattern of light on the wall, and the telescope all form a line that draws our attention to the moon at the top of the open window. While the content of this picture is a bit cluttered, Méliès uses linear perspective to emphasize what is important--the method they'll use to get to the moon, as shown on the chalkboard, and the object of their ultimate destination, the moon itself.   Courtesy the British Film Institute.**

5.2 Raphael. School of Athens. Stanza della Segnatura, Vatican Palace, Vatican State. Photo courtesy of Alinari/Art Resource, NY.

5.2   Previous page, Raphael's *School of Athens* **1509-1512.**

Artists today are concerned with doing more than producing "mirror images" of the world around them. At one time, however, the demand for mimesis and verisimilitude dictated both the subject matter and the techniques that artists were expected to use in their art. One problem any artist will have, when trying to draw or paint an object so it looks "real", is getting a three-dimensional subject to look "natural" on a two-dimensional surface. The two-dimensional surface of paper or canvas forces the artist to use techniques, involving perspective, that will make a flat rendition appear to have depth. This concern for making images look "spatially realistic" imposed some very calculating and restrictive traditions on artists over the centuries. It also has resulted in some clever formulas that artists have come up with to give the appearance of depth. One approach very much in use today, for making an image look three-dimensional, is called **linear perspective** (see fig. 5.2).

Anyone who has seen how parallel railroad tracks appear to come together at a point in the distance will have an idea of the nature of "linear perspective." In essence painters, like Raphael in his *School of Athens* 1509-12, seen in fig 5.2, rendered their pictures in such a way that they appear to have depth. This could be done by having figures in the foreground darker and larger than those in the background. One of the most effective means to simulate depth is to have lines that seem to converge at one point in the distance in the manner of our example of the parallel railroad tracks--linear perspective. If you examine the Raphael painting more closely you will see the floor pattern has definite lines pointing towards the center of the picture. Looking toward the ceiling you will notice there are also lines that are formed at the top of the columns of the room that slant inward. Because we are used to seeing things in perspective our eyes tend to follow these lines, probably subconsciously, to where the painter is directing our attention. Raphael uses other tricks, in *School of Athens*, to get us to look where he wants us to. He centers a bright spot in the middle of the picture, thereby drawing the viewer's eye to that area of the image. He also positions people looking in a particular direction. We are prompted to follow their gaze and look at the object of their attention "in the distance."

The desire to circumvent the principals of verisimilitude and mimesis prompted many artists, in the nineteenth and twentieth centuries, to invent and explore new art forms. Such experimentation led to what became known as "modern art" and influenced the emergence of the abstract/experimental film. Early influential experimental films made in the 1920s, in fact, often were produced by the major modern artists who were recognized as the principal innovators in such important movements as cubism, dada, surrealism, and expressionism.

The classic cubist, dadaist, surrealist, and expressionist motion pictures of the 1920s are useful to the critic and historian because they provide us with some solid examples of what constitutes experimental films when discussing how to classify them. These pictures were not necessarily the first experimental films--one might consider the fantasy pictures of Georges Méliès or the animated cartoons of fellow Frenchman Emile Cohl (1857-1938) as being pioneer works in this category. Nor do these movies enable us to define all the characteristics of experimental film. One would not want to categorize the Conrad and Warhol examples, listed earlier, according to these movements because they were interested in exploring very different concerns. The experimental films of the 1920s do isolate some important principals of abstraction, being explored by modern art at the time, which continue to influence film and artistic expression today.

The modern art movements of the turn-of-the-century involved independent artists who did not always acknowledge one another even when their work shared common goals and interests. While grouping their art together can be a useful means for appreciating their accomplishments and intent, it may create incorrect assumptions about how the artists defined their association with one another. Consequently, the following discussion of these movements will be concerned with isolating general philosophical interests and intentions which critics believe the movements expressed and sometimes shared. These definitions may or may not have been recognized by the artists themselves. There are three broad philosophical concerns which the cubist, expressionist, surrealist, and dadaist films of the 1920s addressed: (1) the external appearance and relationships of objects relative to space and shape; (2) the inner world of the psyche; and (3) the question of what constitutes socially and critically acceptable artistic representation and expression.

Since our discussion of modern art is primarily concerned with helping us identify the nature of experimental film, a strictly chronological examination of its history is not necessarily the most useful strategy for examining the movements we will review. Dada appeared after expressionism and cubism were recognized. It is a useful movement to begin our discussion because of the way it questioned the meaning and purpose of art and what constitutes valid artistic intent. In essence, dada challenged the identity of art itself. This challenge, while very much a concern to the other modern art movements, was central to the philosophy behind the work of the dadaists. By considering the dadaist challenge first, hopefully, the revolutionary qualities of the other movements may be more easily addressed and understood.

II. Dada as an Anti-Art Movement

Stylization and abstraction challenged the notions of verisimilitude and mimesis in general. Dada, shortly after the turn-of-the-century, was an out and out revolt against the rules and regulations of what was considered art. The word "dada" was chosen, in 1916, to define the movement, that was manifesting itself in Zurich and New York City. Dada would also flourish in Paris, Berlin and Cologne before it ended as a movement in the 1920s. "Dada" is a nonsense word whose origin is disputed. Some say it was coined when a French-German dictionary was opened at random and the viewer found a reference for rocking horse. Other informants claim it is Rumanian for "yes, yes." The word also has been attributed to Italian and African origin or a baby's attempt at identifying its father. Whatever its source it is clear that the participants of the movement were more interested in using the quizzical word "dada," to establish the philosophy and spirit behind their art, than they were concerned with finding a word that precisely defined what they were doing.

The Zurich dadaist poets were particularly influenced, and disturbed, by what was then happening in the first world war. Horrified and disgusted by the huge, and what they felt needless, loss of life in the war, these artists questioned how any supposedly rational and humane society could generate such carnage. Not only did they challenge the values of the countries responsible for such abhorrent behavior, they also criticized their art which, they believed, was a reflection and extension of the undesirable society which produced it. Dada, for them, was both a form of social protest and a challenge to the rules and regulations used to define contemporary art.

A key aspect of the dadaist movement was an emphasis on the irrational and inane. Bourgeoisie society's insistence upon rationality and conformity before the world war had not resulted in rational social behavior, the dadaists argued. If it had, why did society systematically engage in the most irrational activity conceivable--the systematic destruction of millions of people in World War I? The dadaists claimed that by _denying_ certain fundamentally irrational aspects of human behavior that need to be manifested--by insisting that people be concerned only with "rational behavior"--society doomed itself to the ultimate irrational act of killing its own people. Dada was dedicated to challenging such counterproductive behavior, attitudes, and rules of bourgeoisie society and its art, by embracing the irrational in its own artistic expression. Emphasizing the absurd and the inane in dadaist art, it was hoped, would remind people that irrationality must be recognized as part of the human condition. Ignoring irrationality could lead to madness.

Because dada's philosophy questioned the basic premises behind reason and rationality, it challenged the logic and perspectives of virtually any society or art. As an anti-art movement, dada produced works which attacked the organizing principles of any artistic pursuit which was not dadaist. Even the style of one of the foremost avant-garde painters could be criticized, as can be seen in Francis Picabia's (1879-1953) 1920 *Portrait of Cézanne*. This collage consisted of a stuffed monkey attached to a board which had the words "Portrait of Cézanne," "Portrait of Rembrandt," "Portrait of Renoir," and "Natures Mortés" scrawled on it. The work questioned, among other things, why a piece suddenly was considered "art," by many people, when it had a famous name like "Cézanne," "Rembrandt," or "Renoir" on it. How can one claim that art by one of these three artists is great, while a painting with someone else's name might be dismissed?

5.3 Portrait of Cezanne, Francis Picabia. Photo courtesy of The Museum of Modern Art, NY.

From 1916 until about 1924, irrational and absurd dadaist works raised their nihilistic questions in Europe and New York. The artist Marcel Duchamp (1887-1968) is considered particularly important as a dadaist. A one-time cubist painter disillusioned with the evolving philosophy of that movement, Duchamp moved to New York from Europe in 1915, where he was instrumental in making that city an early center for dada. One of Duchamp's many contributions to dada at this time was his interest in what he called "ready-mades." Duchamp would find a ready-made object and, through his imagination, take that piece and place it in an unexpected context which challenged existing interpretations of art. In 1917, for example, Duchamp submitted an urinal as a ready-made sculpture he called

Fountain, to an art exhibition organized by the New York Society of Independent Artists. His submission questioned the standards and criteria by which such work was judged and, perhaps, the nature of the art Duchamp may have felt was being exhibited. When *Fountain* was rejected from the exhibition, Marcel Duchamp continued his protest by resigning from the organization which sponsored the show.

Another important dadaist was the American artist Man Ray (1890-1976). A Philadelphia painter and photographer, Man Ray spent much of his life in Paris, where he emigrated in 1921. Like Duchamp, with whom he sometimes collaborated, Man Ray initially was influenced by cubism as a painter but went on to work with other forms of artistic expression such as the ready-made. One of his most famous ready-mades was a 1921 piece called *Gift. Gift* was a laundry iron whose front had the heads of fourteen tacks glued in a vertical row along the middle, the points projecting outward. Among his most notable contributions was the creation of his "Rayographs."

Made without the use of a camera or negative, the Rayographs were created by putting objects on photo sensitive paper which was exposed to light. The shapes and shadows resulting from the process created a one-of-a-kind photograph of abstract images and effects. Besides producing some fascinating images, the Rayograph technique enabled the artist to free himself from the usual restrictions, involving the camera and negative, of the photographic process. Given his interest in still photography it is not surprising that Man Ray considered working with the motion picture medium.

As with a lot of dadaist art, Man Ray's 1923 movie *Retour à la Raison* (*Return to Reason*) utilizes humor. The title of *Retour à la Raison* suggests some cerebral theme but the film's use of abstract imagery belies such association. The majority of *Retour à la Raison* incorporated the Rayograph technique in which the producer placed pins and nails on unexposed motion picture film stock, which was subjected to light, resulting in images which created fascinating abstract patterns when the footage was run through a projector. Made as a joke for a Paris dadaist gathering, the premiere audience was quite vocal in its dislike of the film. Despite this initial negative reaction, the conceptual focus and visual effects of *Retour à la Raison* came to be recognized as interesting alternatives to the restrictions of documentary and narrative formats. *Retour à la Raison* helped filmmakers consider new ways which the properties of the film medium can be employed as a means for artistic expression.

In 1926 Man Ray helped Marcel Duchamp make *Anémic Cinéma.* (See fig. 5.4). *Anémic Cinéma* utilizes disks inscribed with puns which, when spun, create moving spirals that induce hypnotic-like optical illusions. Critics have disputed the intent and effect of the film. According to avant-garde film historian P. Adams Sitney, "Duchamp [in *Anémic Cinéma*] condenses the whole range of sexual event involving emergence and penetration of a plane surface into a model of association between the illusions of gyrating cones and the allusions to breasts, genitals, and defecation." In his book *An Introduction to the American Underground Film,* author Sheldon Renan did not identify any of these perspectives. Other than reflecting Duchamp's interest in exploring perception, Renan felt *Anémic Cinéma* ". . . lacked apparent meaning." [1] The meaning in three other films, which Man Ray made on his own during the 1920s, also has been questioned--an indication of the controversial nature, and difficulty in summarizing the content, of some of the experimental films made at this time. One thing which Man Ray's *Emak Bakia* (*Leave Me Alone*) (1926), *L'Étoile de Mer* (*Starfish*) (1928), and *Les Mystères du Château du dé* (*Mystery of the Chateau of Dice*), (1929) have in common is their use of abstract forms and disorienting imagery to evoke a dreamlike atmosphere more associated with surrealism than dada which, by 1924, had ended as a movement.

5.4 An image from Marcel Duchamp's 1926 film, *Anémic Cinéma*. From the author's collection.

89

Dada's philosophy contained the seeds for its own demise. An anti-art movement, dedicated to questioning everything around it, could only make unorthodox attacks for a short period before its shock value lost its originality and impact. If an artist took the position that he or she was producing anti-art how could they justify, after a time, being associated with art in any form? In reality the dadaists had more problems with bourgeois values than they did with the notion of art as a concept. Initially the purpose of dada, for many poets and artists, was to show their disapproval of the social and political attitudes which led to the horrible inanity of the world war. Their attack on art was a means to voice political protest. For other artists dada was more a question of aesthetics than a form of political discourse. Even these dadaists were less anti-art advocates than they were artists in disagreement with the rules and philosophies of the prevailing forms and styles of artistic expression.

Dada is significant to the history of the experimental film, and the twentieth century, for at least three reasons: (1) it recognized the importance of questioning; (2) was dedicated to challenging social complacency; and (3) created innovative and outrageous ways to get people to think. By 1924 dada was in danger of losing its effectiveness. Most of the dadaists, including Man Ray, shifted their allegiance to the emerging movement of surrealism. No less radical than its predecessor, surrealism was not quite as nihilistic as dada in that it did not advocate anti-art as its basic premise. While it continued many of the forms of artistic expression which the dadaists had introduced, such as variations of the ready-made and the Rayograph, surrealism had a philosophy and focus all its own. The tenets of surrealism will be discussed later in this chapter. Prior to examining surrealism we will consider the important artistic movement which had Marcel Duchamp and Man Ray as practitioners before they became dadaists--cubism.

III. Cubism and the Exploration of Space and Shape

As dada challenged society to think about the meaning of artistic expression, cubism was questioning the way society looked at surface appearance as represented in its art. The term "cubism" was coined from a statement that the artist Henri Matisse (1869-1954) supposedly made--"Toujours les cubes!" ("Always cubes!")--when he rejected a series of paintings submitted by artist Georges Braque (1882-1963), while serving as a judge of a 1908 competition. Rejection of "cubism" by the art world was to be short-lived. Matisse's own work soon reflected the impact of what art historian, and vice president of the Solomon R. Guggenheim Foundation, H.H. Arnason called the most important artistic movement of the twentieth century. [2]

Georges Braque was one of the founders of cubism. Pioneer modern painter Paul Cézanne (1839-1906) is considered to have set the groundwork for the movement. [3]   But it is the brilliant Pablo Picasso (1880-1973) whose name is most commonly associated with cubism.   Picasso's 1907 painting, *Les Demoiselles d'Avignon* (*The Young Ladies of Avignon*)--a reference to a house of prostitution on a street in Barcelona, which a friend jokingly made after seeing the painting--is regarded as his first cubist work. Braque saw the painting in Picasso's studio and at first did not like it. Despite this initial impression his own art was reflecting the influence of *Demoiselles* by the end of that year. One reason the painting is considered so important is that it helped foster a break from the rules of Renaissance perspective which had dictated the form and content of western art for five hundred years.

As we noted in our earlier discussion, linear perspective is the result of the artist's concern for creating a sense of depth when depicting the human figure within a space. This goal resulted in a series of techniques being developed which enabled artists to create an illusion of depth while making the principal subjects stand out from their background. A problem with this strategy is that it forced the artist to subordinate everything to these rules of spatial perspective, that emphasized depth and the diminishing size of objects, which was determined by the distance between subjects. Picasso became aware that art need not limit itself to the Renaissance rules of spatial perspective after seeing African and Iberian art, particularly masks and sculpture.   In *Les Demoiselles d'Avignon*, the   budding   cubist   artist

5.5 Les Demoiselles d'Avignon. Pablo Picasso. The Museum of Modern Art, NY. Lillie P. Bliss Bequest.

experimented with non-Renaissance concepts he found in these alternative art forms. The five female figures in the painting have mask-like or distorted faces, whose proportions are noticeably stylized, and are positioned in a spatially ambiguous environment. Even though these subjects have a kind of three-dimensional quality about them their relationship to one another, and their setting, is different from that found in Renaissance-perspective inspired painting.

The ladies of *Les Demoiselles d'Avignon* appear to be suspended in some amorphous multi-dimensional context with its own laws of space and time. Whatever form of matter allows this world to exist, the ladies apparently are made of the same substance. They look to be a part of their realm rather than prisoners trapped in an alien setting. Both the setting and the ladies were alien to the art world of 1907, but would have a revolutionary impact upon twentieth century expression.

The earliest years of cubism were particularly dominated by Picasso and Braque who, after recognizing that they were interested in investigating many of the same concepts, collaborated closely between 1908 and 1914--their work often being indistinguishable from one another. Between 1908 and 1909 the art of Braque and Picasso systematically explored what this new approach was about, resulting in a period which has been called *analytical cubism*. One of the earliest and most notable characteristics of analytical cubism was the use of sharp linear distortions to evoke the images--an influence of their interest in masks and African and Iberian art. This technique created spatial discontinuity in the work rather than evoking harmony. Painting traditionally had distorted background and landscapes to show depth. As H.H. Arnason has noted, Braque and Picasso now used this distortion to abstract the human being in time as well as space. [4]

An important result of the experimentation, during the analytic cubism period, was that people and objects no longer were the principal focus of a work. The cubists were less interested in rendering a subject than they were in the process and techniques by which it was being rendered. They reduced their images to overlapping and tilting geometric shapes in which subject and environment often were indistinguishable. The emphasis on this reduction, of people and setting into geometrical shapes and planes, and their refusal to define spatial relationships using Renaissance oriented principles, enabled the cubists to get away from single perspectives and embrace simultaneous and multiple points of view. One of the most famous cubist inspired paintings, which attempted to depict simultaneity in space and time, was Duchamp's 1912 *Nu Descendant un Escalier* (*Nude Descending a Staircase*) (See fig. 5.6).

92

5.6 Nude Descending a Staircase, No. 2. Philadelphia Museum of Art: Louise and Walter Arensberg Collection.

5.7 *Cindy Descending a Spiral Staircase.* (1993) **The use of multiple exposure in photography inspired Duchamp to think about creating his painting in the manner he did. Photograph by Carl Hitt.**

Influenced by how the new medium of the motion picture could manipulate space and time Duchamp tried, in *Nu Descendant un Escalier,* to create the appearance of simultaneous movement in a still image. The effect was somewhat comparable to what might be achieved if a person took multiple exposures of a person walking down some steps, and then put these pictures one on top of the other so that the viewer could see all phases of the movement at the same time in one image. (See fig. 5.7). The title reflected the artist's sense of humor. Duchamp provided a couple of fairly recognizable stair steps in the painting, but the figure is rendered so abstractly it is difficult for the average observer to recognize it as a person much less one who is unclothed. Duchamp's title played off viewer expectation and social controversy relating to people's attitudes and objections to nude images.

Nu Descendant un Escalier proved to be a controversial work. For lay people who did not care for modern art it symbolized the absurd, and what many would call frivolous, nature of this kind of activity. The cubists as a group did not like it either. The duplication of a filmic effect in *Nu Descendant un Escalier* demanded the viewer make an association with a mechanical technique outside cubist abstraction. Most cubist artists of 1912 were more interested in abstraction for abstraction's sake than the kind of literal associations with reality, and type of personal expression, that Duchamp was making. They wished their cubist paintings to be self-contained entities which the viewer experienced firsthand rather than representations which brought other images and experiences to mind. The cubists also objected to the title of the painting, apparently, because of its association with social commentary and controversy. These were not concepts which the other cubists wanted to address nor the direction they cared to see their movement take.

Duchamp removed himself from the cubist movement, by 1913, and pursued more personal work which became associated with the emerging dada. Cubism's break from traditional art helped make dada possible but its insular perspective prevented it from addressing social issues of the day. Dada, as we have seen, was able to challenge both the rules and attitudes of the old art forms and question the society which produced it. As Duchamp and the dadaists proceeded with their concerns and interests, the cubists continued to experiment with the tenets of analytical cubism. They attempted to get further and further away from the rules associated with literal representation, Renaissance perspective, and standard artistic spatial conceptualizations. One way they did this was by developing "collage." By 1912, instead of limiting themselves to flat paintings, Picasso and Braque applied three dimensional objects, such as bits of paper, metal, and wood, to the surface of their work.

Art historians have used Braque and Picasso's introduction of collage to identify the second phase of the cubist movement which they call "synthetic cubism." Picasso and other artists would be associated with synthetic cubism for the next twenty years. Other than to separate current work from what had been done during the more identifiable period of analytical cubism, the meaning of "synthetic cubism" is subject to debate. It can be argued that by 1913, when synthetic cubism is said to have appeared, the content of many cubist paintings was not meant to be associated with reality. The cubist works were now intended to be seen as containing separate forms of alternative realities in and of themselves.

The fact that cubism was becoming associated with interesting shapes and patterns, rather than art with specific meaning, may have been a reason why Duchamp left the movement to pursue other concerns. One French cubist who did not feel the need to divorce his work from associations with reality was Fernand Léger (1881-1955). Léger was very cognizant of how industry and machines were so much a part of modern life.

From 1909, and into the 1950s, Léger's cubism employed machine-like representations for subject matter. Sometimes people appeared in robot forms. By taking references from the everyday world Léger was able to continue the cubist interest of breaking the appearance of subjects down

5.8 Fernand Legér's cubist rendition of Chaplin's quaint. From the 1925 film, *Le Ballet Mécanique.* **Frame enlargement.**

into geometrical patterns and shapes while avoiding the limitations of doing abstraction for abstraction's sake. In 1924 Léger used the motion picture to explore some of the artistic concerns he had been working with in his painting, by making a film called *Le Ballet Mécanique (Mechanical Ballet).*

Fernand Léger began his transition from painting to film by animating a cubist cartoon of Charlie Chaplin's quaint while the title of the movie is on the screen. *Le Ballet Mécanique* begins with a rather conventional image of a lady in a swing. Léger then goes against our expectations, for a film narrative, by suddenly bombarding us with a montage of disparate mechanical images edited to form a visual rhythm. As Man Ray had done in *Retour à la Raison* , Léger was structuring his film around a form which did not involve a narrative. Where Man Ray's film was principally meant to challenge the viewer, Léger was also interested in getting the audience to see such things as ordinary kitchen objects in a new way, breaking these images down into shapes and patterns in a very calculated manner, and edited the images to create specific rhythms. One of the most famous parts of the film is the shot of a woman coming up a flight of stairs, towards the camera, which is repeated over and over. The effect is of a person being made into a mechanical object, caught in a cycle, and doomed to repeat the same movement rather than complete it. This mechanization of the woman is an interesting contrast to the objects which have "come alive" through Léger's film techniques. Exceptionally innovative in 1924, the form and format of *Le Ballet Mécanique* is similar to some of the things that can be found in many non-narrative music videos on television today.

Cubism questioned the way we look at things and represent them. Its concern with breaking away from the limitations of Renaissance perspective established an alternative artistic philosophy which brought about many of the innovations in twentieth century modern art. But cubism's emphasis on the abstraction of physical form failed to address other aspects of life that are also important. One area which many modern artists felt needed to be explored, in the 1920s, was the world of the subconscious. This interest became a concern of the surrealists.

IV. Surrealism and the World of the Subconscious

When dada disappeared around 1924, most of its practitioners became associated with the emerging art movement known as surrealism. Surrealism, as is true of so many aspects of modern art, is rather difficult to define. The practitioners themselves often debated its meaning even to the point of charging that an opponent's work was not surrealistic. This debate was partially a concern for keeping the movement revolutionary and dynamic rather than something which could be narrowly defined. Despite conflicting interpretations, generalizations can be made about the surrealist movement and its expression.

Surrealism, unlike cubism, began primarily as a philosophy rather than an artistic style. The surrealists shared the dadaists' irritation with prevailing social and political values. They looked for a unified way to challenge the rules which governed the world. While the surrealists might not care for art which reflected bourgeois attitudes, an anti-art sentiment was not the primary emphasis of their philosophy. Rather, they were concerned about trying to find some alternative perspective to use in their art which avoided the problems associated with current thought, both social and artistic. Dissatisfied with trying to find solutions to their dilemma from the outside world, the surrealists looked for direction from within. They explored the inner world of the subconscious and its relationship to "reality." While investigating the dreamlike environment of the subconscious, the surrealists continued to share the dadaists' dedication in questioning the rules of art and society; need to challenge social complacency; and interest in creating innovative and outrageous ways to get people to think.

The word "surrealism" was first used in 1917 by the influential critic of modern art, Guillaume Apollinaire (1880-1918), when attempting to define an aesthetic that was non-rational. The intended meaning of the new word, and its relation to "reality," was not completely clear. Others tried to define a context for the term, but it was not until 1924, six years after Guillaume's death, that "surrealism" became formally associated with a subconscious condition operating outside or beyond the control of reason. Initially influenced by the work of Sigmund Freud, the surrealists were interested in exploring the irrational, non contextual manifestations of the mind which one sometimes experiences during the course of dreams.

The surrealists, like other modern artists, were concerned with the questions of (1) what is illusion and what is reality; (2) how we differentiate the two; and (3) how we should perceive them. Suspicious of the way society and art had been defining the world, and the way people were told to relate to it, the surrealists looked to the subconscious for answers. Were dreams, with their unorthodox and irrational ways of juxtaposing images, challenging the perceptions of the real world and providing clues for a more truthful perspective of life? If the artist could duplicate the condition of the subconscious, in his or her art, would it be possible to unlock these truths? Believing these points of view to be true, the surrealists sought to find truth in their exploration of the subconscious.

Surrealism was similar to cubism in that it was not concerned with literal representation. It differed from cubism in that the surrealist abstractions represented images and symbols, stemming from the unconscious, which were meant to unlock certain truths. Cubism was concerned more with the act of abstraction than it was with representation. Some surrealists, like Salvador Dali (1904-1989), painted more recognizable objects than their abstract counterparts, but presented this subject matter in dreamlike landscapes. One might, in a dream, see a mountain with a castle on it. Both could be suspended in the sky, without visible means of support, and in defiance of gravity. By depicting this imagery in a painting the surrealist illusionist could get us to (1) examine this subject matter in a conscious state; (2) think about why our subconscious presents us with such a vision; and (3) encourage us to question what are "normal" spatial associations among objects.

Because of the way the motion picture medium can manipulate time and space, while inventing its own worlds, many surrealists were interested in how film could be used to create surrealist images and fantasy. The filmmaker René Clair (1898-1980) made the surrealist movie *Entr'acte* ("*Interlude*," or "*Interval* ") in 1924, which was shown during an absurdist ballet called *Relâche* ("*Canceled*," or "*No Performance*.") Influenced by the films of Georges Méliès and Mack Sennett, the script for *Entr'acte* was written by the dadaist Frances Picabia, had a score by the notable modern composer Erik Satie (1866-1925), and featured such avant-garde artists as Marcel Duchamp and Man Ray as performers. Man Ray, as noted, also helped Duchamp with *Anémic Cinéma* in 1926, and made *Emak Bakia* (1926), *L'Étoile de Mer* (1928), and *Les Mystères du Chateâu du dé* (1929) as surrealist films as well. Of the surrealist motion pictures of the period, few had greater impact on audiences than Luis Buñuel (1900-1983) and Salvador Dali's 1929 *Un Chien andalou* (*The Andalusian Dog.*)

As was true of the other experimental films made up to this time, *Un Chien andalou* was concerned with challenging the conventional attitudes of what a movie should be and do. In making this challenge *Un Chien andalou* questioned the conformity its directors found in other experimental movies, including those made by surrealists. Experimental techniques initially intended for a radical use of the medium were now accepted, Buñuel and Dali believed, as interesting shapes and patterns rather than as thought provoking or revolutionary artistic and social assaults. Opposed to movies that audiences blindly and blissfully accepted without question, *Un Chien andalou* avoided such ineffectual responses by using images which shocked, disturbed, and offended the viewer.

Un Chien andalou literally begins as a visual assault when a man, played by Buñuel, takes a razor and slashes a woman's eyeball--actually the eyeball of a dead pig was substituted during the tight close-up. The rest of the picture continues to proceed in a patently non-narrative fashion. The subtitles give the audience what appears to be useless information. Images of people engaged in activities, both normal and bizarre, are juxtaposed in a seemingly random manner. One of the characters, for example, grabs a couple of ropes and starts pulling two pianos with dead donkeys on them. Behind the pianos a pair of priests--one of whom is played by Dali--are dragged along on the ground. At other times the character who dragged the piano touches his face and removes his mouth, stares at ants coming out of a hole in his hand (see fig. 5.9 and 5.10), and holds up two books that suddenly become guns. He uses the guns to shoot an unarmed individual who looks like himself.

Dali and Buñuel claimed that nothing in the movie symbolized anything. Critics argue that *Un Chien andalou* does use symbolism, whether the directors recognized it or not. The slashing of the eyeball has been described as a metaphor for the way the movie assaults the senses and complacency of the viewer. One observer has compared the hole in the hand with images found in classic paintings of saints who had their hands and feet nailed to a cross--graphic imagery that Buñuel and Dali, who came from Catholic backgrounds, would have been familiar with from childhood.

Though a case can be made that symbolic representation exists in *Un*

Chien andalou, it is questionable how literally one can interpret the movie from such a perspective. More important to the appreciation of the film is the recognition of the vivid and unsettling impressions and associations that the viewer experiences when watching *Un Chien andalou.* The movie recreates some of the same feelings one may get from a dream. A dreamer may become upset with the disturbing, and seemingly incomprehensible, images of his or her nightmare. He or she may feel that the dream means something, even if the meaning is unclear. Like some dreams, *Un Chien andalou* creates an atmosphere that is absurd, unsettling, humorous, threatening, and appears to be saying something. While *Un Chien andalou* works in a non-narrative manner, which defies simple interpretation, it clearly is able to get a viewer to respond strongly to its content for reasons that are not completely understood.

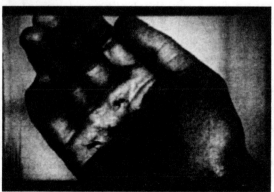

5.9 and 5.10 Ants coming out of the hole in a man's hand. Surrealist images from Buñuel and Dali's *Un Chien andalou,* 1929. Frame enlargements.

99

As a movie meant to shock and offend its audiences, *Un Chien andalou* proved to be an immediate success. When the film premiered in February of 1929, it was soundly booed and objects were thrown at the screen. This reaction was nothing compared to the reception that Buñuel and Dali's second film *L'Age D'Or* (*The Age of Gold*) (1930) was to receive. The script for *L'Age D'Or* was written by Buñuel who also was responsible for most of the direction. Dali's contribution to the film is said to have been minimal since he and Buñuel had a falling out before the picture was completed. *L'Age D'Or* was intended as a surrealist attack on society and religion. It so inflamed one early audience that a riot ensued. Besides the usual boos and flying objects, stink bombs were also in evidence. The outraged viewers damaged the screen by throwing purple ink at it, tore up the seats in the auditorium, and also destroyed an exhibition of surrealist paintings in the foyer. Shortly after the December 3, 1930 incident, *L'Age D'Or* was banned in several countries and generally was unavailable for viewing, even to film scholars, until relatively recent years.

Shock and scandal were part of the surrealistic experience but not the most important aspect. Rather than ends in themselves, the unsettling and controversial elements of the surrealism movement were used to shake viewer complacency and force people to respond to the subjects in question. Buñuel stopped using shock and controversy in films he made after World War II, because he questioned how useful they were in getting audiences to think and respond. Instead of shocking people into awareness there was the danger of audiences becoming even more desensitized after such filmic assaults. They may even become hungry for greater sensationalism in their viewing experiences. Buñuel also questioned how any "shock" artist could compete with the horrors and atrocities perpetuated by the Nazis and the atomic bombings of Hiroshima and Nagasaki. Luis Buñuel continued to make films which challenged social priorities after 1945, but chose to work with images and metaphors more subtle than the slashing of an eyeball.

Surrealism ended as an art movement in the 1940s. Disrupted by World War II, the major artists were unable to maintain a recognizable surrealist philosophy or style despite their efforts to do so. After 1950 the tenets of surrealism were absorbed or overshadowed by other art movements. Though it ceased to exist as a formal movement, surrealism still exerts an influence on the themes, styles, and techniques artists explore, and the way critics define their work. Only a handful of actual surrealist films were made at the time of the movement. Yet surrealism continues to influence such things as "dream imagery" in movies made since the 1920s. One may think of numerous contemporary music videos that employ effects reminiscent of classic surrealism. Despite surrealism's importance, the art movement known as "expressionism" has probably had an even greater impact on the content and appearance of the motion picture.

V. Expressionism as an Art Form of Inner Feeling

Dada was a philosophy which challenged the tenets of art and society. Cubism was an artistic style which questioned the way we look at the form and shapes of things and represent them in art. Surrealism was both a social philosophy and an artistic style that asked us to consider the world of the subconscious and the way it uses images as symbols. One of the oldest of the modern art movements, and actually one of the first to be represented in a motion picture, was "expressionism." Expressionism was concerned with externalizing the mood and emotion of inner despair. Like surrealism, expressionism was interested in depicting an internal condition. What separated the two was their particular emphasis. Expressionism was not working with the subconscious in general so much as it was concentrating on delineating a specific feeling.

5.11   Edvard Munch's *The Scream,* **1893.   Copyright: Munch Museum, Oslo 1993.   Photograph courtesy of Oslo Nasjonalgaleriet.**

Expressionism was a stylistic outgrowth of Norwegian Edvard Munch's (1863-1944) 1893 painting *The Scream*. One of the most famous images of modern art, *The Scream* is now often used in contemporary advertising as a kind of comic cliché for despair. The imagery was not perceived as comic when *The Scream* was first displayed. The focus of the painting consists of a very disturbed person, rendered in a highly stylized fashion, standing next to a railing which recedes into the background. This figure, of undetermined sex, has a skull-shaped head which it holds in its hands. The protruding eyes and open mouth convey an expression of panic, horror, and terror. Behind the individual is a distorted environment in which sky and water swirl in exaggerated waves similar to the twisting lines of the character's body. The solid security of the railing provides a visual contrast to the unsettled world surrounding this disturbed and isolated victim. It is clear that the person is terrified of the swirling environment which is a visual depiction of its internal state--the spinning unsettled background is a representation of how this poor being feels about its world and the way this realm mirrors its feelings.

Munch continued to paint images in which internal feelings were externalized. By the turn-of-the-century his style, which had evolved into an art movement known as "expressionism," had reached Germany and became strongly associated with that country and its culture. Rather than depict "realistic" external environments, the expressionist painters wanted to externalize real internal feelings. Unlike surrealism, which focused on the subconscious, the expressionist painters dealt with gloom, psychological turmoil, isolation, and obsessive terror--conditions which can exist during a wakened state. The formal, stylistic, and thematic elements of expressionist painting were quickly picked up by the other arts in Germany, including literature, poetry, music, and theater, eventually interesting those working in film. The first major expressionist movie, and also one of the first experimental films influenced by a modern art movement, was *Das Kabinett des Dr. Caligari (The Cabinet of Dr. Caligari)* (1919). The international critical and commercial success of *The Cabinet of Dr. Caligari* fostered a German expressionist film movement. Though German expressionism only existed as a cinematic movement from 1919-1925, its influence on film and the other arts continues. A brief examination of the first expressionist film is useful for identifying some of the major stylistic elements of this type of filmmaking.

A movie told from the visual perspective of a mad man, *The Cabinet of Dr. Caligari* has a murdering sleepwalker, an insane psychiatrist authority figure, a protagonist who tries to convince everyone he is not the one who is crazy, and an unsettling set design full of twisted buildings and shapes belying any sense of environmental normality. *The Cabinet of Dr. Caligari* begins with a frame story in which the protagonist, Francis, informs another man he has a strange tale to tell. The movie then cuts to Francis's account. In the story Francis and his friend, Alan, are in love with the same girl, Jane. One day, when Francis and Alan are attending a fair, they visit the tent of a showman named Dr. Caligari. Dr. Caligari's exhibit features a somnambulist, Cesare, who can predict a person's future. When Alan asks Cesare how long he has to live he is told that he will die that night. Cesare's prediction comes true. Alan is murdered--the second person to die a mysterious death since Caligari's arrival in town. Francis investigates Alan's murder, suspecting that Cesare and Caligari are involved. After recounting how the mystery is resolved, the movie cuts back to Francis and his listener in the frame story and concludes with an unexpected plot twist.

The content of *The Cabinet of Caligari* differs from American films of its day in that the story is terrifying and pessimistic rather than romantically optimistic. The movie's plot does not offer escapist fantasy. Where Hollywood films of this time attempted to produce bright and cheerful daydreams, German expressionism portrayed a bleak world reminiscent of a nightmare from which the protagonist knows not how to escape. Besides fashioning a mood and atmosphere contrary to most Hollywood pictures, *The Cabinet of Dr. Caligari* also demands a different formal response from its audience.

The beginning of The *Cabinet of Dr. Caligari* does not appear to be particularly expressionist but the rest of the movie clearly is. The mise-en-scene has a nightmarish appearance indicative that all is not right with this bizarre world. Its strange shadows and distorted shapes exude an atmosphere of mystery, suspense, and alienation. Unlike the form of most 1919 movies, the filmmakers have eschewed a realistic setting for a stylized environment <u>that draws attention to itself</u> as it evokes its particular mood. The typical Hollywood movie, especially before 1960, tries to get the viewer to concentrate on the story rather than think about how the information is being conveyed. The filmmaker <u>**does not**</u> want us to be aware of how the medium is being used to bring us the message. The disorienting images in *The Cabinet of Dr. Caligari* constantly draw attention to themselves, making us aware of this film's mise-en-scene as we watch the movie--an effect that adds to our tension as we try to make sense of this seemingly senseless world. *The Cabinet of Dr. Caligari* forces us to be aware that the formal properties of the film medium are being used to tell the story, while the Hollywood cinema of that day attempts to hide them.

5.12 A scene from the 1919 expressionist film, *The Cabinet of Dr. Caligari*. Notice how the set design adds to the distorted sense of the environment. From the collection of the author.

There were only a few dadaist, cubist, and surrealist movies at the time these modern art movements were in prominence. After the critical and commercial success of *The Cabinet of Dr. Caligari*, expressionism became the predominant style in German film until about 1925. One technique used in *The Cabinet of Dr. Caligari,* which German filmmakers continued to employ in the 1920s, was the practice of shooting everything, including exteriors, inside the studio. Great pains were made to create streets, store fronts, even mountains and streams, in buildings on the studio lot. (See fig. 2.2). Shooting everything inside enabled the filmmakers to have total control over the lighting and atmosphere of the picture. Inside shooting also contributed to the feeling of claustrophobia which is often present in expressionist movies.

Though not always as stylized, the mise-en-scene of the later expressionist films also continued to rely on the shadowy, insecure, and deeply disturbed tone of their 1919 predecessor. Several themes found in *The Cabinet of Dr. Caligari* were adapted in later German films as well. One of the most important motifs in *The Cabinet of Dr. Caligari* involves the strong authority figure who misuses his power, goes mad, and becomes an instrument of evil. Mad doctors and psychiatrists, including a wicked character named Dr. Mabuse, were a familiar element in German films of the

1920s. Some of these movies, as was true of *The Cabinet of Dr. Caligari*, used expressionism for social protest.

By 1925 the rest of the world had become familiar with expressionism and fascinated with its implications. German filmmakers, like the director Fritz Lang (1890-1976) and the cameraman Karl Freund (1890-1969), went to Hollywood where they brought their expressionist style to American movies. The bright and optimistic Hollywood picture began to take on a darker look as a result. The horror and gangster film were two genres directly affected by German expressionism. English filmmaker Alfred Hitchcock was one of several foreign directors affected by the movement. The German innovations of this period continue to influence film today and not just in terms of the dark and moody style they pioneered.

At first German expressionism relied mostly on mise-en-scene to convey its message. By the middle 1920s the German filmmakers became increasingly interested in how the camera could affect the form and content of their movies. This concern would have a revolutionary impact on filmmaking. Chapter Six will consider how the Germans' experiments with the movie camera increased the importance of camerawork as an integral part of filmic communication.

VI. Conclusion

While motion pictures continued to show the influence of modern art, experimental films reflecting the tenets of these movements generally stopped being made by 1930. There were a number of reasons why this cessation occurred. A major factor was money. With the arrival of a world-wide economic depression, artists no longer could afford experimenting with such an expensive medium as film. The expressionist filmmakers worked with popular narrative formats which enabled their movies to be exhibited as a commercial product. Commercialism was not associated with most of the other types of experimental cinema. The dadaist, cubist, and surrealist films were not produced for wide distribution but made to be shown to relatively restricted gatherings. Such experimental films were not expected to find a large audience nor a commercially viable form of exhibition. Consequently, they did not have a market which encouraged more of them to be produced. It should also be remembered that all of these films were made as silent movies, although they usually were shown with some sort of musical accompaniment. After 1930, and the coming of the talkies, filmmaking was done with the more costly sound technology. These added technical complications and expenses further dissuaded potential filmmakers from making experimental films.

Experimental filmmaking went into a temporary decline after 1930, but its influence remained. The modern artists had shown that the motion picture medium could be used in ways which transcended narrative and documentary formats. They proved that movies could be expressive without being tied to a story or preconceived "reality." The pioneer experimental films addressed legitimate questions and interests relating to the arts, fostered a greater exploration and appreciation of the motion picture, and challenged conventional ideas about the relationship of mise-en-scene and editing to space and time. As our Warhol and Conrad examples suggest, later filmmakers would resume their experiments with the experimental film.

ENDNOTES

1. Review of *Anemic Cinema* by P. Adams Sitney, in the 1978-79 Audio Brandon Films *16mm International Cinema Catalog*, p.529; and Sheldon Renan, *An Introduction to the American Underground Film*, (New York: E.P. Dutton & Co., Inc., 1967), p.67.

2. H.H. Arnason, *History of Modern Art: Painting, Sculpture, Architecture*, (Englewood Cliffs, New Jersey: Prentice-Hall, Inc., n.d.), p.124.

3. The author wishes to thank Mr. Ken Stout for reviewing this chapter and sharing his views on cubism.

4. Arnason, pp.121-122.

CHAPTER SIX

GERMAN CINEMA IN THE 1920S AND THE IMPORTANCE OF CAMERAWORK AS AN ELEMENT OF FILM STYLE

CHAPTER OBJECTIVES: *Identify the principal components of camerawork and consider how German filmmaking in the 1920s influenced this major element of film style.*

I. German Expressionism after *The Cabinet of Dr. Caligari*

The Cabinet of Dr. Caligari took a radical approach to art, explored in painting and other media, and successfully brought it to the screen. Unlike the films associated with most of the modern art movements we have discussed, the expressionist pictures were commercially successful. This accommodation to commercialism, as we shall see, was not without its price.

To make their films acceptable to the public the German filmmakers modified, and sometimes abandoned, unique aspects of expressionism which *The Cabinet of Dr. Caligari* pioneered on film. Consequently, *The Cabinet of Dr. Caligari* was to be the "purest," or "most expressionist," of the German expressionist motion pictures. Yet, while some of the radical and abstract elements of the expressionism found in *The Cabinet of Dr. Caligari* were diluted in later pictures, experimentation with other tenets of the movement continued. These experiments, combined with the filmmakers' interest in making expressionism more accessible to a mainstream audience, resulted in an innovative and unique German film style that strongly influenced other national cinemas. One highlight of German filmmaking, which we shall later discuss, is its sophisticated appreciation for the camera as part of film style.

A review of a few of the German pictures which succeeded *The Cabinet of Dr. Caligari* reveals some of the cinematic innovations these filmmakers brought to their art form. One of the most popular expressionist films to follow *The Cabinet of Dr. Caligari* was *Nosferatu, eine Symphonie des Grauens* (*Nosferatu, a Symphony of Horrors*, 1922), directed by F.W. (Friedrich Wilhelm) Murnau (1888-1931) (see fig. 2.2). By comparing *Nosferatu* to *The Cabinet of Dr. Caligari,* we can get a sense of how innovative concepts found in the earlier film were both continued and compromised in its expressionist successor.

Based on the popular novel by Bram Stoker, *Nosferatu* was the first successful film version of the Dracula legend. This familiar horror story allowed Murnau to work with aspects of expressionism, already explored in *The Cabinet of Dr. Caligari,* that might otherwise have been confusing to an audience unacquainted with this art movement. A viewer accustomed to the mood and setting of the horror genre, for example, would not wonder why the tone and environment of this 1922 expressionist picture was unrealistic. Curious shapes and shadows, so enigmatic in *The Cabinet of Dr. Caligari,* seem fitting and even understandable in a horror movie. Audience familiarity with the Dracula myth also enabled Murnau to explore social issues previously considered in *The Cabinet of Dr. Caligari.* A principal theme in *Nosferatu* involves people allowing themselves to be victimized by a depraved authority figure--in this instance the sinister vampire, Nosferatu. A common motif in horror films, this topic also reflects expressionism's ongoing concern with the danger of a complacent and unwary society letting itself become corrupted by evil.

Familiarity with the horror genre could make the expressionism in *Nosferatu* more understandable, to the average viewer, than that found in *The Cabinet of Dr. Caligari.* Catering to increased audience accessibility also risked reducing, or trivializing, the revolutionary effects and impact of the earlier film. One reason *The Cabinet of Dr. Caligari* is considered such an excitingly original movie is because its mysterious appearance does not lend itself to easy explanation. This film depends upon its own unique mood, voice, and vision to convey its story and style. The simplest interpretation for the twisted images, brooding shadows, and foreboding atmosphere of *The Cabinet of Dr. Caligari* is that its mise-en-scene represents the perspective of a mad man.

Any person is capable of becoming a victim of insanity. This fact can make *The Cabinet of Dr. Caligari* quite unsettling to a viewer. It suggests that one's own mental state could someday entrap us in such a world. Putting expressionism in the setting of a horror movie can explain away unsettling tendencies of this sort. *Nosferatu,* it has been argued, lessened the impact of some of the salient expressionist innovative perspectives, displayed *The Cabinet of Dr. Caligari,* by adapting the style to allegory. The terror of expressionism became associated with a fairy tale, making its supernatural impact more fictional and less immediate.

Anyone can be influenced by the trauma of insanity. How many people are affected by vampires?

Associating expressionism with a popular genre could lessen the mystery and efficacy of its form. But expressionism's philosophic and stylistic richness prevented the movement from being solely relegated to fairy tales. Expressionism was interested in more than just the supernatural. It was also concerned with examining disturbed psychological states. Film directors in the Germany of the early 1920s continued investigating how

6.1 The vampire in F.W. Murnau's *Nosferatu* **(1922). Author's collection.**

expressionism could visually represent the internal feelings and problems of real people. A number of filmmakers became interested in combining realistic depiction, and social criticism, with expressionism's stylized representation of internal psychological conditions.   This philosophical trend was actually an outgrowth of a German theatrical style called *"Kammerspiele"* ("intimate theater").

II. *Der letze Mann* **and** *Kammerspielfilm*

Created by the innovative theater director Max Reinhardt (1873-1943) as an alternative to stage spectacle, *Kammerspiele* was drama performed in a space for an audience of 300 or under. [1] This intimate space permitted actors to use subtle gestures and facial expressions, in their performances, that could not have been seen on the stage of a larger theater. Kammerspiele's alternative, to the broad movements and spectacle associated with traditional theater, encouraged the exploration and exposition of acting styles and themes that otherwise might not have been considered. The camera is able to register intimate gestures and facial expression. It is not surprising that German filmmakers, familiar with *Kammerspiele*, eventually explored how the motion picture medium could adapt the principals of this theatrical movement to the screen.

Carl Mayer (1894-1944), one of the two authors of *The Cabinet of Dr. Caligari*, was largely responsible for *"Kammerspielfilm."*   Mayer began writing screenplays in 1921 that sought to use cinematic technique to communicate disturbed psychological states in much the manner that

Kammerspiele used its intimate space on stage. Perhaps Mayer's most successful *Kammerspielfilm* was *Der letze Mann* (*The Last Laugh*) (1924). (See fig. 2.2). The combination of Carl Mayer's script, F.W. Murnau's direction, actor Emil Janning's (1884-1950) screen portrayal, and Karl Freund's camerawork resulted in *Der letze Mann* becoming one of the most innovative and critically acclaimed films up to that time.

Der letze Mann tells a story about an aging doorman at a posh hotel in Berlin. Thoroughly happy with his job, the kind and friendly doorman is respected by family and neighbors because of his employment status. Both the doorman's position in the community and his self-esteem deteriorate in an instant when he loses his job due to advanced age. Ostracized by family and community, the once admired doorman is relegated to a lowly position in the hotel washroom. Dejected and alone through no fault of his own, the doorman's misery and ignominy are graphically depicted in the film. (See fig. 6.2) *Der letze Mann* communicates the doorman's condition through realistic and expressionist renderings of the film's setting and the protagonist's psychological state.

6.2 The doorman's sentence for being too old in *Der Letze Mann*. **Notice how the director employs linear perspective in positioning the row of sinks and rays of light relative to the doorman. Courtesy the British Film Institute.**

Expressionism is used to show the doorman's alienation from his environment when he returns home the first evening after his demotion. The wind blows in an unnatural fashion and the buildings become elongated and twisted as if suddenly reflected in a distorted mirror. The buildings, of course, have not actually become warped. This vision is a product of the protagonist's disturbed view of the world. Because his family is not aware of the doorman's tragedy, life takes a happier turn when he gets home. His daughter has just gotten married and he is able to join in the celebration. During the festivities the doorman gets drunk and expressionism is again used to show his psychological state. (See fig. 6.14). This time the distorted images represent the doorman's ability to overcome his problems at work, in his dreams, which he cannot control in real life. Unfortunately, harsh reality returns the next day. The doorman continues to suffer the opprobrium of demotion at the hotel. His family finds out about his loss of status and throw him out of their home because they feel he has shamed them.

Existing as an unsettling, and not completely understandable, force in *The Cabinet of Dr. Caligari,* expressionism reflects a disturbing subjective condition in *Der letze Mann.* The supernatural elements of expressionism, investigated in *The Cabinet of Dr. Caligari* and *Nosferatu,* are severely tempered in this later film. However, the themes of psychological uncertainty and estrangement that underlined both *The Cabinet of Dr. Caligari* and *Nosferatu*--important considerations of expressionism as a literary style-- are very evident in *Der letze Mann.* Though the source of the doorman's problems seem unusual to us, this film is very much concerned with portraying a depressing psychological condition similar to problems that could be experienced by any ordinary person today. The filmmaker wanted to show suffering related to social injustice. Because of this emphasis, the social criticism of *Der letze Mann* is much stronger than that found in *Nosferatu* and many other expressionist films.

One reason Mayer and his colleagues sought to work with a style of "increased realism" over expressionist abstraction, and adopted the philosophy of *Kammerspiele* in their films, was for purposes of social protest--something they felt lacking in too many contemporary motion pictures. The more stylized and less "real" a film appears to be, like *Nosferatu,* the easier it is for audiences to dismiss its premise as fiction. As is true of any movie, one should question just how "realistic" *Der letze Mann* really is. What appears to be very real looking exteriors of a city's streets, for example, were really a specially constructed set built for the movie inside a studio. (See fig. 2.2). *Der letze Mann* is actually a highly stylized artificial construction that suggests concepts we associate with the world around us. Though an artificial construct, the picture's sympathetic treatment of the problems of age discrimination, and the loss of self-esteem, touch upon social issues that are still relevant.

Critics applauded *Kammerspielfilm* for its handling of social issues. They also recognized the sophisticated way it used the camera for cinematic communication. *Kammerspielfilm* helped change the way filmmakers around the world thought about camerawork's relation to film style. It is interesting that a style associated with an art movement would have such an impact on how filmmakers used their cameras.

Expressionism, like other modern art movements we have discussed, was first affiliated with painting. Given this association one would expect mise-en-scene to be the component of film style most likely to be influenced by expressionism. Of the three principal elements of film style--camerawork, editing, and mise-en-scene--which the directors of *The Cabinet of Dr. Caligari* and *Nosferatu* had at their disposal, the filmmakers were most successful in their use of mise-en-scene. By the time he made *Der letze Mann* in 1924, Murnau did not want to show the protagonist's relationship to inner and outer worlds primarily through the content of the image. Influenced by the theatrical tradition of *Kammerspiele*, Murnau sought dynamic ways the camera could emphasize what the mise-en-scene was trying to communicate. This concern did more than introduce a different type of movie narrative. It revolutionized camerawork as an important element of film style.

One of the ironies of *Kammerspielfilm* is that it was influenced by a theatrical style. A problem with many early movies is that they often relied too much on theatrical convention. Because the filmmakers preferred to record the action on stage, rather than explore the *cinematic* properties of the newer medium, many of these early movies were compromised by the "staginess" of the theater. We saw what could happen to an outdoor scene, when filmed as if it were restricted to the stage, in our discussion of the chariot race sequence in the 1907 version of *Ben Hur*. *Kammerspielfilm* did not impose restrictive stage conventions on the motion picture. Rather, it used the philosophy of a theatrical style to free latent and untapped capacities for communication within the film medium.

Before discussing how *Kammerspielfilm* influenced filmmaking, some time should be spent identifying what constituted camerawork prior to the German innovations. From 1908 onward filmmakers, including the important director D.W. Griffith, sought ways to use the camera for more dramatic effect in their movies. Eventually they discovered that there were three general ways the camera could be manipulated for   filmic communication--**camera placement**, **camera movement**, and **camera adjustment.** A review of these important elements will enable us to better understand how the camera was used prior to *Kammerspielfilm*, and how camerawork has become such an integral part of film style today.

III. Camera Placement and Camera Angle

As indicated in Chapter Three, the camera was used primarily as a recording device in many of the pictures made prior to 1908. The early filmmakers utilized theatrical conventions to guide their expression. Film action, at first, as noted in our *Ben Hur* example, was blocked for the camera in much the same way that theatrical drama was staged for its audience. This tendency resulted in the camera being placed in a stationary position, similar to where a member of the audience might be seated in the theater. The primary function of the camera was to observe whatever was placed in front of it. When used in this fashion the camera was little more than a recording device.

In later pictures the director would film the action from a variety of placements and perspectives. Though made five years before *Ben Hur*, *A Trip to the Moon* was able, on one occasion, to use the camera as more than just a recording device documenting what was happening on the Méliès stage. During the scene where the explorers land their rocket the moon's face physically moves towards the camera, simulating the decreasing distance between rocket and destination. Rather than just *record* the progress of the rocket, the camera is *guiding* our journey through the film's mise-en-scene. This camera effect makes the scene much more effective, dramatically, than if we merely saw the rocket hit the moon's "eye" from a fixed perspective. The decreasing distance between camera and object photographed establishes a constantly changing viewpoint as we appear to get closer to the moon's face. This camera manipulation creates a dramatic *cinematic* effect that could not have been duplicated for members of an audience watching a live performance in the theater. (See fig. 3.5, 3.6, and 3.7).

Camera placement refers to the distance the camera appears to be from the subject. Changing the distance between camera and subject, the filmmakers found, could influence what the viewer sees. A tight close-up on a person's face, for example, provides different information than an extreme long shot where the subject is a substantial distance from the camera. Eventually six major types of placement were isolated--extreme long shot, long shot, medium shot, medium close-up, close-up, and extreme close-up. (See fig. 6.3-6.8).

An **extreme long shot** emphasizes distance and often is used to establish the setting or environment of the picture. If the movie is a western, for example, an extreme long shot may be used to draw attention to the terrain associated with this type of movie. When a character is shown in extreme long shot the director usually wants to show that person's relationship to the environment. Facial expression and much of a character's body language can not be seen in an extreme long shot. Such communication needs a closer placement. (See fig. 6.3 and 4.10).

A **long shot** features all of the subject in the frame, from the top of that individual's head to the bottom of his or her feet. This placement is more concerned with capturing body expression than emphasizing vast distance, as is the case of the extreme long shot. The long shot was the most common placement found in the early movies--a reflection of the tendency to shoot the action as if it were on stage. While more details of the actor's body could be seen in a long shot than an extreme long shot, filmmakers found this placement still was not always the best suited for bringing out what they were trying to communicate in a scene. (See fig. 6.3, 6.4, and 4.11).

A common problem with the very early movies is the ineffectiveness of the acting. A performance, that was very dynamic on stage, often seemed to lose something when filmed. In *Kammerspiel,* as noted, intimate gestures and facial expressions that would be lost in a large theater became an effective form of expression in an intimate space that seated 300 people or less. Conversely, broad gestures that worked well in a large theater could seem overstated and ludicrous when recorded on camera. The knowledge of how altering the distance, between the camera and subject, could effect the filmic message prompted the search for new approaches to screen acting. *Kammerspiel* fostered a new acting style by creating a theater that used more intimate space. It also was an impetus for the developement of *Kammerspielfilm* in the 1920s, in which filmmakers developed new methods of acting for the screen by working with more intimate camera placements.

By the middle 1910s, even before *Kammerspielfilm* was being developed, film directors were already relying less on the long shot as their most common placement. They were now recognizing the versatility of the **medium shot**--a placement that frames a person from the top of his or her head down to somewhere just above or below the knees. This closer employment of the camera permitted more facial expression to be seen while allowing most of the actor's body language to remain visible. The medium shot became the preferred placement, for many silent film directors, but not to the exclusion of the other camera setups. (See fig. 6.5.) Filmmakers were becoming increasingly sensitive to the fact that each camera position has its pluses or minuses, depending upon just what one wishes to communicate.

As the decade of the 1920s progressed, filmmakers demonstrated a greater propensity for closer and more intimate placements. The **medium close-up** became particularly familiar by the end of the silent era. The medium close-up again frames the subject from the top of the head, but cuts them off somewhere in the middle of the chest to the top of the shoulders. This placement enables actors to use facial expressions that would be less visible, at a greater camera distance, while still allowing for some, albeit greatly reduced, body language. (See fig. 6.6 and 6.15).

The **close-up** is often employed when the director wants to express what a character is feeling. Usually consisting of the person's face, the close-up generally does not include more that the very top of the subject's shoulders. This placement can capture very intimate facial expressions and nuance, while drawing attention to details that might not be seen in a longer placement. Forcing us to look this closely at someone's face has more of an emotional impact, on the viewer, than if we see that subject from a distance. A director can orchestrate the dramatic tension, and our psychological involvement with a scene, by using close-ups and long shots to literally physically pull us in, or distance us from, the subject on the screen. (See fig. 6.7 and 3.8).

The definition for an **extreme close-up** has changed since the advent of television. In film it traditionally has referred to a small, or detailed aspect, of a larger entity. A placement emphasizing a word on a page, a fingernail, or the shot of the eyeball in *Un Chien Andalou*, would be defined as an extreme close-up. (See fig. 6.8). Given the smaller, more intimate space of television, "extreme close-up" now is sometimes used to refer to what also is called a "tight close-up." This type of extreme, or tight, close-up occurs when the filmmaker tightly frames a face so that the top and bottom of the head are not visible. As is true with our other definitions, how one defines this camera placement can be fairly relative.

"Camera placement" relates to the distance the subject appears to be from the camera. **Camera angle** is concerned with the position of the camera relative to the subject during filming. The most common camera angle is a **straight-on** shot. With the straight-on shot the camera is generally parallel to the subject. With high and low angles the camera is tilted, or canted, in relation to the subject. In a **high angle** shot the camera is tilted to look down on the subject. (See fig. 6.9).

There is a good example of a high angle shot in *The Gold Rush* following the fight between Big Jim and Black Larson in the cabin. (See fig. 6.11). The camera photographs the majority of the fight with straight-on shots. When Big Jim defeats Black Larson, however, the camera is tilted down to reveal a surprised Larson looking up at Big Jim. This angle effectively does two things. The tilted camera better reflects the position of

6.3　ELS

6.4　LS

6.5　MS

6.6　MCU

6.7　CU

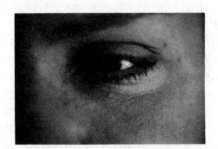

6.8　ECU

6.9　High angle shot

6.10　Low angle shot
Photographs by Carl Hitt and the author.

Larson, relative to his space and the camera, than would a straight-on shot. It also shows the supremacy Big Jim has over the once bullying Larson. Though the director did not choose to do so, he could have further emphasized Big Jim's authority by shooting him from a **low angle** (see fig. 6.10), in which the camera would have been mounted *low*, and looks *up* at the towering Big Jim, from Larson's perspective on the ground.

As can be seen from the above examples, using camera angles to *guide* the viewer's perceptions can be a much more effective form of communication than if the director just positions the camera to record the action in question. By changing the perspective of the camera, the director can influence the viewpoint of the viewer. This change can be achieved by altering the angle or placement from shot to shot, or it can be accomplished by moving the camera.

IV. Camera Movement and Camera Adjustment

The chariot race of the 1907 *Ben Hur* might seem humorous to today's viewers because it does not correspond with how we feel the action of such a subject should be filmed. The director's strategy of placing a stationary camera in the middle of the arena, and only filming what was in front of it, results in our missing the majority of the race. Not only does the camera fail to adequately guide us regarding what is happening, it also is unsuccessful in recording the dynamics of the event. Even before the 1907 *Ben Hur* was released, some filmmakers concluded that it was a better policy to <u>move</u> the camera, and try to follow the subject, rather than consciously miss the action.

6.11 The camera tilts down to view Black Larson from a high angle. Frame enlargement from *The Gold Rush.*

117

One way cameramen found they could follow action was by pivoting the camera on the tripod. Much of the action in *Ben Hur* could have been filmed if the cameraman would have horizontally pivoted, or **panned**, the camera on the tripod head. The **pan** is now one of the most common, and versatile, camera movements available to the filmmaker. Usually the director will simply ask for the camera to pan right or left. On some occasions the direction may call for the camera to turn a specific number of degrees. Thus a half circle would demand a 180° pan and a full circle would be a 360° pan. The vertical equivalent of the pan is a **tilt.** The cameraman would have tilted down to get the high angle shot of Black Larson on the floor, in *The Gold Rush* . (See fig. 6.11). With both the pan and tilt the camera moves, but the tripod's relation to the ground remains unchanged. Eventually filmmakers would come up with another movement, involving a stationary tripod, in which the camera is vertically cranked up or down. This maneuver is called a **pedestal**.

Other types of camera movement encompass moving both the camera and tripod during the shot. This can be accomplished by mounting the camera and tripod on an apparatus with wheels called a **dolly**. In a **dolly shot** the camera often moves while the subject remains stationary. The camera **dollies in** when it moves towards, and **dollies out** when it pulls away from, the subject. A dolly shot is a linear movement. If the camera travels in an arc the movement is called a **crab**. When both the subject and camera move parallel to one another we have a **tracking** or **trucking shot.** In this operation tracks may be laid down on the ground so that the moving camera can smoothly record its subject as they both travel through space.

Throughout the years ingenious inventors have developed elaborate devices to move the camera so that they might come up with more interesting and varied perspectives. As early as the 1910s directors like D.W. Griffith sought ways to put the camera on cranes so that they could increase their camera's versatility. A **crane shot** may involve a particularly elaborate movement which can incorporate and combine virtually all of the camera techniques mentioned above. Cameras can also be mounted on balloons, airplanes, and helicopters for even greater aerial effects than those possible with a crane. One noteworthy camera innovation of the 1970s was the **Steadicam**. By strapping on a steadicam the cameraman can shoot hand-held shots as steady and mobile as those mounted on more cumbersome mechanical devices.

An image is not just effected by the way one places or moves the camera. The type of film used, and the way the camera is adjusted to photograph its subject, will also influence the appearance of the image. Such factors as the light sensitivity of the film stock, and whether it is black and white or color, will affect the final results. Some early filmmakers got around the black and white limitations of the film stock by having their movies colored by hand, frame by frame. Since these motion pictures ran at least 16 frames per second this was no small effort. The more special effects the filmmakers tried to achieve, like color movies, the more the technical capabilities of the medium were expanded. Before such innovations were developed, the filmmakers experimented with techniques and camera adjustments already familiar to still photography. One major form of camera adjustment, carried over from photography, is **focus.**

The purpose of a lens, whether it be in an eye or a camera, is to refract light rays and converge them at a point. This results in an image, of the subject reflecting this light, to form on a "target area." In a camera the target area, where this image is projected, is on the surface of the film. In an eye the target area is the retina, at the back of the eyeball, where the optic nerves take the image and carry it to the brain for processing. People who wear corrective lenses do so because the shape of their eye prevents the image from focusing properly on the retina. A corrective lens further refracts the light to compensate for what the lens of the eye can not properly do on its own. If the light rays do not converge, at the proper distance from the target area, the image will be **out of focus.** Focus depends upon the ability of a lens to refract light rays, the amount of light entering the lens, and the distance the object reflecting the light rays is from the lens.

We are able to control the amount of light that enters our eyes by widening or closing an opening called the iris, located at the front of the eyeball. The iris opening becomes larger in low light conditions so our eye can take in more light. Similarly, a cameraman can open up or close

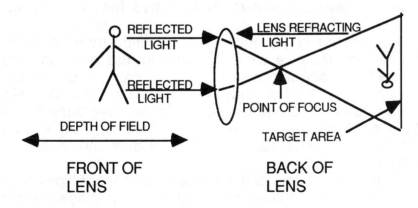

6.12 A lens focusing reflected light rays off a subject on to the target area. The area in front of the lens, which appears in focus on the target area, is called the "depth of field."

down the opening of the camera iris, which is also called a diaphragm, using calibrations known as *f*-**Stops.**

The distance an object is from a lens determines the focus, that a camera or eye has to maintain, if the image of that object is to be clear. If you look at something close to your eyes you will notice that objects further away will be out of focus unless you consciously want them to be in focus. By shifting your attention between the near and far objects you change the way your eyes are focusing. Through expansion and contraction, the muscles of an eye alter the distance of the point of convergence--or focus--of light reflected by the subject on the retina. If this focus is not changed, in accordance with the distance the subject is from the eye, the image will not be in focus. A cameraman controls the focus by physically moving the lens closer to, or further away from, the target area by turning a focus ring. The focus ring determines the alignment, of the point of convergence, of the reflected light relative to the target.

The entire area in <u>front</u> of the camera that appears in focus on the target area is known as the **depth of field**. As the depth of field changes in <u>front</u> of the lens, so does the point of focus <u>behind</u> the lens. In a long or extreme long shot in which everything from the extreme foreground to the extreme background is in focus--an image with a large depth of field--we have **deep-focus**. (See fig. 4.10). At first filmmakers tended to shoot everything in deep-focus. They eventually found that **shallow focus** could also be an effective camera adjustment technique. By using a shallow depth of field the cameraman can draw attention to a subject or action, which is in focus, by placing it within an environment that is out of focus. When part of the frame is in focus, and part of the frame is out of focus, we have a camera adjustment technique known as **selective focus**. (See fig. 4.11, 6.13, and 6.14).

At times a director may want to shift attention from one subject to another during the course of a shot. A situation may exist, for example, where a shot starts out showing a person in the foreground in focus while another individual, in the background, is out of focus. The filmmaker can change the selective focus so that the person in the foreground goes out of focus and the second individual, previously out of focus, comes into focus. Changing the selective focus during the course of a shot is called **rack focus**. (See fig. 6.13 and 6.14).

Placing something in front of the lens allows for other types of camera adjustment that will affect the content and quality of an image. A **filter** is a piece of glass, plastic, or gelatin that alters the light before it goes through the camera lens. Special filters are sometimes used for "**soft focus**" effects. A problem with the early film stock was that it took a great deal of light to get a proper exposure. This harsh light could emphasize the lines in an

120

6.13 and 6.14. "Selective focus" occurs when part of the image is in focus and part of the picture is out of focus. In our first example the foreground of the frame, with Carl, is in focus but the plane with Cindy is not. In the second example we have changed the depth of field so the image of Cindy is sharp, but Carl is now out of focus. The term "rack focus" is used to identify the technique of changing the selective focus. A filmmaker sometimes employs rack focus during a shot to draw the viewer's attention from one subject, in the frame, and direct it towards another. Photographs by the author.

actress's face and make her look older than her years. Cameramen rectified this situation by placing a piece of gauze in front of the lens. This technique diffused the light, softened the image, and gave the actress's face a romantic ethereal glow rather than a harsh appearance. Eventually these soft focus, or **gauze shots**, were accomplished by specially developed **diffusion filters**. A **day-for-night filter** is another example of a filter used for a special effect. A day-for-night filter, as the name suggests, is a dark blue filter that decreases the light entering the lens, enabling the cameraman to shoot a scene in the daytime so it will appear to be occurring at night.

Filmmakers found they could also create some useful and interesting effects by putting a **mask** in front of the lens. A "mask" is an opaque shield which selectively covers part of the lens. The mask will prevent everything but the open area from being exposed, allowing the filmmaker to change the shape of the framed image. By having a mask opening in the shape of binoculars or a keyhole, for example, a cameraman can film a subject so that everything registers black with the exception of the keyhole or binoculars shaped image. The director can then juxtapose a shot of someone looking in a keyhole or through a binoculars with the mask shot, thereby suggesting that the latter image is what the character is seeing. When a shot is presented as being seen from the **point of view** of the character, it is called a **subjective shot**. (See fig. 6.15). The subjective relationship is one of two general points of view the camera can take. In the majority of movies the more neutral perspective of the **objective point of view** is the most common camera to subject relationship.

The **iris** was a particularly common mask effect used in silent film. An iris was usually accomplished by placing a diaphragm in front of the lens. This allowed the center of the image to be exposed but would leave the surrounding area dark. The resulting effect was somewhat comparable to the way old circular frames used to display pictures hung on the wall. The filmmaker could draw the viewer's attention to the information, within a dark circle, while emphasizing the fact that it was obviously part of a larger subject within the frame. The iris was considered to be a rather dated technique by the 1930s. If later filmmakers wanted to draw attention to something, they tended to use a closer placement rather than an iris. We will consider one of the most famous applications of the iris--the iris-in and the iris-out--in Chapter Seven. (See fig. 6.16).

The **matte** is an early camera adjustment that still is commonly used for sophisticated effects. A matte is a piece of opaque material put behind the camera lens for purposes of covering up part of the frame while exposing other areas. (See fig. 6.17 and 6.18). When a director employs a mask, he or she usually wants to permanently leave part of the frame black. In most matte shots the filmmaker is interested in working with multiple

6.15 The drunken doorman's subjective point of view of his aunt in *Der Letze Mann*. Courtesy of the British Film Institute.

6.16 **The camera irises in on the opening shot of** *The Gold Rush.* **Frame enlargement.**

exposures. An early example of a relatively well executed matte effect can be seen in the 1903 Edison film *The Great Train Robbery,* directed by Edwin S. Porter. (See fig. 7.7 and 7.8).

In an early scene involving a telegraph office, no real window actually existed in the office set. The window was made to appear as a natural part of the setting by using the double exposure matte technique. When shooting the scene in the office a piece of opaque material, in the shape of the window, was put behind the lens so that part of the frame would not be exposed. The action in the office would have then been filmed with the "window portion" of the frame covered with the matte. Following this exposure the film would have been wound back in the camera and the "window" matte removed. A new matte would then be used to cover the exposed footage, involving the rest of the telegraph office, while the "window area" was filmed. The footage would then be shot again, this time photographing the window with the train, without affecting the previously filmed telegraph office material. After the film was processed we get an image that gives us the impression that both the telegraph office and the window were always part of the same environment. Today, using sophisticated computers, a single shot in a space adventure from the *StarWars* films or a *Star Trek* episode may be exposed a multiple of times, combining several intricate and "other worldly" matte effects.

One other camera adjustment we might mention is the **zoom.** A "zoom" can instantly change the perspective of subject/camera distance, during a shot, by combining the properties of a **telephoto**, **wide-angle**, and **normal lens.** A "telephoto lens" has a shallow depth of field and is capable of magnifying a small part of a far away image in much the manner that a telescope allows a viewer to get a closer view of the moon's surface. A "wide-angle lens" provides a broad view of the environment before it. A "normal" lens gives a perspective that approximates human vision. By changing the distance among a series of glass or plastic elements that make

6.17 and 6.18. We can get a sense of how matte technique works from this 1890s attachment for a still camera. This special box was placed in front of the camera so that one shut door covered half the lens while the other door was left open. A picture was taken which exposed half the frame and left the other half dark. The film was rewound and the open door was then shut and the shut door opened. The same "frame" was shot again. This time the unexposed half of the film was exposed and the previous exposed section was not subjected to any light. The resulting image, in this instance, is a man fighting with himself. From Hopkins's *Magic*.

up a **zoom lens**, the cameraman is capable of shooting in close-up, wide shot, and everything in between and do it in the same shot without changing the camera's physical distance from the subject. If the filmmaker wants to go in for a close-up without physically changing the distance the camera is from the subject he or she may do so by **zooming in**. If the filmmaker wants a wider shot that can be accomplished by **zooming out**. The cameraman may perform the zoom when the camera is not shooting or it may, like a rack focus, be recorded in the shot.

V.   Case Study in Camerawork Analysis: A Sequence from the *Kammerspielfilm* Picture, *Variety*

By the early 1920s motion picture cameramen had isolated most of the film techniques described above and incorporated them in their work. Throughout the world filmmakers began looking for ways to more actively involve the camera in their cinematic communication. *Kammerspielfilm*, as a movement, sought to use the camera for indicating the psychological nature of the characters while relying less on mise-en-scene to tell the story. We saw how important mise-en-scene was to Chaplin's film style in our analysis of *The Gold Rush*. A close examination of a sequence from a *Kammerspielfilm* picture entitled *Variety*, will enable us to see how camerawork is another important aspect of film style that affects cinematic communication.

Variety is a show business drama directed in 1925 by E.A. (Ewald Andre') Dupont (1891-1956). Because of its intriguing story and innovative use of camera, *Variety* received almost as much international acclaim as *Der letze Mann*. One of the more exotic camerawork innovations, developed for the picture, was putting camera and cameraman on a trapeze to duplicate the perspective of one of the performers.

The film begins with a warden asking an inmate, who was once a catcher for a trapeze act, to tell him how he ended up in prison for murder. The majority of the movie, as was the case of *The Cabinet of Dr. Caligari*, is a flashback of the protagonist's account of his story. From his account we eventually learn that on one occasion the head of the trapeze act, a man named Artinelli, attempted to seduce his catcher's wife. An analysis of the seduction sequence reveals how Dupont used the camera to develop the drama of this important part of the story.

In the following shot breakdown of the seduction sequence from *Variety,* the stylistic elements dealing with camerawork are italicized in bold print to indicate how this aspect of film style complements the information conveyed by the mise-en-scene. Key images from the majority of the shots are reproduced on the pages following this breakdown. It is suggested that you look at these frame enlargements as you read the descriptions.

SHOT BREAKDOWN OF THE SEDUCTION SEQUENCE FROM E.A. DUPONT'S *VARIETY* (1925)

Title #1   The rendezvous where many of the Wintergarten performers spent their afternoons. (Fig. 6.19).

Shot #1   *LS* performers seen through window of cafe. (Fig. 6.20).

Shot #2   *LS* interior of cafe, ***camera pans from right to left***.

Shot #3   *MS* Boss playing cards, surrounded by observers. (See fig. 6.21).

Shot #4   *MCU* Boss smoking a cigar and looking at his hand with an air of confidence. (Fig. 6.22).

Shot #5	*MCU of* opponent, sitting across from Boss, looking at his hand with concern. (Fig. 6.23).
Shot #6	*MS* observers looking at the opponent. (Fig. 6.24).
Shot #7	*CU* opponent looking ill at ease. (Fig. 6.25).
Shot #8	*MCU* Boss, looking at person who has questioned him, replies: (Fig. 6.26).
Title #2	"Artinelli? Oh, he's still sleeping." (Fig. 6.27).
Shot #9	*MS* Artinelli, in dressing gown, looking at the window of his hotel room which he has just opened. *Camera is placed outside the window and is looking in.* Artinelli goes and opens his door to the hall which sets the window curtains aflutter. (Fig. 6.28 and 6.29).
Shot #10	*LS hall. With back to camera* Artinelli, *framed in MS, suddenly leans out of the doorway into the foreground, and* looks down the hall. (Fig. 6.30).
Shot #11	*CU* Artinelli, he bends down. (Fig. 6.31).
Shot #12	*CU, iris* pair of shoes held in Artinelli's right hand being placed on hallway floor. (Fig. 6.32).
Shot #13	*Same placement as shot #11, CU* Artinelli.
Shot #14	*LS, same placement as shot #9,* Artinelli backing into his room and shuts door. (Fig. 6.33)
Shot #15	*CU iris* handle as door shuts. (Fig. 6.34).
Shot #16	*LS* empty hotel hall. (Fig. 6.35).
Shot #17	*CU iris* Bertha's door. Door opens and Bertha comes out. We see only the middle of her body. She is holding what appears to be a hat in her right hand. (Fig. 6.36).

Shot #18   *LS   Artinelli's room, same placement as shots #10 and 14.* Artinelli leaning with his ear to the door. (Fig. 6.37).

Shot #19   *CU* Artinelli with ear to door. *Camera dollies in to ECU of Artinelli's ear emphasizing the act of listening.* (Fig. 6.38-6.42).

Shot #20   *LS, low angle of camera mounted close to floor of hotel hall, Bertha walking towards camera.* Bertha's face has yet to be seen. *This placement shows her from the bottom of her feet to just below her neck.* (Fig. 6.43).

Shot #21   *MCU tracking shot ahead of Bertha walking down the hall.* She is looking towards Artinelli's door. (Fig. 6.44).

Shot #22   *Subjective tracking LS towards Artinelli's door.* He steps out and picks up his shoes with his right hand. He holds a pipe in his left. (Fig. 6.45 and 6.46).

Shot #23   *MCU* Artinelli looking at Bertha as if surprised that she is there. (Fig. 6.47).

Shot #24   *MCU* profile of Artinelli from inside room. With his right hand he throws shoes inside doorway.

Shot #25   *LS* doorway from inside Artinelli's room behind Artinelli as he tosses his shoes inside.

Shot #26   *MCU two-shot* Artinelli, frame left, talking to Bertha, frame right. (Fig. 6.48).

Title #3   "No after effects?" (Fig. 6.49).

Shot #27   *MCU partial iris* Bertha smiling. (Fig. 6.50).

Shot #28   *MCU iris of* Artinelli. (Fig. 6.51).

Title #4	"Our success has already brought me an offer from America." (Fig. 6.52).
Shot #29	*MCU, same placement as #27, of* Bertha. (Fig. 6.53).
Shot #30	*MCU two-shot, same placement as #26,* Artinelli and Bertha. Artinelli goes into his room. Bertha follows but stops at doorway. (Fig. 6.54).
Shot #31	*MCU* Bertha standing somewhat nervously in doorway, holding her hat, and looking at Artinelli. (Fig. 6.55)
Shot #32	*MS* curtains blowing in front of the window, shot from inside the room. (Fig. 6.56).
Shot #33	*MCU* Artinelli with paper, presumably the letter from America. He looks at Bertha and says: (Fig. 6.57).
Title #5	"Won't you please close the door? It's so draughty." (Fig. 6.58).
Shot #34	*MCU* Bertha, *same placement as shot #31.* (Fig. 6.59).
Shot #35	*MS* window, *same placement as shot #32.* (Fig. 6.60).
Shot #36	*MCU* Bertha, *same placements as shots #31 and 34.* (Fig. 6.61).
Shot #37	*MCU* Artinelli reading his letter. (Fig. 6.62).
Shot #38	*MCU Bertha, same placements as shots #31, 34, and 36.* Her face loses its nervousness as she shuts the door behind her. *This action brings her closer to the camera, resulting in her face coming into tighter CU.* She looks intently at Artinelli the entire time. (Fig. 6.63, 6.64, 6.65, and 6.66).
Shot #39	*MS window, same placements as shots #32 and*

35. The curtains go limp. (Fig. 6.67).

Shot #40   *Two-shot,* Artinelli *in MS* in foreground, *frame left.* Bertha is *in LS* in the corner. (Fig. 6.68).

Shot #41   *CU* Bertha, serious look on her face. (Fig. 6.69).

Shot #42   *MS Bertha, camera pans and have two-shot* Bertha and Artinelli. (Fig. 6.70).

Shot #43   *MCU two-shot* Bertha and Artinelli.   Bertha reads the letter, which she holds in her right hand, while stroking her hair with her left. Artinelli watches her intently. (Fig. 6.71).

Shot #44   *MCU in iris* Boss looking at his cards. (Fig. 6.72).

Shot #45   *CU* other card player, looking down unhappily. (Fig. 6.73).

Shot #46   *MS* cards laying in front of opponent's hands. (Fig. 6.74).

Shot #47   *MCU* observers looking down at cards on the table and then at Boss's opponent.

Shot #48   *MCU* opponent.

Shot #49   *MS observers watching, same placement as #47.* Suddenly Boss and his opponent, who have not been visible, lean their heads into the frame and look down at the cards on the table. Boss is on the left and his opponent is on the right, *in MCU.* Their heads block our view of the observers in the background. (Fig. 6.75 and 6.76).

Shot #50   *CU* profile of the opponent, frame right looking to the left, who says: (Fig. 6.77).

Title #6   "You seem to be lucky at cards as well as at love!" (Fig. 6.78).

Shot #51   *MCU* Boss, cigar in mouth, looking in the direction of his opponent as he smiles and nods his head in affirmation. (Fig. 6.79).

129

Shot #52   *Tight two-shot, CU*   Bertha and Artinelli kissing
passionately. (Fig. 6.80).

FRAME ENLARGEMENTS FROM THE SEDUCTION SEQUENCE IN *VARIETY*

The rendezvous where many of the Wintergarten performers spent their afternoons.

6.19   Title #1

6.20   Shot #1

6.21   Shot #3

6.22   Shot #4

6.23   Shot #5

6.24   Shot #6

6.25 Shot #7

6.26 Shot #8

"Artinelli? Oh, he's still sleeping."

6.27 Title #2

6.28 Shot #9A

6.29 Shot #9B

6.30 Shot #10

6.31 Shot #11

6.32 Shot #12

6.33 Shot #14

6.34 Shot #15

6.35 Shot #16

6.36 Shot #17

6.37 Shot #18

6.38 Shot #19A

6.39 Shot #19B

6.40 Shot #19C

6.41   Shot #19D

6.42   Shot #19E

6.43   Shot #20

6.44   Shot #21

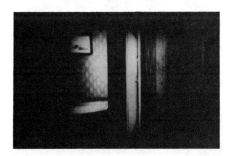

6.45 Shot #22A

6.46   Shot #22B

6.47   Shot #23

6.48   Shot #26

"No after effects?"

6.49   Title #3

6.50   Shot #27

6.51   Shot #28

**"Our success has
already brought me
an offer from America."**

6.52 Title #4

6.53 Shot #29

6.54   Shot #30

6.55   Shot #31

6.56   Shot #32

6.57   Shot #33

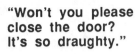

"Won't you please
close the door?
It's so draughty."

6.58   Title #5

6.59   Shot #34

6.60   Shot #35

6.61 Shot #36

6.62   Shot #37

6.63   Shot #38A

6.64   Shot #38B

6.65 Shot #38C

6.66 Shot #38D

6.67 Shot #39

6.68 Shot #40

6.69 Shot #41

6.70 Shot #42

6.71 Shot #43

6.72 Shot #44

6.73   Shot #45

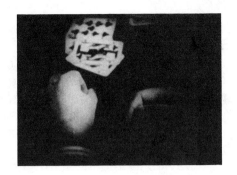

6.74   Shot #46

6.75   Shot #49A

6.76   Shot #49B

6.77   Shot #50

"You seem to be
lucky at cards as
well as at love!"

6.78   Title #6

6.79   Shot #51

6.80   Shot #52

ANALYSIS OF THE CAMERAWORK IN THE *VARIETY* SEDUCTION SEQUENCE

Mise-en-scene criticism could be used to analyze this sequence in and of itself. The mise-en-scene descriptions, however, are rather general when considered by themselves. Combining mise-en-scene criticism with an analysis of the camerawork reveals much more about what is happening in the narrative. The director is, in fact, using the camera to guide us through the mise-en-scene.

Obviously this director could have saved a lot of work for himself by filming everything in a wide shot, from one camera placement, the way the early filmmakers did. A problem with shooting an entire scene in long shot, as we have seen in some of the early films, is that the visual information can be so general that the audience does not get involved with what is happening. While the director starts this scene with two long shots, these placements do more than simply record what is occurring before the camera. They work with the succeeding shots to engage us in this action.

At the beginning of this scene we start outside the cafe, go inside, and eventually focus on Boss. The primary purpose of the first two camera placements of this sequence is to familiarize us with the overall setting . The long shots in shot #1 (Fig. 6.20) and shot #2 establish the environment of the cafe. The pan, in shot #2, enables the director to show us various aspects of these surroundings without having to resort to a wider placement or cut to a series of successive shots. This movement also provides an interesting visual contrast to the other shots which are all stationary. After using these two shots to establish the general setting of this "rendezvous," the director varies the distance his camera is from his subject in succeeding placements. This technique isolates the specific visual information the director feels is most relevant to the story. He does this by employing closer placements that *eliminate* subject matter not germane, to the action, while emphasizing visuals that are.

We can tell, from the director's choice of subject matter and camera placement, that Boss's behavior is the most important theme in this scene. The filmmaker's interest, in essence, is to go from the general--the overall environment--to the particular--Boss's attitudes and actions. The tighter MS of Boss playing cards in shot #3 (Fig. 6.21) directs our concentration on him rather than something else in this setting. Shot #4 (Fig. 6.22) forces us to pay even more attention to Boss, to the exclusion of everyone else, by cutting to the tighter MCU. This placement conveys the idea that the man we are looking at is confident and in control.

The director then establishes the importance of the relationship of Boss, to the person he is beating at cards, by cutting to a MCU of his opponent in shot #5 (Fig. 6.23). The opponent is a study in contrast. His

138

shoulders are slightly stooped and he is looking at his cards with dismay. Clearly there is something of a dramatic confrontation going on between these two men. While Boss and his opponent are the center of this interaction, observers of the game have also been featured in the background of shots #3-5. The MS of shot #6 (Fig. 6.24) concentrates on the observers' interest in the game. The subject matter of this placement emphasizes that there is enough drama in the confrontation to attract the attention of several people.

The difference between Boss and his opponent's reactions to the situation are made even more distinct when we cut to the CU of the opponent in shot #7 (Fig. 6.25). This placement further emphasizes the opponent's feelings of discomfort. The actor could have expressed this same feeling of apprehension in a LS. This CU, obviously, intensifies the mood expressed on his face better than a shot where the camera was placed at a greater distance from him. Again we can see how the camera placement is guiding what we view in the mise-en-scene. The contrast between the opponent's feelings and those of Boss are further accented when the director cuts to shot #8 (Fig. 6.26). The fact that this MCU is further away from the subject helps to suggest a psychological contrast between Boss and his opponent. Instead of centering upon a sad and sagging face this placement features a strong, smiling, and upright body. Boss is the superior party in this confrontation and he, and everyone else, knows it.

Even as this contest at cards is happening, an encounter is taking place between two other principal characters in the film. This other rendezvous proves to have even greater dramatic implications than the one involving the card game. A subtitle at the beginning of our sequence introduced us to the setting where the Wintergarten performers gathered, but all other information, up until now, has been conveyed to us visually. The director makes the transition to this next dramatic scene by using another subtitle. The drama of the card game is temporarily disregarded when Boss is asked the whereabouts of Artinelli. In a subtitle Boss dismisses the question with the statement that Artinelli is still sleeping.

Shot #9 (Fig. 6.28 and Fig. 6.29) is an example of the privileged relationship the camera can have to the subject being filmed. The previous placements could have been duplicated by the perspectives of onlookers. It is less likely that someone would be watching Artinelli at eye level, from outside his hotel room window, particularly when Artinelli is looking through that window himself. The camera's privileged relationship to its subject provides us with information that would not be accessible to onlookers actually at the scene. Interestingly, this unique perspective of Bertha's seduction is also supposed to be part of the story that her husband is telling the warden at the beginning of this film. Obviously Boss could never have known about all of these events, particularly from this privileged perspective outside the window. One could dwell upon this narrative flaw. It is more rewarding to see how the director used this unique camera/subject relationship to communicate what happens in the scene.

One outcome, of the camera's privileged relationship to the subject, is that we observe the upcoming events as "peeping Toms." We literally can look into a window, and watch the most intimate activities within, without fear of detection. The director encourages us to conduct ourselves in a manner that would get us arrested if we behaved this way in everyday life. The ethical questions regarding our voyeurism duly noted, the placement of the camera in shot #9 reveals other important pieces of information relevant to how we will comprehend what is happening in this narrative.

Because of the way the window is emphasized, in shot #9, we eventually become aware that it is an important object in this scene. The character's initial actions make us conscious that Artinelli definitely wants the window open. The subject/camera distance, that determines the placement, is then changed when Artinelli turns away from us and walks to the door in the background. Instead of cutting to a different placement, at this time, the director wants us to consider the relationship of Artinelli to the window. When he opens the door the curtains flutter--a foreshadowing. His energetic, apparently calculated, actions certainly challenge Boss's statement that Artinelli is asleep. Artinelli is wearing a dressing gown. The way he is clothed underneath it, however, raises doubt that he has just gotten out of bed.

Artinelli is interested in his window. His behavior in shot #9 indicates that he is concerned about other aspects of his environment as well. Prior to opening the door Artinelli, who is now seen in LS, bends over to pick up something. He is getting a pair of shoes. As Artinelli opens his door the director cuts to shot #10 (Fig. 6.30)--a LS of the hallway outside his room. Artinelli again changes the emphasis of the camera placement by leaning into the picture so that he is framed in MS. The beginning of shot #10, and Artinelli's lingering stare, indicates that there is something important for him at the end of the hall.

So far our analysis of this sequence has generally restricted itself to information presented in this series of shots. This portion of the film occurs near the middle of *Variety*. Most viewers would have some suspicion about what Artinelli is so concerned with at the end of the hall. From previous scenes they would know that Artinelli is looking towards the room that Boss shares with his wife, Bertha. We are aware that Bertha is not with Boss. Artinelli has been making passes at Bertha which have become increasingly more passionate. Bertha has appreciated Artinelli's attention but so far has remained loyal to her husband. Artinelli appears to be hoping for a confrontation with Bertha. We are not yet sure how he might accomplish this goal or how Bertha will respond to him if he does.

Shot #11 (Fig. 6.31) continues to emphasize Artinelli's interest in Bertha's room down the hall but this time we see his face and in CU. As he looks towards the end of the hall Artinelli leans to the right. Shot #12 (Fig. 6.32) is a high angle CU of Artinelli's right hand putting down the pair of shoes he picked up in shot #9. An iris further accentuates that these shoes are the focal point of some important aspect of the narrative. The motives behind Artinelli's actions will eventually reveal themselves. One motivation for his behavior, familiar to Europeans at the beginning of this century, needs some explanation today.

The act of putting one's shoes in a hallway outside a European hotel room would not have been so mysterious to someone living in Germany in 1925. At this time hotels would polish the shoes of guests who left their shoes outside their rooms. Apparently American hotels did not offer this service. On at least one occasion, during their first vaudeville tour with the Karno troupe in America, Stan Laurel and Charlie Chaplin roomed together. According to Stan Laurel, one night he and Chaplin left their shoes in the hallway outside their American hotel room. Instead of getting polished their shoes were stolen. The next day two confused Englishmen were seen running around in public wearing bedroom slippers. It would not be the last time that Chaplin would do something to call attention to his feet. This lengthy explanation for Artinelli's actions duly noted, it should be observed that the shoes in shot #12 already seem to be adequately polished.

Artinelli's suspicious act of putting polished shoes in the hallway having been emphasized by the director, shots #13 and #14 (Fig. 6.33) repeat previously seen placements as the plotter retires to his room. The CU in shot #13 once again draws attention to Artinelli's scheming face. The LS of him backing into his room distances the viewer from Artinelli. Shot #15 (Fig. 6.34), a CU in iris of the handle on Artinelli's door, further separates us from its owner as we wonder what will happen next.

The director builds on our questions by once again emphasizing the camera's privileged relationship to this environment. Shot #16 (Fig. 6.35) is a LS of the hall. The effect is almost as if we have been locked out of Artinelli's room and not sure where we should go. It also reminds us that the room at the end of this hall probably holds the secret to what next transpires. Indeed, shot #17 (6.36) is a CU of Bertha's door, in iris, that opens to reveal the middle of her body. She is holding what appears to be a hat in her right hand. The fact that we only see the middle portion of Bertha's body is a curious way to introduce a person. Deprived of a head and legs, Bertha seems to be more an unknowing disembodied component of a plot rather than a functioning identifiable person. The camerawork is very concerned with establishing the psychological mood and intrigue in this situation.

It would not hurt to once again consider how much the camerawork molds the way we interpret the mise-en-scene in this sequence. This can particularly be seen in the way the director uses the camera to convey the events in the succeeding shots. The LS of shot #18 (Fig. 6.37) returns to the placement of shots #9 and #14. The open window is seen prominently in the foreground while Artinelli, in LS, is standing with his ear to the door. He undoubtedly is listening for Bertha. The importance of his act of listening is further emphasized in a very fine use of the camera in shot #19 (Fig. 6.38-6.42). The camera starts with a CU of Artinelli, listening intently, and then *dollies-in* to an ECU of the ear itself. The ECU of the ear then dissolves to shot #20 (Fig. 6.43), a low angle placement of the lower portion of Bertha's body, walking down the hall towards the camera.

The way Artinelli's actions relate to Bertha are becoming more clear. The director uses the camera to convey this association in a way that the mise-en-scene could not do by itself. *Variety* is a silent movie yet, by dollying-in on an ECU of Artinelli's ear, the director establishes the presence of sound. By going from the ear to Bertha walking, we get a direct correlation between the act of listening and the subject creating the sound. The camera movement and placements are crucial to the way we interpret the mise-en-scene in this scene. It should be noted that we have yet to see Bertha's face in this sequence--a fact which robs Bertha of an important part of her identity. However, having seen the middle and lower thirds of her body in shots #17 and #20, we finally get to see her head and shoulders--the missing third of her body--in a MCU tracking shot in shot #21 (Fig. 6.44). We finally have confirmation that this person is, indeed, Bertha.

Given the way this scene has been set up, we cannot help but think of Bertha as a victim getting ready to fall into a trap. Bertha appears to be apprehensive as the tracking camera moves ahead of her at the same rate of speed, recording her reactions to the lonely and inhospitable hallway. She is not, however, totally unaware of Artinelli's presence. The camera notes her looking in the direction of Artinelli's room and then cuts to shot #22 (Fig. 6.45 and 6.46)--a subjective tracking shot. The placement reveals that she is looking at the doorway to Artinelli's room in LS. As she approaches the door, presumably planning to walk past, Artinelli suddenly steps out. Seen in LS, he picks up his shoes with his right hand while nonchalantly holding a pipe in his left. The director cuts to shot #23 (Fig. 6.47). It is a MCU of Artinelli, now directing his attention to Bertha as he pretends to be surprised to see her.

The purpose for putting the shoes in the hallway now made clear to us, the director has Artinelli quickly dispose of them. In shot #24, Artinelli is shown in MCU from inside the room. Cutting to a LS, also inside the room, shot #25 has Artinelli tossing the shoes aside. The placement of shot #26 (Fig. 6.48) focuses on a two-shot, in MCU, of Artinelli and Bertha in front of the doorway of his room. This meeting will be instrumental to the outcome of this sequence and the rest of the film as well.

The confrontation begins pleasantly and is seemingly innocent. Artinelli refers to a party they both attended the night before when he asks Bertha if she has any "after effects." This is the first subtitle since Boss was asked of Artinelli's whereabouts. As we saw in our analysis of *The Gold Rush,* silent filmmakers of the 1920s could express a great deal without resorting to sound or subtitles to communicate. We have processed a substantial amount of information since the last time the director resorted to written text. The relaxed and smiling face of Bertha, shown in MCU with partial iris in shot #27 (Fig. 6.50), confirms that she is suffering no ill effects from the night before.

Artinelli, who has been smiling and charming, suddenly changes his expression in shot #28 (Fig. 6.51). He also is seen in MCU with partial iris, which parallels the previous placement showing Bertha. The nature of their conversation has made them equals in their discussion since shot #26. However, where Bertha is dressed in white and is seen as cheerful, in shot #27, Artinelli is dark and no longer smiling. There is an intense look on his face that suggests a dishonorable sense of purpose. In subtitle #4 he tells her that their success has brought them an offer from America. His expression is not what we would associate with this kind of news. Not unexpectedly, Bertha's MCU in the partial iris of shot #29 (Fig. 6.53)--the same placement as shot #27--is one of excitement.

The director, Dupont, returns to the two-shot placement, outside Artinelli's doorway, seen in shot #26. In shot #30 (Fig. 6.54) Artinelli goes into his room, presumably to get the letter from America, and Bertha follows him part way. Artinelli's departure creates tension in the scene as Bertha stands in the hallway, nervously clutching the article in her hand. Bertha is standing to the right of the frame, looking into his room. The space on the left hand side of the frame, where Artinelli had been standing, is now empty. This causes the composition to look unbalanced. The director balances his composition by cutting to a MCU, in shot #31 (Fig. 6.55), of Bertha standing somewhat nervously in the doorway. In the two-shot of shot #26, Artinelli and Bertha were shown as equals who were comfortable with one another's company. Now, once again, she looks like a potential victim on the edge of Artinelli's trap.

The offer from America, as with the business of the shoes in the hallway, is being used by Artinelli to lure Bertha into his room. We now understand how the window is being employed as part of his plan. In shot #32 (Fig. 6.56) we see a MS of the window, this time inside the room, with the curtains blowing. Shot #33 (Fig. 6.57) cuts to Artinelli in MCU, holding a paper that presumably is the offer from America. Artinelli, with a feigned look of innocence on his face, then asks Bertha to shut the door because "it's so draughty." This subtitle begins to clarify why Dupont went to such efforts, earlier, to draw our attention to the window.

We get the impression that Bertha is now aware of the nature of Artinelli's intentions as well. What happens next depends upon how Bertha responds to Artinelli's efforts to seduce her. Shot #34 (Fig. 6.59) is a MCU of Bertha, framed in the same placement as shot #31. This time, however, Bertha is not smiling as she looks at Artinelli intently. Dupont cuts back to a MS of the window with curtains flying. Shot #35 (Fig. 6.60) is essentially identical to the placement and action of shot #32. Shot #36 (Fig. 6.61) returns to the placement seen in shots #31 and #34 with Bertha, in MCU, still looking intently at Artinelli. The repetition of this placement asks us to closely examine Bertha's expression to ascertain how she will react to this man.

Shot #37 (Fig. 6.62) is a MCU of Artinelli looking down at his letter, pretending not to be aware of Bertha's response to his request. The next shot, #38 (fig. 6.63-66), strongly suggests what the outcome of this encounter will be. Returning to the MCU placement of the woman, seen in shots #31, #34, and #36, Bertha's face takes on resolve as she closes the door behind her. The action of shutting the door causes her to come forward, into a tighter CU. She looks intently at Artinelli the entire time. We have not seen Bertha take her eyes off Artinelli since he confronted her in the hallway. Her lack of resistance is metaphorically conveyed in shot #39 (Fig. 6.67). This shot of the window is identical to the placement in shots #32 and #35. However this time, as Bertha is closing the door, the outstretched curtains go limp before the window frame.

Shot #40 (Fig. 6.68) shows both Bertha and Artinelli in the same frame for the first time since their seemingly pleasant exchange in shot #26. In shot #26 they were seen as equals whose intimacy was accented by a MCU. They have not been shown as a spatially close couple since. The succeeding placements, after shot #26, portray Bertha and Artinelli as separate individuals, each framed in his or her own space. This framing asks the viewer to compare and contrast their feelings and attitudes towards one another. We have not seen them united in the same frame, sharing the same interests and emotions, since Artinelli went into his room. The fact that their relationship may be changing adds to the drama of this scene.

In shot #40 (Fig. 6.68) Artinelli is in the foreground in MS, frame left, while Bertha is in LS to the right. While both individuals appear in this two-shot, the distance separating them, and the way they are positioned relative to one another, highlights the tension in their relationship. The expression

144

on Bertha's face, and her hesitation in rushing over to join Artinelli, imply that this woman believes that she has been invited into his room for reasons other than looking at this business offer. The seriousness of her expression is emphasized even more strongly in the relatively tight CU of her face, in shot #41 (Fig. 6.69). She continues to look at Artinelli intently.

Shot #42 (Fig. 6.70) is a MS of Bertha. The way she is clutching the article in her hand continues to convey the tension she is feeling. The camera is further away from Bertha than in the previous shot. This placement is not meant to distance us from her reaction to this confrontation with Artinelli, however. Rather, the director uses this placement to heighten the dramatic tension. Bertha has not come to him. Consequently, Artinelli continues to use the paper of the American offer as a ploy to get closer to Bertha. The camera pans right and the MS of Bertha becomes a M2S with her and Artinelli. Now, in close proximity to one another, Bertha averts her eyes from Artinelli for the first time in this scene. Artinelli, however, is looking very intently at Bertha.

As with his request to shut the door, Bertha continues to accept Artinelli's actions without protest. Shot #43 (6.71) cuts to a tighter MCU of the two, as Artinelli gives her the paper. The expression on Bertha's face lightens as she reads the paper, which she holds in her right hand. The fingers of her left hand gently touch her hair. Prior to this shot the way Bertha has clutched an item has been used to show her tension. She now seems more visibly relaxed. Artinelli continues to observe her expression with studied interest.

Dupont cuts from the MCU two-shot of Bertha and Artinelli to a MCU of her husband, still playing cards. Shot #44 (Fig. 6.72) uses an iris to intensify the way Boss is framed. This emphasis helps to impress upon the viewer the irony being expressed between shots #43 and #44. Even as the confident Boss believes himself to be a winner his partner is trying to seduce his wife. The tighter MCU of the other card player in shot #45 (Fig. 6.73) heightens the sense of irony in the scene. His look of dejection is in stark contrast to what we can see Boss is feeling. Were Boss to know what was happening with Bertha his mood would, of course, be more similar to what the other card player is expressing.

Boss's card playing opponent looks down and shot #46 (Fig. 6.74) reveals the source for his concern. This MS reveals the cards that have made him a loser. Shot #47 is a MS of a couple of observers, also looking at the cards. Their spatial relationship to Boss and his opponent becomes clearer when the latter two lean their heads into the frame, still looking at the cards. Boss is seen in MCU, frame left, while his opponent has appeared frame right. The dynamic way both men break into the frame further emphasizes that they have been involved in a confrontation with one another. While the opponent was partially visible in shot #2, this is the first time they have really shared the same space in this sequence.

Having used a two-shot to show that Boss and his opponent have been engaged in the same activity, the director goes back to framing the two men in their individual spaces. For shot #50 (Fig. 6.79), Dupont cuts to a tighter CU of the profile of the opponent before he ruefully says, "You seem to be lucky at cards as well as at love!" This statement continues to reflect upon the irony of the situation. Our last view of Boss in this sequence is a MCU. Shot #51 (Fig. 6.79) shows Boss, with cigar in mouth, nodding a smiling affirmation in the direction of his opponent. Little does Boss know that his real opponent is his partner, Artinelli. Shot #52 (Fig. 6.80) is a tight two-shot CU of Bertha and Artinelli kissing passionately. Any lingering doubts that we may have had about the outcome of the seduction attempt are succinctly answered.

VI. Conclusion

During the first ten year's of their medium's existence, filmmakers became aware that camera placement, camera adjustment, and camera movement could influence the appearance and content of a picture. With increased experimentation they discovered how to use the camera to convey information in ways that the mise-en-scene, by itself, could not . By the 1920s, as our analysis of the seduction sequence from E.A. Dupont's 1925 German film *Variety* confirms, their technical capabilities with the camera had become quite sophisticated.

In some respects our review of the seduction sequence from *Variety* is fairly thorough. It does not recognize all of the film techniques its director used to make this segment such an interesting piece of cinema. Besides being concerned about how he used mise-en-scene and camerawork to effectively tell his story, Dupont was also very conscious of the manner he juxtaposed the individual shots in *Variety*. Chapter Seven will investigate how Dupont, and other filmmakers, have used editing for cinematic communication.

ENDNOTES

1. Lotte Eisner, *The Haunted Screen,* (Berkeley: University of California Press, 1969), p.17.

CHAPTER SEVEN

FILM FORM AND CONTINUITY EDITING

CHAPTER OBJECTIVES: *Explore the concept of "film form" and identify the major components of continuity editing.*

I. Film Form and the Basic Structural Units of Editing

"Film editing" relates to the physical process of putting a motion picture together. Once this construction is completed the critic is concerned with how a film's editing shapes and influences its content and appearance. This process and outcome are usually described in terms of **"film form."** In essence the form, or structure, of a film determines the way the individual parts of that picture are organized to formulate the whole. Critics also use the concept, of a "film's form," to identify its appearance overall.

To better grasp the notion of "film form" we might compare the construction of a movie to that of a building. How that building is constructed, with bricks, wood, and concrete, is partially determined by the type of structure that is being produced. Likewise a film's form dictates, and is the result of, the editing--building--process.

Taking our analogy further, it is not difficult to instantly conceptualize a general image of a "barn." The overall form and structure of this barn, as a single unit, is fairly clear in our mind's eye. Our mental image of "barn" gets complicated, however, if we are asked to start breaking this structure down into roof, floors, foundation, boards, and bricks. It may become more difficult to envision the "form" of a barn when asked to think about it in this fashion. Remembering the basic image of our barn, as a single unit, can guide our understanding of how its smaller parts contribute to making up the whole. As we noted in Chapter Two, it is good to have a simple "one-liner" to generally describe the content of a movie. Lose sight of a film's basic makeup and the nature of that movie may get lost in a sea of details. This truism given its due, we still need to have some appreciation for the basic brick.

The editor and the critic, like the builder, must proceed with two conceptions in mind--an overall notion concerning the identity of the subject's total structure and an appreciation for its individual parts. The various parts of a film's form can be divided into four primary types: **frame, shot, scene,** and **sequence.** Returning to our building analogy, a movie "frame" could be compared to a brick. A "shot" is similar to a row of bricks. A "scene" could be seen as the equivalent of a room. "Sequences" could

147

relate to the general units of roof, floors, and foundation. A film "frame" contains some of the most minute information relating to a movie, while a "sequence" generally describes a relatively large segment of the picture. The editor uses the smaller units to delineate more specific aspects of a motion picture, while the larger components are employed to identify broader associations relating to its formal structure.

The process of editing, or splicing together, these various parts is referred to as "**cutting**." The word "**cut**" is associated with some of the most basic aspects of filmmaking and criticism. A director yells "cut" when the cameraman is supposed to stop shooting. The editor is said to be "cutting" a picture when she or he splices together the physical pieces of film at the time it is being edited. This term also refers to the transitions, a viewer sees, when one shot "cuts" to the next during the screening of a completed film. The most common division between shots--that is the point where the last frame of one shot ends and the first frame of the next shot begins--is also called a "cut." (See fig. 7.1).

7.1 This is a photograph of two frames from *The Gold Rush* o n a piece of 16mm film. The first image, showing a high angle shot of the ledge collapsing under Black Larson, is the last frame of that shot. The editor then "cuts" to the next shot. The frame line separating the two frames represents the "cut." The first frame of the second shot reveals the collapsing ledge from a low angle. In this example the editor is taking an action, that occurs in one shot, and continues it in the next. This editing technique is known as a "match-on-action." Photograph taken by the author.

148

The **frame** is usually considered to be the most basic unit of a motion picture. We noted, in Chapter One, that a film is made up individual frames, or still images, which pass through a projector gate at the rate of 24 fps. For a ninety minute movie an editor would have to organize 129,600 frames to structure a cohesive and understandable motion picture. As our analysis of individual images from *Variety* can verify, even more minute elements of information in a film can be found in the detailed visuals found within a frame.

While clearly aware of the importance of the individual frames, and the complex data contained within them, a filmmaker seldom writes a script which itemizes the minutia of the frames. Rather, he or she tends to use the more general component of the "shot" to demarcate and enumerate the individual segments of the film. The "shot" is considered to be the next basic unit of filmmaking after the frame. We defined a **shot** as footage photographed during a continuous run of the camera. A shot begins at the point where the camera starts shooting and ends where it stops filming.

Most scripts follow a format similar to the appearance of our shot breakdown of the seduction sequence from *Variety*. At first the shot could be used to adequately summarize the content of a fictional film. *The Hoser Hosed,* for example, told its entire story in the course of one shot. As the structure of narrative films became increasingly complex, however, they needed more shots to tell their tale. Because of the simplicity of the editing structure, the shot in *The Hoser Hosed* is more than just a shot. It is also a "scene."

A **scene** is a self-contained narrative segment in which the action usually happens at the same time and place. To repeat what we stated in Chapter Three, the subject matter of most of the early films, made before 1900, was almost always filmed one shot one scene. Everything we needed to know about the subject was self-contained in that single shot. Once a single shot Lumière film, like *The Hoser Hosed,* finished going through the projector, it would be followed by another shot/scene of a substantially different movie, like *Feeding Baby.* A Lumière program, consequently, consisted of a series of single shot short subjects, spliced together. There was little rationale for the order, or continuity between shots, regarding subject matter. Later films would be comprised of a series of scenes, edited to help the audience relate to the evolving narrative, as the film progressed from shot to shot.

A quick review of Méliès's *A Trip to the Moon* further illustrates how a filmmaker can use scenes to advance the structure of a story. The narrative of this film involves some explorers deciding to go to the moon,

149

building a space ship, landing on the moon's surface, and returning to earth. Each of the segments of this series of actions and events--which take place over a period of some days--constitute individual scenes. Though more complex than the narrative of *The Hoser Hosed*, *A Trip to the Moon* still contains scenes which are completed in one shot. As film narratives became more complex the number of shots, making up a scene, increased.

An examination of our analysis of the seduction sequence from *Variety* suggests that this segment might be broken down into four individual scenes.

Scene #1, of the seduction sequence in *Variety*, starts with Boss playing cards and consists of eight shots. It identifies Boss's attitudes, about himself, and his relationships with Bertha and Artinelli. It also helps to set up the seduction attempt, in scene #2, and the ironic outcome of the sequence. We will justify shot #9 as starting our second scene because it shows a different p<u>lace</u> than the rendezvous where Boss is playing cards.

Scene #2 is the longest of our four scenes. It takes 35 shots (shots #9-43) to constitute this segment. This scene establishes Artinelli's interest in his partner's wife, reveals the elaborate plan he has concocted to seduce her, and uses Bertha's somewhat hesitant reactions to this treatment to build dramatic tension.

Scene #3 cuts back to Boss playing cards at the cafe. Again this scene is relatively short, being only eight shots (shots #44-51) in length. As with scene #1, this segment of the film is designed to emphasize the irony in Boss's situation. He interprets his winning at cards as symbolic of the control he has over the happiness in his life. His attitude is starkly contrasted to the reality occurring in his partner's hotel room. Scene #4 summarizes the outcome of this situation in one dramatic shot.

By breaking our sequence of 52 shots down, into four scenes, we have been able to establish a general outline of what is happening. This allows us to accurately identify some major themes, in a segment of *Variety*, with some conciseness. Our shot and frame analyses, of this same segment, revealed more detailed information than our scene breakdown. They do not, however, summarize its themes as succinctly.

Another way we can examine this portion of the film is by looking at it as a "sequence." Using this type of categorization we are getting closer to what is desired of the production "one-liner" described in Chapter Two. We are trying to quickly define the subject matter in question. Simply and succinctly, this is the "seduction" sequence in the movie. A **sequence** is made up of a number of shots and scenes which form a self-contained narrative unit. This classification, it can be seen, is even more loose and arbitrary than the definition we used to identify the scene. The purpose of breaking a film up into a handful of sequences is to establish a clear, albeit very general, outline of that picture's overall structure.

How many sequences a critic uses to identify the structure of a film is determined by how well we can better understand the picture, as a whole, by using this breakdown. Most films have a structure that enables them to be broken down into at least three basic sequences--a beginning, a middle, and an end. The beginning of *A Trip to the Moon,* for example, starts with the preparations and journey of some astronomers who want to go to the moon. The middle sequence consists of what happens once they arrive there. The end sequence chronicles their return. This outline does not cover many details about the narrative of *A Trip to the Moon.* It does make the structure of the film rather immediately understandable.

The "seduction sequence" is one of nine such units that could be identified as comprising the structure of the film *Variety.* We could outline the motion picture, and label the sequences, in this fashion:

Sequence #1	Frame Story
Sequence #2	Boss and Bertha's Life Together
Sequence #3	Artinelli's Loss
Sequence #4	Collaboration
Sequence #5	Seduction
Sequence #6	Boss's Discovery
Sequence #7	Boss Tries to Cope with his Knowledge
Sequence #8	Death
Sequence #9	Frame Story

These demarcations could be challenged. Some might argue that a breakdown establishing three sequences would provide a better outline of the film's structure. The frame story, for example, could identify the beginning and end of the picture. Units #2-8 constitute the middle sequence using this strategy. Granting that our nine sequence schema is not definitive, this particular choice of segments does reveal information about the structure of *Variety* which our other more detailed analyses have not provided. It also gives us some perspectives about the movie that would be less clear in a three sequence breakdown.

A review of this list of nine sequences indicates certain parallels exist in the narrative structure of *Variety.* Sequences #1 and #9, for example, serve as a frame story that organizes the content of the film. There is an interesting dialectical contrast between sequences #2 and #8. In sequence #2 Boss and Bertha's life together seems blissful. Their relationship in sequence #8, following the death of Artinelli, could not be more troubled. Sequences #3 and #7 concentrate on the common theme of coping. Artinelli must deal with the loss of his brother while Boss struggles with the knowledge of his wife's affair. Our final pair of sequences, #4 and #6, again reflect contrasting perspectives. An apparently workable collaboration is established among the three people in sequence #4. Collaboration changes to conflict, by sequence #6, when Boss discovers that Artinelli and Bertha are having an affair.

By pairing the most outward narrative sequences, at either end of *Variety,* and working inward, we can identify a series of alternating comparisons and contrasts relative to this film's principal themes and structure. Sequences #1 and #9 share similar subject matter. The narrative material in sequences #2 and #8 are in dialectical contrast. The content of sequences #3 and #7 are similar. Sequences #4 and #6 are contrasts. From this reoccurrence, of thematic similarity and contrast, an identifiable pattern emerges suggesting a symmetry in this film's structure. We also find that our schema does not parallel sequence #5 with any of the other segments. An examination of sequence #5, in isolation, confirms how important this sequence is to the film's overall narrative.

Even if we did not break the film into the nine sequences chosen, the seduction segment still occurs, time wise, in the middle of *Variety.* Sequence #5 is, structurally and thematically, the pivotal point of the picture. Everything, preceding this part of the film, has led up to the encounter between Artinelli and Bertha. How Bertha responds to Artinelli's advances will determine what happens in the last half of the film. There is also a symmetry, in this sequence, which parallels the overall structure of *Variety.* Bertha and Artinelli's meeting is framed by a separate set of occurrences involving Boss. This "frame story" within a "frame story" helps us interpret, and better understand, the narrative significance involving the scenes with Artinelli and Bertha.

While camerawork guides how we view a film's mise-en-scene, editing determines what we look at. A film's editing directs what the mise-en-scene and camerawork will communicate. Editing is the element of style most instrumental in determining the choice, and organization, of a film's parts. These, in turn, establish that movie's overall form. We have identified the structural components of frame, shot, scene, and sequence that comprise the form of a film. We have not yet identified the important editing techniques an editor uses to identify and combine these units when structuring a film. Critics have identified these approaches to editing as being of two types: **continuity** and **montage**. We will discuss montage editing in Chapter Eight. The remainder of this chapter will explore the nature of continuity editing.

II. Continuity Editing

There is a truism that "form follows function." The form of our hypothetical barn was dictated by the function which such a building is meant to serve. The shape of an article of clothing is determined by the form of the individual who is to wear it. Likewise the type of editing a filmmaker chooses, to structure a motion picture, reflects the way that movie is meant to function. We can identify some of the basic ways narrative films function by once again looking at *The Hoser Hosed* and *A Trip to the Moon*.

When filming *The Hoser Hosed* the Lumiéres were interested in photographing the actions of their subjects, in a particular space, for a specific duration of time. They were structuring <u>thematic</u>, <u>spatial</u>, and <u>temporal</u> elements to convey their narrative. The form of this simple movie is dictated by the function of the camera and the nature of the story. In this respect *The Hoser Hosed* resembles *A Trip to the Moon*. Méliès's film also tells a story with a beginning, middle and end. This director is also structuring thematic, spatial, and temporal concepts to create a narrative progression in his film. Because they could tell their tale with one shot, the Lumiéres were able to "edit in the camera." As movie narratives, like that of *A Trip to the Moon,* became more complex, so did the nature of film editing.

While *A Trip to the Moon* often relies on the idea of one shot per scene, this picture is more than just a number of shots strung together. The shots are edited to give *A Trip to the Moon* a cohesive form relative to the plot. For purposes of telling its story, each shot of the movie picks up where the last one leaves off. Concepts from preceding shots are added to information that follows, preparing us for what we will encounter in succeeding shots. This continuity may involve story, temporal and spatial relationships, and the **pacing** of the movie. "Pacing" is concerned with the rhythms within a film. During the chase scenes the action of the explorers running, for example, and the physically shorter length of the shots, create a different effect from the more leisurely pace of the earlier scenes. This film's rhythms are affected by the duration of these shots and movement within the frame. A series of three, six frame shots will have a different pace than three, one minute shots. Two shots of equal length, each shown for the same amount of time, will also have different rhythms if one shot contains a stationary subject and the other shot has something moving within the frame.

The themes, action, pacing, and spatial relationships in *A Trip to the Moon* are much more complex than what we have in *The Hoser Hosed*. Méliès was able to develop a more complicated film narrative by using a rudimentary kind of continuity editing to tell his story. **"Invisible,"** **"decoupage"** or **"continuity editing"** are all terms used to identify and classify the same thing. **Continuity editing** is concerned with maintaining spatial and temporal continuity between shots. The continuity editor seeks to make the merger, between the shots, look fluid and unobtrusive. The desired effect is to get spatial and temporal transitions to appear as smooth and flowing as the passage of the frames through the projector gate. This type of cutting is done so that the viewer will not be aware that editing takes place.

Beginning film students may initially find the concept and application of continuity editing to be a bit difficult to grasp. Looking for something in the mise-en-scene, or recognizing how the camera is shooting a subject, is relatively easy to do. Becoming sensitive to the way editing manipulates time and space is somewhat harder to comprehend. This may be due to the fact that continuity editing tries to conceal that editing is taking place. The filmmaker does not want us to be aware that editing is occurring and uses techniques to hide it.

The rationale in making continuity editing "invisible" is somewhat comparable to the point of view of a magician executing an illusion. Usually an illusionist, like Méliès, does not want the viewer to be aware of how the trick is being accomplished. Rather, this trickster prefers that the onlooker relate to the effect of the trick. In the same respect the continuity editor wants the viewer caught up in the effect, of the editing, rather than be conscious of the technique by which it is accomplished.

Decoupage is concerned with maintaining continuity between shots and concealing the fact that these transitions take place. A good way to get to understand continuity editing is by becoming familiar with the techniques used to accomplish these "seamless links." Some of the most common of these editing devices include **master scene**, **match-on-action**, **eyeline-match,** the **over-the-shoulder shot**, the **shot-reverse-shot**, and **parallel action**.

One of the first ways editors learned to structure a film was by employing the **master scene** technique. With this procedure the filmmaker establishes the overall setting of a scene in what often is called a **cover** or **master shot**. The director then cuts to closer placements showing greater detail within this setting. By going from the general to the particular this technique allows the viewer to become oriented to the spatial relationships of the subjects within the overall environment. Usually we are so interested in the subject matter that we are not even conscious that editing has taken place. The continuity editor is very aware of the behavioral and psychological tendencies of a viewer in determining how to direct our response when watching a film.

To get a better sense of the nature of this editing method we might consider its application in *A Trip to the Moon*. At the beginning of the

154

movie Méliès uses a rather wide long shot to establish the setting of the astronomer's meeting. (see fig. 5.1). Instead of cutting to closer placements of the action, by employing master scene technique, Méliès uses the conventional 1902 approach of showing everything one shot one scene. This results in keeping us distanced from specific bits of information, existing in this setting, relevant to the advancement of the narrative. Modern viewers may find this distancing effect a bit frustrating as it also tends to psychologically distance us from getting more involved with the action. Audiences in some theaters of 1902, as we noted in Chapter Three, would have been more involved with the shot because a narrator would have been pointing out pertinent information similar to a speaker describing slides.

As eventually developed, the master scene technique starts with a broad placement and then cuts to closer placements within that setting. The wide placements orient the viewer to the environment while the closer perspectives reveal specific elements of detail in this space. Méliès anticipates, but does not quite accomplish this method, in the shots showing the journey to the moon.

There is a kind of master shot employed in *A Trip to the Moon,* when the rocket is launched from the cannon. In the first shot the cannon is aimed at the moon, which we see in the distance, and fired. (See fig. 7.2). In the next shot we get the famous subjective shot where the rocket approaches the moon's face. (See fig. 3.6-3.8) Our goal is to get to the

7.2   A publicity still showing the first in a series of shots relating to the explorers' journey to the moon. Méliès's series of shots, in this portion of the film, anticipated the concept of master scene technique which would become a standard in continuity editing. Courtesy the British Film Institute.

moon. Méliès's cutting and camerawork brings us increasingly nearer to this objective. Once the rocket hits the moon in the eye, Méliès cuts to a closer placement of the explorers getting out of their craft on the moon's surface. This series of shots almost satisfies what one now associates with master scene technique.

In a true employment of master scene technique the closer placements would be clearly recognizable as part of the setting introduced in the cover shot. Our first two shots, in this segment of *A Trip to the Moon,* accomplish this concern. The face of the moon we are approaching appears to be the same object we saw the cannon pointed at in the previous shot. The moon's terrain in our third shot does not really match the perspective, of the rocket lodged in the moon's eye, as seen in the preceding placement. In the second shot the rocket was very big in relation to the eye of the moon. The rocket is rather small in our third shot. The setting around the rocket does not look anything like an eye. This change in spatial perspective prevents the series from following what one usually expects from a master scene strategy. Yet, because of the emphasis on fantasy in this film, the effect of master scene technique is still accomplished in spirit if not proportionate space. The master scene strategy guides the viewer, from a general setting to specific elements within it, through a series of increasingly closer placements. This series of three shots accomplishes this effect. The fact that the moon's appearance changes from one shot to the next is actually quite plausible in this whimsical world. The change is actually appropriate since it sets us up for the fantastic events which will happen on the surface.

Another continuity editing technique, that Méliès utilizes in *A Trip to the Moon,* is a "**match-on-action**" or "**matched cut.**" A "match-on-action" concentrates on an action, occurring in one shot, that continues in the next. (See fig. 7.1). The continuity between the two placements is established by the action shared between them. Continuity in the master scene technique is largely accomplished by working with space. With the matched cut it is achieved with movement. There is a good example of a match-on-action at the end of *A Trip to the Moon.*

Having escaped the court room of the king's palace, the explorers rush across the moon's terrain towards their ship. The first image, in this matched cut, is a LS emphasizing the moon's terrain. The second shot is a LS of their rocket ship resting on a cliff. The match-on-action occurs when the explorers rush past the left hand edge of the frame, in the terrain shot, and appear frame right in the placement containing their rocket. The action of the explorers running unites the space of the moon terrain placement with that of the cliff and rocket shot.

Méliès's use of match-on-action, in this part of *A Trip to the Moon,* does more than serve as a continuity technique. It also influences the rhythm and timing of this sequence. The chase shots are not on the screen as long as the opening scenes of the film. These shorter shots correspond to the increased speed of the explorers as they run from their pursuers. At the beginning of the film the director used shots, of a relatively long duration, to allow us to become familiar with the environment. The escape is now more important than our savoring of the setting. Méliès uses the action of the chase to dictate the faster cutting of this part of the movie. The matched cuts enable the film's continuity to progress rapidly from scene to scene. The editing of the chase scene helps to give the end of the picture a much different rhythm than that found at the beginning of the film.

Another common early editing transition is the **eyeline-match.** In an "**eyeline-match**" the first shot emphasizes the fact that a person is looking at something. The second shot is a subjective view of whatever that individual is seeing. This technique is a relatively simple, but very effective, method for establishing continuity between two shots. An example of how this technique was used in the film *Variety*, can be seen in Fig. 7.3 and 7.4.

The **over-the-shoulder** shot is something of a variation of the eyeline-match. Not widely employed until the 1920s, this technique emphasizes the fact that a character is looking at something without using a subjective shot when showing it. As the definition suggests, the **over-the-shoulder** shot films what a character is looking at while shooting over his or her shoulder. (See fig. 7.5 and 7.6). By showing part of the character in the frame, the director keeps an objective point of view in the shot.

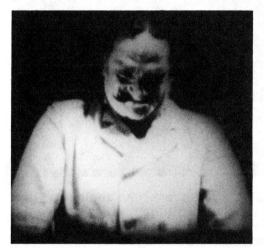

7.3 and 7.4. In this example of an eyeline-match from the movie *Variety* a waiter, shown in MCU, looks down. In our second image we have a high angle subjective shot of what he sees--drawings on the table eluding to the affair between Bertha and Artinelli. Frame enlargements.

The over-the-shoulder shot is also used as part of the editing technique known as a "**shot-reverse-shot.**" The shot-reverse-shot starts with an over-the-shoulder shot of a person, engaged in a conversation with someone, and then cuts to an over-the-shoulder shot of the other individual. This method of filming is also known as **reverse-angle shooting**. It is a dynamic way to cut between two individuals and still maintain a sense of where they are, spatially, in relation to one another.

We have stated that early filmmakers probably learned more about editing from the chase than any other narrative concept. This is particularly true of their development of the important continuity technique of **parallel action.** "**Parallel editing**" is concerned with cutting back and forth, or **crosscutting**, between two or more actions occurring at the same time. We can get a better sense of this technique by reviewing one of the most famous early films to employ parallel action, Edwin S. Porter's *The Great Train Robbery* of 1903.

7.5 and 7.6 These images show examples of the over-the-shoulder shot, reverse-angle shooting, and shot-reverse-shot editing techniques. By shooting over her shoulder, in the first shot (Fig.7.5), the filmmaker makes us aware that Kristy is a part of this conversation but emphasizes that Cindy is the dominant subject in the frame. This sets us up for the reverse-angle, or shot-reverse-shot, when we cut to Kristy's face (Fig. 7.6), now seen over Cindy's shoulder. These techniques are dynamic ways to maintain continuity editing, in a conversation situation, without using subjective viewpoints like the eyeline-match. Photographs by the author.

III.   Parallel Action and *The Great Train Robbery*

The Great Train Robbery was shot in 1903, on location in a rural area outside Orange, New Jersey, which resembled American western terrain. It is eight minutes long and tells its story in fourteen shots. Some existing prints of *The Great Train Robbery* present the shots in the following order. The film begins in a telegraph operator's office. The robbers break in, knock the operator unconscious, and tie him up. Through the window of the telegraph office we see a train come to a stop. In the next shot the four bandits climb aboard the engine. The film then employs parallel action by cutting back to the office where the operator is able to regain consciousness, temporarily. He gets to his feet, attempts to tap the telegraph key with his head, but again passes out. A little girl who comes in, shortly thereafter, is able to untie and revive him.

Aboard the moving train a guard, in the express car, hears two of the bandits. He throws away the key to a strong box and is shot. The thieves blow the cover off the safe and steal the contents. Meanwhile the other two robbers have mounted the coal car. One engages in a fight with the fireman. The robber knocks the fireman down and throws him off the train. The engineer is made to stop the locomotive and uncouple the engine from the rest of the train. Three of the robbers then force the passengers off the train so they can steal their valuables. One of the passengers is shot when he tries to escape. After they finish robbing the passengers, the criminals run to the engine which they use to make their getaway. At this same time, in a nearby dance hall, some cowboys and cowgirls are square dancing. They also amuse themselves by shooting the feet of a "tenderfoot" so they can watch him "dance." When the telegraph operator rushes in, to inform the group of the robbery, everyone immediately leaves.

The robbers are next seen abandoning the engine and running down an incline. Nearby their horses are tied to some trees. The thieves gingerly step on some rocks, as they cross a stream, to get to their horses. The last robber slips and falls in the creek. All the bandits eventually get to their horses. The person who fell in the creek mounts his animal from the wrong side. In the next shot the crooks ride up a trail while pursued by a posse. One of the robbers is shot after falling off his horse. The three surviving criminals apparently believe they lost the posse in the next scene/shot. In this shot the bandits' horses are tied to some trees in the background, in a partially wooded area. The crooks, seen in the foreground, are going through their loot. While engrossed in their ill-gotten gains the posse sneaks up behind them and shoots all three.

There is a fourteenth and sometimes a fifteenth shot, in the film, depending upon whether it is used once or twice. In this shot one of the robbers, in medium close-up, stares into the camera and shoots his six-gun

159

at the audience. Filmed totally for dramatic effect, rather than narrative continuity, exhibitors were told they could put the shot at either the beginning or the end of the movie.

According to film historian Lewis Jacobs, a 1904 Edison advertising catalogue listed some of the shots as appearing in a different order. The shot of the rescue in the telegraph office was not used until after the scene where the bandits cross the stream. The succeeding shot is the one in the dance hall which ends when the telegraph operator informs the group of the robbery. This editing pattern allows more time to elapse between the operator's release and the formation of the posse. It also permits time, to transpire, between the scene of the thieves mounting their horses, at the stream, and the final chase. It still does not explain how the posse could find them so quickly. The abrupt temporal transition between the chase scene and the bandits being surrounded, at the end of the film, seems a bit confusing to modern viewers. The final shot, listed in the 1904 catalogue entry, is the close-up of the bandit shooting at the audience. The description of this shot includes the notation that the exhibitor can use the scene to either begin or end the picture. [1]

The discrepancy between the 1904 listing of the sequence of shots, and the way the movie is sometimes shown today, is indicative of a problem which film scholars must recognize when interpreting any film. Very often movies are re-edited so that the content of the picture is different from what earlier audiences would have seen or the filmmaker intended. This is not just true of early films like *The Great Train Robbery*. Motion pictures shown on television today are re-edited more often than not. The deletion of just one or two shots can totally change the filmmaker's intended meaning. Such changes prevent us from properly interpreting a movie.

The way the film medium is used, in *The Great Train Robbery,* is far removed from the sophisticated story-telling methods we are familiar with today. Modern audiences enjoy this movie as a comic novelty of antiquated charm. This is particularly true when we see a print with "gag" titles that were added many years after the picture's initial release. We now find the dummy, substituted for the fireman thrown off the train, humorously unconvincing. The melodramatic acting of the little girl, when she discovers the bound and gagged operator, would have been considered dated by the 1920s. So, too, the inexplicable twisting of body, and flailing of arms, of the wounded passenger. The clumsy crook who falls in the creek, and mounts his horse from the wrong side, probably was a source of amusement to audiences back in 1903. We might wonder how 1903 viewers responded to the continuity, at the end of the picture, if they did not have a commentator explaining what was happening. The temporal and spatial transitions between the chase with the posse and the final shoot-out now seem awkward and even confusing.

By present filmmaking standards, *The Great Train Robbery* might be considered rather crude. Still, the picture has some fairly complex continuity and narrative techniques which a casual viewing of the movie might not reveal. One of the best effects involves the relatively well executed use of a "matte" of the window in the shots involving the telegraph office. (See fig. 7.7 and 7.8). This window, as we noted in Chapter Six, did not actually exist in the office set. It was made possible through a double exposure technique. This use of the matte process does more that create an interesting effect to help make the scene look realistic. The image in the window also identifies the presence of the train. This information establishes a spatial correlation, linking the two settings, that allows for continuity editing between the first and second shots. When we see the

7.7 and 7.8 The use of the matte in the first image enables the director of *The Great Train Robbery* to employ some rather sophisticated continuity techniques for 1903. The telegraph set was filmed so that the upper right hand corner was covered by a matte and not exposed. The film was then rewound in the camera. The portion of the frame previously exposed was then covered with a matte. The matte covering the unexposed portion of the frame was removed. The film was again shot to obtain the effect of the window with the passing train. This establishes a space outside the telegraph office which is seen in our second image. The two spaces are connected with a match-on-action of the passing train. The existence of these two spaces enables the director to work with parallel action--two actions occurring in separate spaces at the same time. Frame enlargements.

engine pulling up to the water tower in the next shot we know where it came from. The viewer is made aware of where the water tower space is relative to the setting in the previous shot. This matched cut enables the viewer to establish spatial and narrative relationships between the two settings.

When the bandits are seen boarding the train we know who they are and how they got here. We rightly assume that they have left the telegraph office to rob the train. The director has provided us with two settings involving simultaneous activity. He established this association, through his use of a matte shot, by showing the train in the background of the telegraph office. Porter has cleverly set up parallel action in the first two shots. He continues to cut back and forth, between the actions involving the robbers and the telegraph operator, throughout the rest of the film. Most audiences are not aware that they are being manipulated to make these associations. For a movie laughed at for its technical crudity, this is quite a sophisticated editing transition.

Méliès and Porter used editing to structure narrative films before *The Great Train Robbery*. It is questionable whether their previous work was as successful, as this picture, in editing together simultaneous actions. Porter works with parallel action when he alternates between the shots of the bound and gagged telegrapher and the bandits robbing the train. Parallel action is also used in the situations where two of the robbers dynamite the strong box while their accomplices make the engineer stop the locomotive. Crosscutting is again employed to show the dance hall scene while the thieves make their getaway. The rationale for these shifts in action may not always be immediately clear to the viewer, but their relationship to the enfolding story eventually is understood. Parallel action can be a very dynamic continuity technique. One reason it can be dynamic is that it keeps the audience wondering how all of these disparate actions may, or may not, converge at the end of the picture.

A comparison between this film and *A Trip to the Moon* reveals that the editing of *The Great Train Robbery* is, in some ways, the more sophisticated. The Méliès picture sometimes uses a shot as a scene to advance the story. Once he showed a placement, Méliès generally did not use it again in that film. Edwin S. Porter seldom restricts his editing, in *The Great Train Robbery,* to one shot per scene. He also will go back to a setting, like the telegraph office, and use it again. By returning to this placement he reveals additional information germane to the narrative--the bound telegrapher being freed, for example. Porter's use of parallel action adds still another degree of complexity to the editing in *The Great Train Robbery.* Méliès only follows one line of action. The pacing in the Porter movie is also much faster, overall, than in *A Trip to the Moon*. The major exception is Méliès's chase scene where the moon explorers rush back to their ship. The events of the story determine the length of the shots, and the pacing of *The Great Train Robbery*, even more than they affect *A Trip to the Moon*.

The Great Train Robbery is also notable for having some limited camera movement. In the second shot the camera pans slightly to reframe the train as the bandits climb onboard. Another pan is used, to reframe the image, when the thieves cross the stream to get to their horses. The most notable camera movement, in *The Great Train Robbery*, is where the robbers run down the incline to get to their horses. At the beginning of the shot the camera pans left to follow the bandits as they leave the engine. It then tilts down as they quickly descend the embankment.

Exceptionally popular at the turn-of-the-century, *The Great Train Robbery* was also recognized as a technically innovative motion picture. It did not, however, immediately advance narrative filmmaking techniques. *The Great Train Robbery* was actually a bit ahead of its time. Filmmakers knew that the movie worked well in the way it told its story. They could not figure out exactly why. For years they attempted to make imitations of *The Great Train Robbery*, even to copying its camera setups. Most of these imitations were unable to duplicate the original's dramatic achievement. Neither would Porter's future films. Pressures placed upon him by the Edison company, prevented Porter from experimenting with the stylistic elements that made *The Great Train Robbery* so aesthetically interesting.

Eventually other filmmakers built upon the film techniques that *The Great Train Robbery* helped pioneer. Further explorations of parallel editing, by directors like D. W. Griffith, particularly advanced editing as a key element of film style. Later directors were also able come up with techniques to show spatial and temporal <u>discontinuity</u> between a film's parts. The fact that Porter was not always able to indicate a comprehensible passage of time, with his editing, is one of the reasons *The Great Train Robbery* does not always work for modern audiences.

We stated that, in some ways, the editing of *The Great Train Robbery* is more sophisticated than that found in *A Trip to the Moon*. This earlier film does not use the innovative crosscutting of *The Great Train Robbery*, but there are understandable transitions between all the shots. This is not always true of *The Great Train Robbery*. As we observed, the continuity between the chase with the posse and the final shoot-out is somewhat difficult to follow.

At first we get the impression that the narrative of *The Great Train Robbery* is being presented in "**real time**." "Real time" refers to the amount of time it would take for something to actually occur. Events in the latter part of the film do not seem to be happening the way they would in real time and space. The spatial and temporal discontinuity occurring here detracts from the accomplishments of the continuity editing used earlier. We have become <u>aware</u> of the editing and it does not appear to be working.

Continuity editing is concerned with maintaining temporal and spatial relationships between the parts of a film. But not every film shows everything in "real time." "**Slow motion**" photography, for example can capture a recognizable bullet, seemingly suspended within air, gradually penetrating a balloon. "**Stop-action**" cinematography, in a matter of seconds, can show a flower growing out of the ground and bursting into bloom. A ninety minute narrative film may tell a story, of a person's life, dealing with a period of one hundred years. "**Film time**" is not always the same as "real time." The temporal and spatial transitions, at the end of *The Great Train Robbery*, are different from the preceding scenes. Unfortunately the director does not know how to show them as being different.

Editing often must work with spatial and temporal relationships that <u>emphasize</u> changes in time and place. This appears to contradict the notion that continuity editing tries to hide the fact that editing takes place. Ironically, continuity editing sometimes must <u>draw</u> the viewer's attention to changes in place and time. This is particularly true when the editor is cutting between scenes and sequences.

IV. Editing Techniques that "Clue" the Viewer to Temporal and Spatial Transitions Between Parts of a Film

The earliest technique filmmakers used, to indicate transitions in the narrative, was a live commentator describing what was occurring on the screen. When the speaker was no longer utilized in theaters, commentary was often supplied with "subtitles." A **subtitle**, as we are now well aware, is a written caption which represents dialogue or provides the viewer with explanatory information. The year 1905 is generally given as the date when subtitles became common, although they can be found in films made before this date. [2] By the 1920s most silent filmmakers preferred to avoid subtitles, as much as possible, because they felt they interfered with the flow of the visuals. The effect of a subtitle appearing on screen was somewhat comparable to interrupting the middle of a dance with information written on a placard. Directors of the 1920s took great pride in how <u>few</u> captions they needed to tell a story. *Der Letze Mann* is so articulate, in its use of the silent medium, that it has only <u>one</u> subtitle in its entire narrative.

164

A ballet, or theatrical play, generally does not use written subtitles to convey information to an audience. They do often identify scene changes by the lifting and lowering of a curtain. Instead of relying only on subtitles, to tell an audience that such changes were occurring, filmmakers preferred to find cinematic equivalents to the curtain in the theater. They eventually found that the **fade**, **dissolve**, **wipe**, **swish pan**, **iris-in**, and **iris-out** could be used as alternatives to the cut between shots. These techniques can inform the viewer that a change of time or place is occurring at a given point in a film's narrative.

We have already discussed the iris in our examination of camerawork. At first the iris was used as a kind of frame within a frame. The early cameramen created an iris by placing a diaphragm in *front* of the lens. This caused the center of the image to be exposed but would leave the surrounding area dark. The iris effect enabled a filmmaker to draw the viewer's attention to information within a kind of dark circle. The technique also emphasized that the image shown was obviously part of a larger subject within the frame. After some experimentation, filmmakers found that the iris could be used as more than a stationary mask. By opening and closing this diaphragm, which was in front of the lens, they could change the size of the image <u>during</u> the shot. This discovery led to the use of the **iris-in** and the **iris-out**.

The **iris-in** starts as an image in the form of a small circle, in the center of what initially was a black frame, which eventually fills the entire screen. An **iris-out** has the image take the shape of a shrinking circle being enveloped by a black background. The development of this moving diaphragm enabled filmmakers to utilize the iris as more than a means of framing something within the frame. The iris-in and iris-out could frame an entire movie. Film directors employed these iris techniques in the same way the curtain opens and closes a play on stage. Chaplin used the iris-in, to dramatically introduce the ELS of the Chilkoot Pass, at the very beginning of *The Gold Rush* (see fig. 6.16). Treated at first as a useful innovation, the idea of using an iris as a kind of curtain was considered something of a cliché by the 1930s.

The iris-in and iris-out were generally used, in the 1920s, to frame the beginning and end of a film. The fade, dissolve, wipe, and swish-pan were developed to cue the audience that they were observing a change in time or place in the narrative. Usually these techniques demarcate divisions between scenes or sequences. The "**fade**" was one of the most common transitional devices employed.

A **fade** occurs when the cameraman shuts out the light coming into the camera and the frame gradually goes black. This effect is called a **fade-out**. A **fade-in**, conversely, starts with a black frame and the image gradually appears. When a fade-out is used to close one shot, and a fade-in introduces another, the viewer can assume the director is drawing attention to a change in scene, sequence, or time.

A **dissolve** can also be used to show a transition between time and place. This technique is accomplished by superimposing the <u>end</u> of the last shot over the <u>beginning</u> of the next one. During the process of superimposition the first shot gradually disappears as the second shot becomes more visible underneath. As with the fade, this effect enables the dissolve to be used as a transitional device to designate a change in time or place. It is interesting to note that Méliès used dissolves, as an alternative to the cut, in *A Trip to the Moon*. Though it tends to draw attention to itself, the dissolve allows for a kind of "flowing" transition between shots. The dissolve can also be used, within a shot, to make a comparison between two images. (See fig. 7.9 and 7.10). A director might, for example, suddenly superimpose the picture of a sucker over a person, creating a temporary double exposure. Once the viewer has an opportunity to respond to this juxtaposition, the filmmaker will dissolve back to just an image of the individual. The dissolve, in this instance, establishes a comic metaphor that the man is, or has been made into, a "sucker."

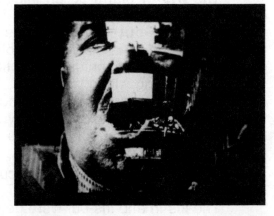

7.9 and 7.10. These two images, utilizing a dissolve, are from the beginning and end of Sergei Eisenstein's film *Strachka (Strike)*. In the first picture a bureaucrat considers the best strategy to get the most work out of his employees. His scheming face is superimposed over the individuals who will be affected by the plan. The second shot reflects an outcome of his actions as strikers are massacred by the police. This dissolve has the laughing face of the evil boss superimposed over a shot of the police violently confronting unarmed workers on some pedestrian bridges. Frame enlargements.

The "**wipe**" is another transitional device an editor can use, between shots, to indicate a change in place and time. A "wipe" occurs when a new shot appears to "push out" the preceding one. Instead of one shot being superimposed upon another, as is true with a dissolve, part of each shot is seen as existing side-by-side within the frame. In this example the wipe exists as a moving "**split-screen.**" Two or more placements are seen-- partially or fully--existing in the same frame, at the same time, without overlapping. Another example of this kind of technique would be a **flip-wipe** where the images are shown as if they were pages in a book. As a "page" is "flipped" away we see the next shot of a "page" underneath. Techniques of this sort are created using special effects. They often are employed to draw attention to their "slickness." MTV videos are particularly noted for their use of wipes. A problem with using an effect, like the wipe, for effect's sake is that it soon loses its freshness and appeal. Various types of wipes periodically come in and out of fashion. A critic can sometimes date a film by the choice of wipes it uses.

Another dated transition is the **swish-pan.** The "**swish-pan**" is a very rapid and sudden pan at the end of a shot. This pan is so fast it blurs whatever is being photographed. When the blurring stops we see a different, undistorted image. Considered a cliché in the 1960s, the swish-pan was used to parody scene transitions in episodes of the "camp" television series *Batman*.

The filmmaker's intent dictates how cinematic techniques fall in and out of favor. When an editor wants us to be conscious of a transition he or she will use something like a wipe or a swish-pan to show a transition between scenes. If an editor does not want us to be aware of a transition a more subtle technique will be employed. We find some early films amusing, in ways that audiences of the time would not, because of their crude or dated appearance. Much of the technical roughness, we associate with films like *The Great Train Robbery* and the 1907 *Ben Hur*, was rapidly disappearing from most filmmaking by 1912. One final look at the seduction sequence from *Variety* will demonstrate how sophisticated continuity editing had become by the 1920s.

V. Case Study of Continuity Editing in the 1920s: An Editing Analysis of the "Seduction Sequence" from *Variety* (1925)

In examining the editing of the seduction sequence from *Variety*, we will once again use our familiar shot breakdown. This time, however, we will present the mise-en-scene descriptions in standard type, have the camerawork material italicized, and represent editing in bold lettering. In reviewing the sequence we will consider how continuity editing effects the manner we perceive the camerawork and mise-en-scene, draws our attention to narrative themes, and guides the way we interpret this information. It is suggested that you review the frame enlargements on pages 129-136 as you read this section.

SHOT BREAKDOWN OF THE SEDUCTION SEQUENCE FROM E.A. DUPONT'S *VARIETY* (1925)

Title #1 The rendezvous where many of the Wintergarten performers spent their afternoons. (Fig. 6.19).

Shot #1 **Master scene technique used in next four shots. Cover shot,** *LS of* performers seen through window of cafe. (Fig. 6.20).

Shot #2 **Continuation of master scene technique. Director cuts from a general placement of the setting to a tighter view of the environment.** *LS* interior of the cafe, *camera pans people inside from right to left.*

Shot #3 **Continuation of master scene technique. The director now concentrates on the most important narrative aspect of this setting.** *MS of* Boss playing cards, surrounded by observers. (Fig. 6.21).

Shot #4 **Continuation of master scene technique. Having gone from a general to a specific view of what is in this environment, the director focuses our full attention on the principal character in this setting. A matched cut starts with the action of Boss, playing cards in MS in shot #3, and continues the action in a** *MCU of* Boss smoking a cigar and looking at his hand with an air of confidence. (Fig. 6.22).

Shot #5 **Reverse-angle,** *MCU of* opponent, sitting across from Boss, looking at his hand with concern. (Fig. 6.23)

Shot #6 **Reverse-angle,** *MS of* observers looking at the opponent. (Fig. 6.24).

Shot #7	**Reverse-angle, eyeline-match,** *CU of* opponent looking ill at ease. (6.25).
Shot #8	**Eyeline-match,** *MCU of* Boss, looking at person who has questioned him, replies: (Fig. 6.26)
Title #2	"Artinelli? Oh, he's still sleeping." (Fig. 6.27).
Shot #9	**Parallel action,** *MS of* Artinelli, in dressing gown, looking at the window of his hotel room which he has just opened. *Camera is placed outside the window and is looking in.* Artinelli goes and opens his door to the hall which sets the window curtains aflutter. (Fig. 6.28 and 6.29).
Shot #10	**Match-on-action of door opening,** *LS of hall. With back to camera Artinelli, framed in MS, suddenly leans out of the doorway into the foreground, and* looks down the hall. (Fig. 6.30)
Shot #11	**Reverse-angle,** *CU of* Artinelli, he bends down. (Fig. 6.31).
Shot #12	**Match-on-action of Artinelli 's movement, to** *CU, iris of* pair of shoes held in Artinelli's right hand being placed on hallway floor. (Fig. 6.32).
Shot #13	**Match-on-action of Artinelli straightening,** *same placement as shot #11, CU of* Artinelli.
Shot #14	**Match-on-action,** *LS, same placement as shot #9,* **of** Artinelli backing into his room and shuts door. (Fig. 6.33)
Shot #15	**Reverse-angle, CU** *iris of* handle as door shuts. (Fig. 6.34).
Shot #16	**Parallel action, cover shot,** *LS of* empty hotel hall. (Fig. 6.35).
Shot #17	**Master shot technique, cutting to a closer placement,** *CU iris of* Bertha's door. Door opens and Bertha comes out.

We see only the middle of her body. She is holding what appears to be a hat in her right hand. (Fig. 6.36).

Shot #18   **Parallel action, master shot technique,** *LS of Artinelli's room, same placement as shots #10 and 14.* Artinelli leaning with his ear to the door. (Fig. 6.37).

Shot #19   **Master shot technique, camera cuts to a closer placement,** *CU of* Artinelli with ear to door. *Camera dollies in to ECU of Artinelli's ear emphasizing the act of listening.* (Fig. 6.38-6.42).

Shot #20   **Dissolve,** *LS, low angle of camera mounted close to floor of hotel hall,* Bertha walking towards camera. Bertha's face has yet to be seen. *This placement shows her from the bottom of her feet to just below her neck.* (Fig. 6. 43).

Shot #21   **Reverse-angle, match-on-action of Bertha walking,** *MCU tracking shot ahead of Bertha coming down the hall.* She is looking towards Artinelli's door. (Fig. 6.44).

Shot #22   **Eyeline-match,** *subjective tracking LS towards Artinelli's door.* He steps out and picks up his shoes with his right hand. He holds a pipe in his left. (Fig. 6.45-6.46).

Shot #23   **Master shot technique, cut to a closer** *MCU* **placement of Artinelli, match-on-action of his movements as** Artinelli looks at Bertha as if surprised that she is there. (Fig. 6.47).

Shot #24   **Reverse-angle,** *MCU* profile of Artinelli from inside room. With his right hand he throws shoes inside doorway.

Shot #25   **Match-on-action on the tossing of the shoes,** *LS of* doorway, inside Artinelli's room, from behind Artinelli as he tosses his shoes inside.

Shot #26   **Reverse-angle,** *MCU two-shot of* Artinelli, frame left, talking to Bertha, frame right. (Fig. 6.48).

Title #3   "No after effects?" (Fig. 6.49).

Shot #27   **Eyeline-match, continuing from shot #26,** *MCU partial iris of* Bertha smiling. (Fig. 6.50).

Shot #28   **Shot-reverse-shot,** *MCU iris of* Artinelli. (Fig. 6.51).

Title #4   "Our success has already brought me an offer from America." (Fig. 6.52).

Shot #29   **Shot-reverse-shot,** *MCU, same placement as #27, of* Bertha. (Fig. 6.53).

Shot #30   **Reverse-angle,** *MCU two-shot, same placement as #26,* Artinelli and Bertha. Artinelli goes into his room. Bertha follows but stops at doorway. (Fig. 6.54).

Shot #31   **Match-on-action on Bertha's actions in the doorway, reverse-angle,** *MCU of* Bertha, standing somewhat nervously in doorway, twisting her hat, and looking at Artinelli. (Fig. 6.55).

Shot #32   **Parallel action,** *MS of* curtains blowing in front of the window, shot from inside the room. (Fig. 6.56).

Shot #33   **Parallel action,** *MCU of* Artinelli with paper, presumably the letter from America. He looks at Bertha and says: (Fig. 6.57).

Title #5   "Won't you please close the door? It's so draughty." (Fig. 6.58)

Shot #34   **Eyeline-match,** *MCU of* Bertha, *same placement as shot #31.* (Fig. 6.59).

Shot #35   **Parallel action,** *MS of* window, *same placement as shot #32.* (Fig. 6.60).

Shot #36   **Parallel action,** *MCU of* Bertha, *same placements as shots #31 and 34.* (Fig. 6.61).

Shot #37   **Eyeline-match, Bertha looking at Artinelli, in** *MCU,* reading his letter. (Fig. 6.62).

Shot #38   **Reverse angle,** *MCU of Bertha, same placements as shots #31, 34, and 36.* Her face loses its nervousness as she shuts the door behind her. *This action brings her closer to the camera, resulting in her face coming into tighter CU.* She looks intently at Artinelli the entire time. (Fig. 6.63-6.66).

Shot #39   **Parallel action,** *MS of window, same placements as shots #32 and 35.* The curtains go limp. (Fig. 6.67).

Shot #40   **Parallel action, master shot technique,** *two-shot,* Artinelli *in MS in foreground, frame left.* Bertha is *in LS in* the corner. (Fig. 6.68).

Shot #41   **Master shot technique, cut to the tighter placement of a** *CU,* Bertha has serious look on her face. (Fig. 6.69).

Shot #42   **Master shot technique, next placement pulls back to** *MS of Bertha, camera pans and have two-shot of* Bertha and Artinelli. (Fig. 6.70).

Shot #43   **Match-on-action relative to Artinelli's movement towards Bertha and her reactions to the letter he is bringing to her.** **Master shot technique to a tighter** *MCU two-shot of* Bertha and Artinelli. Bertha reads the letter, which she holds in her right hand, while stroking her hair with her left. Artinelli watches her intently. (Fig. 6.71).

Shot #44   **Parallel action,** *MCU in iris of* Boss looking at his cards. (Fig. 6.72).

Shot #45   **Shot-reverse-shot,** *CU of* other card player, looking down unhappily. (Fig. 6.73).

Shot #46   **Eyeline-match,** *MS of* cards laying in front of opponent's hands. (Fig. 6.74).

172

Shot #47   **Reverse-angle,** *MCU of* observers looking down at cards on the table and then at Boss's opponent.

Shot #48   **Eyeline-match,** *MCU of* opponent.

Shot #49   **Reverse-angle,** *MS of observers watching, same placement as #47.* Suddenly Boss and his opponent, who have not been visible, lean their heads into the frame and look down at the cards on the table. Boss is on the left and his opponent is on the right, *in MCU.* Their heads block our view of the observers in the background. (Fig. 6.75 and 6.76).

Shot #50   **Master shot technique, cutting to a closer placement, match-on-action of the opponent,** *profile in CU, frame right,* **looking at Boss,** and saying: (Fig. 6.77).

Title #6   "You seem to be lucky at cards as well as at love!" (Fig. 6.78).

Shot #51   **Reverse-angle,** *MCU of* Boss, cigar in mouth, looking in the direction of his opponent as he smiles and nods his head in affirmation. (Fig. 6.79).

Shot #52   **Parallel action,** *tight two-shot, CU of* Bertha and Artinelli kissing passionately. **Fade to black.** (Fig. 6.80).

ANALYSIS OF THE EDITING IN THE *VARIETY* SEDUCTION SEQUENCE

Editing analysis is concerned with identifying what is being emphasized in a shot, and the motivation for the transitions between shots. This emphasis may be concerned with images, ideas, or emotions. Emphasis on "image" involves the appearance of objects, and their spatial relationships to one another within the setting, over time. Such spatial relationships are affected by temporal and rhythmic changes. "Temporal," in film editing, can mean either "real" or "film" time. In the first category the editor tries to duplicate the form of time we live by. For "film time" one might consider the example of how the editing in a musical, or an MTV video, cuts images to music. In this situation the editor's cutting is often guided by the music's rhythm.

Editing, based on spatial and temporal relationships, involves relatively concrete concepts. The editor also works with the more abstract notions of "ideas" and "emotions." "Ideas" are concerned with thematic elements, in a film, while the "emotions" relate to the mood of the viewer. When trying to orchestrate our emotional response, to a movie's content, the editor is working with the feelings of the audience. This goes beyond the physical maneuvering of images and rhythms through the cutting and splicing of pieces of celluloid. Emotional manipulation is trying to mold the response and rapport of viewer to film. In a sense, the editor is trying to edit our attitudes.

An editor's motivation for cutting is determined by the relationship of the emphasis, of a shot, to that which follows. These transitions may continue or discontinue, obtrusively or unobtrusively, narrative, temporal, and spatial associations established before. Cutting between shots, then, is influenced by the themes, rhythms, and emotions with which the filmmaker is working. Using these basic premises, we can analyze the editing in the seduction sequence from *Variety*.

The sequence is introduced with a subtitle which establishes the setting where the Wintergarten performers meet in the afternoon. The director then uses the master scene technique to identify this setting and Boss's spatial and social relation to this environment. In the first four shots the editor starts with a cover shot and ends up concentrating on Boss.

A director sometimes employs camera movement to keep the overall rhythm of a movie from slowing down. The pan, in shot #2, does more than enhance the pacing of this scene. It enables the editor to show us these surroundings without having to cut to a series of successive long shots. The movement, in this instance, provides an interesting visual contrast to the stationary camera, in shot #1, being used to establish this setting. In keeping with the lively action in the cafe, the rhythm of the cutting is quite a bit faster than the pacing of the beginning of the next scene featuring Artinelli.

Another important goal of this scene is to establish the spatial and interpersonal relationships Boss has with his card playing competitor. Boss, the confident "winner," is being contrasted with his dejected opponent. Each individual is framed in his own space, and convey the emotions they are feeling at the moment. Though isolated in their separate individual spaces, their spatial and thematic association is communicated through reverse-angles and the eyeline-match. One of the editor's primary goals is to emphasize the irony that the confident and happy Boss is losing his wife at a time when he thinks he is victorious.

The irony of the situation is then developed through the use of parallel action. Using the second subtitle to get us to think about Artinelli, Dupont concentrates on the subject of the inquiry. The film cuts from a character who projects feelings of confidence and pleasure to a person engaged in curious, even suspicious, behavior. The editor is manipulating our emotions by playing off our curiosity. We can tell Artinelli is engaged in some type of scheme but we are not sure what. Each element of his intrigue is introduced, in the first part of the scene, and its purpose is revealed as the segment unfolds. Once caught up in Artinelli's plot we follow the outcome with increasing interest. Again, more than spatial relationships, character motivations, and temporal and rhythmic transitions are being edited. Our emotional responses are also being orchestrated.

The editor's emphasis in this second scene, then, concentrates on the development and execution of Artinelli's seduction strategy and the shaping of our curiosity as to its outcome. This entails setting up the elements of the plot, which are found in Artinelli's space--his room--and linking them with spaces outside his "lair."

One of the things emphasized in the first shot of this scene is the spatial relationship of the door, of Artinelli's room, to the hallway. Through match-on-action and reverse-angle transitions, the viewer is able to become increasingly aware of how the hall relates to Artinelli's plot. We find that the hallway is a key space linking him to Boss's room and Bertha. Artinelli wants to get Bertha from the neutral transitory space of the hallway into the personal setting of his room. Shots #9-14 are concerned with Artinelli laying out his trap. He now must wait to see if it will work. Shots #16-20 establish Bertha's role as victim.

When Artinelli goes back into his room in shot #14 (Fig. 6.33), after putting his shoes out in the hall, a parallel action develops in this scene. There is the action involving Artinelli, in his room, and the activity he is anticipating at the end of the hall. These simultaneous actions converge when the ECU of Artinelli's ear, listening, dissolves into the low angle LS of the source of the sound--Bertha walking up the hall. The editor could have cut back and forth between the two actions. Instead, Dupont used a dollie and a dissolve, as an alternative to cutting, to bring them together.

In shots #22-39 Artinelli reveals how each of the elements, introduced earlier, affect the execution of his plot. Bertha's reactions to Artinelli are instrumental in influencing the viewer's interest and interpretation. As Artinelli manipulates the space between himself and Bertha, the audience becomes increasingly curious as to how she will respond to his advances. Whether Artinelli or Bertha are framed separately, or share the same space, reflect the nature of their relationship at that time. How close they are to one another, whether Bertha is comfortable or uncomfortable with Artinelli, conveys psychological as well as spatial distance between the two. The length of time it takes for Bertha to respond to each of his requests also structures the pacing of the scene at this time.

By shot #40 (Fig. 6.68), Artinelli has succeeded at getting Bertha into his room/space. The viewer has now figured out Artinelli's motives and it seems unlikely that Bertha is not aware of them as well. Bertha will determine what happens next. The viewer's interest in this scene is now almost fully determined by their curiosity as to how--or when--she will respond to Artinelli's seduction. To heighten our emotional involvement in the situation the director cuts back to the other parallel action occurring at this time--Boss at the card table.

The "frame story" with Boss is used to heighten the irony of the narrative. Boss and his opponent have always been shown in separate spaces. Neither are seen in the frame at the beginning of shot #49. During the course of the shot the two suddenly lean towards one another, sharing the same space, in an abrupt and obtrusive fashion. This action suggests more of a confrontation, between the two, than a comfortable sharing of space. Boss is domineering, confident, and victorious. The opponent is beaten and dejected. Boss's appearance is in ironic contrast to what he would be feeling if he knew what was happening. This irony is emphasized as the editor uses parallel action to show Artinelli and Bertha passionately embracing. Dupont closes the sequence by fading to black.

V.   Summary

Editing is concerned with the process of putting the parts of a film together to shape the motion picture into a cohesive whole. These "parts" can be described as frames, shots, scenes, and sequences. When analyzing the editing of a picture the critic is concerned with identifying the techniques being used to cut the film, what the editor is trying to emphasize in a shot, and the motivations for the types of transitions chosen. There are two basic kinds of editing, "continuity" and "montage." "Continuity" editing is based on a filmmaker's concern with the manipulation of the thematic, spatial, and temporal elements in a film that resembles "real time and space." Also known as "decoupage" and "invisible" editing, this approach to cutting a film is concerned with concealing how the parts of the motion picture are put together. We will discuss montage editing in Chapter Eight.

Endnotes

1. Lewis Jacobs, *The Rise of the American Film,* (New York: Teachers College Press, 1978), pp. 43-46.

2. I am grateful to the British silent film historian, Mr. Stephen Bottomore, for sharing his views about the chronology of early silent film subtitles with me, during conversations we had at the Museum of the Moving Image in London, in the spring of 1993.

CHAPTER EIGHT

SERGEI EISENSTEIN AND MONTAGE

CHAPTER OBJECTIVES: *Explore the nature of editing associated with the word "montage" and identify Russian film director Sergei Eisenstein's contributions in defining it.*

I. Modern Art, Russian Filmmaking, and Sergei Eisenstein

Before discussing the nature of montage editing it might be useful to explore the background of its most famous practitioner, the influential Russian director Sergei Mikhailovich Eisenstein (1898-1948). If film historians had to identify just two or three of the most important names, in motion picture history, it is unlikely that Sergei Eisenstein's name would be absent from the list. While still in his twenties, Eisenstein became internationally recognized as a brilliant scholar, filmmaker, and film theorist. He also is credited with being the first person to categorically define, in practice and on paper, a viable form of film editing which systematically challenged the philosophy behind continuity editing--montage.

As has been true of other major filmmakers we have looked at, Eisenstein's background and early life had a profound effect on the content and appearance of his work. Sergei Eisenstein was born in Riga, Latvia, the only child in a well-to-do family. Though interested in art since childhood, Eisenstein agreed to study engineering at the Institute of Civil Engineering in St. Petersburg, to please his father. Before young Eisenstein could complete his engineering studies, dramatic events occurred in Russia which forever altered the course of world history and Sergei's life.

Russia, at this time, was suffering from its involvement in World War I. Unable to cope with the foreign and domestic problems of the period, Russia's czarist monarchy collapsed in February of 1917. It was replaced by a more democratic form of government, somewhat similar to the limited monarchy found in Great Britain. The new government also proved unable to address the problems facing the country. It fell, in October of that same year, during the Bolshevik Revolution led by Vladimir Ilyich Ulyanov Lenin (1870-1924).

Given the atrocities that the Russian people were to suffer under Communism, it may be difficult for observers of today to imagine what initially attracted thoughtful and caring people to this movement. Sergei Eisenstein, himself, would later suffer disappointment and persecution under the despotic leader who succeeded Lenin, Joseph Vissarionovich Djugashvili Stalin (1879-1953). A major reason that the Bolshevik Revolution occurred, and was so strongly supported in Russia at first, was due to the problems, iniquities, corruption, and incompetence existing in the social systems and governments which preceded it. Had czarist Russia been more responsive to the needs of its citizens, it is possible that Communism would never have seriously been considered as an alternative form of government. Concerned people believed that the pre-Bolshevik Russian governments were not fair to all of the country's citizens, that solutions to their society's problems could be found, and that an alternative system for governing would be better. Tragically, despite their idealism and good intentions, what eventually emerged from the Bolshevik Revolution was a political system which led to more social abuses and the suppression of millions of people.

The initial revolution, to make Russia Communist, was relatively bloodless. Many more lives were lost in the civil war which followed. From 1918 until about 1921, the pro-czarist forces, or "Whites," fought the Communist "Red Army" to gain control of Russia. Nineteen-year-old Sergei Eisenstein was quite apolitical when he joined the Red Army. He enlisted because everyone in his class at the Institute of Civil Engineering was doing so. At this time Sergei's father, ironically, had decided to fight with the Whites. When the latter army was defeated, Eisenstein's father emigrated to Germany.

Despite his initial political ambivalence Eisenstein, like many young Russian intellectuals of his generation, became thoroughly dedicated to the ideals of the Bolshevik Revolution. Eisenstein demonstrated his political enthusiasm, during his army career, by drawing political posters and taking part in theatrical entertainment for the troops. In 1920 Eisenstein was able to leave the army and go back to school at the government's expense. His artistic talent now recognized and appreciated, Sergei decided to study art at the University of Moscow.

The attitudes and goals that idealistic Russians like Sergei Eisenstein brought to their art, in the 1920s, often were similar to the philosophies of modern art movements we discussed in Chapter Four. Many artists of the period, as we have noted, were horrified by the carnage of World War I, and opposed the priorities of the societies which produced it. They questioned whether prevailing art forms were an extension of these social systems. Did traditional art reflect the undesirable values which could lead to war? When they believed that they did, these artists felt compelled to challenge the premises behind the rules and regulations of the current forms of artistic expression. Their "modern art" looked for ways to address social issues, avoid escapist fantasy, and investigate how the media could best express their aesthetics. What made the situation of Russian modern artists different from their counterparts, in other countries, was the political atmosphere in which they applied their theories.

Unlike the heads of state in other countries, Lenin seemed to advocate the nonconformist views of the modern artist. Lenin and the Bolsheviks justified their revolution on the basis that the old form of government they replaced was inadequate. It needed to be supplanted by a new and revolutionary political system. The traditional art forms were associated with the old ways of living. This art needed to be replaced by fresh and innovative types of artistic expression which reflected Russia's modern age. Lenin's government encouraged artists to produce a revolutionary art in keeping with the new political system which now ruled the country. The Russian artists were encouraged to believe that they were pioneers leading the way for the improvement of life in the twentieth century. This atmosphere changed, after Lenin died in 1924, but the shift in the government's support of the arts was not immediate. Artists did not feel the full effects of the emerging Stalinist oppression until the end of the decade.

By the 1930s Russia's artists and artisans were actively discouraged from being innovative in their work. They were now expected to conform to very specific styles and messages dictated by the government. Counter to their original beliefs, they would not see Communism turn Russia into a utopian society in their lifetimes. Their earlier enthusiasm and dreams for its success had, however, led to some exciting developments in the Russian arts of the 1920s. One medium which profited, aesthetically, from this climate was the motion picture. The cinema particularly lent itself to the image which the Bolsheviks initially wanted to project.

At the time of the Bolshevik Revolution, the motion picture medium was not much more than a couple of decades old. Its popularity with the common man gave it a kind of democratic appeal that was different from the sense of elitism sometimes associated with earlier art forms and styles of expression. Because so many average people liked to watch the movies, it was also a particularly useful medium for propaganda. Russia's resources were limited in the 1920s, but Lenin's enthusiasm for film resulted in his giving the country's filmmakers his avid support.

Russia's cinematic innovations in the 1920s have overshadowed the fact that this country had a film history before the Revolution. Film historians are now beginning to examine motion pictures made in czarist Russia, and appreciate their quality. They also are starting to address the fact that numerous White Russian filmmakers, who later had distinguished film careers in other foreign cinemas, came to these countries with a Russian knowledge of their craft. Recognizing that there was a Russian film history before 1917, which deserves fuller attention, we will restrict our examination to what this country's filmmakers did with the medium after this date. We can broadly qualify this investigation by stating that filmmaking in Russia, immediately after the 1917 October Revolution, was affected by three major factors--the shortage of raw film stock, the documentary film work of Dziga Vertov (1896-1954), and the film theory and teachings of Lev Kuleshov (1899-1970).

Because film stock was such a rare commodity in Russia, filmmakers were expected to know exactly what they wanted to do with it before any footage was shot. This concern led to countless discussions as to what film should or should not do. It also prompted the careful study of those films, both foreign and domestic, which already existed. Consequently, the inherent nature of both documentary and non-fiction film were given a great deal of thought before Russia's post-Revolution film enthusiasts even picked up a camera. This seriousness and appreciation strongly affected the philosophy behind documentary and fictional filmmaking in Russia in the 1920s.

Given Lenin's interest in the motion picture, it is not surprising that an effort was made to document, on film, activities involving the new government and current events relating to the civil war. Until raw film stock became more accessible after the civil war, documentary filmmaking was given something of a priority over fictional filmmaking. The major figure in Russian nonfiction filmmaking at this time was Dziga Vertov.

During the civil war Vertov had the responsibility of editing the footage sent to him from the front. At first he cut this footage in a fairly straightforward, chronological fashion. Eventually Vertov questioned this approach and explored ways that editing could make his films more dynamic. Following the civil war, Vertov applied his theories while re-editing his newsreels into three feature films on the conflict. When raw film stock became available, Vertov continued his experiments in the documentaries which he shot. Vertov and his followers filmed subject matter which reflected what they saw as positive and dynamic in Russian society. These documentaries were particularly notable for emphasizing, rather than hiding, the fact that the motion picture medium was being used to express the filmmaker's ideas.

Most documentaries of that time did not want to draw attention to the filmmaking process. Rather, the filmmakers preferred that viewers concentrate on the subject being documented. For Vertov, the fact that the subject was being filmed was part of the event being recorded. We are constantly reminded that we are watching a movie when viewing a Vertov documentary. Shots of the cameraman, people reacting to the camera, and even animated segments where the camera walks away on the tripod are often in evidence. Dziga Vertov's "self-reflexive" attitude, of drawing attention to the film medium, was counter to the philosophy of invisible editing. The dynamic results Vertov obtained, by ignoring the philosophy behind decoupage in his nonfiction films, influenced the way narrative filmmakers in Russia considered their medium as well. We will talk more about Vertov and his work in Chapter Twelve.

Lev Kuleshov, the foremost Russian film theorist and teacher between 1920 and 1925, was the third major influence on filmmaking in that country immediately prior to the emergence of Eisenstein. A filmmaker since before the Revolution, Kuleshov set up his famous Kuleshov Workshop in Moscow, at the age of twenty. The workshop eventually closed in 1925. By then its influence was directing the way people would think about film from that time forward.

Kuleshov and his students, in the early 1920s, were particularly interested in how the motion picture worked as a medium of communication. They questioned what the medium could do, what others had done with it, and how they could use it differently. Besides writing film scripts, and devising set designs on paper, the workshop spent a great deal of time analyzing foreign films. The 1916 American featue *Intolerance,* directed by D.W. Griffith, was particularly influential to the group. *Intolerance* used a complex narrative structure which constantly switched its attention among four separate stories set at different times in history--the fall of Babylon in 538 B.C., the 16th century persecution of the French Huguenots, the events leading up to the Crucifixion of Christ, and a modern story set in an unnamed American city. Besides considering the associations which Griffith was making through his editing, Kuleshov and his students re-edited *Intolerance* to create a new correlation among the parts of the film. By the time the workshop had literally worn out their print of *Intolerance,* the enthusiastic group had come up with some fascinating findings. Kuleshov's insights alone would revolutionize filmmaking.

During his study of editing, Kuleshov came up with a concept that became known as the "Kuleshov effect." Kuleshov found that he could take the same CU of an actor and audiences would interpret the facial expression in different ways, depending upon the content of the shots with which it was juxtaposed. If Kuleshov showed the CU after an image of a person in a coffin, for example, viewers would interpret his expression as one of grief. Replace the coffin shot with one of a bowl of soup and people believed that the actor was expressing hunger. When the CU was juxtaposed to a picture of a baby, spectators felt the man's face was registering love. In all three instances the very same CU was used. Each time the audience imposed an interpretation on the shot which the actor had not been trying to communicate at the time his face had been filmed.

From his experiment Kuleshov concluded that a shot can have two meanings--that which it contains within itself and that which can be imposed upon it through juxtaposition with other shots. Editing can make a shot meaningful in ways that were not intended when that footage was initially filmed. The fact that meaning could be perceived from such quick juxtapositions was particulary appreciated by budding filmmakers with little or no film stock to work with. The Kuleshov effect suggested that one need not resort to an elaborate master scene technique to establish relationships and associations among shots. Instead of filming everything within a setting, and showing how all of it related in a manner suggesting real time and space, filmmakers could create meaning with just parts of the overall information. From this minimal amount of data observers could draw their own conclusions relative to the missing material. The editing was being done in the viewer's mind rather than on screen.

By 1924, Russian filmmakers were able to get access to raw footage. After receiving the necessary funding from the government, they quickly tried to make movies that put their theories and knowledge to practice. Their motion pictures made film history. Of this group Sergei Eisenstein would achieve the greatest fame. One reason for his success was that he took the workshop's questions, and Kuleshov's effect involving juxtaposition, one major step further--he questioned the nature, even the desirability, of continuity editing.

II. The Identity of Montage

The most literal meaning for "montage" is that it is a French word relating to the editing, or "assemblage," of a film. While "montage" can be used to describe editing in general, this same word is used in a variety of contexts internationally. Debates have been waged regarding just what the term "montage" correctly describes. Though some critics dislike limiting the meaning of the word to the effect for which Eisenstein and his contemporaries were striving, American filmmakers often use "montage" to refer to a type of editing sometimes identified as "Russian montage." From this perspective, montage is seen as an approach to cutting which serves as an alternative to "invisible" or continuity editing. Our study will confine the meaning of "montage" to this operational definition, while recognizning that some semantic arguments might prefer a different, even broader, interpretation of the word.

The kind of editing associated with "Russian montage" involves a situation in which the viewer is bombarded with disparate shots which he or she interprets by virtue of their juxtapositions. Montage editing is often used in beverage commercials on television. For example, in the first shot of our theoretical advertisement a character might open a bottle of this "magic elixir." The succeeding shots could then consist of a variety of images where people suddenly appear laughing, dancing, and being ecstatic about life, apparently because they are just hear the sound of the bottle being opened. Each shot represents a different image of happiness and well-being. Where these people are spatially, in relation to one another, in this overall setting probably is unclear. There is no sense of "real time" and "real space." The advertisement shows a montage of disparate, supposedly positive, images trying to suggest that the product being advertised creates a fantastic effect on those in its proximity. Though the product may be hideous in reality, by showing it in the context of positive images we are asked to accept that it is good as well.

Continuity or invisible editing, as we have discussed, depends upon creating the illusion of duplicating spatial and temporal relationships that seem similar to what we experience in the "real " world around us. Montage editing draws attention to the juxtapositions and divisions between shots. The viewer is bombarded with stimuli which draw attention to themselves as associations, rather than shown in the context of duplicating a "real" world. "Real" spatial and temporal correlations frequently are not emphasized. Such editing, in fact, often creates a stylized form of time and space which can exist only in a medium like film. It is ironic that montage, which is associated with Communist film theories in Russia, is now widely used in capitalist advertisements on television and in MTV videos.

"Russian montage" is associated with the Russian filmmakers of the 1920s--particularly Eisenstein. While they refined and developed this concept of editing, they did not invent it. A major example of an early form of montage editing can be found in a massacre scene in D.W. Griffith's 1916 film, *Intolerance*. During the modern story some strikers are suddenly shot at by national guardsmen. The temporal and spatial relationships of the people, shown in the continuity editing of this scene, are suddenly disrupted by a form of montage. We no longer can tell where the individuals are, relative to one another or in the general setting, and real time is replaced by film time. The disorientation the viewer feels is comparable to the chaos we would experience if caught in a riot. Griffith intuitively found an editing style that simulated the frenzy, and the psychological perspective, one would observe if actually involved in such an event. Given the familiarity the Kuleshov Workshop had with *Intolerance*, it is not surprising that this change in his editing style would have caught their attention and impressed them with its effect.

Early examples of montage can also be found in films made in France at this time. *La Roue (The Wheel,* 1921), by the French director Abel Gance (1889-1981), is particularly notable in this regard. The principal character in *La Roue,* a train engineer named Sisif, contemplates suicide by wrecking his locomotive. During the scene Gance rapidly cuts to a myriad of different shots relating to the people on board, the passing countryside, parts of the moving machine, and the troubled engineer. As the train gains speed, and collision seems increasingly inevitable, the tempo of the editing quickens as the viewer's involvement with the various elements of the scene intensifies.

Another fascinating use of montage can be seen in Dmitri Kirsanoff's *Ménilmontant* (1924). *Ménilmontant* is a story about two sisters whose parents are murdered. They move from the country to the Paris suburb of Ménilmontant, where one of the girls becomes a prostitute. The film tells its story through a series of incomplete shots, thereby forcing the audience to contemplate what is missing. By actively imagining what is needed to give the narrative closure, the viewer is asked to complete the story--edit if you will--in his or her mind. Kirsanoff was a Russian émigré who made his film in Paris. The fact that he made his film without any apparent knowledge of the Kuleshov workshop is another indication that the work of the Russian filmmakers before the Revolution needs further research.

One last notable example of montage before Eisenstein, that we might remember, can be found in a picture that was discussed in Chapter 4-- Fernand Leger's *Ballet Mecanique* (1924). This French avant-garde film bombards the viewer with images broken down into the form of geometrical shapes and patterns which Leger edited to a rhythm rather than a story. As we noted, this "mechanical ballet" of shapes and objects is similar to the non-narrative orchestration of objects, abstract shapes, and colors that can be seen in music videos on television today.

One of the reasons Sergei Eisenstein's montage became so notable was due to the systematic and articulate way he defined and developed his approach to editing. Eisenstein came to filmmaking with the notion of challenging previous approaches for using film, and pushing the medium to its most extreme capabilities of expression. Like Vertov, he was interested in drawing the viewer's attention to the medium. This concern for making audiences aware of film enabled Eisenstein to challenge the concept of invisible editing itself. Indeed, Eisenstein was to conclude that the harmonious juxtaposition of shots, in continuity editing, robbed film of its dynamic potential. Instead of trying to maintain spatial and temporal harmony in one's films, Eisenstein advocated that the filmmaker should stress conflict.

Sergei Eisenstein's theory of montage was based on creating conflict in everything from themes in the overall plot right down to contrasting black and white elements within the frame. As had been true of the Kuleshov effect, juxtaposition was the key to the way this approach to editing worked.

Eisenstein experimented with his initial ideas, involving montage, in the first feature film he directed, *Strachka* (1924). When he made his second film, *Bronenosets Potyomkin* (*Battleship Potemkin,* 1925), his theory of montage, and its application in this picture, was incredibly refined. Eisenstein described many of his theoretical concepts, relating to montage, in two important books, *Film Form* and *The Film Sense.*

Continuity editing is based on the illusion of creating the appearance of real time and space in a film, utilizing "invisible" or "seamless" cutting between shots. With this approach there is a harmony and meshing among the various parts. Eisenstein felt that the idea of clash and conflict was much more dynamic than a perspective involving harmony. To him the harmonious nature of continuity editing deprived film of its innate power to excite the audience. Conflict and contrast were at the heart of Eisenstein's alternative form of editing. Sergei Eisenstein identified several basic types of montage, or editing strategies, which could reflect the dynamism he felt film should express. We will concentrate on six of them.

"**Metric montage**," Eisenstein believed, is the easiest way to edit contrast in a film. By alternating the physical length of the shots the editor can impose a tempo on the film regardless of its content. For example, the first shot of our metric montage segment might be five seconds in length, the second shot two seconds, the third shot five seconds, and so on. As one can see, the periodicity of the length of the shots forces a cadence in the timing of the material. Cutting a film to music is a form of metric montage. The MTV video is a very common example of this. The beat, or tempo, created by the physical <u>length</u> of the shots over a particular duration of time dictates what happens with this form of editing. The tempo may, in fact, be more important than the content or "realistic" depiction of the images in metric montage.

In reality a person can not, for example, stand up to look at the Statue of Liberty, in New York, and then sit down to the beat of a song, in the next frame, on top of the Golden Gate Bridge in San Francisco. Such an unusual and discordant juxtaposition of shots is an accepted norm in music videos. With this form of editing the disparate shots may contain no thematic or visual correlation at all. An editor can randomly edit footage, using metric montage, without even looking at the content of the images. The physical length of the shots will determine the tempo and, consequently, the structure of the segment.

"**Rhythmic montage**" was the name that Eisenstein gave for editing movement <u>within</u> the shot. Cutting, in rhythmic montage, is determined by the rhythms and movement seen in the image. This is different from metric montage manipulating the tempo, from outside the frame, by varying the physical length of the shots. Rhythmic montage would be similar to the continuity editing technique known as match-on-action in that it involves being aware of movement in the frame from one shot to the next. Match-on-action takes a movement from one shot and continues it in the next so that the two shots are connected by a <u>continuous</u> action. In keeping with the concerns of continuity editing a match-on-action maintains spatial and temporal relations, between shots, resembling those we experience in reality. The match-on-action often makes it appear that all of this movement is occurring in a single shot--an impression in keeping with "invisible" or continuity editing. The editor has cut the actions together so that the viewer won't notice that editing is taking place.

Eisenstein, of course, was not interested in maintaining the "seamless editing" effect of decoupage. His rhythmic editing was one of the ways that he countered the philosophy of continuity editing. He wanted viewers to be aware that editing was taking place. Rather than using movement to conceal the fact that editing was occurring, as in continuity editing, Eisenstein used this motion to emphasize clash or conflict between shots. In continuity editing a figure may leave frame right, in one shot, and enter frame left in the next. This technique makes the frame line serve the function as a kind of "door frame." With rhythmic montage Eisenstein wanted action to clash within this theoretical doorway. If the action in shot #1 had the movement going from left to right, shot two might have the action moving from right to left (see fig. 8.1 and 8.2). The effect is as if the object doing the movement suddenly spins in a frantic circle, and emerges from the very spot from which it departed, in a fraction of a second, between shots. Instead of watching a smooth flow of movement the viewer finds his or her eyes darting all over the screen, as one tries to follow the action from shot to shot.

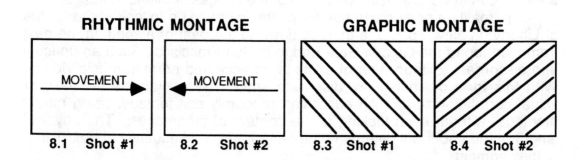

RHYTHMIC MONTAGE   **GRAPHIC MONTAGE**

8.1   Shot #1   8.2   Shot #2   8.3   Shot #1   8.4   Shot #2

8.1-8.4 In the first two diagrams, 8.1 and 8.2, we see how a director can contrast movement to create rhythmic montage. Suddenly changing the direction of a movement, between shots, forces the viewer to shift perspective while watching this dynamic interaction. The third and fourth diagrams, 8.3 and 8.4, show how the filmmaker can employ graphic montage to make vivid visual contrasts between shots.

"**Graphic montage**" is concerned with changing the geometric patterns of lines, between shots, so they visually contrast rather than harmoniously flow together, when the shots are juxtaposed. In essence this accomplishes something of the same effect as rhythmic montage. Where rhythmic montage alternates movement, graphic montage changes the direction, of the dominant lines in the frame, from one shot to the next. We may, for example, have one shot where the lines of some steps diagonally intersect the frame from the upper right hand corner to the lower left. To achieve graphic montage the filmmaker may change the composition by having the lines diagonally intersect the frame extending from the upper left hand corner down to the lower right. When the editor cuts from the first shot to the second we get a dynamic visual confrontation between the two lines (see fig. 8.3 and 8.4). The filmmaker may also seek graphic montage, within a composition, by interjecting a subject that forms a sharp vertical line within a setting emphasizing horizontal planes.

"**Tonal montage**" is also concerned with the physical information within the frame. This type of montage editing is involved with the color and texture of the image. Eisenstein's theory of tonal montage was very much influenced by his study of German expressionism. With this category Eisenstein concentrated on contrasting dark and light elements within a frame or between shots. If the visual information in shot #1 was dark, for example, he could create a dynamic contrast by making his next shot very light. Using black and white for dramatic contrast was also, of course, a variation of standard melodramatic technique. It was not unusual to have an innocent female victim dressed in white, opposed by a villain dressed in darker colors.

"**Overtonal montage**" involves the orchestration of the audiences emotions. While the first three categories are associated with <u>physical</u> elements within a film, overtonal montage reflected Eisenstein's interest in the mood, spirit, and poetry of his editing. We might use an example from one of Eisenstein's own films to identify this concept. In *Strike*, Eisenstein has a scene where two little boys are innocently playing on a pedestrian bridge during a riot. Their joy and innocence is emphasized in one shot. The viewer feels a contrasting emotion, in a succeeding shot, when a Cossack picks up one of the little boys and maliciously drops him off the bridge to his death. As can be seen from this example, with overtonal montage the editor is trying to manipulate the viewer's mood and feelings. Overtonal montage, as was true of Eisenstein's other forms of montage, incorporated dramatic juxtapositions for a particular effect.

"**Intellectual montage**" reflects Eisenstein's concern with the editing of ideas. This part of his theory drew a great deal from Kuleshov's experiments. With intellectual montage Eisenstein explored the way the juxtaposition of two different images could create an association which neither suggested by itself. Again we might use an example from one of Eisenstein's own films to illustrate this concept. *Oktiabr* (1927) (known both as *October* and *Ten Days that Shook the World* in English) was Eisenstein's tribute to the tenth anniversary of the October Revolution. Among the historical figures portrayed in the film was Alexander Kerenski (1880-1970). Kerenski headed the ill-fated government that existed between the reign of Czar Nicholas II and the Bolshevik takeover by Lenin. Not surprisingly, Eisenstein did not have a very high opinion of Kerenski. At one point in the film Eisenstein cuts from Kerenski to the back end of some horses in the czar's stable. The shot with Kerenski does not place him anywhere near the horses. Nor has the setting of the stable really been used for thematic purposes prior to this time. One can conclude, from this juxtaposition, that Eisenstein was making a statement about Kerenski using intellectual montage. He was, literally, comparing Kerenski to the back end of a horse.

Eisenstein did not invent these concepts of montage so much as he systematically identified what other film directors had, often instinctively, already been doing. No one before Eisenstein, however, had been so perceptive in classifying and describing these editing techniques. After establishing these various categories of montage Eisenstein applied them. He proved the viability of his theory, based on "discontinuous" editing, with the release of his second film. *Battleship Potemkin* brought Eisenstein international fame and made film history. We will consider Eisenstein's theory of "Russian montage" by examining part of the most famous portion of this film, the "Odessa Steps" sequence.

III. Montage Editing and Sergei Eisenstein's *Battleship Potemkin*

Battleship Potemkin was based on an actual incident that occurred in 1906 under the government of the czar. As with many Russian films of this time, *Battleship Potemkin* was set in the period before the Bolshevik Revolution. Its story was meant to show problems that existed prior to Lenin's takeover of the government. The sailors of this battleship had actually mutinied because of the intolerable conditions, on the ship, which included being forced to eat spoiled meat. Eisenstein took this situation, from history, and developed it into a dramatic motion picture.

Eisenstein structured *Battleship Potemkin* using his theory of conflict. The principal conflict in the narrative, at first, involves the sailors versus the officers on board. This thematic conflict is expanded to show how the sailors are an extension of the common people while the officers, who are oppressing them, are part of the unfair political system under the czar. Eisenstein stresses this conflict by breaking the structure into five identifiable segments which are given the following specific titles:

I. Men and Maggots
II. Mutiny on the Quarterdeck
III. An Appeal from the Dead
IV. The Odessa Steps
V. Meeting the Squadron

Each sequence identifies the narrative content of that portion of the film and establishes a position in the conflict developed in the film's overall form. For example, "Men and Maggots" refers to the spoiled meat which the men are rebelling against. The sailor's irritation over their food initiates a conflict between them and the officers. The outcome of this dispute is identified in the title of sequence #2, "Mutiny on the Quarterdeck." The title of part #3, "An Appeal from the Dead," recognizes an outcome of the mutiny. We can see from the subheadings that the film follows a narrative progression involving conflict and outcome. The sailors have a grievance, the officers oppose them, and the conflict is resolved through a violent mutiny. Part #3 is the outcome--dead sailors and officers.

The third sequence is the middle, and in some sense pivotal, portion of the film. In this segment the mutineers head to the port of Odessa where they make their case known to the people. The sailors and citizens rally around the body of a sailor, named Vakulinchuk, who was ruthlessly killed during the mutiny. Considered criminals by the government, the sailors are supported by the people of Odessa. The sailors still have to contend with the government, however, and mutiny is punishable by death. Supporting mutineers in the czar's navy is also treason. The governmental backlash, or counter-position, occurs in segment #4--the Odessa Steps Sequence.

Part #3 is a show of solidarity and a kind of "lull before the storm." We get the "storm," or backlash, in part #4. The Odessa Steps Sequence is also structured in terms of conflict and outcome. The first portion of part #4 starts by showing the happiness and sense of solidarity felt by the sailors and the people of Odessa. The "backlash" is the massacre on the Odessa steps. As innocent onlookers watch, their fellow citizens supply the *Potemkin* with provisions. Suddenly unarmed women and children are systematically shot down by the czar's soldiers. After we are shown several scenes of savagery by the troops, the *Potemkin* stops the massacre by turning its massive guns on the headquarters of the army and blow it up.

Part #5 is both a reflection of the outcome of the armed resistance, by the *Potemkin* in sequence #4, and the climax of the film. Given that the

189

sailors have mutinied against their officers, and fired on the czar's troops at Odessa, the full impact of Russia's armed forces will now be employed against them. The "squadron" of the title of this sequence refers to the main fleet of the czar's navy. Clearly this one small battleship is no match for an entire fleet. There are two possible outcomes to the last question waiting to be resolved in this final conflict. Will the *Potemkin* be overpowered by the fleet? Could the squadron join in their rebellion? The audience must wait until the very end of the film to find out.

Eisenstein, of course, does not limit his exploration of conflict to the thematic discord within these segments. He also seeks ways to establish conflict between shots and in the graphic composition within the frames. We can get a sense of these, and his other strategies for bringing conflict to *Battleship Potemkin,* by examining a small portion of the famous Odessa Steps Sequence.

IV. Montage Editing and the "Odessa Steps Sequence" from *Battleship Potemkin*

Few film sequences in motion picture history have been analyzed as much as the Odessa Steps section from *Battleship Potemkin*. The segment we are examining occurs roughly three minutes into the sequence. At this time the citizens of Odessa have gathered on a huge flight of stairs overlooking the harbor. This gathering is peaceful and some of the people are showing their support, for the sailors of the *Potemkin,* by supplying them with provisions.

The following analysis is by no means a "definitive study" of even the short portion of the film we have chosen to investigate. It does allow the student to get both an idea of how Eisenstein's theory of montage works and an opportunity to appreciate the aesthetic richness of this classic film. As was the case when reviewing the shot breakdown from *Variety,* it is suggested that you consult the frame enlargements on pages 210-214 while reading this criticque. An analysis, written in bold type, follows the shot descriptions.

SHOT BREAKDOWN OF PART OF "THE ODESSA STEPS SEQUENCE" FROM SERGEI EISENSTEIN'S *BATTLESHIP POTEMKIN* (1925)

Shot #1   Master scene technique, cover shot, LS of crowd of people on the steps looking towards the battleship, *Potemkin*. A number of white umbrellas are open and seen in prominence. Duration of the shot is approximately 3 seconds. (Fig. 8.5).

190

Shot #2   Continuation of master scene technique, match-on-action. Director cuts from a general placement of the setting to a tighter MS view of the environment. Six people in the foreground are seen in prominence. They are waving at the *Potemkin*. 1 sec. (Fig. 8.6).

Shot #3   Continuation of master scene technique, match-on-action on the action of waving. We now have a 2 shot, MCU, of two women, one of whom is wearing a pince-nez and a white scarf. 2 sec. (Fig. 8.7). **The director is incorporating a variation of master shot technique in this segment. Instead of focusing on where the principal characters are in this setting, Eisenstein is more interested in showing the people as a group. The woman wearing the pince-nez and scarf will be given more emphasis later but she is not the only person whose behavior is emphasized in this segment.**

Shot #4   Continuation of master scene technique. MCU of a wealthy woman wearing a feather hat, and lorgnette in selective focus. She raises her veil to form a line under nose and breaks into a smile. 3 sec. (Fig. 8.8). **Eisenstein is emphasizing intellectual montage by having people of diverse socio-economic backgrounds united in their support of the mutineers on the ship.**

Shot #5   MCU of a woman in a white dress with a white parasol, white hat, black hair, and black gloves. She twirls her umbrella counter-clockwise as she smiles and waves. (Fig. 8.9). 2 sec. **Given the emphasis on people dressed in black in the previous shots, Eisenstein is incorporating some tonal montage in this shot for purposes of visual contrast. The conscious counter-clockwise twirling of the umbrella is also incorporated for purposes of adding some visual diversity to this segment. Note that shot #3 is 2 seconds in length, shot #4 is 3 seconds, and shot #5 is also 2 seconds indicating that Eisenstein is using metric montage to create a kind of rhythm in the editing of these shots. The director may be creating this rhythm to underscore the feeling of harmony that the people are experiencing at this time.**

Shot #6	Low angle, lower two thirds of a couple of women, standing in the foreground on the steps. One wears a white dress, the other is dressed in black. The woman in white opens a white umbrella and lifts it up. Amidst this display of elegant dress a legless man in working clothes comes between the two ladies. 6 sec. (Fig. 8.10 and 8.11). **Eisenstein is employing graphic, tonal, intellectual, and overtonal montage here. The vertical lines of the woman's bodies contrast markedly with the horizontal lines of the steps. The white and dark dresses contrast, as do the women's choice of shoe color. After seeing the women's legs the graphic and emotional contrast of seeing a man without legs is a bit of a shock to the viewer. Eisenstein is both contrasting wealthy with working-class observers, and eliciting our sympathies for this person who is forced to get around without any legs.**
Shot #7	CU of woman with veil whose dark skirt we saw in the previous shot. Camera pans left to reposition her in the middle of the frame. 8 sec. **After assaulting our sense of "normal" space by showing us a man without legs, Eisenstein reorients us to what we usually expect to see in the frame. One of the women cut off below the torso, in the previous shot, is shown to have an upper portion to her body.**
Shot #8	Cut back to placement in shot #6 of legless man waving. 2 sec. **Overtonal montage. The man without legs was introduced in a manner to disorient, if not shock, the viewer. Now that we see him as a smiling person we accept him as another positive member of a diverse group who support the sailors and their mutiny.**
Shot #9	MCU of a little boy in white shirt holding a basket. His mother bends down and points towards the Potemkin. 3 sec. (Fig. 8.12). **Overtonal montage. The director is eliciting more emotional involvement in presenting smiling characters with whom we are expected to relate in a positive fashion.**

Shot #10   Eyeline-match, low angle of a flag flying from the mast of the *Potemkin*. 1 sec. (Fig. 8.13). **Intellectual montage. The flag was hand colored red in the original prints of the film--the color symbolizing revolution. This red color was incorporated in the Russian flag after the Bolshevik revolution.**

Shot #11   Back to placement #9. Mother puts down boy's basket and they wave. 5 sec. **Overtonal montage. We are meant to identify with the little boy, his mother, and the support they are displaying for the sailors and their flag of rebellion.**

Shot #12   MS low angle of a little girl and boy held on people's shoulders and waving. The girl is wearing dark clothing and the boy is wearing a white shirt. Hats are being waved and thrown up behind them. 3 sec. (Fig. 8.14). **Overtonal montage. The continued emphasis on children plays off the natural feelings of attraction we have for them as a group. Their presence underlines the fact that this is a peaceful, "family" event.**

Shot #13   Low angle of the dark dress and white dress cut at the women's waists. The dark dressed woman brings down her white umbrella. 1 sec. **Graphic and tonal montage. The space in the foreground is like a vacuum waiting to be filled. After seeing the previous frames carefully filled with smiling faces this open frame is a bit disconcerting. The open white umbrella in front of the black dress, and the black dress next to the white dress, are tonal contrasts.**

Title #1   Suddenly

Shot #14   CU of a woman violently shaking her head. 1 sec. (Fig. 8.15-8.17). **Metric montage. There are four different close-ups of the woman employed in this shot which give the effect of a violent jerky motion because the slight change in placements happen so quickly. These four "jump cuts" are approximately eight frames, six frames, ten frames, and twelve frames in length. This shift from continuity editing to a discontinuous use of** time and space is designed to create a disorienting, chaotic effect in keeping with the psychological perceptions one might experience in a sudden and unexpected crisis. Another way a filmmaker can purposely disorient a viewer is by using a continuity technique that does not work the way we expect it to such as a "false eye-line-match" or "false match-on-action." These editing methods are often employed to emphasize chaos, or confusion, rather than temporal and spatial continuity.

Shot #15   Low angle straight on shot of the steps. Continuation of shot #13. The legless man crosses in front of the camera from left to right. An open umbrella rushes towards the camera. 3 sec. (Fig. 8.18). **Overtonal montage. The people with whom we have been asked to identify with in celebration are suddenly thrown into panic. By crossing in front of the camera, and rushing down the steps, the legless fills up the open space in the foreground emphasized in shot #13. The umbrella that charges at the camera--us--as if it is going to knock us over underscores the sense of chaos that has replaced what previously was a condition of harmony.**

Shot #16   Low angle perspective from the side of the steps rather than from straight on. Legless man is seen rushing down the side of the steps. 4 sec. (Fig. 8.19). **Overtonal montage. It is very disconcerting to see a person, so helpless and vulnerable, being forced to run like this. We can not but wonder who would be so mean as to attack such an individual.**

Shot #17   Reverse angle, high angle LS at the top of the stairs. A statue of the czar has its back to the camera. The "czar" has his right arm up as if he is signaling his troops to attack. A line of soldiers are marching down the steps with rifles drawn. 2 sec. (Fig. 8.20). **We now know who is responsible for the chaos which has disrupted a previously friendly gathering. Rhythmic montage is used to emphasize the conflict by reversing the action previously going down the steps <u>towards</u> the camera at the <u>bottom</u> of** the steps. Now the camera is <u>behind</u> the action at the <u>top</u> of the steps, looking <u>down</u> on the action which is going <u>away</u> from the camera. **Intellectual and overtonal montage are used to emphasize that the czar and his cold-blooded soldiers are the enemy shooting at innocent women, children, and physically disadvantaged people of diverse socio-economic backgrounds. The soldiers make up the cruel machine that coldly shoots the unarmed and helpless victims but the statue symbolizes who is responsible for their actions. Interestingly, we have the czar's statue as one symbol at the top of the steps and a church as a contrasting symbol at the bottom. Tonal montage is employed to further differentiate and separate the soldiers, in their white uniforms, from the people in their predominantly dark clothing. The director will continue to emphasize that this confrontation pits government vs. the people throughout the remainder of the sequence.**

Shot #18   Reverse angle, low angle, perspective on the steps. One individual is sitting on the steps, where she apparently has fallen. She gets up and runs. The people are represented by what appear to be disembodied legs and feet. We are aware of how well dressed they are. 2 sec. **Rhythmic montage, overtonal montage, intellectual montage. The action in shot #17 was going away from the camera, this movement is coming towards it. Emotionally we view these people as victims who have lost their humanity to the point of becoming "disembodied" fleeing legs and feet. Intellectually, we can interpret the presence of these "well-dressed" feet as an indication that the czar does not care whether his victims are poor, middle, or upper-class.**

Shot #19   ELS from bottom of a flight of steps. The foreground is empty as a body of people rush down the steps and eventually fill up this space. 5 sec. (Fig. 8.21). **Match-on-action. Eisenstein is alternating shots of chaos with wider perspectives of the action. The position of the troops methodically and systematically moving down the steps from the back, while their victims rush** frantically in front of them, generally allows us to orient ourselves to the action and space.

*   *   *

Shots #20-37 concentrate on the panic and casualties of the massacre. These shots represent the depersonalized behavior of the soldiers and the horror experienced by the victims. We see an occasional familiar face but mostly the people in these shots are treated as part of an overall group. Eisenstein changes this strategy, in shot #38, by reintroducing us to the mother and boy that we saw in shots # 9 and 11. From this point Eisenstein will alternate between showing us group experiences and the specific encounters of recognizable individuals.

*   *   *

Shot #38   Tracking shot down steps. The camera follows, in LS, the little boy and his mother whom we last saw in shot #11. (Fig. 8.22). 4 sec. **Rhythmic montage, overtonal montage. This is the first time that Eisenstein has used a tracking shot to isolate specific individuals since we started analyzing this sequence. The director is singling these people out for special attention.**

Shot #39   Low angle side perspective of a row of rifles shooting downward at the fleeing figures. 1 sec. (Fig. 8.23). **Overtonal montage, intellectual montage, graphic montage. Will the mother and child get shot? The lines of the guns firing down provide an interesting contrast to the lines of the steps in the previous shot.**

Shot #40   Match-on-action, high angle LS of little boy falling into frame after being shot. 1 sec. (Fig. 8.24). **Overtonal montage, graphic montage. This time the victim is someone with whom we are somewhat acquainted. The innocent little boy's body harshly intersects the lines of the stone steps.**

Shot #41   Match-on-action, eyeline-match, almost a continuation of the tracking shot in shot #38 except the mother is running without the little boy. She is not yet aware that he is not with her. 1 sec. (Fig. 8.25). **Overtonal montage, metric montage.**

The little boy falls and watches as his mother runs away. We are aware of the mother's tragedy before she is. We can imagine how she will react when she finds out what has happened to her son. Eisenstein is using metric montage by cutting shots #39-42 so they are of one second duration--a way of emphasizing that the events, and the mother's current behavior, are happening in an almost mechanical fashion. This tempo will change when she discovers that her son is not with her.

Shot #42   Straight on CU of little boy with wound to the head clearly yelling, "Mama." 1 sec. (Fig. 8.26). **Rhythmic montage, tonal montage, overtonal montage. The camera is looking straight at the boy instead of following a downward movement of people from the side. The boy's white shirt is in stark contrast to the dark figures running down the steps in the previous shot. The blood on his head indicates he probably has a serious wound.**

Shot #43   Same tracking placement, as shot #46, showing the mother and others fleeing. The mother stops and turns. 2 sec. **Rhythmic montage, tonal montage, overtonal montage. We wait to see when the mother will discover the tragedy.**

Shot #44   Match-on-action MCU of mother turning her head looking for her child as she responds to his cry. There is a look of horror on her face. 1 sec. (Fig. 8.27). **Overtonal montage. The director builds the tension as we watch her response.**

Shot #45   Eyeline-match, same placement as shot #42. The boy cries out and then his head falls down. 2 sec. **Overtonal montage.**

Shot #46   Same placement as shot #44. The mother puts her hands to her head and screams. 1/2 sec. **Overtonal montage, metric montage. The mother's trauma over the loss of her son adds a new dimension to the terror, confusion, and psychological disorientation presented in this sequence. The short duration of this shot dramatically alters the pacing.**

Shot #47 Eyeline-match, low angle LS of boy lying on the step as feet and legs step over and around him. 2 sec. **Overtonal montage. Is he dead or will he get hurt worse? We are made to feel the mother's anguish as we watch how these people remain oblivious to his condition and, perhaps, add to his pain.**

Shot #48 Tight CU of the mother's horrified reaction. 1 sec. (Fig. 8.28). **Overtonal montage. Eisenstein emphasizes her feelings by forcing us to look closely at the mother's face.**

Shot #49 LS of children running down the steps. 2 sec. **Overtonal montage. A reminder that the little boy in the previous shot no longer can run like this and that other children are in danger of sharing his fate.**

Shot #50 MS of the little boy's leg, straddling the step, being stepped over. 1 sec. **Overtonal montage. The vulnerability of the innocent child continues to be emphasized.**

Shot #51 CU of the boy's shoulder and hand. The hand is stepped on. 1 sec. (Fig. 8.29). **Rhythmic montage, overtonal montage. The movement of the leg stepping over the boy's body in the previous shot goes from the lower right hand corner to the upper right hand corner. In this shot the movement is from the upper left hand corner and moves to the lower right as the boy's hand is stepped on. The effect suggests that the boy is being subjected to a series of violent physical abuses from all directions. Our discomfort for him is made greater when his hand seems to expand as the foot presses it into the step. Is the boy suffering from this pain or is he dead?**

Shot #52 Same placement as shot #51. The mother, with her hands to her head, walks towards the camera. 1 sec. **Metric montage, overtonal montage. The director has conveyed the last three shots in the same amount of time creating a constant rhythm as he shows these shocking images.**

Shot #53   High angle LS. The placement is similar to shot #49 showing panic stricken people running down the steps. 1 1/2 sec. **Rhythmic montage, overtonal montage.**

Shot #54   Jump cut, similar placement, similar group, emphasizing a distortion of space between this shot and shot #53. 2 sec. **Rhythmic montage, overtonal montage. The director is again relying on spatial and temporal discontinuity to give us a sense of the disorientation, chaos, and shock that the victims are feeling. Visually, spatially, and temporally, things are not right in this place and time.**

Shot #55   High angle MCU of the boy dangling over a step. A man walks over him and the lifeless body rolls over out of the frame in the upper right hand corner. 2 sec. (Fig. 8.30). **Rhythmic montage, overtonal montage. The way the boy is being treated in this chaotic, horror filled situation shows how the dehumanized behavior of everyone is escalating. We continue to experience extreme discomfort at the way this boy, whether dead or alive, is being treated.**

Shot #56   Reverse angle match-on-action MCU, as the boy rolls from the upper left hand corner into the frame an unknown woman, wearing expensive shoes, walks on top of his body. 1 sec. (Fig. 8.31). **Rhythmic montage, overtonal montage. The disorienting movement, and the fact that the people stepping on the boy are oblivious to the fact that he is there, adds to the nightmarish unreality of the situation. There is definite spatial discontinuity in the cutting between shots #55 and 56, and this creates an unsettling effect.**

Shot #57   Tight CU of the mother's face, similar to placement in shot #48. 1 sec. **Overtonal montage.**

Shot #58   High angle LS of crowd continuing to rush down the steps from the upper right hand corner of the frame to lower left hand corner. 1 sec. **Overtonal montage, metric montage. As the mother looks in horror at the body of her child** being kicked and trampled, the majority of the crowd are oblivious to her situation and running for their lives. Eisenstein helps give a mechanical pace to these events by making shots #56-58 each a second in length.

Shot #59   Low angle LS of people gathering around the mother as she goes up the steps. They are aware of her anguish and try to help when suddenly they turn and run down the steps as she continues to go back for her son. 4 sec. **Rhythmic montage, overtonal montage. The swirling motion of the people trying to help the mother and then turning in a circle to flee is indicative of the confusion of the situation. They are caught between feeling sympathy for the mother, wanting to help, and fearing for their own lives. The initial movement up the steps, by the mother, is counter to the trend of running down them. The mother's shock, as she looks down on her son, is strongly in evidence.**

Shot #60   Eyeline-match, CU of the boy. Same placement as shot #55. 1 sec. **Overtonal montage. This could be described as a continuity error if we were concerned with continuity editing. In the last shot, where we saw the boy's body, he was lying face up. This time he is again face down. We could rationalize this change in position by noting that his body could have been knocked over again. Eisenstein is not, of course, overly concerned with precision in his continuity editing. More important than our response to his body position, of course, is the way we empathize with how the mother feels seeing her son being treated in this fashion. It is this effect, and not a concern for creating the impression of "real" time and space, that Eisenstein is striving to achieve in this segment.**

Shot #61   LS of mother leaning over to pick up her son as people ignore them and rush, from upper frame left to lower frame right, behind her. Same placement as shot #59. 1 sec. **Overtonal montage.**

Shot #62   LS of people rushing down the steps, largely from upper frame right to lower frame left. 3 sec. **Rhythmic montage, overtonal montage. Eisenstein is using parallel action here to contrast the mother's behavior with the way the majority of people are responding to this situation.**

Shot #63   Same placement as shot #61. The mother raises her head into the frame as she picks up her boy's body and carries it up the stairs. She confronts the wave of people rushing down from the upper left hand corner towards the lower right hand corner of the frame. She stops, turns, and calls to them. 3 sec. **Rhythmic montage, overtonal montage. The director continues to use movement as a means to separate the mother's perspective from that of the other people. He is using his editing to orchestrate our concern for her disturbed condition in this dangerous situation.**

Shot #64   ELS of a mass of confused people, intermixed with bodies, rushing down the steps from the upper right hand corner toward the lower left hand corner of the frame. 4 sec. **Rhythmic montage, overtonal montage.**

Shot #65   LS of the woman in glasses and scarf, last seen in shot #28, still crouching with her two companions. She raises her head to look up the steps. 1 sec. **Rhythmic montage, overtonal montage, tonal montage. The woman's dark clothing stands out in stark contrast to the white wall behind her. The sharp horizontal line of the wall provides a sense of security when compared to the open, milling activity, occurring on the steps. She is conducting herself with a sense of confidence that is quite different from the way the other victims are behaving. Eisenstein is using this other familiar character, introduced at the beginning of the sequence, to establish another parallel action. He draws attention to this new emphasis by using this establishing LS as a master shot.**

Shot #66   Match-on-action as the woman continues to rise. 1 sec. **Intellectual montage. Eisenstein wants us to start**

thinking about what this woman is doing and why.

Shot #67 MCU of woman. She continues to look up the steps frame left. 1 sec. **Intellectual montage. The director's sudden use of master scene technique suggests we are supposed to focus on this woman and her behavior but we still are not sure why.**

Shot #68 LS, side view of the steps. The mother stops in MS, with son in arms, apparently asking for help. 3 sec. **Overtonal montage. The plight of the mother and child continue to be important to the director and the audience.**

Shot #69 MS woman with glasses and white scarf also making an appeal to those around her. 5 sec. **Intellectual montage, metric montage. We get the idea she wants to confront the soldiers rather than flee from them. After the previous rapid cuts Eisenstein is extending the pace, suggesting that the drama of the massacre is slowing down a bit if still not actually stopping.**

Title #2 "Let us appeal to them!"

Shot #70 Same placement as shot #69. Some of the people are starting to rally around her. 1 sec. **Intellectual montage. We wonder both how they plan to make their appeal and what manner of persuasion could have any impact on such merciless killers.**

Shot #71 LS of the majority of people, who continue to pay no attention to the woman in the scarf, running away. 2 sec. **Rhythmic montage, overtonal montage, intellectual montage. Eisenstein continues to establish people's perspective through the direction of their movement. Our feelings for their fate, and our doubts about their future, bring both our emotions and intellect into play while interpreting this scene.**

Shot #72 Same placement as shot #70. Some of the people around her look at the woman in the white scarf as a kind of visionary leader. She rises to stand and her head goes out of frame. 3 sec. **Intellectual montage, overtonal montage. The** terrified people are desperately looking to her for hope even though questions remain, at least for the viewer, as to the viability of her plan. We continue to sense the terror and desperation of the people around her.

Shot #73   Tighter placement on the faces of the crouching people who are rallying around the lady in the white scarf. One young woman clutches the lady's legs in childlike fashion. They look up at her with a growing sense of hope. 2 sec. **Intellectual montage, overtonal montage. Continuation of themes described in previous shots.**

Shot #74   Eyeline-match CU of woman's face that people have been looking at in the previous shot. She looks down at them in a maternal fashion. The woman is becoming more emphatic in assuming the role of a person with the correct vision. She looks frame left, up the steps towards the descending troops, with confidence. 2 sec. **Intellectual montage, overtonal montage. Continuation of themes described in previous shot. Eisenstein is relying on conventional continuity techniques to emphasize the development of the theme of this woman as self-proclaimed leader and visionary.**

Shot #75   High angle CU of the heads of the people who are rallying. They follow her direction by turning to look up the steps. 1 sec. **Intellectual montage, overtonal montage. We continue to wonder about the wisdom, and the outcome, of this woman's plan. Won't these people be submitting themselves to even greater danger by confronting the enemy?**

Shot #76   Eyeline-match, low angle LSof a line of soldiers descending the steps with guns pointed at the people. They move forward like an unthinking machine. (Fig. 8.32). 3 sec. **Rhythmic montage, intellectual montage, overtonal montage. The movement of the soldiers conflicts with the movement of the people--both figuratively and literally. In the face of this approaching threat we continue to question the prudence of the "visionary's" plan and the safety of those who are listening to her.**

Shot #77   High angle tracking MCU of mother holding her boy and walking up the steps pleading for help. 1 sec. **Rhythmic montage, overtonal montage, intellectual montage. The upward movement of the shocked and grieving mother is putting her in greater jeopardy of being harmed by the military machine. The director is emphasizing four parallel actions: the activities of the visionary and her group, the upward movement of the mother, the downward movement of the soldiers, and the overall downward movement by the majority of anonymous victims.**

*   *   *

Shots #78-86 concentrate largely on the activity of the visionary and her followers. The group appear to be watching both the mother and the descending troops as they rise to their feet from their crouching positions. The visionary has convinced these terrified people to accept her plan that they need to appeal to the soldiers to stop shooting. They turn and, like the mother, walk up the stairs to confront the troops as they come down. One of the followers is on crutches and has only one leg--an indication of the vulnerability of these people. Meanwhile the soldiers are continuing their systematic descent, stopping at times to fire their rifles in unified action. The behavior of the soldiers, and the majority of the people running from them, indicate nothing has happened to modify the way the fleeing individuals should relate to this situation. We can't help but feel that the visionary's group and grieving mother may be advancing towards an ominous fate.

*   *   *

Shot #87   Return to placement in shot #77. Tracking high angle MS of mother carrying the body of her son and asking for help. 2 sec. **Rhythmic montage, overtonal montage, intellectual montage. She has survived the last volley fired by the troops. We are skeptical about the soldiers giving her any assistance, despite her poignant pleas for help, as she continues to walk towards the troops.**

Shot #88 Match-on-action, similar high angle MS of movement of the visionary's followers, going up the steps and pleading to the soldiers not to hurt them. 3 sec. **Overtonal montage, intellectual montage. Two of the parallel actions are now seen as being united by a common goal--the two parties asking the soldiers to help them. The similarities in the way that the two parties are filmed--from a common high angle, tracking shot recording action moving in the same direction--contributes to our sense that these two parallel actions share something in common.**

Shot #89 Match-on-action, same placement as shot #87. Mother exits, frame left, and we see the carnage on the steps behind her. 2 sec. **Overtonal montage, intellectual montage. The mother's strategy of asking the soldiers for help seems very dubious given the evidence of the victims whom they have killed.**

Shot #90 High angle LS, diagonal composition of the shadows of the row of soldiers intersecting the horizontal lines of the stairs and the bodies of their dead victims. The soldiers march in formation over the bodies as if they were not even there. 4 sec. **Rhythmic montage, overtonal montage, intellectual montage. The soldiers are once again portrayed as a soulless entity as dead in spirit as the bodies they nonchalantly step over. We are made more aware of the deadliness of this machine, the lack of compassion these men have for their victims, the impractical nature of the visionary's plan, and the decreasing distance between the troops and those individuals who are coming up the steps.**

Shot #91 Match-on-action, low angle, ELS from the middle of the steps. The line of descending soldiers have entered at the top of the frame and the mother, still carrying her son, enters the bottom of the picture. In between them are numerous bodies. An open white umbrella is in the lower left hand frame. 4 sec. **Rhythmic montage, overtonal montage, intellectual montage, metric montage. For the first time we see the soldiers in the same physical space as the mother and child. The distance between them is not**

great given the destructive power of their rifles. The bodies in the frame underscore the danger the distraught mother is in. Too draw out the danger of the confrontation Eisenstein has increased the duration of the shots. Shots #90-92 are all four seconds in length--a rather extensive amount of time given the fact that most of the shots in this sequence have been from one to three seconds in length.

Title #3   "Listen to me! Don't shoot!"

Shot #92   High angle LS emphasizing the bodies lying on the steps and the soldiers moving down them. There is no indication that they are paying any attention to what the mother is saying. 4 sec. **Rhythmic montage, graphic montage, intellectual montage, overtonal montage. The tension mounts as the outcome of the inevitable confrontation becomes more immediate.**

Shot #93   High angle tracking shot of the mother marching up the steps. She walks past the dead bodies on the steps and into the shadows of the assembled line of soldiers who are now stationary. The shot ends as we see the officer's raised arm holding a sword, commanding his men to halt. 11 sec. **Rhythmic montage, overtonal montage, intellectual montage, metric montage, graphic montage. Considering how rapid most of the shots have been, in this sequence, this is a particularly long one. Tension continues to build as the mother tries to reason with the aggressors. Their representation as regimented shadows forming a calculated pattern on the steps serves to both dehumanize the soldiers and give them a menacing quality. The fact that they have stopped suggests that they may be capable of responding to the woman.**

Title #4   "My child is hurt!"

Shot #94   Continuation of shot #93. The woman has pretty much stopped moving but the camera pulls back to reveal the row of guns with fixed bayonets pointed at her. 3 sec. (Fig. 8.33). **Overtonal montage, graphic montage. Their shadows** still conveying a menacing quality, the soldiers now look like a firing squad ready to execute the target facing them--a distraught and vulnerable mother holding the body of her child. Notice how the officer's arm and drawn saber graphically intersect the line of the shadows of those he is commanding.

Shot #95 Parallel action, high angle tracking MS of the visionary's group moving up the steps with hands in air pleading. 3 sec. **Overtonal montage, intellectual montage. The visionary's people now appear very much as a support group for the grieving mother. Rather than disparate elements in a tragedy, we are seeing people combining forces to create a unified position counter to that of the regimented troops.**

Shot #96 Same placement as shot #94. The officer signals to fire and the mother starts to fall. 1 sec. **Rhythmic montage, overtonal montage, intellectual montage, metric montage. Our worst fears have been realized and Eisenstein picks up the pacing, through metric montage, by decreasing the duration of this shot compared with the length of the previous ones.**

Shot #97 Match-on-action, high angle LS, closer placement, of the woman falling on top of her executioners' shadows. About 1/2 sec. (Fig. 8.34). **Metric montage, overtonal montage, intellectual montage. When Eisenstein wants to concentrate on a theme he will often resort to continuity editing to emphasize the situation. Here he uses metric montage, in the form of a very short shot, to dramatize the explosive violence directed at the vulnerable mother.**

Shot #98 Parallel action, new placement showing a side view at the bottom of the steps We see a LS of victims running down the steps and past the camera in chaotic fashion. Galloping horses sometimes go in front of the camera and block our view. This frenzied activity is in stark contrast with, and a direct result of, the regimented downward movement of the troops at the top of the stairs. 2 sec. **Rhythmic montage, intellectual montage, overtonal montage. Clearly the only viable** behavior for these victims is to flee. **What has happened to the visionary and her group? When will this carnage end? What will persuade the soldiers to stop killing?**

Shot #99   Same placement as shot #97. The mother continues to fall backwards. The body of the woman, still holding her child ends up on the ground. The shadows of three of the soldiers are on top of them. 3 1/2 sec. (Fig. 8.35) **Rhythmic montage, overtonal montage, overtonal montage, graphic montage. The chaotic action of the running people in the previous shot is contrasted with the irreversible movement of the dead mother. The identity of her executioners is clearly established with the presence of the shadows. The formation of shadows of the soldiers is meant to visually contrast with the bodies of their innocent victims.**

Title #5   Cossacks

Shot #100   Same placement as shot #98. We now find that the presence of the horse in the earlier shot is the result of the czar's cavalry, or Cossacks, being brought into play. This parallel action indicates that the Odessa steps victims are surrounded by danger. Troops are firing from the top of the steps and Cossacks, armed with sabers, are attacking the individuals at the bottom. The people are rushing from right to left as the horses are moving left to right. 2 1/2 sec. **Rhythmic montage, overtonal montage, intellectual montage. The brutal and unnecessary treatment of the people by the czar's forces continues to be emphasized as new dangers to the victims are introduced.**

Shot #101   Match-on-action of movement of the horses, ELS at the bottom of the steps. As people run chaotically Cossacks on horses, enter from frame left, and attempt to systematically attack them. 5 sec. (Fig. 8.36). **Rhythmic montage, overtonal montage, intellectual montage. We continually are made aware of the fact that this is a calculated response by the army, against the people, and not some spontaneous action. The soldiers are being ordered to massacre their victims and are**

uninterested in pursuing any humanitarian alternative.

Shot #102   High angle LS of the line of troops, who shot the mother, moving down the steps to "squeeze" the pursuing victims between themselves and the Cossacks below. In the process of moving down the steps they walk over the bodies of mother and child as if they were merely another step. 6 sec. **Rhythmic montage, overtonal montage, intellectual montage. More evidence of the calculated efforts on the part of the military against the people.**

Shot #103   LS of wounded and dying victims, at the base of the steps, in front of a fence. Behind them people try to run past the fence to escape the Cossacks. 4 sec. **Rhythmic montage, overtonal montage, intellectual montage. More emphasis on the sense of entrapment the people are feeling in this situation. They are desperately trying to gain control of a situation full of chaos and frenzy. The viewer is being directed to take clear sides in this conflict.**

Shot #104   Parallel action, high angle shot of the woman with the scarf standing on some steps. 1 sec. **Rhythmic montage, intellectual montage, overtonal montage, metric montage. Now that the mother and child no longer are a theme in the upcoming events the director returns us to the parallel action of the visionary and her group. Metric montage is employed by reintroducing the group in a shot of relatively short duration. We last saw the woman self-confident and assuming control. We now see her in the midst of chaos.**

Shot #105   Low angle LS of a row of guns pointing down the steps. They fire. 1 sec. (Fig. 8.37). **Graphic montage, rhythmic montage, overtonal montage, intellectual montage. The primary focus in this image is on the guns. The disembodied soldiers are extensions of the weapons rather than vise versa. The carefully composed lines of the guns are in stark contrast to the composition of the confused group below. The strength and** authority of the guns, seen in this position, are juxtaposed to the vulnerable appearance of the peace advocates. The juxtaposition of these shots, and the nature of the previous events, bode ill for the visionary and her followers.

Shot # 106   Match-on-action, same placement as shot #104. All but the visionary are hit by bullets and fall around her feet. 2 sec. (Fig. 8.38). **Rhythmic montage, overtonal montage, intellectual montage, graphic montage. Eisenstein is clearly playing off the irony that the visionary is the only one who is not harmed by following her ill-conceived plan.**

Shot #107   Return to placement in shot #105. The killing machine continues to march down the steps. 1 sec.

As can be seen from our analysis of this sequence, Eisenstein's montage incorporates an editing strategy different from the system of decoupage employed in E.A. Dupont's *Variety*. With continuity editing the filmmaker works for harmonious transitions between shots. A concept, or theme, is established in a preceding shot and <u>continued</u> in the succeeding one. Montage is concerned with creating associations through the <u>juxtaposition</u> of shots. We are constantly being asked to make comparisons between the two shots and interpret what is happening as a result of this juxtaposition. Montage can be based on the tempo, or pacing, of footage through the alteration of the physical duration of the shots (metric montage). It may be developed from the manipulation of geometric patterns within the image (graphic montage) or the "darkness" or "lightness" of the compositions (tonal montage). Montage can also focus on the orchestration of emotional or intellectual responses of a viewer to the shots (overtonal and intellectual montage).

The complex ways a viewer can respond to the editing in the Odessa Steps Sequence from *Battleship Potemkin*, are indicative that Eisenstein's theory of montage works. He not only proved his approach to editing was a viable alternative to continuity editing, Sergei Eisenstein created a dynamic and exciting classic film in the process.

FRAME ENLARGEMENTS FROM THE ODESSA STEPS SEQUENCE IN *BATTLESHIP POTEMKIN*

8.5   Shot #1

8.6   Shot #2

8.7   Shot #3

8.8   Shot #4

8.9   Shot #5

8.10   Shot #6A

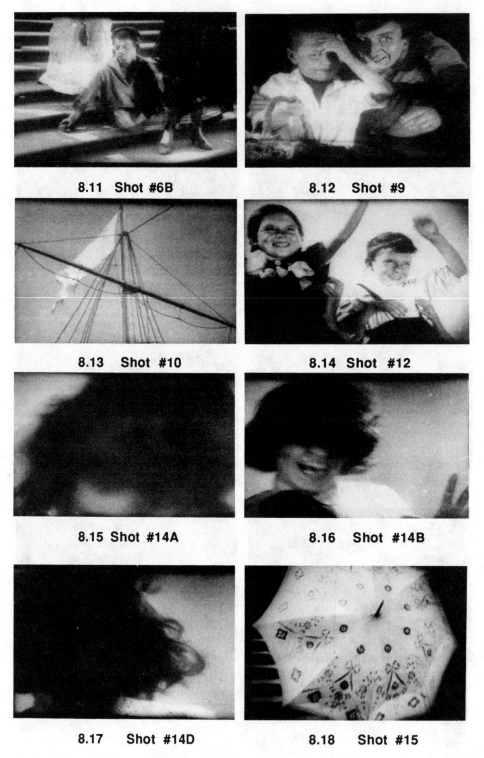

8.11　Shot #6B

8.12　Shot #9

8.13　Shot #10

8.14　Shot #12

8.15 Shot #14A

8.16　Shot #14B

8.17　Shot #14D

8.18　Shot #15

212

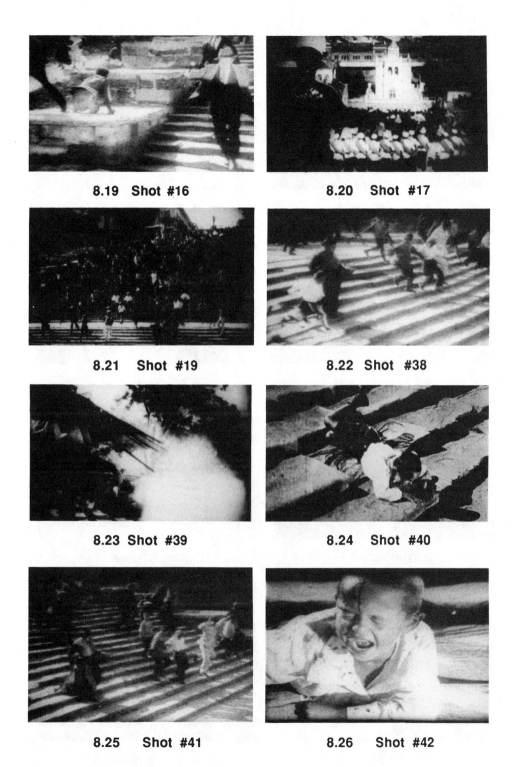

8.19 Shot #16

8.20 Shot #17

8.21 Shot #19

8.22 Shot #38

8.23 Shot #39

8.24 Shot #40

8.25 Shot #41

8.26 Shot #42

213

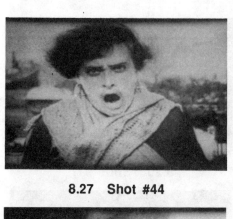

8.27　Shot #44

8.28　Shot #48

8.29　Shot #51

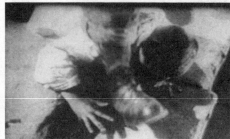

8.30　Shot #55

8.31 Shot #56

8.32　Shot #76

8.33　Shot #94

8.34　Shot #97

214

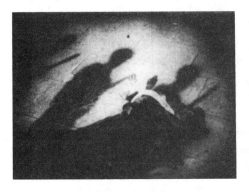

8.35 Shot #99

8.36 Shot #101

8.37 Shot #105

8.38 Shot #106

V. Summary

"Russian montage" was developed as an alternative to continuity editing. Continuity editing harmoniously establishes the connections between the parts of a film, while montage involves conflict. Rather than show spatial and temporal relationships, among the shots, montage bombards the viewer with disparate images. The unfinished nature of this type of cutting forces the spectator to complete the editing process in his or her mind. This is done by forming associations, among the parts of the film, based on the juxtapositions of the images.

Sergei Eisenstein did not invent the idea of "montage." He was the first filmmaker and theorist to systematically codify and film the various forms of montage which he isolated and identified in the middle 1920s. Radical and revolutionary in its day, Eisenstein's approach to editing forever changed the way filmmakers relate to their medium. Before the end of the decade, montage had become a standard tool of filmmaking in national cinemas around the world. Important and influential as it is, montage would not have the far-reaching impact on film aesthetics of another stylistic development of this time--the coming of sound.

CHAPTER NINE

"TALKING PICTURES" AND FILM GENRES

CHAPTER OBJECTIVES: *Examine the history and development of the "talking picture," identify the meaning of "film genre," and explore chronological changes relating to the genre of the movie musical.*

I.   Warner Brothers and the Introduction of the Sound Picture

In 1926 the Warner Brothers Studio realized Thomas Edison's dream by experimenting with commercially viable sound motion pictures. Interestingly, the studio did not envision using sound for <u>talking</u> pictures at first. Rather, they saw sound technology as a means for providing smaller theaters with music comparable to what audiences heard, when live orchestras accompanied silent movie projection, in large city auditoriums.

Silent films were not shown silently. In the smallest theaters a viewer would have watched films with piano accompaniment. Intermediate sized theaters showed their films with a Wurlitzer organ. In the largest urban theaters, one would watch a film with a full orchestra. Going to the movies, in the 1920s, was comparable to attending a concert. If a viable technology could be developed, Warner Brothers believed, the symphonic scores that the city audiences enjoyed could be reproduced in the smallest theaters across the country.

Though Edison and W.K.L. Dickson had experimented with sound in the early 1890s, and sound films did exist at the turn-of-the-century, none of these processes proved to be commercially feasible. Edison and Dickson had been able to mechanically synchronize their Kinetoscope with the Edison phonograph, but the system had problems. The excitement of seeing a sound picture, in a peepshow format, was not much greater than watching a silent movie. Combining a phonograph with the Kinetoscope increased the cost of the apparatus and greatly added to the complexity of its mechanics.

While sound movies could be shown, in the peepshow format of the Kinetoscope, projecting these films was not possible at first. The major problem was amplifying the sound. It was not until 1907, and the invention of the **audion tube** by Lee de Forest (1873-1961), that sound amplification was technically possible. With this process sound was translated into electrical impulses which were sent through the audion tube. This glass tube contained a metal filament, housed in a vacuum, which could amplify the electrical signals before they were sent through a speaker. The vibrations of the speaker retranslated the electrical impulses into recognizable sound. This invention did not affect just the development of the talkies. It also made possible the existence of radio and, later, television.

The technology began to be available for the development of talkies by 1907, but was not really explored as a commercial approach to filmmaking for another twenty years. Audiences appeared to be quite satisfied with silent movies at this time. The expense, and complexity, of adding this technology to filmmaking did not seem to be commercially worthwhile. There was not, in short, a recognizable market for sound films until the Warners discovered that there was one.

In 1926 the Warner Brothers produced a program of sound films. The program included some short subjects, using "lip-syncing sound," that preceded the feature film, *Don Juan*, which had a synchronized score. **"Synchronized sound"** refers to the precision matching of sound to image. **"Lip-syncing sound"** relates to the precise matching, or synchronizing, of sound to the movement of a person's mouth.

Don Juan was essentially a silent costume drama, involving castles and sword fights, starring John Barrymore--grandfather of the actress Drew Barrymore--in which the musical score and sound effects were added after the picture was shot. Although this process did not create many changes in the way the picture was filmed, the experiment was not cheap. Warner Brothers was very concerned that the failure, for sound pictures to catch on commercially, might break their company. Besides the expense of the technology for recording the sound in the studio, theaters had to be supplied with the appropriate speakers and projecting equipment for exhibition.

The reaction to *Don Juan* was positive and Warners embarked on a second sound feature, *The Jazz Singer*, starring the singer Al Jolson (1886-1950). Released in 1927, *The Jazz Singer* was also primarily a silent picture with a sound track added. Unlike *Don Juan*, *The Jazz Singer* featured some lip-synced segments involving songs which Jolson sang before the camera. During one of the numbers Jolson spoke the words, "You ain't heard nothing yet!" Meant to refer to more songs and music by the character Jolson was portraying in this movie, the line was used as a prediction for the future of the talkies.

The Jazz Singer proved to be a major hit and the demand for more talkies was immense. Warner Brothers had a head start in the production of sound pictures and became one of America's most financially successful studios of that period. Audiences, in the late 1920s and early 1930s, preferred the novelty of the technically crudest talkie to the most polished silent. Between 1927 and 1932, Hollywood made the transition from silent filmmaking to the manufacture of talking pictures.

217

It is interesting to speculate what would have happened to the history of the talkies if Warners had not made the transition to sound when the studio did. By 1929 America was hit by a major economic depression. At first the film industry was somewhat depression-proof because people were seeking entertainment as a means to forget their troubles. By 1932, however, people could not afford to go to the movies. Hollywood suffered major financial losses, during this year, and some of the studios went into receivership. No one had the revenue, nor would have dared the costly experiment, to test the commercial viability of talkies until after the depression. By then the country was involved in World War II. Experiments were being made with television at this same time. It would not be marketed until 1948. It is possible that talking pictures would not have been developed for another ten or even twenty years if the Warners had not decided to release *Don Juan* and *The Jazz Singer* before 1929..

Though Hollywood was not inclined towards making talkies before Warner's success, inventors had been continuously exploring the possibility of synchronizing sound with the moving image since Edison's experiments in the 1880s. By 1926 there were two basic technologies being used to obtain sync sound--the sound-on-disk and sound-on-film systems. The sound-on-disk system, which the Warner Brothers initially used, incorporated a phonograph in a manner similar to the procedure for exhibiting sound pictures that Edison and Dickson envisioned. A phonograph was mechanically connected to the projector and each reel of film was synchronized to a large record. Shooting a film, when using this process, was not without its problems.

Since the sound was cut directly on a record, it could not be easily edited. Once the record started to be cut, they could not stop and start the recording. The filmmakers had to shoot continuously for ten minutes until they reached the end of the reel. If someone made some mistake nine minutes into a scene, such as a performer stumbling over a line, the filmmakers had to stop and shoot everything all over again. If the director wanted to cut to another angle, he or she had to have two or more cameras continuously shooting the scene at the same time.

Technical modifications had to be made with the cameras as well. Instead of relatively small, fluid cameras, like those used for silent filmmaking, the talkies had to be shot with rather cumbersome stationary devices covered with soundproofing. This soundproofing material was necessary so that camera noise was not picked up by the microphones. It was so hot, in these soundproof boxes, that the cameraman was in danger of fainting. Shooting would have to stop, during intervals of half an hour or so, to allow the cameraman to revive.

Placement of the microphones was another problem. At times they were hidden in telephones, vases, and other props on the set. In one of the first sound westerns shot outdoors, a movie called *In Old Arizona* (1928), the microphone is said to have been hidden in a cactus. The way the actors positioned themselves to talk in front of these inanimate objects was not always realistic.

Such shooting conditions placed a fair degree of stress on the actors and actresses. Performers with European accents, certain American dialects, and high pitched voices could not always make the transition to talkies because of the way their speech sounded on film. There is a story that Frank Capra, one of the first directors to make sound films at Columbia, was troubled by a noise that continuously appeared on the soundtrack in the rushes of his early talkies. After some investigation Capra discovered that the actors were so nervous they were getting upset stomachs. This caused a rumbling which the microphone was picking up. Capra solved the problem by making sure there was plenty of ginger ale on the set during shooting.

All of these technical demands resulted in major aesthetic changes in the appearance of the movies. Given the fluid camerawork, intricate editing, and detailed composition relating to the film style of the late silents, the early talkies were, in fact, often aesthetically retrogressive. The bulky sound camera did not lend itself to movement--not even pans--and the resulting style was not dissimilar to the appearance of the 1907 version of *Ben Hur*. Actresses and actors had to perform in a restricted, space before the camera, creating a perspective similar to what a viewer would see while sitting in a seat in the middle of the theater. Most of the action was shot in the studio. During silent filming the director could shout directions over the camera. Now everything had to be quiet during the shooting of a scene. The result was a stagy, static, and very "talky" movie.

Though very popular in their time, most of the early talkies look technically crude and dated when viewed today. Audiences of the time enjoyed them, but the people making these movies were aware of their limitations. These filmmakers did not want to give up the aesthetic accomplishments achieved during the silent period. They sought to free the camera from the shooting restrictions imposed upon them by the technical limitations of their changing medium. New technologies and approaches to filming the talkies were sought. One major breakthrough was the sound-on-film process.

Experiments with the sound-on-film process were being conducted even before Warners decided to test the commercial feasibility of the sound-on-disk system. The sound-on-film system uses a technique in which sound vibrations are translated into a pulsating light focused on a portion of the unexposed movie film left for the sound track. As the light flashes, or pulsates, in accordance with the vibration of the sound, it exposes dark areas on the track, where there is no sound, and gray and white patterns where there is sound. These patterns represent a visual record of the various sounds imprinted on the film. When the film is projected it passes over a device called a "sound head" which is sensitive to light coming from a lamp, known as an "exciter bulb," located above it. As light from the exciter bulb hits the film it penetrates the light and dark areas of the sound track in accordance with their density. The sound head translates the pulsating light into electrical impulses. These electrical impulses are converted into sound when as the go through a "speaker."

While the fidelity of the sound-on-disk system might have initially been better, the sound-on-film process was more versatile in terms of filming, editing, and projection. One important advantage was that sound-on-film allowed the sound track to be edited. This meant that the filmmaker was no longer restricted to shooting everything in a long take. Also, part of a shot could be used in the finished film even if there might be problems with the rest of this particular footage. It was more difficult to salvage shots with problems filmed sound-on-disk.

Exhibition of the film was also easier with sound-on-film. With this system the projectionist did not have to worry about operating a phonograph player, working with the disks, putting reels of films on the projector, and keeping everything synchronized. The projector now handled both image and sound because everything was self-contained on the film. Unless sound and image had not been properly synchronized when initially printed on the film, the projectionist had little fear that the picture would lose lip-sync. By about 1932 or so the sound-on-film process became the norm and the sound-on-disk was no longer used. With the exception of formats that use a magnetic track, the optical sound-on-film process is still used today.

By 1932 filmmakers had regained much of the camera mobility and visual quality that marked the aesthetics of the silent movies. New microphones and sound systems had now been developed which made for a crisper sound track. The bulky soundproofing had been eliminated and the cameras, that once took up a good share of the studio space, were once again made portable. Filmmakers were also able to identify certain strategies to make the most of sound as a new element of filmic expression.

II. Aesthetics and Film Sound

As filmmakers began making talkies, they developed certain ways that sound could be utilized. All sound could be placed in two general categories--"**synchronous**" and "**asynchronous**" sound. These groupings were influenced, in part, by the way sound is recorded and mixed. "**Synchronous sound**," as we have indicated, is sound that matches the visual source--such as the lips of a speaker--which produces it. Film theorist David Bordwell has used the word "**diegetic**" as another term to identify this type of sound. "**Diegetic sound**" can be heard by the characters in the film and is indigenous to the visual setting that the viewer can see on the screen.

"**Asynchronous sound**" is usually not recorded at the time a scene is filmed but mixed in the soundtrack later. Very often asynchronous sound is <u>not</u> indigenous to the setting and is usually <u>not</u> heard by the characters on screen. Professor Bordwell has described this use of asynchronous sound as "**non-diegetic.**" Examples of non-diegetic sound would be an unseen narrator commenting about what is happening, on the screen, or background music which is added for mood. We normally would not expect to see a full orchestra in the desert during the chase scene in a western even though one often hears such music. There are, of course, exceptions. One does actually see Count Basie and his orchestra playing in the desert, in Mel Brooks's comic western *Blazing Saddles* (1973), at one point while we are watching the chase.

Within the two general contexts of diegetic and non-diegetic sound there are four general types of sounds which a filmmaker can use. These fairly self explained categories are (1) voice, (2) music, (3) sound effects, and (4) silence. All of these sounds can be used in conjunction with individuals and objects we see on screen, or to denote "**off-screen space.**"

"**Off-screen space**" literally refers to the space around the borders of the frame which the viewer can not see. Usually we do not consider this space because we are concentrating on what the filmmaker is asking us to look at in the frame. We assume that if there is something beyond the frame, with which we should be concerned, the director will bring it to our attention. This can do this by showing us the space with a new camera position or by suggesting its importance through a technique like "**off-screen sound.**"

When a film only focuses its attention on what is occurring in the frame, the area outside the frame lines can be referred to as "dead space." This dead space can be made more dynamic, and add to the information we get from a scene, through the use of off-screen sound. For example, we may have a situation involving two individuals, on camera, who are looking for a third person. This third character may suddenly reveal his or her presence through off-screen sound. In fact, the <u>distance</u> that person is from the other two can also be implied through the volume of this sound off-screen. The off-screen space that this person occupies, which we have not yet seen, may take on all sorts of meaning in our imagination. A whole new spatial dimension is made available for audience interaction, through this technique, which had little or no meaning before.

It is relatively easy for the viewer to envision off-screen space when the off-screen sound helping to define it is diegetic. Non-diegetic off-screen sound creates a more complicated perspective, from a spatial and philosophical standpoint. How do we relate to a disembodied voice? From what dimension is this authoritative narrator speaking? How is this "otherworldly" dimension connected to the space we are seeing on the screen? Does the fact that we cannot see the speaker give us a different perspective, of his or her presence, than if that individual was incorporated as a diegetic element?

As viewers we usually don't spend a great deal of time asking such questions. Critics and filmmakers are quite concerned about how we relate to, and are affected by, non-diegetic sound. Some documentary filmmakers, for example, dislike the idea of the disembodied voice because it implies a kind of "godlike" authority which tells the viewer how to respond to the content of the film. They claim it is better for the material on-screen to speak for itself, and for the audience to interpret it for themselves, rather than have an off-screen narrator tell them how to relate to the information.

The question of how we respond, or should challenge, the presence of the authoritative off-screen voice suggests that sound can be used in two general ways--for literal representation and for persuasion. "Literal sound" is concerned with conveying information to the audience--like dialogue where one person tells another that she is going to the store. An example of persuasive sound would be a situation where music is added to create the mood the filmmaker wants the viewer to feel. Very often, of course, the sound in a film is both literal and persuasive.

Needless to say the addition of sound to the filmmaker's stylistic tools greatly altered the appearance and form of the motion picture. The talkie was literally a different type of movie, than the silent, even though both worked with camerawork, editing, and mise-en-scene. Filmmakers had to learn new ways to express themselves, with this new medium, and the content of their films changed accordingly. One aspect of filmmaking greatly affected, by the coming of sound, was the form and content of the film genres in which the filmmakers now worked.

III. The Film Genre

"**Genre**" refers to narrative categories that several movies can be placed. Examples of film genres would be the gangster film, the horror movie, the western, science fiction, and the musical. "**Genre criticism**" involves the study of films seen as belonging to these particular groups. A movie like *The Great Train Robbery* of 1903, for example, can be compared with *Butch Cassidy and the Sundance Kid* made sixty-five years later, because of common generic themes and elements. In this instance both films contain a train robbery and the blowing up of a safe--a familiar situation in westerns from the earliest days. The genre critic takes such films as a group, and determines how and why they are similar or different.

One thing that the critic, and the viewer, considers when watching a genre film are its "conventions." A "**convention**" is a common trait associated with a particular genre. Genre conventions may be an object, image, a type of behavior, or narrative theme. A cowboy hat, the American desert with the western hero riding off into the sunset, and the shoot-out between the good guy and bad guy at high noon are all examples of western conventions.

One complaint about genre films is that they sometimes seem to be variations of the same movie. Even the most loyal fan can find it a bit tedious when it takes the characters most of the movie to figure out that their friends are dying from vampire bites, who Dracula is, or what they need to do to kill him. Clearly a genre can not just rely on convention if it is going to keep an audience. Genres can go out of favor until someone comes up with a new way to tell an old story. It may be several years between major westerns, musicals or gangster films because viewers have become tired of this type of movie. Yet, as critics have pointed out, genre films are not always the same. The fact that there are differences, between *The Great Train Robbery* of 1903 and *Butch Cassidy and the Sundance Kid* of 1968, suggests that genres do experience changes over time.

Whenever a director comes across a new element for a genre film we have an "**invention**." *Butch Cassidy and the Sundance Kid*, for example, is in color and has sound whereas *The Great Train Robbery* is silent. Sometime between 1903 and 1968 sound and color changed the appearance of black and white silent westerns. The anecdote we discussed in Chapter Two, about the same song played over and over again in *High Noon*, is another example of an invention in the western. After 1952 the incorporation of a theme song in a western became a familiar convention within this genre. We might think of the song "Raindrops Keep Falling on My Head," in *Butch Cassidy and the Sundance Kid*, or the familiar music in the "spaghetti westerns" starring Clint Eastwood--*A Fistful of Dollars* (1964) and *For a Few Dollars More* (1965)--as examples. When an invention is repeated in succeeding movies, to the point that it is familiar, it has become recognized as another convention.

One last major concept associated with genre criticism, that we will consider, is the "**symbol**" or "**icon**." When a convention takes on significance or meaning beyond its surface appearance, or function, it becomes more than a repeated element within the genre. Professor David Bordwell has used the word "**icon**" to describe the phenomenon of what happens to a convention when it takes on symbolic meaning. This use of the term "icon" is a reference to a type of sacred painting associated with the Russian Eastern Orthodox religion. These religious paintings--or icons--are seen as symbolic of the religious subjects that they visually portray. Given this connection to a venerated figure, such as Jesus or Mary, the icon is more than just a painting. It is a sacred extension of the subject it represents. While they obviously do not contain the same religious significance as the Russian icon, certain movie conventions are also recognized for having a kind of symbolic meaning.

A cowboy's white hat, for example, is no longer considered just an article of apparel in a western. It is now considered representative, or symbolic, of the hero's purity. Another western symbol is the notched six-gun. The notches are symbolic of the prowess of the person who has shot it. In some instances a person can even become "iconic." Real life gunmen Jesse James, Billy the Kid, Wild Bill Hickock, and Wyatt Earp have taken on mythic proportions in the western. Because of his unique personality and recognizable philosophy, the actor John Wayne (1907-1979) also achieved the status of an icon. At the height of his popularity no other actor could give a film character the same dimensions, values, or perspective that John Wayne could. Audiences, in fact, watch John Wayne westerns with certain expectations in mind. The convention makes a genre familiar. The icon, or symbol, gives a convention extended layers of meaning.

Most movie genres existed in another medium before being adapted to the screen. Conventions in the western genre were being developed in "dime novels," paintings, plays, and "wild west shows" even before the motion picture was invented. The western, horror story, and gangster genres experienced further change when modified to meet the demands of silent filmmaking. As with every other type of movie, these genres underwent even greater transformation with the coming of talkies. One genre particularly affected by the emergence of the talkies was the musical-- a genre which, obviously, could not exist on film prior to the advent of sound.

IV. Sound and the Early Movie Musical

The musical, as a genre, developed on stage before it evolved on film. When Hollywood found that the talkies were a fact of life, they looked to the New York stage as a source for film product. In the late 1920s numerous musicals, which had just finished their run or were still being produced, were purchased for the screen. Often the performers associated with them were hired as well. The Marx Brothers filmed their musical *Coconuts* (1929) in a New York studio during the day while performing their hit *Animal Crackers* on Broadway at night. When *Animal Crackers* finished its stage run, it became the vehicle for their second sound film. The rest of the films the

Marx Brothers made were based on original scripts and shot in Hollywood. Numerous other New York actors, directors, and writers made the transition to Hollywood at this time. James Cagney, Humphrey Bogart, Edward G. Robinson, George Burns and Gracie Allan, were just a few of the stage performers who began successful careers in the early talkies.

Obviously there were only so many stage musicals which could be adapted for the screen. One form of musical which Hollywood made to supplement their adaptations of Broadway shows, in the late '20s' and early '30s', was a format sometimes described as the "all star revue." The all star revue was a kind of variety presentation in which a master of ceremonies introduced several numbers in the course of the movie. There generally was no real plot in these films. The MC and various acts would openly address the camera. The performances might involve an elaborate chorus routine, led by a star, or a modestly staged magic act, in which Laurel and Hardy messed up the tricks.

As had been the case with the early Edison movies, which tried to attract viewers on the basis of novelty, audiences eventually tired of the all talking, all singing, all dancing musicals. The content of too many of these musicals were uninspired and film patrons became bored with them. If depression audiences decided to spend money on a movie, by 1932, they were more discriminating about what they would see. The musical went into a decline, about this time, until some innovative filmmakers found the necessary inventions to bring it back as a popular genre. Once again it was Warner Brothers that came up with a new approach to filmmaking.

In 1933 Warners produced a picture entitled *42nd Street*, directed by Lloyd Bacon. *42nd Street* was not meant to be a musical so much as it was a story about the lives of people, and the process behind, putting on a show. The musical numbers were saved for the big show at the end of the movie. It was these creative productions which helped infuse new interest in the genre. Choreographed by a former drill sergeant, named Busby Berkeley (1895-1976), the dance routines featured scantily clad chorus girls performing kaleidoscopic patterns obtained through the positioning of their arms and legs. These images often were captured by suspending the camera above the stage while the dancers achieved these movements lying on their backs. These self-contained numbers--which had little or no relation to the film's overall story--contained images, short narratives, and special effects which make them forerunners of today's music videos. While interesting from a cinematic standpoint, there is no way that the people sitting in the theater could have seen these routines from the perspective we see on the screen. Despite this contradiction, the audience in the movie applauded enthusiastically. Movie-goers were enthusiastic as well.

Based on the success of *42nd Street*, Bacon and Berkeley went on

225

to produce a number of musicals of this type for Warners, individually or as a team. Their "gold digger" series (*Gold Diggers of 1933*, *Gold Diggers of 1935*, and *Gold Diggers of 1937*) particularly became associated with the formula which made these musicals so popular. As with *42nd Street*, this "formula plot" consists of the behind-the-scene lives of show business people--the poor chorus girls and hoofers as well as the rich backers. The narratives are usually quite forgettable because the principal point of these musicals is the elaborate, often surreal, numbers performed at the end. What attracted the movie-goer was the suggestive dialogue; the scantily clad chorus line; the catchy music; and the cinematic, imaginative, and spectacular staging of the climactic musical numbers. Not everyone, of course, appreciated the suggestive dialogue and scantily clad chorus lines. As we shall see in Chapter Ten, this type of musical underwent substantial change when a wave of censorship influenced the content of American film, after 1935.

The Warners musicals juxtaposed the gritty, and decidedly unglamorous, world in which the chorus girl and hoofer lived, with the elaborate spectacles they were involved with on stage. A much different world could be found in the RKO musicals of Fred Astaire (1899-1987) and Ginger Rogers (b. 1911) being made at this time. While the RKO musicals are usually identified with both Rogers and Astaire, it was the latter who was largely responsible for their choreography. The first film in which Astaire and Rogers appeared together was *Flying Down to Rio* (1933). They finished their collaboration with *The Story of Vernon and Irene Castle* (1939). Interestingly, Ginger Rogers also appeared in *42nd Street* . Though *42nd Street* is often credited with revitalizing the genre in the early 1930s, an equal case can be made for the importance of the Astaire and Rogers musicals at RKO.

Where the Warners musicals had a depression-affected America influencing its content, the RKO musicals showed a world of glamour and wealth. The chorus line established the principal kind of music in the Bacon and Berkeley musicals. The Ginger Rogers and Fred Astaire films often centered on variations of ballroom dancing. Berkeley and Bacon saved the best music for the end of the film. Astaire and Rogers performed intricate and often glamorous numbers throughout the entire movie. There is a sense of realism reflected, at times, in the Warners films. The RKO musicals are pure fantasy throughout.

As with the Warner musicals, the plots of the Astaire and Rogers films are often slight. Fred sees Ginger and, after a lot of resistance and misunderstanding, they dance happily away at the end of the movie. Both people are usually incredibly well off, financially. Their hotel rooms have the space of small auditoriums. The amount of money spent on their clothing, it seems, would have comfortably supported a middle class family of four through much of the depression. Why depression-racked America wanted to see such movies has intrigued scholars for decades. The most common answer is that viewers wanted escapist fantasy to help them temporarily forget the harsh economic realities thwarting most peoples' lives at this time.

By 1933 filmmakers had overcome many of the technical problems they had been experiencing with sound. Directors and choreographers, like Berkeley and Astaire, were no longer interested in re-staging musicals done on the Broadway stage as a kind of "canned theater"--a limitation of many of the earliest musicals. They sought to explore ways to combine sound with the properties of the cinema to make the musical cinematic. The talkies, by this time, had regained much of the aesthetic quality of the late silents. The camera was more mobile and less stage bound. Montage and continuity editing could be executed as smoothly as they had been employed in the late 1920s. Set designers and actors once again had more options regarding how they would manipulate the mise-en-scene. Rather than a restrictive element, sound provided new aesthetic avenues for the filmmaker to explore. A brief review of one of the Astaire and Rogers musicals of the period, *Top Hat* (1935), directed by Mark Sandrich, reveals how the other elements of film style could be influenced by sound.

V. Film Sound and the Aesthetics of *Top Hat* (1935)

Top Hat depends upon the polish and fluidity of its film techniques for its particular form. It is so much a musical that the visuals and narrative are orchestrated to flow with the songs. This relationship of camerawork, editing, and mise-en-scene to sound is clearly established at the beginning of the film.

The plot of *Top Hat* is slight. Fred Astaire plays a famous song and dance man named Jerry Travers. In the opening scene Jerry is waiting for his friend, Horace, at the latter's club. Ironically Jerry, who is associated with lively activity and song, is severely restricted by the club's insistence on quiet. Even the slightest noise that Jerry makes is met with irritation by the clubs elderly and elegantly dressed members. The use of silence in a talking picture very much draws attention to itself in this opening scene. When Horace finally comes, to take his friend away from this situation, Jerry gets even for being made to feel uncomfortable. As they are leaving Jerry breaks into a loud tap dance which throws the whole club into a state of disruption. The mise-en-scene in this opening scene, and the comic emphasis involving the sound, quickly establishes the fact that this a highly stylized movie. The director has immediately developed a very unrealistic, artificial, even comic atmosphere which is continued throughout the rest of

227

the picture.

After utilizing a "silent" scene to begin a talking picture, *Top Hat* uses sound and music to link all the parts, characters, and elements of the narrative. Jerry's life is almost totally involved in dancing. His pent-up energy seems to constantly want to release itself by having him break into a dance. He disrupts the silence of the club with his tapping. Later, when he dances in Horace's hotel room, he disturbs Gale Fremont (played by Ginger Rogers), whom he does not know, who is trying to sleep in the room beneath. This "musical disruption" is a means of introducing Gale's character as the love of Jerry's dreams. Our hero's tendency to disturb people, at this point in the film, is played as a humorous contrast to Fred Astaire's image of polish and sophistication.

We soon see that Jerry's proclivity for bothering people is not really part of his character. Jerry is basically a likable and charming man. If he gets carried away with his singing and dancing its because he is so full of essentially positive energy. Jerry's infectious and lighthearted spirit, reflected in the nature of the songs to which he sings and dances, exists as a dominant theme in the film. His ability to infect others with his ebullient spirit is demonstrated by an audience's enthusiastic response to a dance act he does on stage. Though irritated with him at first, Ginger Rogers's heroine is soon taken with Jerry as, indeed, he is with her.

The next day Gale tries to find out more about the charming young man who disturbed her sleep. She discovers, to her regret, that the person who has the room above her is Horace, the husband of Madge, one of her best friends. When Jerry tries to become better acquainted with Gale she wards off his advances because, unbeknownst to anyone, she thinks he is Horace. Her behavior puzzles Jerry because he can not understand why she does not find him charming like everyone else in the picture. The more he tries to charm her the more attracted to Jerry she becomes. This makes Gale feel guilty because of her friendship with Horace's wife.

Finally Gale feels compelled to tell her friend about Horace's behavior. Madge does not give any credence to the charge at first. Eventually she comes to believe that Horace is trying to have an affair, behind her back, and blackens her husband's eye. The likable and devoutly monogamous Horace is now even more befuddled, if possible, than he was before. After everyone becomes involved in numerous other complications, based on this misunderstanding, Madge eventually figures out what has happened and explains the situation to the other characters. Instead of apologizing to Horace, however, she suggests that he take the black eye as a lesson--as if he ever needed one.

While the comic plot in *Top Hat* is slight, it does not mean the film is not good. This light, funny, and improbable story is less integral to the form of the film than the music and dance numbers. It is the music, more than the plot, which dictates the structure of *Top Hat*. In essence the music is designed to do three basic things: (1) Establish the romantic spirit and highly stylized nature of the film. (2) Underscore the personalities and conflicts surrounding the love interests. (3) Keep the mood of the film as pleasant and flowing as possible. The form and effect of the music really sets the tone of *Top Hat*, while the other filmic elements are shaped, and made subordinate, to it.

All elements of the motion picture are organized to make the mood of *Top Hat* light and cheerful. Even when the characters' spirits are at their lowest we have no doubt about the film's eventual happy and romantic outcome. The dialogue is witty and good-natured. The integration of the songs, and the mood of the music, reflects the characters' attitudes and emotional states. The highs and lows of Jerry and Gale's romantic involvement are highlighted by the music. When they feel something, more often than not, they will burst into a song and dance that reflects their feelings, accompanied by a symphony orchestra that can be either diegetic or non-diegetic. The fact that they can hear this music, when other characters in the film probably can not, merely underscores the sense of fantasy which governs their world.

The style of *Top Hat* is meant to be as smooth and flowing as the music which sets its mood. Overlapping sound is often used between scenes and sequence, linking the two segments in a fluid manner. The editing, too, is designed to minimize abrupt transitions from part to part. Visual dissolves are often incorporated so that the action can proceed smoothly from one scene to the next. The camera, which usually is quite mobile, is also utilized to add to this flowing effect. It often is choreographed, like a dancer, to move with the music.

Much more could be said about the aesthetics of this film. We will conclude our discussion by repeating that what makes *Top Hat* so interesting, for our purposes, is its use of sound in developing this movie's particular form. The film is structured through its songs. The songs set the mood for the picture, help establish the personalities of the characters, indicate their feelings and conflicts, and tell us how their problems are resolved at the end. The three elements of style so important to silent filmmaking--camerawork, editing, and mise-en-scene--are subordinate to, and complementary with, the newly explored fourth element of sound in this most musical of early Hollywood musicals.

VI. The Movie Musical as a Genre after 1935

The post-*42nd Street* 1930s musical was characterized by unrealistic cinematic effects designed to provide depression audiences with escapism entertainment. Innovative, technically polished, and fun, this type of musical no longer was as popular by the end of the decade. As we noted earlier, certain elements in American society took exception to aspects of the Warners Bacon and Berkeley musicals--a reflection of how genres must change with the times and are a reflection of the period which produces them. The end of the depression, and the advent of World War II, demanded a different type of entertainment from that desired in the 1930s..

The content of the American musicals of the 1940s was marked by patriotism, national pride, and nostalgia. Many musical narratives centered around a number of dancers and singers playing members of the armed forces, appearing on stage in rousing numbers, and supporting America's war efforts in a format similar to the earlier all star revue. Historians and critics usually view these musicals as interesting artifacts of the time rather than "classic" pictures. The cliché of "Lets put on a show!" is often associated with an overused convention employed by the musicals of this period.

One of the best musicals of this time was *Meet Me in St. Louis* (1944), directed by Vincente Minnelli and starring Judy Garland. Filmed in color and set in a St. Louis of the 1890s, *Meet Me in St. Louis* was a nostalgic celebration of the family and America's past. Its memorable tunes, excellent use of color and set design, and appealing performances enables this film to still be enjoyable to audiences today. *Meet Me in St. Louis* was produced for MGM by Arthur Freed (1894-1973), and is representative of the kind of film which this producer became famous for in the 1940s and 1950s. Freed's unit at MGM, in fact, developed some of the most successful Hollywood musicals of all time.

The talent that Freed was able to utilize, at MGM, was one reason for the success of his musicals. Fred Astaire, Gene Kelly, Judy Garland, and Leonard Bernstein are just a few of the names who collaborated on MGM musicals of this period. Because of competition from the new medium of television, Hollywood felt compelled to give audiences an experience in the theater which they could not enjoy at home. Television screens at this time were very small and only showed programs in black and white. Hollywood's answer, in the 1950s, was to produce films in color, wide-screen, and sometimes 3D, featuring stories that involved fantasy and spectacle. The musical particularly lent itself to this type of movie.

As with the Astaire and Rogers films of the 1930s, the MGM musicals were developed as cinematic vehicles for the screen. A great deal of pride was demonstrated in the technique and polish relating to the way the film medium was used. Particular attention was paid to color and set design, with the purpose of making these films a feast for the eyes. Where Astaire's earlier musicals concentrated on an upper-class make-believe world of elegance and ballroom dancing, the fantasy settings and stories for these later pictures vary greatly. *An American in Paris* (1951) featured George Gershwin's music in an idealized Paris. *Brigadoon* (1954) takes place in a completely magical world. *Singin' in the Rain* (1952) was set in a Hollywood of 1929, and features a thoroughly enjoyable fabrication of the problems the industry had in making the transition from silent movies to talkies. Though these pictures were quite successful, Hollywood shifted away from this kind of musical by the middle of the decade.

By the late 1950s and early 1960s filmmakers once again decided to look more to Broadway for material for their musicals than develop properties of their own. *Oklahoma!* (1955), *South Pacific* (1958), *West Side Story* (1962), *My Fair Lady* (1964), and *The Sound of Music* (1965) are examples of stage musicals adapted for the screen at this time. Produced for large sums of money, these films took advantage of the fact that audiences were aware of the music before the property was even made into a picture. All of these movies were quite popular and, *The Sound of Music* in particular, made the studios a substantial financial return. This prompted Hollywood to continue the strategy in the latter part of the 1960s with disastrous results. Films like *Star* (1968) and *Good-bye Mr. Chips* (1969) lost millions and Hollywood ended up wanting to avoid the genre altogether.

As we have noted, to be successful a genre must change with the times. There were at least three reasons why the Hollywood musical suddenly became unpopular after the middle 1960s. One reason was that audiences just did not find many of these films all that appealing. Another problem was that Hollywood was doing the same thing it had done in the early 1930s--making too many pictures of the same type and viewers had grown tired of them. A third consideration is the social condition of the country at this time. America was involved in the Vietnam War. The youth were finding their own culture and music while Hollywood was concentrating on musical formats rapidly becoming associated with an older generation.

The musical, as a genre, did not die in the 1960s, but it underwent some major transformations. Some of the most successful music films from this time were not traditional musicals as much as they were motion pictures--often in documentary format--involving concerts. In some respects the Beatles film *A Hard Days Night* (1964), which was made in England, might be seen as a transitional picture of this period.

A Hard Day's Night is a wacky, unrealistic account of a day in the

231

life of the Beatles. This film is very conscious of cinematic techniques but does not utilize them in the slick and highly polished manner of the musicals we have been discussing. Rather, *A Hard Day's Night* draws attention to zooms and flashbacks, for comic purposes, in much the way that we described the "camp" television series *Batman* in Chapter Six--a program which *A Hard Day's Night* and the Beatles' second film *Help!* (1965) undoubtedly influenced. After being chased by adoring fans, and engaging in comic exchanges, the Beatles at one point rush on stage to perform some numbers. They no more than get through their set when the mob of fans appear and the Beatles rush out again. The tongue-in-cheek, almost home movie, atmosphere of the film enabled audiences to enjoy the personalities of the Beatles, and their music, without having to try and make sense about how their world and the film's plot operated. The Beatles continued this approach, in short films developed around their songs, in a format we now call music videos.

A Hard Day's Night was a fresh way of making a motion picture which allowed fans to enjoy the Beatles and their music. Their second film, *Help!*, does not work quite as well. *Help!* looks more like a film where everyone is self-consciously trying to imitate cartoon characters than a picture designed to showcase these musicians and their music. We get a much better sense of this type of artist; the appeal of their music; and the actual interaction of music, musician and fans; in specialized documentaries that documented concerts of this period. D.A. Pennebaker's *Don't Look Back* (1965) is a "behind the scenes" account of a Bob Dylan tour. Albert and David Maysles' *Gimme Shelter* (1971) documents a death at a Rolling Stones concert. Martin Scorsese's *The Last Waltz* (1979) captures a farewell tour of The Band. The most famous of these concert musicals was Michael Wadleigh's *Woodstock* (1970). The last Beatles film, *Let it Be* (1972), was also a non-fiction picture. It documented some of their last recording sessions as a group.

The music documentaries of the 1960s and 1970s avoided the musical's tendency of creating an artificial world for enjoying the music. Instead they focused on actual musical events involving people enjoying the music. A problem with this format is that there are only so many ways one can film a concert. Its future was limited. Audiences avoided many of the movie "blockbuster" Broadway stage adaptations in the late 1960s, but that did not mean it was the end of the musical as a fictional genre. Nor did it mean that stage musicals could no longer be adapted for the screen.

One of the most successful film director/choreographers, to achieve commercial and critical success in the 1970s, was Bob Fosse (1927-1987). His *Cabaret* (1972), starring Liza Minnelli, mixed music with realism to create a thought provoking musical about the rise of Nazism in Hitler's Germany. This perspective went against the musical's traditional approach of being "light and charming," in a manner that was more in keeping with the period's interest in social concerns. Fosse's *All That Jazz* (1979) is also a film with a bleak message.

In some respects *All That Jazz* is based on the old convention of, "Hey, lets put on a show!" and is reminiscent of the plot of *42nd St.* As with the earlier film, *All That Jazz* deals with the trials and tribulations of the principal choreographer putting on a show. In this picture, however, the choreographer is a self-destructive workaholic who pops pills and plays Russian roulette with a bad heart. This condition provides a grim contrast to the sense of fun we usually associate with dance numbers. The fact that this is an autobiographical work--the part played by Roy Scheider is based on Bob Fosse himself--makes *All That Jazz* even more disturbing.

Milos Foreman (b. 1932) is another director who was able to make successful musicals at this time. His *Hair* (1979) was an interesting adaptation of the popular stage production from the 1960s. With *Amadeus* (1984) Foreman not only brought a play to the screen, he showed Mozart as a personality who could be appreciated by audiences who otherwise would not be interested in the life of a classical composer.

The 1980s was a decade interested in break dancing and MTV, yet not a lot of this popular culture reached the big screen in the form of musicals. *Flashdance* (1983), a story about a working-class girl trying to be taken seriously as a dancer, did well at the box-office but did not inspire successful imitators. It also dated very quickly and does not stand up well today. *Dirty Dancing* (1987) is one of the last musical of this decade to do well commercially. Like *Hair* and *Amadeus*, *Dirty Dancing* was not really concerned with adapting current music and dance forms to the screen.

So far the 1990s have not contributed any really innovative musicals to the screen if we limit ourselves to films involving live actors. As some critics have pointed out, the most successful musical format of our decade is the animated film produced by Disney. *The Little Mermaid* (1989), *Beauty and the Beast* (1991), and *Aladdin* (1992) use conventions we associate with the musical as a genre. Also, since nothing in a cartoon "is real," the animated musical is less apt to be criticized when non-diegetic music comes from nowhere whenever the hero and/or heroine burst into song. Like every other genre, the musical of the future can be expected to take on new permutations to meet the interests of a changing contemporary audience.

VII. Summary

The ability to combine sound with filmic image created an entire new dimension of expression in the motion picture medium. Once audiences recognized this element they no longer were satisfied with films that did not "talk." Today the uniqueness of seeing a film without sound, for most viewers, is as great as the novelty audiences experienced when hearing the first talkies. Since there no longer was a market for silent movies, Hollywood frantically made the transition to talking pictures between 1927 and 1932. The technical change was generally accomplished by 1929, but it took another three years before most filmmakers were proficient with this new form of exposition.

While all film genres were influenced by the coming of sound, the musical was the most affected. Musicals had existed on the stage before 1927, but the movies had no real equivalent genre before then. Though the musical was very popular as a result of the novelty of sound, filmmakers soon found that this format had to be adapted to reflect the changing tastes and interests of the film audience. Over the years the movie musical, like every other genre, has had to rework its conventions and symbols and come up with workable inventions to function as a viable form of filmic expression. Because genre films are constantly changing, while in some ways also staying the same, the critic can look at these old films and identify the tastes, attitudes, and interests of the societies for whom they were intended.

Audiences have interests and expectations regarding film that can change over time. On occasion some people do more than dislike certain movies and subject matter. They do not want to see this material and do not think anyone else should view it either. As we noted, Busby Berkeley and Lloyd Bacon had to modify aspects of their kind of musical, after 1935, because of protests from some segments of American society. In Chapter Ten we will explore the problems and history of film censorship, in America, and consider how it has affected the content of the Hollywood movie.

CHAPTER TEN

FILM CENSORSHIP

CHAPTER OBJECTIVES: *Examine the questions and problems behind censorship and its history in American film.*

I. Censorship

As we have seen, the motion picture is a medium of communication which carries messages to an audience. Viewers experience an emotional, intellectual, and physiological involvement with the medium when assimilating these messages. This process has an effect on a person, but no one can knows exactly what this influence entails. We may, for example, forget the content of a movie in a matter of days or have memories of it for the rest of our lives. Since each of us responds differently to a film, these memories may be positive or negative. Censorship is concerned with limiting the content of the motion picture when certain critics claim the effect is bad.

Movies have always been controversial. There have been people who have complained about the content of films almost from the time the first moving picture was shown to the public. What subject matter should be limited in film, how it should be limited, and who determines and enforces these restrictions are questions which are continuously debated. They have never been resolved to everyone's satisfaction and probably never will. By reviewing the issues and history we can, however, get a sense of how the responsible film consumer should deal with the important subject of film censorship.

There are two general positions which people have taken in the debate regarding what should or should not be shown in the movies. The most conservative argument is that there are some subjects which are objectionable and should not be shown at all. The opposite position is that audiences should decide for themselves what they want to see. This latter argument is often linked with the right to freedom of speech. As is invariably the case, the subject is much more complicated than these two rather simply stated positions suggest.

Clearly there are situations and subjects which society and the responsible film consumer does not want to have on film. Child pornography exploits those people's rights, as individuals, at an age when they can not properly exercise control over their own lives. Society must protect children from abuse in those instances when certain adults will not.

Our example relating to child pornography is one of the few instances, relating to film censorship, where groups advocating either censorship or free speech would be in general agreement. Adherents of freedom of speech would accede that any privilege must be limited when it infringes upon another right. One's right to carry arms, for example, does not give a person the freedom to limit the life, liberty, and pursuit of happiness of others by shooting them. Everyone's basic freedoms must be protected even if it means limiting certain other freedoms.

Censorship based on the infringement of other rights is sometimes justified. It is not so easy to defend calls for censorship when the infringement of these other rights is not so clear. Let us take a situation where children are involved as viewers rather than as participants in a film. We all know that children respond to film and television differently than adults. It is possible for a child to have frightening nightmares, after watching a movie, while most grownups could see the same film without experiencing any problem. Does this fact give censorship advocates the right to say that society must protect children, from these movies, because some adults will not? We justified banning the production of child pornography films on these grounds. Why not censor scary movies as well?

In our "scary movie" example the argument of the infringement of children's rights is certainly less valid than in the situation involving child pornography. By preventing scary movies from being made, because some child might see them, we are depriving a potential adult audience from viewing that subject. To say that a film should be censored because someone objects to it, or that all movies should be made for children, severely limits what this medium can do. Some censorship advocates might not have problems with this. Freedom of speech adherents would argue that such censorship limits the exchange of ideas and is an infringement on the rights of other audiences.

Social responsibility should be at the heart of any debate regarding censorship. Those involved in such debates are often concerned about how a given medium can best serve society. Unrestricted use of the media, it has been argued, can result in the infringement of some people's rights and lead to the perpetuation of values--or lack thereof--which are not in society's best interests. Censorship can control content but it stifles dialogue and debate in the process. Dictatorships rely heavily on censorship to control what they want people under their rule to believe. Alternative viewpoints may not be popular and even objectionable, but they still provide perspectives for the conscientious person to make balanced judgments in pursuit of the truth.

Ultimately censorship involves the limitation of freedom. A society may sometimes deem this loss of freedom as necessary. It should not surrender this freedom lightly. To give up fire, because someone might get

236

burned, means losing all the positive things that can be done with this force. Restricting or doing away with any form of expression, which is what censorship is designed to do, is not a desirable goal. It is always better to use freedom responsibly rather than lose it altogether. Rather than have the censor dictate what we see, the responsible film consumer should assume the obligation of ascertaining the accessibility, quality, and content of the message.

One way a society defines itself is by what it decides to censor. Historians can determine the values and priorities of a society by examining its censorship policies and analyzing the content of the films which viewers wanted and/or were allowed to see in a given period of history. The following historical overview of American film censorship is concerned with three issues. First, it enables us to get a sense of social priorities and contemporary feelings about film in the United States, from its origins to the present. Secondly, this examination addresses the problems and concerns relating to censorship that affected film content and society in the past. Finally, and perhaps most importantly, it is concerned with making us question our own attitudes and social responsibility regarding how film should be used today.

II. Early Film Censorship in America up to the "Mutual Decision," 1893-1915

One of the first films to create a "scandal" was the 1896 Vitascope short entitled *The May Irwin-John C. Rice Kiss* or, as it usually was referred to, *The Kiss*. The two actors--mentioned in the longer film title-- appeared in a Broadway play entitled *The Widow Jones*. Film historian Terry Ramsaye described their stage activities in his book, *A Million and One Nights* as follows:

> *The Widow Jones* had its high moment in a prolonged kiss between the principals. It was one of those persisting, adhesive osculations, doubtless made more delightful by the sweeping model of the hero's mustache, a hirsute ornamentation of the type which reached its zenith among British Cavalry officers in India and among the Texas Rangers. It was also a high-vacuum kiss, attended at its conclusions by sounds reminiscent of a steer pulling a foot out of the gumbo at the edge of a water hole. It was in brief--and in length--the world's greatest kiss as of that date.

Vitascope saw commercial potential in the kiss but were not interested in the rest of the play. The company was able to get the two stars to perform the kiss in front of the camera and made it into a film. *The Kiss* was fifty feet in length which would have been under a minute in playing time. It was, however, a major film hit in 1896.

Not everyone liked the film. Herbert S. Stone, who published a periodical in Chicago, was less than enchanted with *The Kiss*. He was to write:

> In a recent play called *The Widow Jones* you may remember a famous kiss which Miss May Irwin bestowed on a certain John C. Rice and vice versa. Neither participant is physically attractive, and the spectacle of their prolonged pasturing on each other's lips was hard to bear. When only life size it was pronounced beastly. But that was nothing to the present sight. Magnified to gargantuan proportions and repeated three times over it is absolutely disgusting. All delicacy or remnant of charm seems gone from Miss Irwin, and the performance comes near to being indecent in its emphasized vulgarity. Such things call for police interference. Our cities from time to time have spasms of morality when they arrest people for displaying lithographs of ballet-girls; yet they permit, night after night, a performance which is infinitely more degrading. . . . The Irwin kiss is no more than a lyric of the Stock Yards. While we tolerate such things, what avails all the talk of American Puritanism and of the filthiness of imported and English and French stage shows? [1]

Criticisms of this sort are indicative of the type of public propriety expected of Americans and their entertainment at this time. Eventually American attitudes would change regarding middle-aged couples kissing on screen. The intensity of the challenges being made, against certain subjects on film, would not.

Another early incident, relating to a call for film censorship, concerned a nickelodeon short usually identified as *Fatima's Dance*. "Fatima" was one of the sensations of the Chicago Columbian Exposition of 1893. Her specialty was a belly dance. In keeping with the dress styles of the day, Fatima wore a long skirt that nearly touched the ground. Her blouse had long sleeves that went to the end of her wrists and its neck covered her throat. One could see her face and hands. Where Fatima's clothing was different, from most women's apparel, was that her navel region was also exposed.

The Edison Company heard about the excitement regarding Fatima's exposed navel and decided to make a film of her dance in 1897 which, like their other subjects, ran less than half a minute. Fatima and her navel attracted a great deal of attention, comment, and subsequently, calls for censorship. The Edison Company responded to the pressure but, interestingly enough, did not withdraw the film. Instead they scratched white lines across the offending oscillating regions. The effect was now somewhat comparable to seeing Fatima dance behind a picket fence. This interested viewers even more. Apparently, they assumed, if the company had gone to so much trouble to conceal what was going on, it really must be worth seeing. Audiences now became even more attentive as they tried to catch a glimpse of what Fatima was displaying behind her unusual fence.

Though innocent by today's standards, the criticisms against *Fatima's Dance* and *The Kiss* related to public deportment. Later calls for censorship involved larger, and often less tangible, issues. By the 1910s popular interest in the motion picture had grown at a phenomenal rate. Now seen more as a passion than a novelty, some critics were becoming concerned about the sociological, psychological, and physiological impact film had on these devoted viewers. As the film historian Robert Sklar has noted, in his book *Movie-made America*, educators, reformers, clergymen, and intellectuals were writing countless articles hypothesizing about the deleterious effects of a medium that they were afraid was running out of control. This supposed damage was not limited to its impact on society. There was also anxiety relating to "physiological harm" falsely associated to the motion picture medium itself. Doctors wrote of their concern about increased nervousness, harmed vision, and organic disturbances they thought might be occurring as a result of attending the movies.

Such theories were based on speculation rather than any scientific or systematic study of data. Instead of isolating actual dangers, associated with the medium and its content, these challenges reflected the fears of the challengers. In many instances the people questioning the movies were not people who went to see the pictures themselves. Most of these middle class critics, at the turn-of-the-century, sought amusement at the theater, concerts or even vaudeville rather than from the movies. Filmmakers had yet to learn how to work with film in an articulate manner. Consequently, most of their audience was from the poor and working-class who had no other available amusements. The middle-class critic was often suspicious of these people, their neighborhoods, and their cinematic entertainment that was experienced in a dark and decrepit room.

For the most part the audiences who went to the movies were made up of basically good people enjoying an innocent amusement. But the movies were also going off in their own direction, satisfying an audience which the upper-classes neither understood nor trusted. Middle-class critics, who saw themselves as responsible for defining respectable standards of culture, felt it was their duty to make sure that film be controlled. Demands were made for federal regulations to be placed upon the content of the movies and the industry itself.

Unlike many countries, there never has been a federal board of censorship regulating the content of motion pictures in the United States.

Other restrictions on film have existed, including state and local boards of censorship, but not one run by the <u>federal</u> government. There have been numerous requests for such a board, however. In the early years of this century the Pure Food and Drug Act, established under Theodore Roosevelt's administration, was seen as a possible precedent for federal film censorship regulation. The Pure Food and Drug Act established national regulatory standards for the sale and packaging of consumable goods. Some critics thought the same philosophy should extend to the ideas being consumed by people's minds. It was, however, easier to show how tainted meat affected one's system than demonstrate how movies can hurt you.

Most of the people promoting censorship in the 1910s thought they were acting in a responsible manner. Too often, however, these reformers' actions were based on fear rather than a rational and objective examination of the situation. Their crusades frequently were marred by an elitist bias which failed to realize how poor and working-class people benefited from what was generally an innocent entertainment. They did not succeed in establishing a federal board of censorship, but they did create comparable state and local organizations. Pennsylvania passed the first law creating a state board of censorship in 1911, and Ohio and Kansas followed in 1913. These organizations reviewed the content of films, excised portions of films they felt were unsuitable, and even prevented some movies from being shown in their jurisdiction altogether.

Not surprisingly the developing American film industry was disturbed by this trend of outsiders dictating what was to be the content of their motion pictures. The president of the Mutual Film Corporation, Harry E. Aitken, took the state of Ohio to court claiming that it had no right to censor the films made by his company. The case of *Mutual Film Corporation v. Industrial Commission of Ohio* went as far as the United States Supreme Court. In 1915 the Supreme Court ruled unanimously, in what has come to be known as the "**Mutual Decision**," that film <u>did not</u> come under the protection of the First Amendment which protects freedom of speech. Governments could censor film if they felt it necessary. The Mutual Decision was the first Supreme Court ruling dealing specifically with motion pictures. It would not be the last. Much of the furor, involving film censorship in 1915, focused on one film--D.W. Griffith's *The Birth of a Nation*.

III. D.W. Griffith, *The Birth of a Nation* and Media Distortion Today

D.W. Griffith was one of the most important of the early American filmmakers. Born near Louisville, Kentucky in 1875, David Wark Griffith was the son of a Confederate Colonel--"Roaring" Jake Griffith--who had distinguished himself in the War Between the States. Griffith idolized his father and was deeply hurt when Jake Griffith died when David was still a boy. He spent his childhood dreaming of becoming a famous person of whom his father would have been proud. David decided the best way to do this was to become the Shakespeare of his day.

D.W. Griffith was able to earn a modest living as an actor at first, but his plays never did prove successful. By the early 1900s he found it difficult to find acting jobs as well. Griffith ended up working as a film actor for Edwin S. Porter at Edison, in a 1907 picture entitled *Rescued from an Eagle's Nest*. In the film an eagle swoops down on a baby and deposits the child in its nest. The baby's father, played by Griffith, climbs down a rope to the nest, battles the bird, and rescues the child. The film's "special effects" are a source of much mirth for modern audiences. Given Griffith's aspirations of becoming the Shakespeare of the American stage, appearing as a film actor in movies of this type must have been rather irritating experiences.

While Griffith did not think much of the movies, he appreciated the financial remuneration associated with the profession. Griffith left Edison for Biograph where he got work as a director. Between 1907 and 1913 D.W. Griffith directed approximately 485 films, most of them short subjects of between ten and twenty minutes in length. During this period he experimented with mise-en-scene, camerawork, and editing. So successful was Griffith, in developing a filmic language at Biograph, that some critics have called him the "Father of the Motion Picture."

When Griffith left Biograph, he was recognized as one of the top-- perhaps the top--film directors in the world. While his body of work at that company was considered a major achievement, Griffith was not happy with many of these films himself. The enormous output he was expected to produce, and the limited budget he had to work with, prevented him from making the really fine pictures he felt he was capable of directing. When Biograph balked at supporting his efforts to direct feature films, instead of short subjects, Griffith departed.

D.W. Griffith made four feature length pictures before embarking on his most famous film, *The Birth of a Nation*. *The Birth of a Nation* was based on two novels, *The Clansman* and *The Leopard's Spots,* written by a minister named Thomas E. Dixon, Jr. at the turn-of-the-century. Purporting to tell the story of the American Civil War and Reconstruction from a Southern point of view, these novels were very popular and very racist. The fact that these novels were written by a clergyman, popular, and fostered so little complaint, is indicative of how racist America was at this time.

D.W. Griffith was very enthusiastic about turning Dixon's work into a movie. A Southerner himself, and proud of his father's participation in the war, Griffith saw the situation as an opportunity to tell Jake Griffith's story.

The spectacle of the subject, D.W. Griffith's personal interest in the Civil War and Reconstruction, and the promised financial backing that would enable him to do it well, led the director to believe that this opportunity would allow him to make a really artistic motion picture. Commercially, the popularity of the books had led to an earlier stage production. This promised that there would be an enthusiastic audience for the picture. Interestingly, the play received some criticism for being racist even though the books had not. This may have been due to the different type of visibility which the stage medium had with the public or, perhaps, a reflection of changing racial attitudes among some Americans.

The Birth of a Nation proved to be the artistic success Griffith hoped it to be. For audiences used to modest films of ten and twenty minutes in length, the impact of *The Birth of a Nation* was overwhelming. His training in, and appreciation for, 19th century melodrama and stage convention enabled Griffith to construct a story in which the viewer felt an optimal emotional involvement with the characters. One way Griffith accomplished this effect was by filming sequences with certain musical nuances in mind. A special score was then composed to emphasize the emotional feelings he desired from his audience. More than just a period melodrama, the director's knowledge of the South and the Civil War a film with a very striking, often authentic, feeling for the period. What helped to make it a great movie, however, was the self-assured and articulate way D.W. Griffith executed the film techniques, he first developed at Biograph, to communicate his story. Today this movie is considered the first major cinematic tour de force. Eighty years after its production, viewers still can get involved with the story and appreciate the experience Griffith was trying to create, with *The Birth of a Nation* . Unfortunately *The Birth of a Nation* is also an artistic masterpiece with a tragic flaw.

In telling a story based on a racist work from a bigoted viewpoint, D.W. Griffith made a racist film. Unconsciously racist himself, Griffith was surprised that certain black groups, particularly the newly formed National Association for the Advancement of Colored People (NAACP), took exception with the way members of their race were portrayed. To Griffith's credit much of the virulent racism of Dixon's novels was absent. Enough racism remained to disturb some viewers, of the time, and most audiences today.

The story of *The Birth of a Nation* centers on two families, the Camerons from the South and the Stonemans of the North. They become acquainted after a friendship develops between the eldest Cameron and Stoneman sons at school. When the Stoneman sons visit the Camerons, at their plantation in the South, the family bonds become stronger. Shortly after their visit the Civil War breaks out. The sons fight one another, and some of them die together, on the battlefield. The eldest Cameron son is wounded, taken prisoner, and eventually meets his friend's sister, Elsie Stoneman, in a Northern hospital. Just when the families think they can resume their friendship after the long war, Abraham Lincoln is assassinated. This tragic incident ends the first half of *The Birth of a Nation* .

While black stereotypes exist in the first half of the film, their treatment in the Reconstruction portion of *The Birth of a Nation* is what particularly disturbed those sensitive to racism in 1915. The blacks of this picture are seen as trusting individuals who are persuaded to turn against their former masters by unscrupulous and misguided people from the North. According to the picture, the South forms the Ku Klux Klan as a necessary vigilante group to "protect" innocent whites. During the height of the story's upheaval, the Ku Klux Klan "rides to a last minute" rescue in a situation comparable to another racist convention in Hollywood movies of this time--the cavalry saving whites from "marauding" Native Americans. The picture ends with four of the Stoneman and Cameron sons and daughters marrying, thereby uniting North and South in "the birth of a new nation."

An underlying problem with *The Birth of a Nation* is that it gives a distorted view of who blacks were during this or any time. Those upset by the film were bothered by the way the picture slanted themes and historical events to support an underlying racist philosophy. Whites rather than blacks, for example, are seen as victims of what happened in the South of this period. The picture suggests that blacks were perfectly satisfied being slaves until this lifestyle was disrupted by the Civil War and Reconstruction. This perspective leads to a number of underlying assumptions that are both untrue and disturbing.

People are people. Sociologists, scientists, humanitarians, and others who have studied the problem have all concluded that no group of people is inherently better or worse than any other, genetically. Any race, nationality, or country is capable of producing people of genius, talent, quality, or the adverse. Racism does not recognize this undeniable fact. It prefers to make false value judgments based solely on the surface appearance of a group of people. Unfortunately, D.W. Griffith unknowingly was guided by this bias when he made *The Birth of a Nation* .

While Griffith and many other people did not see the racist elements in his film, they are quite apparent to most viewers today. One thing that strikes us as ludicrous is the use of obviously white performers in black makeup. Most, although not all, of the actors in *The Birth of a Nation* are not black and their makeup makes them look like a parody, rather than an accurate depiction, of this actual group of people. Instead of seeing these individuals portrayed the way they were in the 1860s, we are given a distorted view which the movie asks us to accept as the truth. The tradition of white performers appearing in black face was part of a nineteenth century American entertainment known as the minstrel show. An unfortunate aspect of the minstrel show was that blacks were portrayed only as clowns rather than as regular people. This practice continued throughout most of the twentieth century. Al Jolson, for example, put on black face in *The Jazz Singer*. The black face tradition did not really disappear from American film and television until the 1960s.

Clearly the majority of Americans no longer accept the perceptions of blacks which D.W. Griffith, and too many other people, had when *The Birth of a Nation* was first released. This fact makes the movie an important, albeit disturbing, picture for conscientious and concerned viewers to see today. There are three important justifications for watching this film aside from the argument that *The Birth of a Nation* is considered one of the most influential and technically innovative movies made anywhere in the world up to that time. To begin with it documents the racist attitudes which a lot of otherwise good people took for granted in America at the turn-of-the-century. By observing how people thought at the time we can get a sense that people's attitudes have changed for the better since 1915, regarding certain aspects of racism, although we certainly have not come far enough.

A second reason for watching the movie is to isolate the strategies that Griffith uses to get us to think in ways we now know to be wrong. We know blacks are not like this. Only racists could now envision the Ku Klux Klan as a heroic group that rides to someone's rescue. Most individuals currently associate the Klan with racial harassment. Having formed a different interpretation of what happened during the war and reconstruction, and knowing Griffith's interpretation is not correct, how is the director using the film medium to "sell," or try to get us to go along with, his viewpoints? How are these same strategies being used to get us to buy distorted ideas today?

This last question brings up a third and very important justification for seeing *The Birth of a Nation* today, despite its incorrect and irritating treatment of its subject. Millions of otherwise good people once watched *The Birth of a Nation* and found nothing wrong with it. Can we, as equally good and conscientious people, be watching things which are false but accepting them as true? Audiences today are, understandably, irritated when Klansmen are portrayed as the heroes executing the last minute rescue. How many viewers get upset when they see the cavalry conduct a last minute rescue to save endandagered whites from Native Americans in a western? In how many westerns is the convention of cowboys vs. Indians based on a racist premise?

Since 1915 some critics have said that *The Birth of a Nation* should be censored because its content is disturbing. The problem with banning the film is that we will not be able to learn from it if we do prevent it from being seen. The history of racism in America, people's apathy towards bigotry, and the concern that people become more sensitive to these problems will not be positively served if all prints of *The Birth of a Nation* are locked away. No conscientious person will become a racist by watching this film. Conscientious viewers can become more aware if they learn how filmmakers distort the truth in the way the media is used, both yesterday and today.

IV. The Influence of *The Birth of a Nation* on the American Film Industry

Pressure was placed on D.W. Griffith, by the NAACP and other groups, to cut some of the most racist scenes in the earliest version of *The Birth of a Nation,* which he reluctantly did. Calls for further censorship of the film also prompted him to write a monograph entitled *The Rise and Fall of Free Speech in America.* Yet, despite some public outcry, the controversy did not lead to major immediate changes in the way the content of film was regulated in America. Rather than offend most middle class audiences and critics, *The Birth of a Nation* tended to please them.

People were drawn to the film by the millions. Awed by its use of the medium and thrilled by its story, *The Birth of a Nation* attracted the middle class to film theaters like no movie before it. Giving the buying power of the dollar at the time--$1 in 1915 money conservatively equals what $20 is worth today--and the lax methods of keeping financial records regarding admissions, it is probable that *The Birth of a Nation* remains one of the top grossing films of this century. The fact that middle-class critics advocated film censorship, but were not offended by the this picture, is a strong indication of the social acceptance of racism in the America of this time. It also raises questions regarding the value system behind these peoples' demands for censorship. Some viewers could get upset when they saw kissing on the screen but have little problem with the racist depiction of minorities.

The Birth of a Nation probably had more impact on the way movies were constructed and viewed in America than it did on promoting suppression of the medium. This film attracted a larger and wealthier audience, than the poor and working-class, and the industry wanted to keep this group in the theaters. Before *The Birth of a Nation,* many of the calls for censorship related to films which most upper-class people did not see, produced for lower and working-class audiences of which the critics were not a part. Larger theaters in better neighborhoods were now being built in great numbers, as Hollywood made films that the middle-class wanted to view. Federal censorship did not come about, in part, because the industry tried to keep the critics happy by catering to the audience's desires. If there were too many complaints about a certain kind of movie it was more profitable to avoid making it. Happy filmgoers were ignoring the complaints of those calling for the regulation of films. Film content was largely being regulated by supply and demand.

At Biograph D.W. Griffith systematically isolated, polished, and in some instances invented the techniques of filmmaking--such as the iris, flashback, close-up--that became identified as the language, or grammar, of narrative filmmaking. As a result of the success of his methods for storytelling, in pictures like *The Birth of a Nation*, Griffith has also been called, "The Man Who Invented Hollywood." In essence, Griffith's method of filmmaking was a cinema of emotional involvement.

A principal concern, of Griffith's "cinema of emotional involvement," was to provide characters, either appealing or sinister, with whom the audience could become emotionally involved. Once their personalities were established the story thrusts them, along with the viewer, into emotion packed situations. D.W. Griffith did not want the audience to think about the filmmaking process, the plausibility of the narrative, nor alternatives relating to the issues presented. The emotional involvement of the film spectator might be seen as somewhat comparable to what is experienced by a thrill seeker strapped in a roller coaster and swept away by the mechanics of this amusement. While the event is actually happening, the rider is more concerned with the sensation of the ride than with the moral and philosophical implications of the effect. This emphasis on emotional involvement would be the guiding principle behind the majority of Hollywood films produced after *The Birth of a Nation*.

A problem with this "roller coaster sensationalism," in film involvement, is suggested at the beginning of a sentence in the previous paragraph--"The filmmaker did not want the audience to think. . . ." The viewer is asked to get caught up in the experience and carried away by the thrills and sensation which the cinematic roller coaster is providing. There is nothing inherently wrong with escapist entertainment as a concept. However, the filmmaker and audience do have a responsibility in questioning the messages--and the impact of the ride--on viewers as they observe the techniques and concepts carrying them along.

With this Hollywood type of emotional involvement, a director like Griffith would make characters appealing, surround them with kittens and puppies, show them to be "victims" of an attack by Native Americans or members of the Ku Klux Klan. Because of our emotional associations, with such "good" people, we are expected to go along with the roller coaster of assumptions and sensations, in the Hollywood film, without thought or question. The director is asking us, in the above situations, to see Native Americans as the "bad guys" and the Ku Klux Klan as good, even when we would disagree with such generalizations in more rational contexts.

The Griffith inspired Hollywood film is exciting, spectacular, and sensationalistic. It appeals to our emotions while often asking us to accept stereotypes and simplistic generalizations which are not always true or in society's best interests. Too often these stereotypes and generalizations are made at the expense of the actual people being stereotyped and generalized. Despite this problem, the Hollywood film has attracted an international audience. While *The Birth of a Nation* raises serious questions about its content and this approach, it attracted millions of people to the theater and helped establish a broader American audience for Hollywood film. Many middle class viewers became more comfortable with the content of what was being shown on the screen, after 1915. Hollywood tried to give the viewers what they wanted rather than produce films that were objectionable. Despite this catering, certain critics still called for stricter regulation and the creation of a federal organization for censoring films.

V. Hollywood Scandals in the 1920s, Roscoe "Fatty" Arbuckle, and the Hays Office

After the middle class audiences went to the movies in increasing numbers, following the success of *The Birth of a Nation,* the demand for censorship modified somewhat but did not altogether stop. By 1921 the cries for censorship became very vocal, indeed. The end of World War I ushered in the "Roaring 20s" and a number of conservative groups were upset about the changes in American lifestyles. A number of scandals also happened in Hollywood at this time, which protesters pointed to as proof for the need for greater Hollywood regulation.

One of the first of these unfortunate incidents, involving a Hollywood personality, was the death of a popular leading man, Wallace Reid (1891-1923), from heroin addiction. Reid had risen to fame after playing the part of a blacksmith in *The Birth of a Nation.* Heroin addiction was not at all consistent with Reid's screen image of "an all American boy." Questions also arose when one of Hollywood's favorite comediennes, Mabel Normand (1894-1930), innocently became associated with a series of events that occurred prior to the murder of a director named William Desmond Taylor (1877-1922). Taylor turned out to have had a dubious past and his murder was not solved. Despite her innocence, Mabel Normand's reputation was badly damaged by association. The incident was taken, by critics, as further proof that Hollywood was a den of iniquity, the people who worked in movies were immoral, and that their films should be regulated. The fact that the movies of people like Wallace Reid, Mabel Normand, and William Desmond Taylor contained nothing that would give most people offense was not considered in these arguments.

The Hollywood scandal most responsible for precipitating change, in the way the content of films were regulated in America, involved a famous screen comedian named Roscoe "Fatty" Arbuckle (1887-1933). The world's most popular comedian after Charlie Chaplin, Roscoe Arbuckle was charged with the rape and murder of a young actress at a party he gave in a hotel suite in San Francisco. Arbuckle and a few friends had rented some hotel rooms for a party during Labor Day weekend in 1921. One of the guests, Virginia Rappe, became ill and was put to bed. The woman subsequently died from a ruptured bladder.

Virginia Rappe's condition existed before she came to the party and Arbuckle had not touched her. Seeing the situation as an opportunity to gain publicity at the famous comedian's expense, a corrupt public prosecutor and some of the guests at the party charged Arbuckle with rape and murder. Roscoe "Fatty" Arbuckle was innocent of any wrongdoing but the lurid spectacle printed in the newspapers condemned him. Despite being cleared of any charges in court, Roscoe Arbuckle's career was over. His movies, blameless of any impropriety, were withdrawn from circulation.

Roscoe Arbuckle spent the rest of his life working to pay off the huge legal fees he had accumulated when defending himself. Twelve years after the incident he had paid off all of his creditors. Warner Brothers gave him an opportunity to resume his film career in front of the camera. The evening following the signing of his contract, Roscoe Arbuckle died of a heart attack. Denied of the right to make films that would renew his image, the comedian's reputation is still associated with a crime he did not commit.

A somewhat comparable situation occurred a few years ago which affected the career of comedian Paul Reubens. Reubens, who performed under the name of "Pee Wee Herman," was arrested for indecent exposure in an adult cinema. Even though there was no objectionable behavior in the Pee Wee Herman films and television programs, Reubens's TV series was dropped by the network. As of the date of this writing, Paul Reubens still has not made any movies or television programs using the character of Pee Wee Herman.

Although Roscoe "Fatty" Arbuckle was innocent of any crime in 1921, the public outcry against him was great. Demands for a federal board of censorship for regulating Hollywood films was one outcome of the scandal. Fearing that they would have to subject its product to outside control, the American film industry decided to convince the critics that Hollywood could regulate itself. The studio heads, in 1922, invited a man named Will Hays (1879-1954) to head an organization that would censor their motion pictures. Hays had not been affiliated with the film business prior to this time but, as the postmaster general of President Warren G. Harding's administration, had an image of respectability. Ironically, Harding's presidency is now considered one of the most corrupt administrations in American history and Will Hays has been accused as being one of the dishonest offenders. Reality aside, Hays had the appearance of virtue at the time, and that was what Hollywood needed to be associated with in 1922.

Hays agreed to help give Hollywood a "clean image" and became head of the new self-regulatory organization. Entitled the Motion Picture Producers and Distributors of America (MPPDA), this self-censorship body was usually referred to as the "Hays Office." The Hays Office drew up a list of "don'ts" for the American film industry, and worked to ward off the creation of a federal board of censorship. This satisfied many of the more vocal protest groups. Ironically, the content of Hollywood film was not much affected by the new organization in the 1920s. Things would change substantially during the next decade, however.

By the late 1920s, and the coming of sound, American films were less restrained in their use of sex and violence. This shift reflected the content of material imported from the New York stage. It also was an attempt by Hollywood to attract audiences during a time of decreased revenue as a result of the depression. The gangster film was a particular popular genre at this time, and some critics complained that movies were glorifying crime. In an attempt to stave off these criticisms, the Hays Office came out with the "Hays Code" in 1930, which tried to specifically spell out what Hollywood films should not do. Despite these efforts, some faultfinders did not feel that the industry was paying enough attention to respectability in its films.

There were two major reasons why the Hays Office could be criticized as a less than effective regulatory body at this time. Set up by Hollywood as a voluntary organization to regulate Hollywood, there was no way the Hays Office could ensure that its demands would be enforced. If a studio wanted to ignore recommendations or decrees from the Hays Office the MPPDA could not make that company follow its dictates. A second element, which weakened the Hays Office's image as a censoring body, was the fact that the industry saw it as something of a public relations entity. The industry was more interested in the Hays Office serving to reassure outside critics that Hollywood was responsible, and open to their suggestions, than having Will Hays tell filmmakers what they could or could not do.

Eventually one outside group decided that Hollywood was not addressing criticisms against the content of its films and measures needed to be taken. In 1933 people connected with the Roman Catholic Church formed the National Legion of Decency. This organization drew up a list of objectionable films. By 1934 the organization threatened to have members of the Catholic Church boycott any theater showing these motion pictures. Not only would the theater be boycotted at the time the displeasing film was being shown, the National Legion of Decency would ask its members not to attend that movie house for several weeks after the picture had left.

Hollywood was very much affected by the economic depression America was suffering in the 1930s. This threatened boycott was something that the industry took very seriously. Once again the studio heads decided it was better to oversee any regulation of their films in Hollywood, rather than be subjected to guidelines from outside. They invited prominent Roman Catholics to join the Hays Office and help run the newly created Production Code Administration (PCA). This organization would determine what could or could not be shown in American films for the next twenty-five years.

When the Catholic Church joined forces with the Hays Office, the MPPDA ceased to be just a kind of public relations organization. It became a full-fledged regulatory body with the threat of fines and economic boycott behind it for power of enforcement. These censors were very serious about what they objected to and they expected filmmakers to conform to their demands. Standards were drawn up, scripts were reviewed, and films were carefully screened by the PCA before a picture would be awarded a certificate of approval. Restrictions against nudity, violence, suggestive sexual activity, and profanity were imposed and enforced. All of Hollywood's product was expected to conform to what the PCA felt was suitable for a family audience. Mature themes had to correspond to PCA standards which bore little resemblance to reality. A bedroom scene featuring a married couple, for example, usually involved two single beds. If both people were seen on a bed, one of them had to have one foot on the floor. Such restrictions often made it difficult for filmmakers to tell a credible story.

Despite the difficulties this censorship policy placed on Hollywood, most movies conformed to the Hays Office dictates in the late 1930s and the 1940s. There were two interesting challenges to the PCA and MPPDA's power at this time. Producer David O. Selznick refused to remove the word "damn" in Rhett Butler's parting sentence to Scarlett O'Hara in the 1939 picture, *Gone with the Wind*. The Hays Office eventually allowed *Gone with the Wind* to be released with a restricted rating. The other film to defy Hollywood's own censors was *The Outlaw*, made in 1941 by the eccentric millionaire inventor and film producer, Howard Hughes. After substantial debate the MPPDA finally gave the film a rating and it was released in 1943. *The Outlaw* used an advertisement campaign that drew attention to actress Jane Russell's cleavage and contained some suggestive dialogue and sexual situations. Viewers today tend to find *The Outlaw* more humorous than salacious and the film has been shown on cable's Christian Broadcasting Network (CBN).

Though Selznick and Hughes were unique in the way they challenged the Hays Office, they were not the only Hollywood filmmakers irritated with the restrictions placed on their work at this time. By the end of World War II sophisticated motion pictures, containing mature themes that could not have been dealt with in American films, were coming out of Europe. To make matters worse, by the late 1940s and early 1950s, family audiences were staying at home and watching a new form of entertainment called "television," rather than going to the movies. Filmmakers needed to produce films that would bring people back to the theaters. Censorship organizations, including their own Hays Office, was preventing them from doing so. Ultimately it was a controversial European film that enabled Hollywood filmmakers to overcome this impasse.

VI. The Miracle Decision and Changes in American Film, 1952-1966

In 1948 a respected filmmaker in Italy, named Roberto Rossellini, made a short film called *Il miracolo* (*The Miracle*). The movie tells the story about a retarded shepherdess who thinks she is visited by St. Joseph while she is tending her sheep. After she discovers she is pregnant, the woman is convinced that her baby is holy despite the skepticism of others. An exhibitor named Joseph Burstyn brought *The Miracle* to the United States in 1950. The state of New York objected to its being shown because some felt the film to be sacrilegious. Burstyn questioned the ruling and took his case all the way to the United States Supreme Court.

The resulting 1952 **"Miracle decision"** was the first Supreme Court case involving film, since 1915, and essentially reversed the Court's position established in the Mutual decision. In this instance the Supreme Court ruled in favor of the film interests and agreed that motion pictures did come under the First Amendment's protection of freedom of speech. Joseph Burstyn's right of freedom of speech had been transgressed with the censorship of this film. *The Miracle* could now be exhibited.

As can be seen from this history, financial interests had as much to do with Hollywood's self-censorship as moral and aesthetic concerns. The demands of a changing audience dictated the content of the industry's films. By 1952 the types of restrictions placed on Hollywood pictures were no longer satisfactory. Encouraged by the Supreme Court ruling, some Hollywood filmmakers decided to make some movies that openly challenged the restrictive standards of the day. As David A. Cook notes in his book *A History of Narrative Film,* the director Otto Preminger deliberately released two films that were denied the Production Code certificate of approval. *The Man with the Golden Arm* (1955) involved heroin addiction and *The Moon is Blue* (1953) contained the forbidden

251

word "virgin." Both films did well commercially. A further blow against the censors' threats occurred with Elia Kazan's 1956 picture, *Baby Doll*. The Catholic Legion of Decency publicly condemned the movie but the organization's censure, if anything, only added to the picture's substantial box-office appeal. [2]

Social and business demands meant that Hollywood's old methods of self-regulation had to be modified. The Legion of Decency continued to make viewing recommendations to its members. But its advice and approval no longer served the industry. There was no need to have representatives of the Catholic Church working with what had been the Hays Office. Eric A. Johnston, onetime president of the United State Chamber of Commerce, had succeeded Will Hays as head of this body in 1946, when the name of the organization was changed to the Motion Picture Association of America (MPAA). In 1966 Johnston was replaced by current head Jack Valenti. With Valenti's arrival the old Production Code was abandoned.

VII. The MPAA and the Regulation of the Content of American Film after 1966

Rather than make all American films conform to one standard for a general audience the MPAA decided, in the middle 1960s, that there was a need for a broader range of motion pictures for more diversified types of patron. At first American films were identified by two categories--"M" and "G"--representing "mature" and "general" content. Eventually this classification was broadened into five categories--"G," general audiences; "PG," parental guidance for children under 17; "PG-13," parental guidance, children under 13; "R," restricted to individuals 17 or older unless accompanied by an adult; and "X," restricted to people over 17. While audiences might object to the content of some of these films, the MPAA saw the ratings as a means of preparing the potential viewer for what could be expected from a picture in the given categories. The responsibility for what one saw was on the viewer, not some outside watchdog.

The new ratings system allowed Hollywood filmmakers to experiment with subject matter and themes that the old Production code prohibited. Hollywood's output since 1966 has not been totally exemplary despite the benefit of these increased freedoms. While the situation has allowed concerned artists to make thoughtful studies of important issues, this new freedom has also resulted in sensationalistic froth with dubious merit. Before one blames the ratings code for this type of film, and call for a return of the old Hays Office days, one should remember that sensationalism without thought has been fundamental to Hollywood filmmaking since Griffith. If there was not a market for this type of movie, Hollywood would not make it.

252

Despite experiments with different types of regulation and categories of film content, the Hollywood market seems to allow, if not advocate, a large body of films of mediocre merit. While the categories of G through X were meant to encourage a variety of film styles and quality pictures, each classification has tended to foster an almost predictable type of movie. Instead of becoming a vehicle which invited filmmakers to make progressive and challenging motion pictures the "X" rating, for example, became mostly associated with films of a sexual nature.

In the 1980s some prominent film critics, which included Gene Siskel and Roger Ebert, petitioned the MPAA to add a new category which would prevent progressive films from suffering what had become the stigma of an "X." On September 26, 1990 the old X rating was replaced with NC 17--no children under 17. As had been the case with some of the early films made under the X rating, the early NC 17 category was used to classify some thought provoking pictures. Early NC 17 pictures of this type include *The Cook, the Thief, His Wife and Her Lover* (1990); *Henry and June* (1990), and *Henry, Portrait of a Serial Killer* (1990). The NC 17 proponents wanted this category to separate artistic films from movies concerned with "sex for sex's sake." The MPAA has not made this distinction. Numerous censorship proponents, understandably, have labeled the NC 17 as merely the old X rating with a new name.

Critics, like Siskel and Ebert ,were quite upset with this development since it allowed for no improvement over the old X classification. Requests to Jack Valenti and the MPAA to differentiate "serious" NC 17 pictures from X rated "porn" have been rejected because the organization says it is not their responsibility to make aesthetic value judgments relating to a film's content. Rather, the MPAA claims its job is to categorize films based on broad classifications relative to certain types of subject matter. The MPAA will not differentiate "good nudity" from "bad nudity." If nudity is present in a film that movie will get a specific type of rating. The interpretation of how it is being used is to be made by critics like Siskel and Ebert and, it is hoped, the responsible film consumer. Despite good intentions, the NC 17 classification appears to be doomed to the fate of the old X rather than used as a means for aesthetic demarcation.

The ratings system has allowed broader types of filmmaking. The Miracle decision provides film with First Amendment rights. But film censorship in America still exists. As we noted, the unfair suppression of the acting career of comedian Roscoe "Fatty" Arbuckle, in the 1920s, has parallels in the way Paul Reubens has been prevented from making films and television programs using his character of Pee Wee Herman. The controversy surrounding the exhibition of Roberto Rossellini's *The Miracle*, in the late 1940s and early 1950s, is not dissimilar to the reaction surrounding Martin Scorsese's 1989 picture, *The Last Temptation of Christ*. Both films explore a topic, associated with religion, that some critics have found thought provoking, others as sacrilegious. Rather than allow viewers to watch the film, and make up their own minds, the pro-censorship forces demanded that the controversial film not be shown at all. Where the Supreme Court expressly allowed *The Miracle* to be exhibited, another Court decision has permitted *The Last Temptation of Christ* to be suppressed.

In 1973 the Supreme Court made a third ruling relating to film. This time the Court ruled that the definition of obscenity can be decided by "community standards." Since there was no specific definition of what constitutes a "community," this decision allows a rather broad latitude as to <u>who</u> can suppress <u>what</u> they do not want others to see. Despite the fact that intelligent critics have claimed *The Last Temptation of Christ* is a thoughtful and responsible work by a respected artist, dissenters have prevented it from being shown at theaters, on television, or made available in video rental establishments. The Supreme Court said *The Miracle* could be shown in 1952. There seems to be less interest in making *The Last Temptation of Christ* accessible to audiences today.

VIII. Conclusion

Censorship is concerned with regulating the content of motion pictures. Social responsibility is at the heart of the conflict between those who want to control film content and those concerned with freedom of expression. Some feel it is more responsible to restrain the subject matter in film. Others believe such restrictions dangerously limit ideas and information. Censorship can purge odious material. Too often it accomplishes this by abolishing channels of communication.

Critics of *The Last Temptation of Christ*, for example, have insisted that this film's version of the New Testament should not be shown because it does not conform to some people's interpretation. Other critics, equally conscientious, have found *The Last Temptation of Christ* to be thought provoking and not sacrilegious at all. Censorship of films like *The Last Temptation of Christ* may satisfy those who want a narrow interpretation of a subject, but it also deprives the responsible viewer from getting access to information. Conformity of description can be a high price to pay for sanitizing a message. Whatever one's position regarding censorship, it is healthier for a society to maintain an ongoing debate of what it wants, accepts, or refuses to be shown in film, than it is to put major restrictions on such questions altogether.

While our examination of censorship has involved fictional films, the question of whether the _truth_ is being served, in the promotion or suppression of a point of view, is often present in these debates. Even though the word "fiction" implies a kind of alteration of reality, both free speech and pro-censorship groups claim to be interested in promoting the truth. Fiction allows some modification of reality but, critics would argue, it should not fundamentally alter the truth. How film can modify reality and still be true is, of course, something of a contradiction.

One way some filmmakers have sought to use the film medium, in the pursuit of truth, is by making "non-fiction" films. The "non-fiction," or "documentary," motion picture goes to the "real world" for its subject matter rather than stage material before the camera to produce fictional accounts. Upon initial reflection the documentary format might appear to allow the filmmaker to create an inherently more "truthful" interpretation of a topic. Yet the matter of how "realistic" a documentary film actually is, as we shall see in Chapter Eleven, is not as straightforward as one might originally think.

ENDNOTES

1. Terry Ramsaye, *A Million and One Nights,* (New York: Touchstone, 1986, pp. 256-259.)
2. David A. Cook, *A History of Narrative Film,* (New York: W.W. Norton & Co., 1990, pp. 535-36.)

CHAPTER ELEVEN

DOCUMENTARY

CHAPTER OBJECTIVES: *Examine the history and makeup of the non-fiction film.*

I. The Nature and Biases of Non-fiction Film

One of the first things about the motion picture that fascinated inventors and observers alike, as we noted in Chapter Three, was the unique manner film created a recognizable image of the subject it was recording. The way film could make identifiable facsimiles of the subjects it photographed prompted many early observers to believe--incorrectly--that this medium was more "truthful" in its interpretations than other media. Painting and sculpture, for example, depend upon an artist's impressions and skills at interpretation when recording a subject's likeness. Because photography uses a mechanical method, to reproduce what is before the camera, these commentators believed that the filmmaking process was more "objective" than other interpretive procedures. Today critics are less likely to share this assumption.

Motion picture footage from W.W.I, for example, has a great deal of credibility as a record of that conflict. This material contains images of the actual participants, in the genuine environment, at the specific time this event took place. For many viewers today this is what World War I looked like. Yet, do these films show the truth? Looking at this footage we get the impression that everything was black and white in those days. People moved in a jerky fashion and they were not able to hear anything since this world was silent. Despite the benefit of the camera being there, and the resemblance the cinematic document has to aspects of what it recorded, no film exactly duplicated what was happening at this time. There is a <u>bias</u> in the way the cinematic record has documented the event.

We have a tendency, as viewers, to accept documentary films as being a truthful record. Though the mechanical process of filming can record aspects of what is before the camera with some objectivity, there is still a built in bias in how and what the motion picture documents. Rather than accept what is before us as the truth, the viewer needs to look for the distortions--the way the medium, or the filmmaker has misread or falsely interpreted the subject. Our World War I film account is a silent, two-dimensional, black and white account. The environment it recorded was actually three-dimensional, in color, and contained sounds, smells, changes of temperature, and other sensations which people were experiencing. Every time the camera was pointed at something that was happening it was not examining other activities going on at the same time. Even if the technology documenting this event could have been more advanced--if someone could have taken one of today's camcorders to the scene, for example--its record still could not have exactly duplicated everything that "actually" was there. The limitations and format of a motion picture or video technology, and the choice of what the filmmaker decides to shoot or not to shoot, all create biases that influence the trustworthiness of the chronicle. The responsible film consumer should question the reliability of the record, and look for and be aware of the biases and distortions in the documentary, even as she or he is appreciating the factual information that can be obtained from the filmic interpretation of the subject.

Today critics are less likely to believe that one medium is more truthful than another. Motion pictures of the battlefields of World War I give us certain insights about this conflict while the poetry, short stories, cartoons, paintings, newspaper accounts, and interviews provide equally valid "truths" that the films--by themselves--often do not provide. A medium is not inherently honest. How well it conveys its information depends upon the honesty, and skill, of the person working with it. A non-fiction film may record what is before the camera, but what we see is still the result of the manipulation of what the filmmaker wants us to see. The fact that there is a manipulation of the way the subject is being recorded can make the so-called non-fiction film as biased as the fictional motion picture.

The novelty of a new medium tends to impress the observer with the effectiveness of what it can do. Later, as a medium or format is replaced by newer technologies, we often become more critical of the quality of the earlier record. It is much easier to criticize methods of interpretation from the past than it is to be aware of the biases and distortions of what we are seeing now. As was the case with our review of *The Birth of a Nation*, and other early film narratives, the perspectives we get from looking at these older movies often can be used to question contemporary motion pictures that we now view. The filmmakers' objectives when making these films frequently were the same as those of producers today, even if the manner of communication is different.

This chapter will review the history of non-fiction film from its origins to the present, consider some of the perspectives the filmmakers had when making these documentaries at the time, and explore how our understanding of the non-fiction film has changed over the years or has remained the same. During the course of our discussion we will also identify important questions that need to be asked concerning the relation the non-fiction film has to the subject it often portends to be "realistically" portraying.

II. Early Non-Fiction Film, *In the Land of the Headhunters,* and the Development of the Feature Length Documentary, 1890-1914

We already discussed the earliest years of the non-fiction film in Chapter Three. Non-fiction movies were, as we noted, the first type of motion picture that the inventors of the film technology tended to make. When experimenting with their new device it was easier to film what already existed around them than it was to stage something for the camera. One unique aspect of the new medium was the fascinating way film created an image of its subject. Audiences and filmmakers alike were intrigued with moving picture interpretations of everyday activities. After awhile the idea of seeing a train come into a station, or parents feeding a baby, ceased to excite many viewers. As interest in common subject matter declined early non-fiction filmmakers of the turn-of-the-century, like the Lumière Brothers, shot more exotic subjects such as President William McKinley in the United States, Queen Victoria of England, Kaiser Wilhelm II of Germany, Czar Nicholas II of Russia, battle footage of the Spanish American War, and devastation from the 1906 San Francisco earthquake.

The subjects listed above were chosen because of their fame or novelty. Movies gave audiences an opportunity to see people and situations they found interesting, or had read about, but probably would otherwise not get the opportunity to see. The fact that filmmakers recognized and responded to such interests is comparable to the reasons television journalists shoot the kind of "actualities" produced today. Prior to 1907 the non-fiction film was the most common type of motion picture. After 1907 the fictional film was the most popular movie being made. Viewers appreciated the way film could reproduce situations that occurred in reality, but they enjoyed spectacle and escapism even more.

Non-fiction films continued to be shot despite the growing popularity of fictional movies. By 1910 the Lumière type of nonfiction actuality had evolved into the format known as the **newsreel**. Through the 1950s, and even in the 1960s, movie audiences expected to see a ten minute newsreel of news and novelty stories before viewing the feature film. Most Americans had access to television by the 1970s and there really was no longer a need for the newsreel in the theater. They could see the same news items at home on TV. The newsreel was replaced by the television news actuality.

The newsreel format, an extension of the Lumière kind of early actuality, was the most common type of non-fiction film prior to 1922. There were other kinds of non-fiction film shown, during this time, but they were exhibited on a much more limited basis. One format was an extension of the magic lantern lecture in which a traveler or an explorer would show images of an exotic place, he or she had been, and verbally interpret what was on

258

the screen as the pictures were shown. This type of film program was not very common because making motion pictures was expensive and not everyone had the expertise to shoot them. This format also depended upon the filmmaker actually being present which limited the number of screenings that could be given. Despite these limitations this type of presentation proved that it was possible to use film to provide a more detailed examination of a subject than was possible with newsreels. It also anticipated another approach to non-fiction filmmaking.

Feature length fictional films, of an hour or longer, became increasingly familiar to audiences after 1912. It was only a matter of time before a non-fiction filmmaker attempted a feature length documentary that could be shown sans commentator. Before such movies could be made filmmakers needed to develop the necessary techniques to convey the information without narration. There was also the question of marketing. Was their an audience for this new product if, in fact, it could be created?

One of the first filmmakers to try and make a feature length non-fiction film was a still photographer named Edward S. Curtis. Curtis had, at the turn-of-the-century, tackled the assignment of photographing every Native American tribe in the United States. His classic photographs have been seen by anyone who has looked at books or documentaries on Native Americans. During his travels Curtis became particularly interested in the Kwakiutl tribe, in the northwestern portion of the United States, who were noted for their wood carving, weaving reeds, and for the fact that their ancestors had been cannibals. In 1914 Curtis made a feature length film, entitled *In the Land of the Headhunters,* in which members of the tribe re-enacted the lifestyle of their ancestors in a romanticized story that the director devised.

In the Land of the Headhunters does not resemble what most of us identify as a documentary today. The film was structured around a fictional narrative and the people in it performed before the camera rather than had their actions recorded as a situation "actually" happened. The format and content of this picture was strongly influenced by Hollywood melodrama and Griffith style film language and effects. *In the Land of the Headhunters* was different from the fictional films of the day in than it used actual members of a particular Native American tribe, recreating the lifestyle of their ancestors, for purposes of creating an anthropological record of their culture as well as entertainment. In this sense Curtis's motion picture was meant to serve some of the same functions as his still photographs of Native Americans.

While *In the Land of the Headhunters* got good reviews it did poorly at the box-office. A commercial failure, Curtis's film did accomplish some of the things it tried to do. Although unavailable for many years a reconstructed version of the film now exists entitled *In the Land of the War Canoes*--the new name avoiding the Hollywood sensationalism implicit in the previous title. The film provides students with a fascinating visual record of an earlier lifestyle of this tribe as performed by actual tribal members. It also enables us to analyze Edward S. Curtis's romantic biases in interpreting this culture. Equally important, *In the Land of the Headhunters* pioneered a feature length non-fiction format. Among the few people who got the opportunity to see this feature was Robert Flaherty (1884-1951). It would be Flaherty, not Curtis, who ultimately produced the first feature length documentary that was both commercially and critically successful.

III.   Robert Flaherty, *Nanook of the North*, and the Lyrical Feature Length Documentary, 1922-1929

Robert Flaherty was an explorer who was hired to look for mineral deposits in Canada during the early part of this century. During his visits he became friendly with the "Inuit" people of the region, as they call themselves, or "Eskimos," as outsiders usually describe them. He became intrigued with the idea of making a movie about these people, particularly after having seen *In the Land of the Headhunters*. Flaherty took a quick course on motion picture photography, went to the region and shot a substantial amount of footage, and came back to the United States with the idea of trying to make a film from this material.

One thing that his filmmaking course apparently did not adequately impress upon him, or prepare him for, was that motion picture film stock was highly flammable in those days. On one occasion, while Flaherty was sitting looking at his film and smoking a cigarette, he accidentally set fire to the majority of footage and burnt himself as well. Many people would have given up the project at this point. The footage had been obtained with a great degree of difficulty. Life in the Canadian Arctic was very harsh and Flaherty had encountered substantial problems when filming. Besides nearly freezing to death he had to contend with thawing out his equipment, when the grease in his camera froze, and the film would sometimes get so cold it would become brittle and break. He also had the option of attempting to develop the exposed footage there, under impossible conditions, or bring it back to America undeveloped, not knowing whether or not he had gotten the proper exposure.

Besides being a patient man, Robert J. Flaherty was also pragmatic. After some reflection Flaherty decided he did not like what he originally had shot anyway. His initial footage was basically a **travelogue**--a series of images of a place with no unifying philosophical or narrative perspective. This concept was OK, in and of itself, but Flaherty did not feel that this series of unconnected shots really presented his subject matter to its best advantage. The impeded, but not yet beaten, filmmaker felt he should go back to the Arctic and do the job correctly. After persuading a fur company called Revillon Frères to finance a second film attempt, in 1920, Flaherty returned to the Arctic to shoot footage of the Inuit with a different type of picture in mind. The result, two years later, was *Nanook of the North*.

Nanook of the North resembles *In the Land of the Headhunters* in several ways. Flaherty took native people and asked them to portray the lifestyle of a previous generation. These "re-enactors" were not professional performers but they did stage events and situations for the camera. Curtis ended up with a rather melodramatic narrative that resembled Hollywood pictures of the time. Flaherty was also strongly influenced by Hollywood film techniques, particularly in the way that he structured his film around the personality and adventures of a heroic central figure. However, even today, the viewer is so caught up in the fascinating lifestyle, which enabled Nanook and his family to function in their harsh environment, we generally are unaware of the Hollywood type of manipulation that exists in this film.

When Flaherty finished *Nanook of the North* he had difficulty getting it distributed. The film distribution people he contacted, in the industry, were not sure if there was a market for the picture. Eventually the Pathé company decided to take a chance on it. Ironically *Nanook of the North* became one of the most commercially successful films of 1922, as well as one of the most critically acclaimed. *Nanook of the North* was so influential, and its director's approach to filmmaking was seen as so important, that some critics have called Robert J. Flaherty the "Father of the Documentary."

One immediate outcome, of the success of *Nanook of the North*, was a series of feature length motion pictures that tried to duplicate this film's commercial and critical achievements. Flaherty himself was hired by Paramount to make another non-fiction feature. Rather than risk freezing to death, or suffering further physical hardships, Flaherty chose to go to Samoa where he shot footage of topless women in an idyllic setting. The resulting film, *Moana* (1926), has its poetry but lacks the excitement of the life and death struggle for existence found in *Nanook of the North*.

Moana did not do well at the box-office but had its critical defenders. In a 1926 review of the film a British commentator, named John Grierson (1898-1972), coined the word "**documentary**" to describe the picture. The term caught on and today "documentary" is the word most often used to identify this type of film. The retrospective use of the word "documentary," to describe non-fiction films made before 1926, creates some confusion. Even though many non-fiction films were produced before 1922, *Nanook of the North* is sometimes described as the "first documentary" because of its critical and commercial success. Historically speaking, the first film to be called a documentary was *Moana*, in 1926. These facts duly noted, it is considered acceptable to use the word "documentary," to describe any non-fiction film no matter when it was made.

The success of *Nanook of the North* immediately influenced a succession of feature length documentaries, set in exotic locations, using native people to portray themselves or their ancestors' lifestyles from a bygone age. Often these films were closer to Hollywood fiction than they were ethnographic studies recording vanishing cultures for posterity. All of these pictures are very interesting, some are excellent, but none matched the poetry and commercial success of *Nanook of the North*.

One of the first of the "lyrical" features, made by someone other than Robert Flaherty, was a picture entitled *Grass* (1925). Filmed by the team of Merian C. Cooper and Ernest B. Schoedsack, *Grass* dealt with tribal migration in Persia. After completing this picture Cooper and Schoedsack went on to make *Chang* (1927), which focused on survival of people living in the jungles of Siam. These two filmmakers are probably most famous for their 1933 picture *King Kong*, which is definitely <u>not</u> a documentary.

The Silent Enemy (1930) was one of the most poetic re-enactment pictures filmed at this time. This movie featured Native American life in the Hudson Bay area before the coming of the white man. *The Silent Enemy* was similar to *In the Land of the Headhunters* in that the film was structured around a fictional narrative which attempted to recreate the lifestyle of an earlier generation of Native Americans. *White Shadows of the South Seas* (1929) and *Tabu* (1930) also used fictional narratives. These two films were set in Tahiti and initially involved Robert Flaherty. Flaherty pulled out of both pictures when their content proved to be too melodramatic and Hollywood oriented.

Nanook of the North had been influenced by Hollywood but it attempted to get away from some of the unrealistic fantasy often associated with that type of movie. What Flaherty did not like was the trend for these lyrical features to become more and more like Hollywood style pictures, shot on location as opposed to in the studio, rather than anthropological examinations of their subjects. The genre was becoming more a mirror of Hollywood fantasy and less reflective of documentary realism. This criticism duly recognized, the films are still interesting interpretations of their subjects. One of the most intriguing of these pictures is Karl Brown's *Stark Love* (1927).

Karl Brown had worked for Griffith as a cameraman, on both *The*

Birth of a Nation and *Intolerance,* before moving to Paramount. While at this studio Brown became intrigued with the idea of making a film about a group of people, in rural Kentucky, whose lifestyle had not changed in hundreds of years. Brown persuaded Paramount to allow him to make a movie there, using local people as on-screen talent. While one might not think of comparing remote parts of the United States, in the 1920s, with the exotic cultures of Siam or Tahiti, Brown showed a world much different from that which most Americans were accustomed. An intriguing film to watch today, and an innovative motion picture for its time, *Stark Love* was not a commercial success.

The failure of *Stark Love* at the box-office was rather typical of the fate of many of the lyrical non-fiction features. While *Nanook of the North* did extremely well, commercially, no other motion picture of this type was as financially successful. The feature length lyrical documentary went into decline, at the end of the 1920s, for two reasons. The financial return did not merit the expense of the costly on-location shooting. The coming of sound also made the technical problems of shooting in remote areas prohibitive. During the economic depression, of the 1930s, it was much cheaper to shoot escapist fantasy in the studio than spend a lot of money in some isolated land. Though the lyrical feature length documentary, as a popular approach to filmmaking, faded with the coming of sound, its influence continued. A particularly interesting feature, in the lyrical tradition inspired by *Nanook of the North,* was one of the last pictures made at the end of the movement-- Sergei Eisenstein's *Que Viva Mexico* (1931-32).

IV. The Lyrical Feature Length Documentary Becomes Propagandistic--Sergei Eisenstein's *Que Viva Mexico* (1931-1932)

Following the international acclaim of his *Battleship Potemkin,* film director Sergei Eisenstein went on a worldwide trip with his cameraman, Eduard Tisse, and assistant director, Grigori Alexandrov. The trio were welcomed by filmmakers in every major city they visited. When in Hollywood they were offered financing for a documentary, by the socialist author Upton Sinclair, to be made in Mexico. Though Hollywood, as a film industry, was showing less interest in making this kind of movie, political activists like Eisenstein and Sinclair believed the format had a great deal of potential for expressing their ideological viewpoints.

Eisenstein embarked upon a brilliantly conceived motion picture that never was completed as a result of a misunderstanding between Sinclair and himself. Sinclair knew nothing about the cost and techniques of making movies and Eisenstein had never worked under the limitations that this type

263

of financing created. Before Eisenstein could finish shooting the picture Sinclair stopped his funding of the project and the Russian filmmaker returned to his country in disgrace. The fact that Eisenstein never had the opportunity to edit the completed footage of *Que Viva Mexico,* into the film he envisioned, was one of the personal tragedies of his life. Eisenstein never finished this documentary but years later his assistant director, Grigori Alexandrov, got access to the footage and put together a documentary he believed was close to what the director wanted.

As with other lyrical features, *Que Viva Mexico* was shot on location in an exotic--at least to most western and urban audiences--localeusing members of the local populace to play people indigenous to the area. The film begins with scenes that reveal the timeless nature of Mexico, its pyramids, and ancient statues with faces closely resembling those of the Mexican people today. Idyllic images of an Eden-like Mexico followed, showing man and animal living in harmonious balance. The desirability of this world and its ancient ways are further emphasized with images of who are people wearing costumes, and engaged in local rituals, from time immemorial.

The idyllic lifestyle of Old Mexico is then disturbingly contrasted with the native people being exploited and raped by corrupt landowners and business interests. This is Eisenstein's interpretation of modern Mexico in the 1920s and 1930s. The end of the film calls for a revolution, against the inequitable system of the present, and a return to the ancient harmony shown at the beginning of the motion picture.

Que Viva Mexico resembles the other lyrical features of this period in that it was shot on location using local amateurs, rather than professional actors, as performers. Eisenstein, like the other lyrical non-fiction feature filmmakers, also imposed a kind of fictional narrative on his location footage. What separated Eisenstein's lyrical documentary, from others of this genre, was the propagandistic nature of *Que Viva Mexico*. This motion picture is not interested in providing melodramatic entertainment, like *White Shadows of the South Seas*, or duplicating Flaherty's concern for creating an ethnographic record of a vanishing culture, as seen in *Nanook of the North*. Rather, Eisenstein was using the lyrical approach to documentary filmmaking to make a political statement calling for social change.

Eisenstein's poetic imagery, depicting the ancient Mexican's relationship to animals in a kind of Eden, was a romantic rather than realistic depiction of the actual situation. This lyrical technique ignored and misrepresented how these people actually related to their world--a criticism which can be leveled against all lyrical documentaries. This distortion of reality in a "non-fiction" format probably did not bother the Russian filmmaker. Instead of emphasizing the fact that he was showing a reality as such, Eisenstein wanted audiences to think about <u>ideas</u> relative to what he was portraying. For Eisenstein, the lyrical feature was more interesting as a <u>vehicle for social change</u> than as a means for recording data for posterity or creating illusion for illusion's sake.

Our examination of the lyrical feature raises a number of questions relating to responsible use of the film medium and our reactions when viewing such motion pictures. Flaherty's lyrical documentaries, *Nanook of the North* and *Moana,* proved that fascinating anthropological studies could be made using the medium. However, Flaherty's methods of conveying his information were influenced by Hollywood and his own individual poetic style. These created personal biases, in his interpretations, which the viewer must consider before accepting the validity of Flaherty's filmed accounts. These tendencies towards sentiment and romanticism were biases which became even more pronounced in the lyrical Hollywood features. Eisenstein's concern for using the film medium for positive social change is admirable. Yet, for those who think the function of the non-fiction film is to convey the truth, the idea of a documentary-like film working as propaganda is troubling.

Today viewers tend to think of the documentary as a type of film that tells the truth while propaganda is something which distorts it. The "propagandistic documentary," like the "fictional documentary" or "docudrama," suggests a contradiction in terms if not philosophy. Yet, as we shall see, for much of its history the documentary film has been used for purposes of propaganda. We should once again remember that film, like any medium, manipulates and distorts what it interprets. The idea that the documentary is "more truthful" than other forms of filmic expression is a dangerous bias that the film consumer should avoid thinking. Just because the subject matter of a given movie looks realistic does not mean that what we are seeing is unbiased or completely true. As viewers we should always **question what** we see when watching a film, whether it be fictional, experimental-abstract, or documentary. Just how the documentary has been used for propaganda and distorted perspective will be the subject of much of the rest of this chapter.

V.   Propaganda and Dziga Vertov's "Kino-eye," the Urban Documentary, and John Grierson

Eisenstein's approach of using non-fiction filmmaking, in *Que Viva Mexico,* for propaganda purposes had to have been influenced by the work of Dziga Vertov. During the time Flaherty was laboring on *Nanook of the North*, Vertov had finished three feature films using newsreel footage shot during the civil war in Russia. As we noted in Chapter Eight, Vertov had the responsibility of editing the footage sent to him from the front. Rather than present the material in conventional newsreels, Vertov explored how editing could make the footage more dynamic. Dziga Vertov's "self-reflexive" attitude, of drawing attention to the film medium, led to a philosophy of filmmaking called "kino-eye."

Most documentaries of that time did not want to draw attention to the filmmaking process, preferring the philosophy of invisible editing. Vertov believed the fact that the subject was being filmed was part of the event being recorded. The audience is constantly reminded that it is watching a movie when viewing his films. In his most famous picture, *Chelovek s kinoapparatom* (1929) (*The Man with a Movie Camera*), we see shots of the cameraman, people reacting to the camera, the footage being edited, and animated segments where the camera "walks away" on the tripod. Vertov's approach is concerned with documenting the experience of what is happening at the moment. Filming, for Vertov meant including the presence of the film medium itself.

One important aspect of Vertov's form and style, which makes his work so different from what other non-fiction filmmakers were doing at the time, was his openness in presenting many of his biases on film. Vertov and his group believed that they were part of a dynamic new political system that would fix society's ills. This belief underlined everything they shot. The Vertov documentaries celebrated life in Russia under the new regime. Using hidden cameras they filmed ordinary people engaged in everyday activities--a kind of early version of "candid camera." The intention of this type of filmmaking was to capture the feeling of vibrancy and energy of contemporary Russia. They believed that life in their country was not yet perfect. There were still problems left over, from czarist days, before their government took power. Vertov, at first, filmed these lingering concerns with the idea that if they were brought to public attention so that they could be corrected. Later, when many believed that these problems should have been rectified, Vertov and others were prevented from filming any reference to them at all.

Kino-eye did not restrict itself to exotic locations or newsworthy events for its material. It sought to celebrate the vitality of everyday life and the filmmaking process that could record it. It was propagandistic, in the manner it promoted its political views. The style was honest in that it did not try to conceal its filmic techniques with invisible editing or create the illusion of "reality" in the manner of Hollywood melodrama. Most non-fiction filmmakers have been concerned with exploiting, rather than questioning, how the medium seems to record reality in a truthful way. Dziga Vertov prided himself, and tried very hard, in his efforts to provide an accurate view of what he saw within the context of his openly declared interests and bias.

No matter how much one agrees or disagrees with Vertov's politics, we should appreciate his attempt to honestly present his views in a manner that questioned the way the motion picture medium distorts what it photographs.

However intriguing his kino-eye philosophy may be, there was an inherent problem in the way people responded to it. Most audiences preferred to see escapist Hollywood fantasy to Vertov's documentary interpretation. Also, when the new regime did not take care of social problems, like those which Vertov documented at first, it was more difficult to blame their existence on the previous Czarist government. As Stalin gained power in Russia he became more insistent on dictating what films could and should not show. Vertov was increasingly deprived of his freedom, to honestly explore his subject matter, because of governmental restriction.

The lack of audience for the documentary, as compared to fictional film, has dictated the kind of movie that has been made throughout most of the medium's history. If popularity at the box-office can not financially support making documentaries, the filmmaker must get financing from a sponsor. This sponsor, however, usually will expect certain attitudes to be reflected in the motion picture which will ultimately dictate its content. Given this situation it is not surprising that the documentary would become associated with propaganda, following the decline of the lyrical--usually Hollywood financed--feature film. A major filmmaker involved with propaganda documentaries, in the early 1930s, was John Grierson--the British social scientist who originally coined the word "documentary" to describe Flaherty's *Moana* in 1926.

Having been interested in the motion picture as a teaching tool since the early 1920s, John Grierson both appreciated and deplored the way he saw the medium being used. Grierson was impressed with the technical capabilities of Hollywood, but found the content of their movies wanting. As a social scientist he had a "love/hate" relationship with Flaherty. He welcomed the subject matter of Flaherty's documentaries but was irritated with their lack of social perspective. While Grierson could relate to the way Vertov's filmmaking projected a political agenda, he would have liked more pedagogy in the way Vertov's films taught viewers about the particular subject on the screen. Eisenstein's approach to non-fiction filmmaking, as attempted in the ill-fated *Que Viva Mexico,* probably came closest to Grierson's interests in how he felt the medium should be used. John Grierson saw himself as a teacher and this perception was at the heart of his relationship to film and the focus of his work.

To produce the type of documentary he wanted to see, John Grierson persuaded the British government to finance a unit that could make short educational documentaries reflecting his country's way of life. In many respects Grierson created an environment for non-fiction filmmaking similar to the one in which Vertov made his movies. The arrangement allowed the pictures to be made without their having to make money in return. The films also resembled Vertov's in that they often were filmed in one's "own backyard" rather than in some exotic locale.

Vertov's tendency to shoot locally, particularly in metropolitan locations, was picked up by a number of other filmmakers around the world leading to a genre that has been called the "urban documentary." The 1926 French picture *Rien que les heures*, and the German *Berlin die Symphone einer Gross-stadt* (1927) (*Berlin: Symphony of a Great City*) documented the "life" of a city--Paris and Berlin respectively--in the course of one day. Paul Strand's 1921 picture *Manahatta* featured shots of New York, structured around Walt Whitman's poem of the same name. These films were vehicles for exploring filmmaking techniques, and showing the vitality of the urban center. Grierson's documentaries were meant to educate the viewer about their subjects. Nor did he restrict the material to urban areas.

Rather than functioning as a filmmaker as such, Grierson served as a producer who made it possible for others to make the kind of films he wanted to see. Grierson worked with the British government to get financing, provided the facilities for the documentaries to be made, and assisted directors like Alberto Cavalcanti (1897-1982) and Basil Wright (1907-87) in developing their projects into completed films. These documentaries included *Drifters* (1929), a picture about the English herring industry; *Night Mail* (1936), which showed the process of overnight mail delivery by train; and *Housing Problems* (1937).

As the titles and descriptions of these pictures suggest, the Grierson inspired documentary sought to educate the viewer concerning how institutions and processes affected the British way of life. Their purpose was to make audiences appreciate these subjects more and, in some instances, address existing problems. In reviewing the content of these documentaries one does find more process films than pictures focusing on social problems. Because the pictures were funded by the government, Grierson had to be careful that he did not produce something that would get his sponsor upset. While the British government did not insist upon the kind of propaganda expected by Stalin, this relationship did put restrictions on the content and type of picture which Grierson made.

VI. The Documentary as Government Sponsored Propaganda, Leni Riefenstahl's *Triumph of the Will*, and the Non-fiction Film in W.W.II

The trend for government sponsored documentaries in the 1930s resulted in the non-fiction film being largely associated with propaganda for the next thirty years. Hollywood, and other commercial interests, found a continued market for newsreels but balked at making feature length documentaries to the degree it had in the 1920s. Government funding exerted an influence over the content of the Grierson documentaries, but it did not dictate the type of propaganda that regimes like that of Stalin's expected. The way the non-fiction film could be manipulated to actually distort reality, while appearing to tell the truth, became particularly evident in 1936 with the release of the German documentary *Triumph des Willens* (*Triumph of the Will*), by Leni Riefenstahl (b. 1902).

Leni Riefenstahl is often acknowledged as the greatest woman film director of all time. Few filmmakers' work have been more damned. A dancer and film actress, Leni Riefenstahl turned to film directing in the late 1920s. Her achievements caught the attention of Adolph Hitler, who asked Riefenstahl to direct a motion picture of the 1934 Nazi rally in Munich. Riefenstahl has claimed she declined his request, fearing that she would not be able make the picture the way she wanted. Hitler supposedly agreed to her demands, Riefenstahl accepted, and a masterpiece in cinematic propaganda was made. The director had unlimited access to the film technology she needed and the million and a half people who gathered for the rally were positioned to accomplish the visual effects Riefenstahl wanted to achieve. The event was made to look like a spiritual experience in which Adolph Hitler was treated as if he were a god. Principal messages in *Triumph of the Will* emphasized that everyone should totally support Hitler, that any challenge to his authority was treason, and that life was supposedly idyllic under the Third Reich.

The film begins with Adolph Hitler flying to Munich to meet with the party faithful. Instead of showing an airplane, we get the impression that the camera is floating through the clouds and Hitler is some sort of ephemeral deity without a physical body. Soft, spiritual music is played as Germany's "savior" "wings" his way to the city. Later, when he gets closer to the "adoring masses," this ethereal entity takes on a material shape so that the people can see him. The physical Hitler is shown as a loving and much loved man. Women swoon, babies give him the Nazi salute, and everyone else shows their awe and appreciation. Throughout the film Riefenstahl uses every camera technique she can think of to emphasize the relationship of the "great man" to his subjects. All aspects of her film style are designed to make the Nazi party look good and Adolph Hitler authoritative and even godlike.

The film is, in a sense, an incredibly expensive commercial, for Hitler and the Nazi party, in which over a million people allowed themselves to be choreographed to create a massive spectacle staged for the camera. The products being sold--Hitler and the Nazis--are portrayed as gods who "know what is best" for the "superior people" which make up Germany. The power structure presented suggests a kind of pyramid with the people at the base, the party officials above them, and Adolph Hitler at the very top. To maintain harmony in this situation everyone must go along with the dictates of those above. Anyone who would question or challenge this hierarchy and its dictates is not part of the symmetry of Nazi Germany and, consequently, an enemy of the people and the system. The consensus of a dictatorships allows for things to get done in a government. The resulting decisions of such a process, however, often fail to be in the best interests of a society or humanity as a whole. What happens if the top of the pyramid says that Jews and other ethnic minorities do not conform to the pyramid? The result, in Germany, was the deaths of millions of innocent people.

The pyramid government portrayed in *Triumph of the Will* reflected a censorship perspective taken to an extreme. Conformity to narrow standards were strictly defined, in Nazi Germany, at a horrible expense. After W.W.II, Leni Riefenstahl has repeatedly been asked to explain why she made this totally distorted film praising a dictator who created so much horror in our world. Riefenstahl, who is still alive at the time of this writing, claims she never was a Nazi, was not aware of many of the events occurring in Germany at the time, and views her film from an "artistic standpoint" rather than as a form of political expression. Riefentstahl's critics feel that her position is indicative of a failure to take moral responsibility for her film's message.

As stated earlier, Leni Riefenstahl is considered one of the greatest film directors of all time and the most famous woman filmmaker. Riefenstahl's refusal to be accountable for the misinformation and deception in *Triumph of the Will*, has prevented her from enjoying the respect of a great artist. Riefenstahl claims she willingly produced the film and the person most responsible for making it this way. Though she professes to be the author of *Triumph of the Will*, Leni Riefenstahl refuses to assume responsibility for what the movie's distorted perspective that persuaded others to be part of the Nazi cause. Her critics feel that Riefenstahl lent her name and art to promote a terrible lie. She is in no position to say that what happened in Germany, after fully endorsing this propaganda, was not in anyway her fault. Everyone in a society must assume responsibility for what his or her government does. Riefenstahl's close association with Hitler and the top Nazi officials make her all the more culpable in this matter.

Besides serving as an incredibly big budgeted advertisement for Hitler and the Third Reich, *Triumph of the Will* influenced critics and filmmakers in two ways. *Triumph of the Will* raised questions about the moral responsibility of a filmmaker, regarding the content of his or her films, and became a model for others wanting to make propaganda. Even as critics were thoroughly contemptuous of this movie's glorification of Hitler and his dictatorship, and found the way *Triumph of the Will* portrayed its subject totally inexcusable, they were overwhelmed by the film's use of lyrical poetry and its technical brilliance. Hollywood director Frank was particularly influenced by *Triumph of the Will*.

Before joining the Army during World War II, Frank Capra was one of the most commercially successful American film directors in the business. Capra's films, in a verification of the American dream, glorified a common man rising to success. His popular films include *It Happened One Night* (1934), *Mr. Deeds Goes to Town* (1936), *Mr. Smith Goes to Washington* (1939), *Meet John Doe* (1941), and the Christmas classic, *It's a Wonderful Life* (1946). Having made commercially successful Hollywood movies, noted for their great emotional appeal, for decades, Capra suddenly found himself being asked to make "information" films for the United States Army. Capra had never made a documentary. He was shown enemy propaganda pictures, including *Triumph of the Will*, to get an idea of what was expected of him. Frank Capra found himself facing something of a moral dilemma following these screenings.

Like many American directors who saw this film, Capra must have been taken aback with how Leni Riefenstahl was using the persuasive film techniques, developed by Hollywood, to induce viewers to accept her subject matter without question. Where Hollywood employed these methods to sell escapist fantasy, Riefenstahl was marketing a "little jerk"--as Frank Capra described him--as some kind of god. Tragically, some people were buying the idea. Charlie Chaplin's initial reaction to Hitler, it is said, was one of extreme irritation that the dictator had stolen his makeup. By World War II Hollywood filmmakers saw Hitler as more than some competitor, who was stealing their ideas. He was a threat to world democracy.

It was one thing to use the persuasive film style of Hollywood for escapist fantasy. It was another thing to use these devices to make propaganda that lied, as had Leni Riefenstahl. At first Capra was at a loss regarding how he could make Army information films that would compete with the Riefenstahl product. A dictatorship sees no problem with lying because the ends supposedly justify the means. People in a democracy, Capra rightly believed, expect the truth from their government. How could Capra make films that told the truth and, for a small sum of money, challenge the big budget propaganda of Leni Riefenstahl? Eventually Capra decided the best strategy in combating Riefenstahl's propaganda was turning it, and its lies, upon itself.

Frank Capra, like John Grierson, saw himself as an educator. Taking footage from *Triumph of the Will* and other enemy propaganda films, Capra made a series of seven documentaries for the Army entitled *Why We Fight*. Capra used the same film that his adversaries had produced but re-edited it to reflect a democratic perspective. By doing this Capra was able to show his audience what the enemy was saying, give the Allied perspective, and teach the viewer why America and her partners were fighting in this war. Because he was using footage that Riefenstahl and others had, unwittingly, made for him, Capra's production expenses involved little more than the cost of editing and narration. It was a relatively inexpensive, and ultimately very effective, series of films that succinctly informed the viewer about the history and nature of the war. Originally meant as orientation films for American soldiers entering the Army, the *Why We Fight* series eventually was shown to civilians in the United States. They also were seen, overseas, by Allied audiences in the millions.

Given the priority of the war, it is not surprising that the propaganda documentary was the predominant type of non-fiction film being made during the 1940s. The educational documentary, which too often had a strong propagandistic emphasis, was one of the most prominent forms of "non-fiction" film in the 1950s. By 1959, as the result of the work by a French anthropologist named Jean Rouch (b. 1917), a new approach to documentary filmmaking was developed that tried to counter the propagandistic bias.

VI. *Cinéma-vérité* and Beyond

Jean Rouch was interested in making anthropological films in Africa. After completing some of his earlier documentaries he was disturbed to find that the people appearing in them did not always agree with the way he interpreted their culture. Concerned that his misinterpretation and biases were falsely influencing the integrity of the information in his films, Rouch radically changed the process in which he produced his pictures. Instead of allowing a preconceived perspective to dictate how he would put his ethnographic studies together, Rouch actively involved the subjects, being photographed, in determining what would be said. Rouch would shoot some footage, ask the subjects to interpret what was on the screen, and invite suggestions concerning how they could make the most truthful film possible. If different footage was needed to accomplish this goal, Rouch and his subjects would produce it. The same process was utilized in post-production. The subjects would look at the edited film, make suggestions, and Rouch would rearrange the footage to reflect their concerns.

Instead of producing propaganda, or creating questionable educational documentaries with a dubious bias, Jean Rouch tried to use non-fiction film to make objective interpretations of his subject matter. Rouch took full responsibility for the content of his films and developed a means to become more sensitive to his own prejudices and incorrect assumptions. The integrity of the subject matter's treatment was a foremost concern in his approach to filmmaking. Because of this interest, Rouch looked back to the work and philosophy of Dziga Vertov as a model. Rouch eventually came up with the term *cinéma-vérité*--"cinema truth"--in 1959, to describe what he was doing.

"*Cinéma-vérité*," as the term suggests, attempts to define a philosophy in which the filmmaker tries to be as objective about the subject being filmed as possible. Vertov's kino-eye sought to work around the biases of the motion picture medium when he was making his documentary films. The earlier Russian director was, however, very open and not at all apologetic about the political bias in his films. Conversely, Rouch was very concerned about how his personal biases could color and distort the filmed depiction of his subject matter. He came up with his *cinéma-vérité* style of filmmaking to work around what he saw as a deficiency.

By the 1960s *cinéma-vérité* was being widely practiced outside of France, including in the United States. Practitioners saw this approach to non-fiction filmmaking as a desirable alternative to propaganda, stilted educational films, or short newsreels that were incapable of covering a subject in depth. Going back to the spirit of Flaherty and *Nanook of the North*, the *cinéma-vérité* filmmakers were using the film medium to study and explore a subject--to learn from the experience--rather than manipulate the motion picture to reflect a preconceived bias. The development of lightweight, and relatively inexpensive, motion picture equipment and new film stocks enabled filmmakers to shoot subjects that previously would have been inaccessible. The growth of television also provided a market, for this product, which heretofore had not existed.

While there were variations in the way *cinéma-vérité* filmmakers made their films, most of them approached the process of shooting their subject as a learning experience. Instead of knowing exactly what they wanted to film and how, these directors shot what occurred before them. After completing their shooting the filmmakers looked for some type of structure, for a film, hidden in the substantial amount of footage they had accumulated. In this fashion the form of the *cinéma-vérité* documentary was determined by events and the process of learning about the subject, rather than from a preconceived bias or script.

Cinéma-vérité challenged previous forms of documentary and gave the concern for objectivity a higher priority than it had in most previous forms of non-fiction filmmaking. However, by the end of the 1960s, the notion that a director could be unbiased, even when using *cinéma-vérité* techniques, eventually was questioned. Critics argued that a filmmaker's decision to turn on a camera, for filming, or leave it off, is in itself a bias. The way a subject is filmed also constitutes a bias. The preference of using certain footage for the completed film, while discarding other shots, is another form of bias. The particular order in which the footage is spliced together is still another instance where the filmmaker imposes a perspective on the completed motion picture. While objectivity is an admirable goal, these critics maintained, it is impossible for a filmmaker's attitudes and prejudices to be absent from his or her film.

Today's filmmakers still use many of the *cinéma-vérité* methods. Journalists, for example, often shoot a news story in progress to produce programs in which they are not sure of the outcome. Treating a subject as an open-ended film does enable the director to learn from the process--and become more sensitive to what the subject entails--than if the motion picture was filmed entirely from a very specific pre-written script. The claim that a process of filmmaking can make a documentary more objective is now treated with suspicion. Rather than rely on a process to make the filmmaker objective, most critics believe it is more honest for the filmmaker to be clear about his or her rationale in making a given movie. The filmmaker should acknowledge and accept responsibility for the message, perspectives, and biases in his or her work. It is also the responsibility of the viewer think about the quality, of a film's message, and the biases inherent in that film.

VII. Conclusion

The documentary or non-fiction film has been a popular type of filmic expression since the invention of the motion picture. Although viewers tend to associate the documentary with a "truthful" documentation of events in the "real" world, the non-fiction film has often been associated with propaganda and calculated distortions of the truth. Our review of the history of the documentary indicates that the film viewer should question the messages and biases found in the non-fiction film as strongly as those in "staged" narratives. Indeed, documentaries have often been carefully staged for the camera.

One important narrative filmmaker who questioned the way audiences relate to documentaries, and explored how "non-fiction" film can be staged to suggest "honesty" and "realism," was Orson Welles. Welles structured his first picture, *Citizen Kane*, around an apparent newsreel and incorporated faked "non-fiction" footage in this movie as well. Besides challenging the way we watch and interpret movies, Orson Welles revolutionized the manner films would be made from that time onward.

CHAPTER TWELVE

CASE STUDY: *CITIZEN KANE*

CHAPTER OBJECTIVES: *Examine how this classic picture can be seen as a culmination of many of the developments in film history, prior to 1940, and consider how it can be used for a case study that can identify various types of film criticism.*

I. How Should We Study *Citizen Kane* ?

Before addressing the question of <u>how</u> to study *Citizen Kane* we should ask <u>why</u> we are devoting our last chapter to this film. One reason is because this motion picture has received so much critical attention. During those occasions when critics have been asked to name their top favorite ten films of all time, *Citizen Kane* has generally been near the top of the list. Made in 1941, this movie is seen as a benchmark in motion picture history. No film of its period succeeded so well in summing up, stylistically, what the cinema had been doing up to that time. It was more than just a synthesis of current film styles, however. After building upon its cinematic precedents *Citizen Kane* attempted to be innovative in every area of filmmaking that its collaborators could define. Most critics would argue these filmmakers more than succeeded. *Citizen Kane* was, to say the least, a brilliant film debut for its twenty-six year old director, Orson Welles.

An extensive examination of *Citizen Kane* can be justified, as the last chapter in this book, for at least three reasons. (1) The fact that *Citizen Kane* is recognized as a classic, by so many critics, makes it worthy of study in its own right. (2) The movie's unique position as a "synthesizer" of trends in film history enables us to use it to review most of the critical themes and perspectives described in the previous chapters. (3) Finally, because *Citizen Kane* can be examined from so many critical perspectives, our study can serve as a method for recognizing several analytical approaches that may be used to critique other films. Given these factors, the following chapter is not so much an examination of one film as it is meant to serve as a model for identifying approaches to film research and analysis that you might like to address in the future.

There are two general ways that a critic can analyze a film. One approach is to do a close analytical study of the form and style of the motion picture in question. This perspective can consider the movie as a closed body of information. The other approach is to examine the film in the context of outside information--to judge the film on the basis of some category such as genre or national cinema. We will begin by considering how one would approach a stylistic analysis, of *Citizen Kane*, without benefit of any outside data or information regarding its content.

A good way to structure our stylistic analysis of *Citizen Kane* is to consider the movie from the perspective of our four basic questions outlined in Chapter One: (1) *What is the film about?* (2) *How is the film conveying its information?* (3) *Why is the filmmaker interested in stating the ideas expressed?* (4) *How successful is the film in achieving its particular goals in this communication process?* You will notice that the order and phrasing of these questions is not identical to what we presented in Chapter One. We made these modifications to better address progressive changes in your critical skills.

When considering the question of who a film is about one must first place the picture in one of the three general categories: narrative, documentary, and experimental. *Citizen Kane* is considered a Hollywood narrative. Its emphasis on experimentation, and use of concepts associated with documentary, makes it a highly unusual narrative motion picture, however. In a narrative the "what" usually involves a plot in which some conflict needs to be resolved. Our strategy of devising a "one-liner," for identifying the general nature of a movie, is one good way to isolate this principal conflict. We might describe *Citizen Kane* as a movie in which: *A reporter tries to understand a famous media mogul by finding the meaning behind his dying word, "rosebud."* Much more could be said about *Citizen Kane*, if we wish to do our first principal question justice. Just "what" we determine a film is about depends upon how we analyze the picture. This calls for a more detailed understanding of this movie's form.

Besides giving us a general sense of what a movie is about, the "one liner" is useful for helping us get an idea regarding the form of the film. We find that *Citizen Kane* is actually structured around the investigation of a reporter, named Thompson. He is trying to understand who newspaper mogul Charles Foster Kane was based on the meaning of the mysterious dying last word that Kane uttered--"rosebud." The manner in which Thompson conducts his investigation determines the form of the film. Most of the major sequences of the picture center around interviews and research, that Thompson pursues, relating to people associated with Charles Foster Kane. When considering an analysis of the form of a film it is always useful to think about the significance of the title and the first and last shots of the movie. The first shot sets us up for everything we will see in that

276

picture. The last shot contains the last information we take away from the film.

"Form follows function" and the stylistic elements of a movie are manipulated to accomplish the effect which that film is trying to achieve. Of the four elements of style, editing is most involved with the way the various parts of a film are put together to create its overall form. *Citizen Kane* has a very unusual form in that it is structured around the reporter Thompson's investigation. We do not get to know Charles Foster Kane by observing his behavior, from one perspective, in standard linear progression. That is the form which most movies take. Rather, *Citizen Kane* starts with Kane dying and we then get to know him through the observations of <u>several</u> people associated with him. Our understanding of Kane develops the same way a researcher gets to know his or her subject over time--by virtue of multiple perspectives as presented in the different sources found in one's research. An analysis of the editing in *Citizen Kane,* then, would identify the film's form, consider how this structure effects the picture's content, isolate the relationships the director creates between the movie's parts, and reflect on why these associations are being made.

The mise-en-scene of *Citizen Kane* is concerned with showing viewers the world of Charles Foster Kane, the various places which the newspaper reporter must visit during his investigation, and the people associated with Kane. More than just establishing setting, the mise-en-scene in *Citizen Kane* is also interested in evoking the mood and spirit of the film, and the personalities, interests, and problems of the characters. An analysis of the mise-en-scene would identify these effects and consider why the director wants to convey such impressions to the viewer.

Camerawork, as we noted in Chapter Three, <u>guides</u> the viewer through the mise-en-scene. The camera is used to isolate what the director wants us to observe. This element of style can be considered in terms of camera adjustment, camera placement, and camera movement. In each instance the filmmaker is working with a particular camera effect to direct the viewer's attention to certain visual information. Again, the analyst should consider <u>how</u> the filmmaker is using the medium to communicate with the viewer, <u>why</u> he or she is doing this, and <u>what</u> effect results from this attempt at communication. As we will see in our examination of the production history of *Citizen Kane,* the camerawork in this film was considered particularly revolutionary at the time the movie came out.

Sound is the fourth element of film style which a filmmaker can use to communicate information to an audience. Film sound is of two general types--"diegetic" and "non-diegetic." Diegetic sound is a natural part of the environment, while non-diegetic sound occurs off-screen and cannot be heard by the people seen in the frame. Non-diegetic sound is most closely associated with an off-screen narrator or music. These non-diegetic elements impose a commentary, or a mood, on the content of the film which is designed to manipulate how the viewer interprets what is on the screen. An analysis of the sound in *Citizen Kane* should identify <u>what</u> Orson Welles is seeking to achieve, with this element of style, and consider <u>why</u> the non-diegetic sound is being used in this manner.

After identifying the form and style of *Citizen Kane* the analyst needs to assess his or her findings. This filmic communication either works, for the viewer, or it does not. If it does, why has it worked? If it does not, is the problem with the message, the transmission, or the receiver? It is the responsibility of the critic to try and honestly ascertain, and assess, what has transpired and why.

The above discussion has considered how we could analyze *Citizen Kane* as a closed body of data. As our studies have shown, access to information outside a film's content can also add to our understanding of the viewing experience. One way we can get a broader perspective of what a movie is about is by putting that film in a category and comparing it with others of its type. We discussed a number of these categories, that can be used to classify films, in Chapter One. The three most basic types of film are narrative, documentary, and experimental. A movie can also be examined in relation to national, auteur, genre, and classical distinctions. Does *Citizen Kane* reflect the philosophy of an auteur? If so, we would research Orson Welles's background and interests to see if we can isolate an underlying philosophy, or theme(s), that may make this film more understandable. Can *Citizen Kane* be seen as a part of a genre? Genre study involves the recognition of a common narrative shared by a group of films. What, in the case of *Citizen Kane*, could this common narrative be? Since *Citizen Kane* is considered such an innovative <u>Hollywood</u> film, is it more of an "experimental" picture than a standard narrative? Why is it a "classic"? What makes *Citizen Kane* different from other movies? What was the outcome of its being different? Did Hollywood change, because of this film, or did *Citizen Kane* remain a one-of-a-kind phenomenon? Such questions demand that *Citizen Kane* be examined in contexts outside of itself. This involves researching and defining the categories of Welles as auteur, the genre of which *Citizen Kane* may be a part, and the nature of Hollywood films before and after "*Kane.*"

The following chapter will suggest some ways that *Citizen Kane* can be analyzed from all of these perspectives and more. This movie, as we shall see, can also be examined by comparing it with attitudes relating to documentary film, of the time, and from the standpoint of censorship. Our discussion by no means provides the definitive list of approaches for analyzing *Citizen Kane*. This chapter can only show the film consumer some of the many different, and productive, ways one can look at the same movie. We will begin our discussion by providing some perspective on the background of Orson Welles, the director of *Citizen Kane*, as auteur.

II. Orson Welles as Auteur

Orson Welles was born on May 6, 1915. His father was an eccentric inventor and his mother was a pianist. Considered a child prodigy from infancy, Welles spent much of his childhood in adult company. Young Orson's interest in art and theater was encouraged by his family and friends. When at the Todd School for boys, in Woodstock, Illinois, fifteen-year-old Orson produced a stage play, built around *Richard III,* in which he incorporated lines from other Shakespeare plays. The result was an unusual, and highly original, adaptation that anticipated his later Shakespearean screen and theater productions.

At the age of sixteen, Orson Welles embarked on a walking trip of Ireland where he intended to occupy himself painting Irish landscapes. After running out of money, he developed second thoughts about his romantic undertaking. When Orson decided his career as a painter seemed to be leading nowhere, the ex-painter sought employment, as an actor, at the well known Gate Theatre in Dublin. Orson Welles had been praised and encouraged all his life. This support prepared Orson to present himself with a supreme self-confidence, belying his years, that impressed the theater's producers. He was immediately hired for one of their plays. Orson exercised this same bravura--which would forever be associated with the man and his work--in performance. His acting debut in Dublin was, in short, a great success.

Welles went to New York, following his triumph in Dublin, and was disturbed by this city's lack of interest in him. It would not be too many years before New York's attitude towards Orson Welles would change. While pursuing the type of theater roles he felt desirable, Welles spent the early 1930s getting paid to do voice work in countless radio dramas being aired at the time. Though unbilled, his versatility with voices enabled Orson to go from a marginal living to a salary of $1,000 a week, almost overnight. [1] By the age of twenty Orson Welles was recognized as a gifted professional in radio and was also developing the reputation as a brilliant director of experimental theater.

The young artist was a whirlwind of activity, during these years, rehearsing Shakespeare productions in the daytime and doing live radio at night. Often he would do several shows in the same evening for different networks. To work around the logistical problems, of getting to the programs on time, Welles is said to have hired an ambulance for transportation--a practice that was made illegal when the authorities found out about it. Such audacity was typical of Orson Welles's brash, unorthodox, and self-confident way of doing things. Eventually this brashness would create a controversy that made international headlines.

For a Halloween broadcast on October 30, 1938, Welles thought a radio version of the H.G. Wells (no relation) 1898 novella, *War of the Worlds,* might be amusing. He also thought it would be interesting if they presented the program in a format resembling a news broadcast. *War of the Worlds* began fairly conventionally. An announcer introduced Welles, who talked about our world being watched by alien beings, existing outside our planet, who have an intelligence far greater than our own. The format then shifted to what appeared to be an actual weather report, to a program of music by "Ramón Raquello and his orchestra," to a news bulletin about atmospheric disturbances over Mars, back to the music program, and ending with a series of increasingly intense news bulletins relating to what finally was identified as an invasion of our world by Martians.

For those who tuned in late, and listeners did so by the hundreds of thousands, Welles's Halloween program was interpreted as a series of actual news broadcasts. People panicked. Highways were jammed by those trying to escape. Men, ready to defend their families, patrolled their property with shotguns. Other individuals put wet towels around their windows and doors to keep out the poisonous gas Welles's broadcast claimed the Martians were unleashing upon their victims. Some sought to spend their last moments in church. Finally, after the broadcast was over and listeners discovered that other stations were not providing live coverage of the destruction of the earth, things settled down. Many people were now quite upset with Orson Welles, however. Numerous lawsuits were filed but, given the lack of precedent for such litigation, they were eventually all dismissed. Most descriptions of the incident say that no one died from the ensuing panic. Given the large number of people involved in the scare, however, some critics have been skeptical that there was no loss of life.

Orson Welles's famous 1938 broadcast continues to be viewed as controversial. Some accounts have treated it as a kind of prank--an indication of how naive audiences were back then. Others have praised it as an innovative means of challenging the media--a way of getting people to strongly question what they are told. The respected radio producer Charles Chilton, who was working for the British Broadcasting Corporation at the time Welles broadcast his program in America, views it as neither. In a conversation with the author, in July of 1993, Mr. Chilton described Welles's methods, in this instance, as irresponsible.

Mr. Chilton's criticism of Welles appears to be based upon the position that both the transmitter and the receiver have certain responsibilities in the communication process. As the "transmitter," Orson Welles took a format of radio communication associated with information--the news bulletin--and purposely employed it in a misleading context. Audiences expect news formats to be used in a truthful manner to convey the news. Welles had changed the rules, without their realizing it, and betrayed this trust. For Mr. Chilton there was nothing innovative nor admirable in someone purposefully breaking down this communication process. Since the receivers had no framework for interpreting his message, other than to assume it was true, it is no surprise that confusion and panic ensued.

Throughout his career the personality, interests, philosophy, and iconoclasm of this man would be associated with innovation and/or controversy. Since childhood Orson Welles had been a self-confident, brash, articulate individual, fascinated with the arts and the media used to communicate them. At age fifteen young Orson had no qualms about rearranging Shakespeare's writings to fit his own sense of what could be interesting. At sixteen Welles went to a foreign country and, self-assured beyond his years, performed in one of Ireland's top theaters with intelligence and skill. While at the Gate Theatre in Dublin, Welles also developed the philosophical perspectives, regarding his art, that would influence his work from that time forward.

According to his biographer, Barbara Leaming, one of the things about "the Gate" that fascinated Orson Welles was its emphasis on stylization over realism. This company did not want to create an illusion of reality. Instead they took pains, in their productions, to remind audiences that they were watching theater. The viewer was forced to think about how this medium worked, even as he or she was relating to the story of a play. [2] The Gate's formalist emphasis in theater, in the middle 1930s, was similar to the philosophy behind Vertov's documentaries, and Eisenstein's montage, a decade earlier. As a director Orson Welles's plays, and later his films, would also draw attention to their medium.

Throughout his artistic career, Welles continuously looked for the dramatic essence of a work and would do everything he could to bring it out. He did this even if it meant rearranging Shakespeare or rewriting how a medium was to convey its message. Sometimes, when he broke the accepted rules in dealing with a particular form or format--as was the case with the "news broadcast" in *War of the Worlds*--he got in trouble. Welles gloried in being a maverick and an iconoclast. His unorthodox methods often made him enemies. It also brought him fame.

Following the *War of the Worlds* controversy the RKO film studio decided that Orson Welles's name recognition might be what they needed to reverse a trend in disappointing receipts at the box-office. They offered him an unprecedented contract to use their studio to make movies any way he wanted. Orson could write, produce, direct, and/or star in these movies or wear all four hats at once. The twenty-five-year-old Welles had never made a movie. He accepted their offer and moved to Hollywood in 1940. After considering some projects, which he later abandoned, Orson Welles eventually produced the movie *Citizen Kane*.

III. Preproduction: The Genre of the "Newspaper Film" and the Form of *Citizen Kane*

Orson Welles was an artist who was particularly intrigued with how a medium, and an audience's expectations regarding it, influence the communication of its message. He was also interested in how people who controlled the media, like Adolph Hitler--and some would say Orson Welles himself--could misuse a medium and distort the message. Given these interests, it is not surprising that Welles would embrace a story about a newspaper mogul for his first movie. As innovative as *Citizen Kane* would prove to be, this picture was not the first to focus on people associated with newspapers for its subject matter.

Many analyses of *Citizen Kane* do not consider this picture in the context of a "newspaper genre." A review of popular plays and films of the time reveals that such a genre did exist. First produced in 1928, *The Front Page* was one of the most influential of the newspaper plays. In fact, *The Front Page* was turned into two film versions prior to *Citizen Kane--The Front Page* (1931) and *His Girl Friday* (1940). A remake of *The Front Page*, set in 1920s, was produced in 1974, and a modern version entitled *Switching Channels,* which took place in a television station, was made in 1988. An examination of *The Front Page* can help to define the general form, and many of the conventions of the "newspaper genre."

Written by former journalists Ben Hecht and Charles MacArthur, *The Front Page* was a black comedy in which cynical newspaper reporters do anything to get a story. They are much more interested in covering the hanging of an accused man, Earl Williams, than considering the fact that Williams probably is innocent. The play portrayed the newspaper man as brash, misanthropic, and insensitive towards those whom they write about. Rather than offering a pious condemnation of an impenitent character, this drama reveals the peculiar qualities of the newspaper reporter through the use of humor. Though distasteful, this particular animal is not shown as innately vicious. The reporter exists this way because society encourages the callous behavior and sensationalism he or she provides. When the play debuted in New York, reviewer Brooks Atkinson believed *The Front Page* to be "realistic," but denounced its use of language because it ". . . degrades those who speak and hear it." When *The Front Page* was given a New York revival in 1946, Atkinson looked back on his previous comments with "amusement." [3]

Initially, Brooks Atkinson saw *The Front Page* as a disturbing comedy dealing with ". . . the skepticism, the callousness, the contempt, the vague dissatisfaction with their lot, the boorishness, the brutal jesting and the omniscience. . ." of the newspaper reporter. Atkinson blamed his feelings of uneasiness on the foul language. An argument can be made that what made the play disturbing was the way it asked an audience to question its own acceptance of this work's dispassionate atmosphere. One can laugh at an innocent person, being hung, but the nature of one's laughter should be carefully considered. Callous reporters mold public opinion and it is this callousness that allows unfortunate victims, like Earl Williams, to suffer the consequences. By 1946 neither the language nor the cold portrait of the reporter, in the black comedy of *The Front Page,* was disturbing to Atkinson. These conditions were accepted as recognizable standards of the newspaperman's behavior. Indeed, the type of discomfort that Atkinson initially felt may have been a minority reaction. Given the success of *The Front Page,* audiences appeared to have embraced this interpretation almost as soon as it debuted.

As is true of any successful work, *The Front Page* encouraged imitations. While *The Front Page* was the most successful newspaper play to use a comic format, stage productions like *Five Star Final* continued exploring concepts we can associate with the newspaper genre. When Hollywood needed writers and stage actors for the talkies, in the late twenties and early thirties, they looked to the New York theater. Many of these theater people had been associated with the newspaper plays. Working or former journalists, including Hecht and MacArthur, were also recruited by Hollywood to serve as screenwriters at this time. Not surprisingly, the newspaper genre was well represented among the popular types of motion picture then being made. An examination of the output of the Warner Brothers Studio, in the 1930s, reveals that over thirty of their feature films have plots involving reporters and the press. A number of these pictures, like *Five Star Final*, were adaptations of popular Broadway plays.

The newspaper genre centers around a stereotype of the reporter. This individual is brash, energetic, articulate, self-confident, focused, very conscious of the sensational, and willing to let the ends justify the means--

descriptions that have also been used to describe the personality and behavior of Orson Welles. Exceptionally receptive to minute elements relating to a story, the reporter can be equally insensitive to the feelings, or the fate, of the people he or she is writing about. The reporter feels an almost pathological need to be "on top of things" and is extremely suspicious of any attempt to be misled or "played for a sucker." This suspicious nature usually results in the reporter exuding an air of callous skepticism. Often this type of newspaper reporter indulges in self-righteous justification when countering allegations that he or she is self-centered and insensitive.

The plot of a newspaper genre picture centers around the personality and behavior of the reporter. Frequently the reporter's "tunnel vision" for getting the story at all costs is central to the newspaper picture's structure. Many of the films in this genre concentrate on the abuses of the media, and the tragic consequences that can occur, when people are made expendable for a story.

It is not surprising that Orson Welles became interested in making a film about a newspaper mogul. The genre had produced some popular movies. "William Randolph Hearst" and "Joseph Pulitzer" were names that the public followed, with interest, in the very papers these newspaper magnates controlled. Welles was very much aware of how the media, and the communication process, was being abused by demagogues like Hitler. He also was concerned about how people were, at times victims of irresponsible media manipulation by Hearst, Pulitzer and, some critics would argue, Welles himself. A newspaper film which focused on a fictional newspaper mogul would allow the new film director to explore these issues.

A genre will determine, in part, the form its movies will take. Few newspaper narratives ever used the genre to create such a fascinating form as that found in *Citizen Kane*. Orson Welles, and scriptwriter J. Herman Mankiewicz, largely developed the structure of the movie around the process by which a reporter researches a story. The film can be broken down into eight principal parts. The first segment uses an omniscient camera to invade the private domain of Charles Foster Kane--a stone castle-like mansion called "Xanadu." Through the privileged perspective of the camera, we see Kane in bed. He says his dying word, "rosebud," and drops a paperweight which shatters on the floor. Sequence #2 is in the form of a newsreel being projected for some reporters in a theater. The newsreel tells of the death of Charles Foster Kane and summarizes his life and career. As David Bordwell and Kristin Thompson have pointed out, in their analysis of this film, this newsreel is a blueprint for the structure of the overall movie. [4]

The traditional skepticism of the newspaperman prevents the reporters from being satisfied, with what they have seen, when the movie finishes. While the documentary has given them surface details, regarding media mogul Charles Foster Kane, they feel that there is a lot more about the man which they have not been told. The reporters speculate that if they can identify the meaning of the mysterious word "rosebud" they will be able to figure out who Charles Foster Kane really was. A reporter named Thompson is given the task of interviewing the people who knew Kane best. Segments #3-8 are sequences involving Thompson's interviews and research. Part #8 ends with all the reporters gathering together again, this time at Xanadu, to discuss Thompson's findings. This last sequence also involves an omniscient camera, which provides the viewer with privileged information.

The structure of *Citizen Kane* was quite unique for its time and is still considered highly unusual today. It was very uncommon to have the principal character die at the beginning of the movie in 1941. Instead of getting to learn about the protagonist from one point of view, the audience is asked to understand him through a series of multiple, retrospective, perspectives. Like the researcher, or the newspaper reporter, we learn about our subject by putting together "pieces of a jigsaw puzzle." It was a brilliant script and, when combined with the production methods which Orson Welles used to realize his vision, the foundation for a brilliant movie.

IV. Production: The Style of *Citizen Kane*

In an article he wrote for the February 1941 issue of the film journal, *American Cinematographer*, the cinematographer for *Citizen Kane*, Gregg Toland, described what he and Welles were trying to accomplish during the production of their picture. According to Toland, the " . . . keynote [of *Citizen Kane*] is realism. As we worked together over the script and the final, pre-production planning, both Welles and I felt this, and felt that if it was possible, the picture should be brought to the screen in such a way that the audience would feel it was looking at reality, rather than merely at a movie. . . . He [Welles] instinctively grasped a point which many other far more experienced directors and producers never comprehend: that the scenes and sequences should flow together so smoothly that the audience should not be conscious of the mechanics of picture-making. And in spite of the fact that his previous experience had been directing for the stage and for radio, he had a full realization of the great power of the camera in conveying dramatic ideas without recourse to words." [5] In keeping with a revolutionary script, and while working with their strategy of making *Citizen Kane* look as realistic as possible, Orson Welles revolutionized every aspect of mise-en-scene, editing, sound, and camerawork in his first movie.

Of all the elements of its film style the camerawork, in *Citizen Kane*, received the most attention. As Toland notes in his article, the other components of film style were adapted to allow the camerawork to make everything look realistic. "The first step," in this production process according to Toland, "was in designing sets which would in themselves strike the desired note of reality. In almost any real-life room, we are always to some degree conscious of the ceiling. In most movies, on the other hand, we see the ceiling only in extreme long-shots--and then it is usually painted in as a matte shot. . . . Therefore, the majority of our sets for *Citizen Kane* had actual ceilings." [6] This, as Toland noted, prevented them from employing the usual methods for lighting a set and recording the sound. Indeed each time a particular effect was desired, for *Citizen Kane*, and a technique was devised to accomplish it, new problems were created that had to be resolved. This was particularly true in regard to the lighting.

Usually a room set involves three walls without a ceiling which enables lights and microphones to be hung from above. The filmmakers got around this difficulty by making the ceilings out of muslin. This translucent and porous material allowed the microphones, and some of the lights, to continue to be suspended above the set. While the quality of the sound was not affected, the muslin did cut down some of the intensity of the lighting. The cinematographer needed a great deal of light to get a proper exposure within these deep sets. Welles's concern for realism made Toland's job of obtaining the proper image, in his shots, one of his most difficult tasks during production. The way they addressed this challenge added to the distinctive and innovative "look" of *Citizen Kane*. Nor was this problem with lighting limited to the way they could photograph deep sets.

Because the filmmakers were filming a larger area than what usually was photographed in conventional films of the day, the lighting designer had to provide more illumination than most movie sets generally needed. More lights were added. This increased brightness could bring out flaws in props, costumes, and makeup that went undetected in situations requiring less light. Costumers had to design clothing that looked "realistic" in *Citizen Kane*. Makeup artist Maurice Seiderman had a particular challenge because several characters in the film are shown at different ages. Welles's character of Charles Foster Kane, alone, was seen in twenty-seven stages of life. Seiderman developed special latex makeup to convincingly emphasize these particular transformations. One element that Welles was concerned about was that the elderly characters' eyes look like those of an aged individual. Welles felt that, too often in films, the young actor's eyes belied the age, of the older person, which the otherwise successful makeup was trying to suggest. They got around this in *Citizen Kane*, according to writer Harlan Lebo, by using special ". . . contact lenses veined with tiny lines of paint and filled with a milky substance to stimulate the rheumy-eyed look of the very old. . . ." [7]

286

Mise-en-scene was not the only element of style, in *Citizen Kane*, which was affected by Gregg Toland's innovative camerawork and Orson Welles's concern for "realism." One editing technique, which Welles used to good advantage in *Citizen Kane*, was the dissolve. A dissolve, as we have discussed, is a superimposition of the end of a shot, which gradually disappears, over the beginning of the shot that succeeds it. This transition is often used to indicate a division between scenes or sequences, informing the viewer of change in time and/or place. Rather than use the dissolve as just a temporal and spatial transition between shots, Welles sometimes employed this device, in *Citizen Kane,* to <u>draw attention</u> to thematic relationships between the images being juxtaposed. A good example of Welles's thematic utilization of the dissolve is in his division between the sequence where Thompson reads Thatcher's written memoirs, relating to his association with Charles Foster Kane, and the reporter's interview with Kane's close associate, Bernstein.

To gain access to the wealthy late banker's unpublished memoirs, Thompson must read the original handwritten copy in the mausoleum-like setting of the Thatcher Memorial Library. The script for *Citizen Kane* describes the setting as, ". . . a room with all the warmth and charm of Napoleon's tomb." [8] The sequence begins with a low angle of a statue. After tilting down the stone figure to show Thatcher's name written on the bottom, the camera dollies back to reveal a stern and authoritarian woman, seated in front of the statue, who is dictating to Thompson what he can and cannot read from the manuscript. Attempts by Thompson to politely describe what he is looking for are cut off, by the waspish woman, before he can finish his sentences. She leads Thompson behind a heavy metal door to a table, illuminated by light rays streaming from high windows above the square stone walls. In the rather distant background a guard is getting the manuscript from a safe. There does not seem to be anything else in this large, empty room. Apparently the sole purpose of this vast "temple" is to store Thatcher's text and provide a place for it to be studied on very rare occasions. Solemn music is played as the guard gently carries the manuscript as if it is a holy relic. The manner in which the guard lays the book down on the table, acknowledges the woman, and then withdraws, is performed like some sort of ceremonial ritual.

The director shows us images, described in Thatcher's narrative, as Thompson reads the manuscript. We get a sense that the stone statue of this man, the funereal setting of the library, and the no-nonsense behavior of the woman administrator, reflect the rather cold personality of Thatcher. His written memories outline a stormy relationship between himself and Kane. At the beginning of Thompson's reading, Thatcher describes going to the Mrs. Kane's boardinghouse. He has gone there to assume guardianship

287

over the young boy, Charles, and to meet him for the first time. Charles's mother has come into a fortune. A defaulting boarder left a supposedly worthless deed to a mine in lieu of payment for his room. A family of modest means prior to this windfall, Mrs. Kane believes that her son needs to move away and become educated if he is to handle the fortune in a responsible manner. The child is taken away from his parents. This forced estrangement from his mother will color Kane's attitudes toward Thatcher for the rest of his life.

In the last written account, which Thompson reads in Thatcher's memoirs, the banker describes a meeting with Kane at a time when the latter's power had been compromised by the economic turmoil of the 1929 depression. Once again Thatcher is assuming control over Kane's finances--this time because the depression has pushed Kane into bankruptcy. During their conversation Kane offers the suggestion to his business associate, Bernstein, that if he hadn't been so rich he might have been able to have become a really great man. When Thatcher asks Kane what he would have liked to have been the latter replies, "Everything you hate."

Following Kane's pronouncement the film dissolves back to a high angle over-the-shoulder shot of Thompson. The white pages of the manuscript on the table are in front of him in the oppressive and guarded room of the Thatcher library. The director then employs a reverse-angle. This reveals that the previous shot could have been an "eyeline-match" of the guard, who is standing beside a huge closed door. The previous over-the-shoulder shot may also represent "Thatcher's perspective," as seen from the position where a painting of the banker is hanging on the wall. The entire time Thompson has been reading the manuscript the painting of Thatcher, as a bald-headed old man, has been "looking" over the reporter's shoulder from its place of reverence by the door. Frustrated that Thatcher's memoirs have not supplied him with answers to his questions, Thompson irreverently asks the painting if he is "Rosebud," and leaves the vault-like confines of the gloomy room. The shot, with the image of the painting of Thatcher dominant in the frame, then dissolves to a long shot of Bernstein's office where Thompson is now interviewing this close business associate of Kane's. The "Thatcher sequence" ends, as it began, with an image of Thatcher. Interestingly the "Bernstein sequence" begins and ends with a painting of Kane, as a bald-headed old man, hanging prominently in Bernstein's office.

The way the painting of Thatcher dissolves into one of Kane provides an interesting thematic comment on the relationship of these two men. The two paintings, of the deceased capitalists, are displayed like venerated icons. Throughout the "Thatcher sequence" we learn about Kane through an understanding of the personality of Thatcher and his opinions about his onetime ward. Thatcher was an efficient, cold, impersonal, and guarded banker. Kane had rebelled against the man, and what he stood for, since childhood. When Thatcher asked the younger man what he most wanted to become Kane tells his former guardian, "Everything you hate." Ironically, as seen in this painting, Kane's appearance does not look that much different from Thatcher's. As we will see later in the film, Kane became very much like Thatcher--everything he hated. Orson Welles is able to help make this thematic association by superimposing Thatcher's picture over Kane's in this dissolve.

We have already described the revolutionary form--which is directly related to the editing--of *Citizen Kane*. Besides questioning the way most narrative films were structured at that time, Welles was not comfortable with how Hollywood editing was linking shots in a manner that supposedly represented the way we see the "real" world. In reality we view what is happening around us in what might better be described as one "continuous action" rather than as a series of shots. The appearance of continuous, rather than segmented, action is also the effect one sees on stage. Cutting from shot to shot in film, even with invisible editing, can spatially disrupt the flow of the images presented. Welles did not want his movie to look like a series of obviously linked shots--a concern in keeping with this director's interest in avoiding artifice and concentrating on what looked "real." He got around this through deep focus.

Most Hollywood films of the time concentrated their action in a center plane within the frame. Frequently the background will be out of focus. This effect is not how we "view reality." When we look at the world around us we see things, in the distance, in a series of planes. Our eye automatically adjusts its focus on whatever our mind commands it to see. According to Toland, writing in 1941, ". . . the focal settings most frequently used in studio work (on the average picture, between 8 and 10 feet for the majority of shots)--is very small. Of course, audiences have become accustomed to seeing things this way on the screen, with a single point of perfect focus, and everything falling off with greater or less rapidity in front of and behind this particular point. But it is a little note of conventionalized artificiality which bespeaks the mechanics and limitations of photography. And we wished to eliminate these suggestions whenever possible." [9] Toland avoided selective focus and shot scenes which emphasized, or gave the impression of, great depth of field. Deep focus was the rule, rather than the exception, in *Citizen Kane*. By presenting the subject matter in a series of planes, in the same shot, the viewer had the opportunity to examine whatever information, in any portion of the frame, which he or she chose to contemplate at that moment.

By wishing to make their film look more "realistic," Welles and Toland were placing new demands on the technology and current methods of filmmaking. Each aesthetic concern changed the "way of doing things" which, in turn, affected the way the final film looked. There were four general ways the filmmakers created the appearance of a greater sense of depth in their images. These were: (1) Experiments with lighting to properly illuminate the large physical spaces being photographed. (2) The use of newly developed light sensitive film stock--Super XX. (3) Employment of lens treated with a new "Opti-cote" non-glare coating which made their cameras more sensitive to light. (4) Incorporation of special effects, or "film tricks," such as layered mattes in a shot which gave the impression that everything had been filmed in the same setting. Their efforts to give the impression of deep space were so distinctive that Toland, as cinematographer, felt compelled to write about the results, as innovations, in one of the industry's most respected journals. Gregg Toland's deep focus photography was immediately recognized as one of the major cinematic accomplishments of *Citizen Kane*. We can get some sense of the effect from an analysis of one of the scenes.

Where most directors would communicate associations and relationships through a series of juxtaposed shots, *Citizen Kane* explored these associations <u>within</u> the shots themselves. By using deep focus, Welles's layered his subject matter in various planes within a shot. Instead of isolating characters in separate spaces and cutting back and forth, Welles had us consider these individuals all at the same time and in the same general space. A good example of how this technique could work can be found in a key scene, at the beginning of Thatcher's memoirs, where the banker describes meeting the boy, Charles Foster Kane, for the first time. While his future is being decided, young Charles is outside playing in the snow. Mr. and Mrs. Kane and the banker are inside Mrs. Kane's boardinghouse. Mr. Kane does not want his son to leave but is too ineffectual to prevent Mrs. Kane, who is very strong willed, from sending Charles away with Thatcher. The new guardian's businesslike personality seems very unsuited for someone assuming the role of a surrogate parent.

This scene represents a major turning point in the life of Charles Foster Kane. All four individuals are key players in this event. The director could have cut back and forth showing the relationships of the characters, to one another, and the parts they have to play in this drama. Instead, Welles shows all four in the same shot, simultaneously, through the use of deep focus. In the extreme background, through the boarding house window, Charles can be seen innocently playing outside. He is oblivious to this momentous event in his life. In the next plane, within this same shot, Charles father stands complaining about his son being taken away but is ignored. In the center of the frame Thatcher is sitting at a table with Charles's mother. Mrs. Kane is sitting to Thatcher's left, in the right hand corner, in the extreme foreground of the frame. Thatcher instructs Mrs. Kane how to fill out the contract that will make him guardian of her son. Young Charles will be taken away, raised by Thatcher, and the fortune will be administered by this banker until his ward comes of age. Cutting from individual to individual would have forced us to recognize specific interpretations, about the characters and their relationships, that the editor would want us to make. By employing all these characters in the same frame, using deep focus, the director allows us to concentrate on whichever personality or relationships we choose to consider.

Citizen Kane is a very visual film. Since Welles made this movie, after having worked in radio, it is not too surprising that *Citizen Kane* also contains some exceptionally innovative sound techniques for a motion picture of that time. In radio dramas the producer tries to create the impression of distinctive environments using sound. A pastoral setting, for example, has a different "presence" than the interior of a church. Radio narratives, in the 1940s, were concerned about making aural distinctions between such surroundings but filmmakers generally did not. The "presence" would all tend to sound the same, no matter what the setting shown in the movie. Given his interest in realism, Welles wanted the environments to sound like they would in reality. The tomb-like marble rooms of the Thatcher Memorial Library, for example, should have a cavernous kind of sound. Welles was able to suggest this reverberating vibration by having his actors voices recorded through a device known as an "echo chamber." When he cuts to images of the young Charles Foster Kane playing in the snow, we can hear the wind blowing. These wind sounds are lessened as the camera moves into the boardinghouse and concentrates on Thatcher and Mrs. and Mr. Kane, inside. The director also effectively used overlapping sound--the aural equivalent of the visual dissolve--between scenes to emphasize thematic associations. Before ending our discussion of sound, as any element of style, it should be noted that any analysis of *Citizen Kane* must recognize Bernard Herrmann's excellent, and innovative, film score.

As with the other critical perspectives, considered in this chapter, our purpose in describing Welles's use of form and style in *Citizen Kane*, has been to show the reader how a stylistic analysis of this film can be pursued. It is up to the analyst to take these suggestions and apply them to a more detailed examination of *Citizen Kane*. The few examples we have isolated, in addressing these considerations, have not begun to explore the rich nature of this truly exceptional film. Filmmakers, from the very first, were very impressed with the revolutionary manner Orson Welles used the medium in

Citizen Kane. Not everyone, in 1941, appreciated the movie, however. Major efforts were actually made to censor the film.

V. Censorship and Exhibition: Reaction to *Citizen Kane*

We made a great deal about the fact, in our preceding discussion, that Welles and Toland wanted a film style that looked realistic. It should be noted that Orson Welles did not want realism for realism's sake in *Citizen Kane*. In earlier efforts Welles had been involved with formalistic theatrical styles designed to remind audiences that they were watching theater. The viewer was asked to think about how this medium worked, even as he or she was comprehending the message of the play. One supposed justification for creating chaos in another medium, relating to his *War of the Worlds* broadcast, was that it forced listeners to question the truth of what they heard on the radio. With *Citizen Kane* Welles avoided old forms of filmic technique. But wasn't his "more realistic" approaches to filmmaking just replacing previous forms of illusion with new types of artifice? This was true in a sense. What prevented Welles from being called just another Hollywood trickster was that *Citizen Kane* was also asking the audience to question how its medium was being used.

While our one-liner suggests that the movie is about a reporter trying to find the meaning of "rosebud," it fails to recognize that Welles was exploring other concepts as Thompson sought an answer to his question. More important than the "mystery of rosebud" is the question of the identity of "Citizen" Kane. One of the most controversial aspects of this man is that he is a newspaper mogul who misuses his medium. To establish the identity of this figure, Welles used the format of a documentary newsreel to describe this man's life. This "film within a film" resembles a popular newsreel series of the day called *March of Time*. In the "newsreel" Kane is seen, at various times, in front of the White House; standing on a train, with Theodore Roosevelt; and appearing on a balcony, next to Adolph Hitler. This all looks very realistic yet, as we know, Charles Foster Kane was a fictitious film character played by Orson Welles. This "documentary," like Welles's earlier *War of the Worlds* "news broadcast," is a lie.

Though Orson Welles and Gregg Toland took great pains in making their movie look realistic, our auteur wanted his audience to question the truthfulness of this representation. Even if a viewer does not contemplate the falseness of the newsreel, the most casual observer could not come away from *Citizen Kane* without being aware of how this mogul misused his power and promoted lies in his newspapers. The fact that Kane resembled an actual newspaper mogul, William Randolph Hearst, resulted in demands for the film to be censored.

Welles claimed that the character of Kane was not meant to represent Hearst alone, but was a composite of tycoons. There is also a question as to whether or not Hearst himself actively demanded that the film be suppressed. No matter what the actual connection with the newspaper magnate, Hearst's friends and employees--particularly film critics Louella Parsons and Hedda Hopper--claimed they needed to "protect William Randolph Hearst" from what they said was the "slander" of the movie. To its credit, RKO refused to bow to this pressure and censor the film. As a result of the controversy, Hearst papers refused to advertise *Citizen Kane*. The negative publicity undoubtedly affected the amount of money the film made during its initial release. Orson Welles's career may have been hurt as well.

According to author Harlan Lebo, before the film was even released, Welles suddenly found himself being investigated and questioned about his supposed "Communist sympathies." The Hearst papers contacted "patriotic" groups and suggested that they look into the director's political background. There was some question as to whether theaters, that tried to show the picture, might be picketed. Comparable protests and boycotts were to force Charlie Chaplin to permanently leave America eleven years later, in 1952. Eventually *Citizen Kane* was released and some of Hollywood's most prominent individuals endorsed it. But damage had been done. The controversy made its distribution more difficult and may have overshadowed people's reaction to its technical brilliance. Reviewers, for the most part, were quite taken by the film, but it did not do well with a mass audience when first released. [10]

Orson Welles was able to make one more excellent film for RKO, *The Magnificent Ambersons* (1942). Welles was released from his contract before he could finish the third film of their three picture agreement. *The Magnificent Ambersons,* which had yet to be released, was also taken away from him and the studio tacked on a totally unsuitable ending. Despite this tampering, most of the film reflected Welles's vision. The question of why RKO let him go at this time is open to speculation. *Citizen Kane* no longer was the source of controversy that it had been but Orson Welles still was. One reason RKO hired Welles in the first place was because of his flamboyance. It appears that he may have been fired for the same reason.

As an auteur, Orson Welles's challenged the rules, and presented his art, in iconoclastic ways. This both excited and irritated his critics. Welles delighted in being a maverick and this often resulted in his alienating the very people who had been most vocal in their praise of him. On rare occasion Welles would be able to get a directing assignment, with a studio, and given the freedom to make a film the way he wanted. Very often events surrounding the filming, or the content of the movie itself, would involve some conflict between Welles and the studio. This situation prevented Welles from getting another directing assignment. Unable to work well within the system as a director, Welles preferred to accept acting jobs or do the narration on documentaries. His work, in such projects, was often done more for the money than for the art. He used his earnings to finance low budget independent film productions which he directed. Welles's Shakespearean pictures *Othello* (1952) and *Chimes at Midnight (Falstaff)* (1966) were made under these conditions. Considered as being two of his very best pictures they are, indeed, two of the best film adaptations of Shakespeare ever made.

The fact that this genius was only able to produce a dozen or so films worthy of his talent, during a relatively long lifetime, is cited by historians as one of the tragedies of American film history. That it was a tragedy partially of Orson Welles's own making can not be ignored. Given Welles's propensity for challenging the very basis of the medium with which he was working, and Hollywood's interest in establishing rules for standardization, perhaps this tragedy was inevitable.

Orson Welles was to experience both success and disappointment in his career after *Citizen Kane*. Recognition that *Citizen Kane* was a classic came before the end of the decade in which it was made. Following World War II, the film was distributed in Europe. It was quickly hailed as a work of art, particularly in France. [11] After *Citizen Kane* began to be shown on television in America, in the 1950s, it gained a public following there as well. The place of *Citizen Kane* in film history, and the hearts of movie buffs, was forever assured.

VI. Conclusion

While this chapter addresses many of the ways we can look at *Citizen Kane*, it has not considered all the possible analytical approaches that can be used to examine this movie. Nor does this chapter fully investigate how each critical approach we have isolated, can identify much of what is happening in this film. An auteur approach, for example, should look at <u>all</u> of Welles's films and fully define this director's formalist approach to filmmaking. We have only mentioned a handful of Welles's other works. A genre study requires a detailed examination of most of the major films in this category, the principal themes that enable this group to exist, audience expectations of the genre, and should define chronological changes that this form of narrative has experienced over the years. We have argued that *Citizen Kane* is part of this genre. We have not fully explored why.

Hollywood films were based on invisible editing--a technique which created the illusion that the film was showing a real time and place. Welles produced a film that looked <u>more</u> realistic than the typical Hollywood picture. We have said that Welles examined every aspect of film style and sought to make each element look more realistic. We have given some examples to indicate what Welles was doing. A proper stylistic analysis of this film needs to take this critique further.

It is evident, even from a casual viewing of *Citizen Kane*, that this movie has an exuberant film style. From our discussion we find that part of this exuberance is a result of its iconoclasm--breaking the established rules. Welles's film style even questions the way we have divided film up into three principal categories--narrative, documentary, and experimental. This supposedly Hollywood narrative is structured around what appears to be a documentary newsreel. But the newsreel in *Citizen Kane* is, itself, fiction. If we can't even trust these basic distinctions, what can we believe on the screen? Though considered a narrative, Orson Welles film methods were highly <u>experimental</u>. How does this picture differ from the experimental films of the that day? While these questions do not suggest that this film should be classified as something other than a narrative, they do prompt the analyst to take a closer look at what documentary and experimental films were doing, at that time, as compared to *Citizen Kane*.

Once he had "out Hollywooded Hollywood" in making his movie look realistic, we have claimed, Welles audaciously questioned the nature of this illusion itself. His newsreel was not to be trusted. The movie argued that media moguls who used their medium to distort the truth, like Charles Foster Kane, could not be trusted. By producing this movie, and emphasizing these arguments, did Orson Welles present himself as a maverick whom Hollywood could not trust? Was it an irony that *Citizen Kane* would, itself, be threatened by censorship, or an inevitable outcome given its message? Did Welles not consider that he, himself, might become a victim of the system he was describing? We have explored some of these issues in this chapter. To properly address these questions the analyst should compare *Citizen Kane* with traditional Hollywood films, made before and after this picture, and consider whether such flagrant abuses were occurring within the media. Such a study would also call for a careful consideration of what subject matter was being censored at this time and why.

As we have seen, *Citizen Kane* is considered a great film because of its timeless power of expression. Its history and content can also be examined in several contexts relating to film study. The form of *Citizen Kane* asks the viewer to consider its subject from a multiple of perspectives. We find, after seeing these various interviews and reflections, that no one impression of "Citizen Kane," the man, is definitive. Each "Kane observer's" point of view offers different attitudes, about this person, even when it shares certain ideas in common with the others. In the same sense we find that no one analytical approach to *Citizen Kane* provides the best means for fully examining this movie. Each method offers interesting perspectives, about the picture, but also has its limitations. The more critical approaches we have, for looking at *Citizen Kane,* the better we are able to appreciate this picture. This is also true of film criticism. No interested movie consumer can learn everything there is to know about any film. But we can always ask questions. By asking questions we can continue to discover more things, about the movies, that will add to our appreciation and enjoyment of this medium.

ENDNOTES

1. Barbara Leaming *Orson Welles: A Biography*, (New York: Penguin Books, 1986), p.115.

2. Ibid., pp.53-55.

3. Brooks Atkinson, *New York Times Theater Reviews*, August 15, 1928, 19:2; August 26, 1928, VII: 2.1; and September 15, 1946, 11:21:1.

4. David Bordwell and Kristin Thompson, *Film Art: An Introduction*, (New York: McGraw Hill, Inc.), pp.86-91.

5. Gregg Toland, "Realism for *Citizen Kane,*" *American Cinematographer*, February 1941, reprinted in *American Cinematographer*, August 1991, p.37.

6. Ibid., p.38.

7. Harlan Lebo, *Citizen Kane: The Fiftieth Anniversary Album,* (New York: Doubleday,) 1990, p.91.

8. Pauline Kael, *The Citizen Kane Book,* (Boston: Little, Brown and Company,) 1971, p.133.

9. Toland, p.39.

10. Lebo, pp.144, 176-178.

11. Ibid., pp.183-184.

GLOSSARY

Actuality Short visual documents relating to a newsworthy item or human interest story. Actualities are shot to illustrate news stories while the reporter gives a voice over describing the nature of the story or event.

Art-for-art's-sake Art specifically made to be art. A body of work with no apparent cultural context or direction.

Assistant Director Person who assists the director during shooting. The "A.D." often serves a liaison between, director and crew, while seeing that the director's wishes are being carried out.

Asynchronous Sound Sound which usually is not recorded as synchronized sound, at the time a scene is filmed, but mixed in later. Non-diegetic sound is asynchronous. (See "non-diegetic sound.")

Auteur Criticism Criticism which treats the director as the "author" of a film. Developed in France following World War II, the "auteur critics" identified certain Hollywood directors--like John Ford and Alfred Hitchcock--whose distinctive film styles enabled all of their movies to be placed in a category deemed significant for study.

Best Boy See "gofer."

Camera Angle Camera angle is concerned with the position of the camera relative to the subject. The most common position is a "straight-on" shot, in which subject and camera are generally parallel to one another. A "high angle" shot looks down on the subject while a "low angle" is a perspective in which the camera is looking up.

Camera Adjustment Adjustments, that can be made to the camera, that will affect the image. These include putting filters

297

over the lens, the type of film stock chosen, and manipulations of focus.

Camera Movement   Types of camera movement which include the tilt, pan, dollie, and tracking shot.

Camera Placement   The distance the camera appears to be from the subject. Some common camera placements are closeup, medium close-up, medium shot, and long shot.

Camerawork   One of the four basic elements of film style. Camerawork guides the viewer through the mise-en-scene. This category includes such concerns as camera adjustment, camera placement, and camera movement.

Cinematographer   Person in charge of camerawork. The cinematographer is concerned with helping the director accomplish the type of image desired during shooting by providing such things as the proper lenses, lighting, and film stock.

Cinéma-Vérité   ("Cinema truth.") Type of documentary defined by the French anthropologist Jean Rouch in 1959. An approach to documentary filmmaking where the filmmaker attempts to be as objective, and open-minded, about a topic as possible, while it is being filmed. The *cinéma-Vérité* filmmaker tries to be as unbiased as possible about the topic during production. The perspective of the film is gleaned from the footage during postproduction.

Classic Film   A film that is so powerful and articulate in its force of expression, that it is capable of giving the viewer a unique experience. The quality of the classic is so strong that its power to move the viewer does not diminish with the passage of time.

Close-up   A camera placement usually associated with recording a person's face. In a CU we see

298

everything from the top of the subject's shoulders to the top of his or her head.

Continuity Editing

Also known as Hollywood editing, invisible editing, and decoupage. Continuity editing is designed to create the illusion of real time and space between shots. It uses techniques designed to conceal the editing so that the viewer is not aware that editing is occurring.

Convention

A common object, image, theme, or type of behavior associated with a genre. A cowboy hat, shoot-out at high noon, and the hero riding into the sunset are conventions relating to the western.

Costumer

Person responsible for providing the proper costumes for a shoot.

Cover Shot

See master shot.

Crab

A camera movement in which the camera moves in the form of an arc.

Crane

Type of shot in which the camera is mounted on a crane.

Cubism

Modern art movement that explored geometrical shapes and patterns while eschewing linear perspective. Pablo Picasso and Georges Braque are credited with initiating the movement, around 1907-1908, but Paul Cézanne's work also anticipated cubism. Painter Fernand Legér's cubist movie *Ballet Mecanique* (1925) is credited with being one of the first important experimental films.

Cut

The division, represented by the frame line, between shots. This is also the word that the director calls when she or he wants filming to stop. A third definition pertains to editing. An editor is said to "cut" the film when putting the various parts together.

Dada   Modern "anti-art" movement that developed in Zurich, New York, Paris, and Berlin, around 1916, in direct response to World War I. The movement challenged society's insistence on rules and behavior, that resulted in the shocking and absurd carnage of the war, while denying the place of absurdity in art. This absurdist movement was eventually succeeded by surrealism in 1924. The movement resulted in some experimental films being made by Marcel Duchamp and Man Ray.

Day-for-night Filter   Usually a dark blue filter that enables scenes, shot in the daytime, to appear like that they were filmed at night. With the advent of more sensitive film stocks many filmmakers preferred not to use this filter after the 1970s. Though workable it is not as effective as actual night photography.

Deep Focus   Image in which everything from the extreme foreground to the extreme background is in focus. This term is usually restricted to LS and ELS placements.

Depth of Field   Area in front of the camera that appears in focus on the target area behind the lens.

Diegetic Sound   Sound that is "indigenous" to the setting. This is sound that the characters in the picture can hear.

Diffusion Filter   See "soft focus filter."

Director   The person responsible for the way a final film looks. The director makes the artistic decisions, regarding how a film is shot, and often is responsible for determining who will be working on the film. The director "calls the shots."

Dissolve   A transitional editing device which the editor can use, between shots, usually to indicate a change in time or place in scenes. A "dissolve" is accomplished by superimposing the end of the last shot over the beginning of the next one.

Documentary Term coined in 1926 by the British social scientist, John Grierson, to describe Robert Flaherty's film *Moana*. The word is now used to define the category of "non-fiction" film. (See non-fiction film.)

Dolly Movement where the camera moves but the subject remains stationary. If the camera physically moves in towards the subject it "dollies in." The camera is said to "dolly out" if it pulls back from the subject.

Editing One of the four elements of film style. Editing is concerned with the way the various parts of the film are put together to make that picture a cohesive entity. These parts include frames, shots, scenes, and sequences. The two basic kinds of editing are "continuity" and "montage."

English Music Hall A form of live "vaudeville" or "variety" stage entertainment that was popular in England during the nineteenth, and early twentieth centuries. Charlie Chaplin and Stan Laurel got their start as stage comedians while working in the English music hall.

Experimental Film One of the three principal divisions which motion pictures can be categorized--the other two are narrative and documentary. Also referred to as "abstract" and "avante-garde," this type of motion picture relies on experiments with film, or the unique cinematic effects which the medium can produce, to give a motion picture its form. Films which come under the other two categories are structured around information of a narrative or non-fiction nature. Because of the way it depends upon the film medium for its existence, the animated picture is usually placed in the experimental category, even though cartoons often contain a narrative.

Expressionism

Modern art movement largely an outgrowth of the Norwegian painter Edvard Munch--particularly his 1893 painting, *The Scream.* Expressionism attempted to externalize such internal psychological conditions as despair, isolation, and terror. Beginning as a movement in painting, expressionism spread to the other arts. The 1919 German picture *The Cabinet of Dr. Caligari* is generally considered the first expressionist film. This picture was so well received that a highly innovative, and commercially successful German expressionist film movement existed in that country from 1919-1926.

Extreme Close-up

This definition has changed since the advent of television. In TV an extreme close-up refers to what often is called a "tight" close-up. In film it traditionally has referred to a small part of a larger object. An image of an eyeball or a word on a page would be described as an ECU in film terminology.

Extreme Long Shot

An "ELS" is a placement that emphasizes distance. It is often used to establish setting, such as a desert in a western.

Eyeline Match

A continuity editing technique where the subject matter in a second shot is linked to the first by emphasizing that someone is actively looking at something in this previous shot. When the editor cuts to the subject in the second shot we assume that is what the person is looking at.

ƒ-Stop

Reference to the calibration used to describe the size of the opening allowing light to come into a camera lens. Each ƒ-stop either halves or doubles the light of light, coming into camera, when compared to the calibration on either side of it.

Fade

A transitional editing device which the editor can use, between shots, usually to indicate a change in time or place in scenes. A fade occurs when the cameraman shuts out the light coming into the camera and the frame gradually goes black. The effect is called a " fade-out." A "fade-in," conversely, starts with a black frame and the image gradually appears.

Fiction Film

A narrative film "staged" for the camera.

Film

A strip of transparent acetate with individual still images printed upon it called "frames."

Film Criticism

Process by which we assess our response to the content and quality of a motion picture.

Film Form

The structure of a film. The form of most films can be broken down into three basic sequences-- beginning, middle, and end. The most basic element of film form is the "frame." Of the four elements of style, film form is most associated with the editing.

Film Time

One of two types of time that can exist in film. See definition for "real time."

Filter

A piece of glass, plastic, or gelatin that alters the light before it goes through the camera lens. A "diffusion" or "soft focus" filter is one example.

Frame

Individual still image printed on transparent acetate film. When projected at the rate of 24 fps, in sound films, these individual frames give the illusion of "moving images." The frame is considered the most basic element of film form.

Gaffer

Person in charge of providing electricity for a shoot.

Gate

The area directly behind the lens, and in front of

the shutter, where the film is transported in a camera or projector.

Gauze Shot   See "soft focus."

Genre Film   Group of films that share certain narrative elements in common. Examples of film genres would include westerns, horror movies, musicals, gangster, and science fiction movies.

Gofer   Also known as a "best boy." Individual who fetches items on a set. The "gofer" "goes fer" this and that.

Grip   Person who moves the property on the set. The "key grip" is the person in charge with seeing that the grips have arranged everything the way the director wants.

Icon   A genre convention whose symbolism goes beyond its surface appearance or function. "Icon" originally referred to a type of sacred painting associated with the Russian Eastern Orthodox religion. These religious paintings--or icons--are seen as symbolic of the religious subjects that they visually portray. While not containing the same religious significance as the Russian icon, certain movie conventions are also recognized for having symbolic associations. Examples of some icons in the western would be the good cowboy's white hat, "Robin Hood" outlaw Jesse James, and actor John Wayne.

Intellectual Montage   One of the principal types of montage identified by Eisenstein. Intellectual montage juxtaposes ideas presented in two shots and asks the viewer to combine the concepts to form some type of conclusion. An example of intellectual montage in Eisenstein's Odessa Steps Sequence in *Battleship Potemkin* (1925), involves a statue of the czar overlooking the massacre of his subjects on the steps. The juxtaposition of this symbol of the czar, with the carnage done in his name, would support his association with this tragedy.

Invention

A new element added to a genre. An interesting invention, explored in *The Rocky Horror Picture Show* (1975), was combining the horror film with the musical to create a "musical horror movie." When an invention is repeated in succeeding movies, to the point that it is familiar, it has become recognized as another convention.

Iris

An effect accomplished by putting a diaphragm in front of the lens. This allows the center of the image to be exposed but leaves the surrounding area dark. The resulting effect is somewhat comparable the way old circular frames used to display pictures hung on the wall. The iris also was used as a transitional device, between shots, usually to indicate a change in time or place in scenes, by opening and closing the diaphragm during the shot. The "iris-in" starts as an image in the form of a small circle, in the center of what initially was a black frame, which eventually fills the entire screen. An "iris-out" has the image take the shape of a shrinking circle being enveloped by a black background. The iris was considered something of a dated effect by the 1930s.

Kammerspiele

Type of theater, created after the turn-of-the-century, by the great German stage director, Max Reinhardt. *Kammerspiele* was designed for an intimate space seating and audience of no more than 300. This enabled Reinhardt to develop an acting style of intimate gesture and subtle facial expression that could not have been observed in the traditional space of the typically large theaters of the time. *Kammerspielfilm* was a direct outgrowth of Kammerspiele.

Kammerspielfilm

Type of German film developed in 1921. Filmmakers took the concepts of *Kammerspiele* and applied it to the cinema. The camera was

305

positioned closer to the actor's face and an acting style was developed to emphasize communication through the use of subtle facial expression and restrained gesture. *Der Letze Mann (The Last Laugh)* (1924) and *Variety* (1925) are two good examples of *Kammerspielffilm*.

Key Grip   See "grip."

Kinetograph   Name of the first workable Edison movie camera, patented in 1893.

Kinetoscope   Name of the first Edison peep-hole projection device.

Kino-Eye   ("Cinema eye.") Documentary film style developed by the Russian filmmaker, Dziga Vertov, in the 1920s. While attempting to be objective, Vertov emphasized the involvement of the film medium during the making the documentary, because it was integral to the event. Notable for its obvious incorporation of "trick photography"--i.e., an animated camera taking a bow and "walking away" on the tripod.

Linear Perspective   Technical "trick," for verisimilitude, of making a two-dimensional image appear three-dimensional. A common device is to have "parallel" lines, in the foreground converge to a point, in the background. This duplicates the effect one observes when standing on railroad tracks and looking where they go to in the distance. Also called "Renaissance perspective," because it was during this time that many painters perfected the techniques.

Lip-syncing sound   Precisely matching the sound of a voice to the proper movements of the speaker's lips.

Lighting Designer   Person in charge of designing the lighting for a film. The lighting designer is concerned with both providing illumination and proper "atmospheric mood" with the lighting in a film.

Long Shot

The LS is a placement which shows the person's entire body in the frame. Although relatively distanced from the camera, that individual is still the principal subject in the frame. A LS is not like an ELS where distance itself is being emphasized.

Lyrical Documentary

Inspired by the commercial and critical success of *Nanook of the North* in 1922, this type of feature length documentary featured exotic people and locales. They often involved native people reenacting the lifestyle of their ancestors. The lyrical documentary pretty much ended as a movement by about 1930 and the coming of sound.

Mask

An opaque shield that covers the lens so that the camera only records part of an image. A binoculars mask and a keyhole mask are sometimes used to photograph images in these particular shapes. The iris is the most common form of mask.

Master Shot

Also referred to as "cover shot" and "master scene technique." Continuity technique in which the filmmaker employs a shot, to show the overall setting, and then cuts to progressively closer shots to emphasize where the principal subject is in regard to this environment.

Match-on-action

Continuity technique in which the action in an opening shot is continued in the next one. Also called a "matched cut."

Matte

A camera adjustment in which something is filmed with part of the frame covered. Unlike a mask effect, where that area will remain permanently black, the matte will later be removed, the film rewound, and shot again. Before this subsequent exposure a .matte will be placed over the area previously filmed. When developed the two separate exposures will appear to be part of the same environment, all of which was filmed at the same time.

Medium
Means by which communication is conveyed from the transmitter to the receiver. Film, television, radio, and newspapers are examples of media that are used for "mass communication."

Medium Close-up
A MCU is a placement that frames the person from the top of the individual's head to below the shoulders, somewhere in the middle of the chest.

Medium Shot
A MS is a placement that frames the person from the top of the individual's head to somewhere above or below the knees.

Metric Montage
One of the principal forms of montage identified by Eisenstein, metric montage is accomplished by alternating the physical length of the shots to impose a "tempo" in the film. For example, the first shot might be of five seconds duration, the second shot one second, and the third shot five seconds. The timing of such a segment is determined by the duration, or physical lengths of the shot, rather than the content.

Mimesis
The act of imitating that which is seen in "reality." The object is to give an interpretation the appearance of being real or true--a condition known as "verisimilitude." Mimesis was the basis for defining art throughout most of history.

Miracle Decision
1952 United States Supreme Court decision that reversed the Mutual decision, by claiming that film was protected by the First Amendment. It did not, however, dispute the question of a government's right to censor motion pictures.

Mise-en-scene
One of the four elements of film style. Mise-en-scene refers to the composition of the image.

This element of style is concerned with such things as lighting, costume, setting, props, acting, and the position of the characters within the frame.

Montage

The most literal meaning for "montage" is that it is a French word relating to the editing, or "assemblage," of a film. Often used to refer to "Russian montage," the type of editing that Eisenstein and Kuleshov developed in the 1920s. An alternative to continuity editing, "Russian montage" bombards the viewer with disparate shots which he or she interprets by virtue of their juxtapositions. See metric, rhythmic, tonal, overtonal, and intellectual montage.

Mutual Decision

(*Mutual Film Corporation v. Industrial Commission of Ohio* .) The 1915 United State Supreme Court decision that claimed that film did not come under the protection of the First Amendment which safeguards freedom of speech. The Court later reversed itself on this position. The Mutual decision also validated a government's right to censor film if it felt necessary. This right continues to exist today.

Narrative Film

See fiction film.

Newsreel

Early form of actuality in which short movies of newsworthy events or special interest stories were edited into a film of about ten minutes in length. This "newsreel" was shown prior to the narrative feature that people specifically came to see. Newsreels were common in theaters from 1910 until the middle 1960s. After that time people depended upon television for this type of visual news story.

Non-diegetic sound

Asynchronous sound which the audience can hear but the characters in the film can not. Examples of non-diegetic sound would be a voice over narration and mood music.

Non-fiction Film	Alternative description for identifying "documentary" films. The non-fiction film is concerned with recording events or processes with the camera rather than relying on using fictional narratives, or filmic effects, to structure the form of that movie's content. (See "documentary.")
Normal Lens	A lens that photographs its subject so that the resulting image approximates that seen by the human eye. See telephoto and wide-angle lens.
Objective Point of View	One of two types of point of view that the camera can take. The other is subjective point of view. The objective point of view is most common perspective, and is a neutral recording recording of a subject.
Off-screen Space	Space beyond the frame line which is not visible on the screen.
Off-screen Sound	Sound which is produced off-screen. Non-diegetic sound is always off-screen sound.
One-liner	A sentence in which the "essence" of an entire movie is summarized.
Over-the-shoulder Shot	Continuity technique where the filmmaker shoots over the shoulder of a person towards the subject to which that individual is directing his or her attention. By showing that person in the frame the perspective remains an objective point of view. If the director cut to what the subject was looking at we would have a subjective point of view--we would see the object from the perspective of the subject.
Overtonal Montage	One of the principal types of montage identified by Eisenstein. Overtonal montage is concerned

with the manipulation of the emotional responses of the viewer. Shot #1, for example, might emphasize the desirability and vulnerability of a subject, such as a baby. Shot #2 would show a villain jeopardizing or even harming the infant, thereby increasing the viewer's dislike for that individual.

Pan   Left or right horizontal movement of the camera on a stationary tripod. The extent the pan is sometimes described in degrees. A half circle, then, would be a 180° pan while a full circle would be a 360° pan.

Parallel Action   Two actions occurring at the same time in different places. When the editor cuts back and forth between these actions he or she is using a technique known as "crosscutting."

Pedestal   Camera movement where the camera is cranked vertically in the air on a stationary tripod.

Photoplay   Term used to describe film narratives during the silent period.

Phi-phenomenon   Theory describing a physiological process, which psychologists have not yet adequately explained, which enables us to perceive "movies" as moving. The phi-phenomenon suggest that the human mind is capable of retaining the memory of a still image, for a fraction of a second, while a shutter is closed, and the film is moving prior to the next frame is exposed. Before the preceding visual is forgotten, the mind "blends" its subject matter, with the information in the next frame, in such a way that the two pictures are part of one continuous action.

Pop Art   Popular work whose worth is determined by whatever is commercially popular.

Postproduction   The phase of the filmmaking process in which the film is edited and made availabe for distribution and exhibition.

Preproduction

The "planning phase" of making a motion picture. The development of the idea for a film, the writing of the script, the planning for the shooting, the hiring of the personnel, and the preparation of the budget would all be part of preproduction.

Producer

Person who is usually responsible for the initial idea for a movie. The producer guides the production of a film from initial idea to completed picture. Besides being involved with all phases of the production process, the producer is usually responsible for the funding, logistics of the shooting, and the hiring and firing of personnel.

Production

The phase of filmmaking where the film is actually shot.

Quaint

Eccentric "red nosed," "baggy pants" comedian that was popular in the English music hall. Charlie Chaplin played this type of comedy on stage and adapted a variation of the character for the screen.

Rack Focus

Changing the selective focus during a shot. (See selective focus.)

Real Time

One of two types of time that can appear in film. Real time is the amount of time it takes for things to happen in reality. "Film time" is time that is artificially speeded up or slowed down. "Slow motion" and "stop action" photography are techniques used to create various forms of "film time."

Receiver

That which receives communication, from a transmitter through a medium, during the communication process.

Rhythmic Montage

One of the principal types of montage identified

by Eisenstein. Cutting, in rhythmic montage, is determined by the rhythms and movement seen in the images. This is different from metric montage where manipulation of the tempo is determined from outside the frame, by varying the physical length of the shots. In rhythmic montage, where Eisenstein wanted "clash" rather than "continuity," if shot #1 had movement going frame right, shot #2 would have the movement going from right to left.

Scene
A self-contained narrative segment in which the action usually happens at the same time and place. At first most films were one shot, one scene. As film narratives became more complex it became possible for a scene to contain over a hundred shots.

Screenplay
See "script."

Script
Also called a "screenplay." A complete written description of all the shots and dialogue in the film. A "shooting script" is what the director follows when filming.

Scriptwriter
Person who writes scripts.

Selective Focus
Situation in which part of the frame is in focus and part of the frame is out of focus.

Sequence
Major units of a film that contain several scenes. The purpose of breaking a film up into general sequences is to be able to outline its overall form. Most films can be broken down into three principal sequences--a beginning, a middle, and an end.

Set Designer
Individual who stages the environment that will be shot in a film.

Shot
After the frame, the shot is the next basic unit of film form. A shot starts where a filmmaker begins

shooting and ends when the cinematographer "cuts." The editor assembles the shots, in post-production, to give a film its overall structure. A motion picture is also said to be "shot" during filming.

Shot-reverse-shot
Also known as "reverse-angle shooting," this continuity technique starts with an over-the-shoulder shot of someone talking to an individual. The filmmaker then reverses the situation and cuts to a placement over the shoulder, of the person whose face was emphasized previously. We now see the face of the individual whose shoulder was in the foreground of our first shot.

Shutter
A mechanism which opens and closes, behind the lens of the camera or projector, which enables an individual frame to be exposed to light. The intermittent opening and closing of the shutter gives still images the illusion of being "moving pictures."

Slow Motion
A type of photography which enables filmmakers to slow down real time.

Soft Focus Filter
Diffusion filter traditionally used to film the leading lady. Because the film stock needed harsh lighting to get an exposure, actresses were sometimes made to look older than they actually were in scenes. It was found that a piece of gauze placed over the lens would diffuse the light, making a more romantic image. This effect is often referred to as a "gauze shot."

Sound-on-disk
Early "talking picture" technology involving the synchronization of phonograph with a film projector to obtain synchronized sound.

Sound-on-film
"Talking picture" technology that rivaled, and eventually replaced the sound-on-disk. This format involves printing the sound trap on a special track, located next to the frames, on the

film itself.

Sound Track Portion of the film, next to the frames, in which the sound is either optically or magnetically stored.

Special Effects "Trick photography" that enables the filmmaker to create the illusion of reality.

Steadicam Apparatus developed in the 1970s that enables a hand-held camera to get exceptionally steady and fluid shots.

Subjective Point of View One of the two points of view that the camera can take--the other is "objective." With a subjective POV the camera is viewing something from the perspective of one of the characters, or possibly the director.

Subtitle A written caption which represents dialogue or provides the viewer with explanatory information.

Surrealism Modern art movement that replaced dadaism in 1924. The surrealists were interested in exploring the dreamlike world of the subconscious. By looking at the inner world, they were asking us to question the "reality" of the outer one. One of the last important experimental films of the period from 1919 to 1930 was the surrealist film *Un Chien Andalou* (1929), by Luis Buñel and Salvador Dali.

Swish-Pan A very rapid and sudden pan at the end of a shot. This pan is so fast it blurs whatever is being photographed. This technique is now seen as something of a cliché and was used as such in the 1960s TV series *Batman*.

Symbol See "icon."

Synchronized Sound Precision matching of sound to image.

Telephoto Lens	Lens with a "shallow" depth of field that enables a filmmaker to photograph an object a long distance away. A binoculars incorporates a telephoto lens.
Three-o'clock	A timetable, posted in the afternoon, often at various locations in the hotel where members of the production are staying. It identifies what is going to be done, the following day, where the film will be shot, and who is expected to show up.
Tie-in	Commercial items sold that relate to the release of a new feature film. The tie-in may be in the form of candy, books, music or toys.
Tilt	Vertical movement of the camera on a stationary tripod.
Tonal Montage	One of the principal types of montage identified by Eisenstein. Tonal montage is concerned with the contrasting textures between shots. If a preceding shot contains a great deal of white, in the image, and the editor wants to create tonal montage, the second shot would emphasize dark imagery.
Trailer	Also called a "preview." Short film describing the nature of a "coming attraction" which is shown before a feature in the theater.
Transmitter	Source of the communication that will be conveyed, through a medium, to the receiver in the communication process.
Travelogue	A type of documentary emphasizing images associated with a journey or a vacation.
Treatment	A rough outline of a film, which is seldom more than a few pages. The treatment is the intermediate phase between a "one-liner" and a "script."

Urban Documentary	Documentary trend in the 1920s to shoot films involving metropolitan areas or subjects. Urban documentaries include *Rien que les heures* (1926) and *Berlin Symphony of a Great City* (1927).
Verisimilitude	See "mimesis."
Wide-angle Lens	A lens that enables the filmmaker to photograph a broader view of a setting than what can be seen with the normal perspective of the human eye.
Wipe	A transitional editing device used to indicate a change in time or place in scenes. A "wipe" occurs when a new shot appears to "push out" the preceding one. Instead of one shot being superimposed upon another, as is true with a dissolve, part of each shot is seen as existing side-by-side within the frame.
Zoom Lens	A lens with a series of glass or plastic elements that can be adjusted thereby shifting the perspective from normal, to telephoto, to wide-angle, and any combination in between. When the camera operator changes the zoom ratio, during a shot, so that we go into a telephoto effect, he or she is said to be "zooming in." Conversely, "zooming out" would refer to going into wide-angle mode.

BIBLIOGRAPHY

Adeler, Edwin, and Con West. Remember Fred Karno? London: John Long Limited, 1939.

Arnason, H.H. History of Modern Art: Painting, Sculpture, Architecture. Englewood Cliffs, New Jersey: Prentice-Hall, Inc., n.d.

Atkinson, Brooks. New York Times Theater Reviews. August 15, 1928, August 26, 1928, September 14, 1946.

Bacon, James. Hollywood is a Four Letter Town. New York: Avon Books, 1976.

Bailey, Peter. Leisure and Class in Victorian England: Rational Recreation and the Contest for Control, 1830-1885. London: Routledge & Kegan Paul, 1978.

Balio, Tino. The American Film Industry. Madison, Wisconsin: The University of Wisconsin Press, 1976.

Balio, Tino. United Artists: The Company Built by the Stars. Madison: University of Wisconsin Press, 1975.

Barnouw, Erik. Documentary: A History of the Non-Fiction Film. New York: Oxford University Press, 1993.

Bordwell, David, Janet Staiger, and Kristin Thompson. The Classical Hollywood Cinema: Film Style and Mode of Production to 1960. New York: Columbia University Press, 1985.

Bordwell, David, and Kristin Thompson. Film Art: An Introduction. New York: McGraw Hill, Inc.

Brownlow, Kevin. The Parade's Gone By. New York: Alfred A. Knopf, 1968.

Calthrop, Dion Clayton. Music Hall Nights. London: John Lane the Bodley Head Limited, 1925.

Chaplin, Charles. My Autobiography. New York: Pocket Books, 1966.

Chaplin, Charles. My Life in Pictures. New York: Grossett & Dunlap, 1975.

Churchill, Winston. "Everybody's Language." Colliers, October 26 1935, reprinted in Donald W. McCaffrey (ed.) Focus on Chaplin. Englewood Cliffs, New Jersey: Prentice-Hall, Inc., 1971.

Cook, David A. A History of Narrative Film. New York: W.W. Norton & Co., 1990.

Eisenstein, Sergei. Film Form and The Film Sense. New York: Meridian Books, 1968.

Eisner, Lotte The Haunted Screen. Berkeley: University of California Press, 1969.

Ferguson, Francis. ed. Aristotle's Poetics. New York: Hill and Wang, 1961.

Frye, Nortrop. Anatomy of Criticism: Four Essays Princeton: Princeton University Press, 1957.

Gallagher, J.P. Fred Karno: Master of Mirth and Tears. London: Robert Hale & Company, 1971.

Guiles, Fred Lawrence. Stan: The Life of Stan Laurel. New York: Stein and Day, 1980.

Hopkins, Albert. Magic: Stage Illusions and Scientific Diversions Including Trick Photography. New York: Munn & Co., Inc., 1911.

Jacobs, Lewis. The Documentary Tradition. New York: W. W. Norton, 1979.

Jacobs, Lewis. The Rise of the American Film. New York: Teachers College Press, 1978.

Kael, Pauline. The Citizen Kane Book. Boston: Little, Brown and Company, 1971.

Lahue, Kalton C. Mack Sennett's Keystone: The Man, the Myth, and the Movies. Cranbury, New Jersey: A.S. Barnes, and Co., Inc. 1971.

Leaming, Barbara. Orson Welles: A Biography. New York: Penguin Books, 1986.

Lebo, Harlan. Citizen Kane: The Fiftieth Anniversary Album. New York: Doubleday, 1990.

London, Jack. The People of the Abyss. New York: Grossett & Dunlap, 1902.

Lyons, Timothy J. Charles Chaplin: A Guide to References and Resources. Boston: G.K. Hall & Co., 1979.

McCabe, John. Charlie Chaplin. New York: Doubleday & Co., 1978.

McCabe, John. The Comedy World of Stan Laurel. Garden City: Doubleday & Co., 1974.

Mander, Raymond, and Joe Mitchenson. British Music Hall. London: Gentry Books, 1974.

Miller, J. Hillis. Charles Dickens: The World of His Novels. Cambridge, Massachusetts: Harvard University Press, 1958.

Ramsaye, Terry. A Million and One Nights. New York: Touchstone, 1986.

Renan, Sheldon. An Introduction to the American Underground Film. New York: E.P. Dutton & Co., 1967.

Robinson, David. Chaplin: His Life and Art. New York: McGraw-Hill, 1985.

Scheide, Frank. The Comedy of Chaplin and Keaton. Educational television series produced by the Department of Independent Study, the University of Arkansas-Fayetteville, 1982.

Scheide, Frank. "Legitimate Theater vs. the English Music Hall: The Legal Repression of Dramatic Expression on London's Variety Stage, 1899-1912." Free Speech Yearbook, 1990.

Toland, Gregg. "Realism for Citizen Kane." American Cinemagographer, February, 1941.

INDEX

321

323